NARRATOLOGY AND TEXT:
SUBJECTIVITY AND IDENTITY IN NEW FRANCE
AND QUÉBÉCOIS LITERATURE

PAUL PERRON

Narratology and Text
Subjectivity and Identity in
New France and Québécois Literature

UNIVERSITY OF TORONTO PRESS
Toronto Buffalo London

© University of Toronto Press Incorporated 2003
Toronto Buffalo London
Printed in Canada

ISBN 0-8020-3688-0 (cloth)

Printed on acid-free paper

Toronto Studies in Semiotics and Communication
Editors: Marcel Danesi, Umberto Eco, Paul Perron, Peter Schulz,
   Thomas A. Sebeok

National Library of Canada Cataloguing in Publication

Perron, Paul
   Narratology and text : subjectivity and identity in New France and
   Québécois literature / Paul Perron

   Includes bibliographical references and index.
   ISBN 0-8020-3688-0

   1. New France – History – Sources.   2. Canadian fiction (French) –
   Quebec (Province) – History and criticism.   3. Nationalism in literature.
   I. Title.

   PS8073.P47 2003   C840.9′358   C2002-902985-6
   PQ3901.P47 2003

University of Toronto Press acknowledges the financial assistance to
its publishing program of the Canada Council for the Arts and the
Ontario Arts Council.

This book has been published with the help of a grant from the Humanities
and Social Sciences Federation of Canada, using funds provided by the
Social Sciences and Humanities Research Council of Canada.

University of Toronto Press acknowledges the financial support for
its publishing activities of the Government of Canada through the
Book Publishing Industry Development Program (BPIDP).

Contents

PREFACE   vii

Part I. Narratology

1 Introduction to Narratology   3
2 A.J. Greimas and Narratology   18

Part II. Discovery, Conversion, and Colonization

3 First Encounters and Myth Making: Jacques Cartier's *Voyages* to New France   41
4 Settlement and Conversion: Jean de Brébeuf's *Jesuit Relations* of 1635 and 1636   57
5 Founding Nations: Jesuit–Huron Relations in Seventeenth-Century New France   77
6 Narrating and Reading the Body: The Martyrdom of Isaac Jogues   103

Part III. Historiography and the Novel: Nation and Identity

7 Before and after the Fall – The Historical Novel: *Les Anciens Canadiens* (*The Canadians of Old*)   131
8 Family, Group, and Nation in the Nineteenth-Century Agrarian Novel: *La Terre paternelle* (*The Paternal Farm*)   152

9 Nationalism and the Novel of Colonization: *Maria Chapdelaine* 166
10 On the Margins of Nation – The Realist Novel: *La Scouine* 192
11 History and the Urban Novel: *Bonheur d'occasion* (*The Tin Flute*) 208
12 Utopia, Family, and Nation – The Wilderness Novel: *Agaguk* 230
13 Conclusion 255

NOTES 259

GLOSSARY 313

BIBLIOGRAPHY 317

INDEX 329

Preface

This work grew out of the graduate seminar I gave every year in the Department of French at the University of Toronto on narrative theory, and I would like to dedicate it to my students, who constantly challenged and pushed me to clarify my positions. It represents many of my intellectual preoccupations in terms of both the theory and the corpus that I have chosen to study and to use, in part, as an illustration of a method that has proven over the years, for me, to have a decidedly heuristic value. Its theoretical foundations reach back to Plato and Aristotle, Edward Morgan Forster and Henry James, but also to Jean-Paul Sartre, whose philosophy and reflections on literature influenced so many intellectuals of my generation. These include especially his brilliant essays on contemporary authors in *Situations I*, notably 'La Temporalité chez Faulkner,' published in 1939, the opening paragraph of which contains the memorable lines 'The technique of a novel is always grounded in the novelist's metaphysics. The task of the critic is to uncover the former before assessing the latter.'[1] In his analysis, Sartre considers that the formal features of *The Sound and the Fury* at the level of expression articulate an ontological dimension at the level of content: notably, temporality conceived of as the infrastructure of the author's consciousness.

Then came the epistemological break of the mid-1960s when structuralism assailed the bastion of phenomenology. Roland Barthes, Michel Foucault, Jacques Lacan, Algirdas Julien Greimas, Julia Kristeva, the Tel Quel Group with Philippe Sollers, and many others, all under the impact of Saussurian linguistics, contributed to the neutralization and relativization of phenomenology on the Parisian intellectual scene, especially as represented by Sartre, even in spite of the rearguard strategy of his impressive four-volume study on Gustave Flaubert, *L'Idiot de la famille*. The publication of Barthes's *L'Analyse structurale du récit* in 1966, with an introductory essay by Barthes, and with contributions by A.J. Greimas, Gérard Genette, Umberto Eco, Claude Bremond, Tzvetan Todorov, and Christian Metz, to name those who would, indeed, alter the course of narratological studies in the latter half of the twentieth century, transformed the critical landscape. It should be added that both Todorov and Kristeva, who arrived in Paris from Bulgaria in the mid-1960s, played a major role in introducing the Russian formalists and the Prague School to French and, I dare say, many Western intellectuals. In his introductory essay to the volume he edited in 1966, Barthes begins by remarking that narratives are numberless, transhistorical, and transcultural, and he ultimately links the appearance of story telling in the child to the advent of the Oedipus complex. Yet his great contribution consists not in establishing the prolegomena for a structural analysis of narrative *per se* but in freeing textual analysis from what he called the constraints of traditional temporal considerations: 'dechronologizing' the narrative continuum and 'relogicizing' it, making it dependent on what Stéphane Mallarmé, the hermetic nineteenth-century poet, called with regard to the French language 'the primitive thunderbolts of logic.' In fact, what he wished to do was to give a structural description of the temporal effect in narrative, considering it only in terms of its functionality – in other words, as an element, among others, of a complex semiotic system.

Most narratological theory of a structuralist bent, stemming from the pioneering work of what I would like to label the 'Paris School,' tended to bracket off the philosophical and psychological underpinnings of discourse, especially with respect to the author and reader. As a result, Greimas and his numerous followers thought of written discourse as a simulacrum of the speech act itself, a phenomenon that should be studied independently from the actual conditions of its production and reception, and they tended to focus, first, on a narrative semiotics of action, then on a semiotics of cognition, and, in the end, on one of passions, progressively rewriting the entire system in terms of a simulacrum of intersubjectivity and of enunciation, bracketing off, in effect, both the referent and all psychological considerations on the actual author.

The narratological theory and methodology presented in this volume[2] owe much to the Parisian narratologists of the 1960s and 1970s, building on some of their most innovative discoveries and models.

However, one of my major departures in this work from the narratological theory of the Paris School was to rethink their contributions from the point of view of Émile Benveniste's ground-breaking work on enunciation, or subjectivity in language. Traditionally, French theoreticians made the distinction between third-person historical narrative, which was supposedly 'objective,' and first-person narrative, which was said to be 'subjective.' Examining examples from Balzac's novels, Benveniste demonstrated, through linguistic analysis, that third-person historical discourse was shot through with subjectivity, or the presence of an enunciating narrator and narratee, thereby laying this specious distinction to rest for good. Taking his inspiration from structural linguistics, Benveniste then posited the existence of a subject in and by language: '"Ego" is one who *says* "ego."' In this foundational act of subjectivity, by saying *I*, the subject both positions her/himself in relation to a *you*, and an absent person, *her/him* – who is the referred to, the one who is not present in the actual communicational act – and appropriates all of the resources of language. From this perspective, *I* exists only in and by language, and in a relationship of intersubjectivity. *I* also is a virtual *you* since, when the *you*, by saying *I*, appropriates all the resources of language, the initial *I* is relegated to the position previously occupied by *you*, who can, in turn, muster up virtually the same linguistic resources. In addition to these deixes of personal pronouns that found subjectivity, Benveniste explores the function of temporal and spatial deixes in the institution of subjectivity. What this profoundly innovative linguist does is to define subjectivity within a system of positions. In coming into being through their actual and virtual appropriations of all the resources of language, *her/him*, the spoken about, is positioned outside this act of intersubjective communication, but is none the less still there. To complete such a theory of subjectivity in and by language, what still remains to be done is to invest the ever-evolving and -switching positions, or poles (deixes), ontologically, historically, ideologically, psychologically, and so on.

In this volume, another step I took in elaborating a more complete narratological theory was to examine the major advances in the works of Barthes, Bremond, Genette, Todorov, but especially Greimas, and remodel them with respect to Benveniste's theoretical writings on enunciation, thus rethinking them in terms of a more global theory of production and reception. What, in turn, becomes clear, is that intersubjective relations do not exist directly between an actual and a virtual subject as such, but are always mediated through a sign system and, in the case in point, a text considered as a complex sign system. Such a textual sign system is produced by an enunciator and addressed to an enunciatee, and both of these roles can be assumed by the same actant. Hence, it became essential to shift my analysis from the enunciator and its production, and to attempt to uncover the underlying coherence of the enunciative strategies that characterize each text, an undertaking that of necessity, for me, presupposes a syntactic, semantic, and pragmatic reconstruction of text on the part of the enunciatee-reader and/or critic.

It is mainly Paul Ricœur's monumental three-volume work, *Time and Narrative*, that served as a matrix to reconceptualize and rework the Parisian narratologists whom I had as a first step retheoretized through Benveniste. In the most simple terms, Ricœur's originality was to produce an integrated global theory that could account for how, through narrative, we make sense of our experience of the world, for how the experiential is configured in texts, and for how, through the act of reading, we reconfigure texts to make sense of them. Starting with Aristotle's concept of mimesis and Augustine's notion of time, Ricœur defined narrative as temporalized action by which, in our daily lives, we conceptually organize our lived experience (*Mimesis I*). He then defined both fictional and historical narratives as the configuration, through emplotment, of temporalized action, the only difference between the two being that the goal of historical discourse is to tell the truth, which is not necessarily the claim made for fiction (*Mimesis II*). Finally, he considered the act of reading and interpretation as the reconfiguration of the emplotted textual temporalized actional configurations by and through how the reader makes sense and organizes meaning in terms of his/her own temporalized actional configurations (*Mimesis III*). In this way, an ontology of being in the world, a theory of text, a theory of reading, and a theory of interpretation are all founded upon a coherent theory of narrative as temporalized action. It should be noted here that, in contrast to the earlier narratologists who, we saw, downplayed the role of narrative as a means of making sense of the world, along with the role of the reader, and also gave little consideration to temporality, in order to focus only on the text as system, Ricœur reintroduces these fundamental dimensions in his general theory. For the sake of argument, though, it could be pointed out that Gérard Genette, in *Figures III*, founds his poetics of the novel on the temporal features of the text. However, all Genette does is to ground his theory on temporal markers, a strategy which, at the level of the form of expression, enables him to determine the temporal structure of the form of content. What I have attempted to do in this work is to expand Ricœur's definition of narrative as temporalized, actional, cognitive, and passional emplotment and to concentrate on the enunciative strategies and mechanisms established in each text to position, to manipulate cognitively, and to move the enunciatee-reader. In a sense, I will not say that I have come full circle from a theoretical perspective – that is, back to Sartre and a phenomenology grounded in an ontology that posits temporality as the infrastructure of consciousness. Yet the theory of reading and interpretation that I have worked out here owes much to a phenomenology that is first of all informed by a theory of the sign and the text – which is certainly not the case with Sartre, who remained rooted in an antiquated notion of language as symbol, contrary, for example, to Maurice Merleau-Ponty, who integrated the linguistic theory of his times into his philosophical system. The theory also, as I stated above, owes a great deal to some of the innovative contributions of structural linguistics and narratology that have been integrated into Ricœur's theoretical frame in order to construct a coherent methodology that, I believe, has a real discovery value.

During my encounter and dialogue with Ricœur, and through my experience of textual analysis over the years, I was struck by the fact that Aristotle's theory of action and Augustine's of temporality were insufficient to account for such complex narratives as novels, since cognitive, passional, as well as enunciative dimensions had to be integrated into the model. It also became apparent that the Saussurian definition of sign that consisted in a signifier and a signified remained much too abstract to account for the actional, cognitive, and sentient dimensions of narrative that were always incorporated in acting, thinking, and feeling characters. Hence the need to have recourse to a phenomenology that could integrate the perceived and felt semantic universe by and through the body. It became progressively evident that a signifier signifies only when it is incorporated in a perceiving, thinking, and feeling body. I also applied this shift, from a dualistic to a triadic concept of the sign in action, to the enunciative strategies and semionarrative structures at play in a text that position and provoke a cognitive, sentient, and embodied enunciatee-reader.

This book has a three-part structure. The first, consisting of chapters 1 and 2, gives a historico-notional overview of what I believe to be the major contributors to the theory of narrative in the twentieth century. There are undoubtedly some flagrant oversights, but I have concentrated on critics whom I have encountered, especially those whose theories I have applied over the years and who have contributed to my own reflections on the theory of narrative. Chapter 2 deals in some detail with A.J. Greimas, who, for more than thirty years, gave a bi-monthly research seminar on semio-narrative theory at the École Pratique des Hautes Études in Paris, attended by well over fifty graduate students and colleagues from around the world, who all contributed to the elaboration of this exemplary, theoretically coherent body of work. Even some ten years after Greimas's death in 1992, the seminar continues to meet on a bi-monthly basis, further investigating, exploring, and refining the global theory. The reader who does not wish to dwell on this theoretical construct can, in fact, pass directly on to the next ten chapters, chapters that I hope illustrate and clarify the import of this theory, based on, and grounded in, a coherently elaborated structural semantics.

The second and third parts of this volume deal with a corpus of texts written on and in New France and, after the Conquest of 1759, in Quebec, spanning some four centuries. In part two, I examine the very first texts, Jacques Cartier's *Voyages* of 1534 and 1535, dealing with first encounters. In fact, this and all subsequent chapters could fall under the category of reading and writing the body. Chapter 3 focuses on the presuppositions and preconstructions underlying the discoverer's discourse on the other and on otherness. It also closely follows how the other is constructed as otherness, reduced to violent, uncontrolled gestures, dances, and cries, read as pure transparency: *terra incognita* being rewritten and transformed into *terra nullius*, inhabited by half-naked 'barbarians' as they and their land are projected by the discoverer onto a wished-for historical trajectory of European colonization and cultivation. The next three chapters deal with the *Jesuit Relations*, written some one hundred years after Cartier's exploration narratives. These I have defined as ethnohistorical discourse, as the missionaries attempt to convert to Catholicism the Huron at war with the Iroquois. A shift occurs in these texts, since as a potential source of danger the other is seen as both a docile virtual convert, who willingly awaits and accepts revelation, and as one who can unexpectedly turn on the missionary; in turn, the missionary is depicted as one who suffers incredible hardship, and even torture, in spreading the Word. The *Relations* are meant to move their French readers, in their innermost being, to support the missions of New France; in them, racked, bleeding, mutilated bodies, cruelly tortured by the 'enemies' of the church, are displayed in gruesome detail, reacting unflinchingly and stoically, thereby demonstrating unbelievably heroic qualities in the name of the Saviour: 'Let thy will be done' and 'Into thy hands I commend my spirit.' These models of heroic behaviour will be reactivated, presented, and consolidated in the French-Canadian imaginary in writing some two hundred years later, with the return of the Jesuit order to Quebec,[3] and more particularly with the emergence of the novel and historiography towards the middle of the nineteenth century.

Part three examines in detail six exemplary novels written in Quebec from the mid-nineteenth century until the end of the Duplessis era that inaugurated the Quiet Revolution. All of these novels belong to the canon, and four of them can be considered as best sellers, since they were, and continue to be, widely read in Quebec and abroad. These texts emplot cognizant and sentient bodies to a degree, and establish particular spaces where characters can realize their potential and fulfil their own individual and collective aspirations. They constrain their main protagonists to positively and negatively moralized physical, cultural, and historically referentialized spaces that foster the emergence of individual or group identity. Three of the novels – *La Terre paternelle* (*The Paternal Farm*) (1846), *Les Anciens Canadiens* (*The Canadians of Old*) (1865), and *Maria Chapdelaine* (1914) – clearly project the desiring subject into a social constellation where duty (faithfulness to the past) regulates will and where all heterogeneous values are neutralized and eliminated. These narratives set in place a body politic of censorship, of the control of desire that transforms the subject who, in taking up all the resources of language, says 'I want for me,' into a collective being, constrained by the symbolic social and historical structures of language, who is forced into saying 'I want for us.'

A striking exception to these three major novels, in which individuals are programmed by long-term homogeneous transcendental values that guarantee the survival and prosperity of the group (unity of language, race, and religion), is *La Scouine* by Albert Laberge. This 'curious' work, which has intrigued critics with respect to both its form and its content, was published privately by the author in 1918, with a run of fifty volumes for personal distribution. Although official censorship did exist (i.e., the Index), Laberge and the small number of others who wrote what the clergy considered to be subversive works exercised, in effect, self-censorship, knowing all too well that their creations could not and would not be sold by book dealers in the province.[4] The novel unfolds as a series of vignettes that, at first glance, are not integrated within the unity of a single action. Here, most of the male and female subjects are depicted as instinctive, violent, conflictual beings who attempt to dominate all those, including family members, with whom they interact. Cut from a Hobbesian cloth, they are nasty, brutish, and short, and, throughout the novel, no transcendental values succeed in motivating and transforming them. A degraded form of the family continues, in the Name of the Father, with the weak and sterile being marginalized and even, eventually, eliminated. In fact, the symbolic structures that attempt to assign each subject his or her role in the social order are always present, but the subjects refuse these roles, through violent reaction. At this level, the form of expression of the work is isomorphic to the form of content, since the novel subverts the grand narrative of the integrated, homogeneous family/group/nation and succeeds only in producing a fractious and fractured tale of the survival of the fittest.

Bonheur d'occasion (1945) by Gabrielle Roy (translated as *The Tin Flute*) tolls the knell of the moribund novel of the land as its subjects definitively migrate to the city, a migration that corresponds quite closely to the actual demographic distribution and movement of the population of Quebec at the end of the 1930s and the beginning of the 1940s. The novel deals with a large cast of characters linked by multiple intertwining intrigues, but focuses mainly on the Lacasse family, poor and generally ill-educated individuals in an underprivileged district of Montreal at the outbreak of the Second World War. The father is unemployed and the mother desperately seeks to keep the increasingly dysfunctional family together as it is forced by economic need to move from one dilapidated house to another. Everyone feels the effects of the Depression, most men have temporary jobs or are unemployed, while all who can sign up for military service do so in order to send money back to family, thereby ensuring its continuity. Most of the characters walk the maze of the city by day and night, trying to find ways to survive and give some direction to their lives. In their daily social, economic, and personal lived experience, each and every one of them has to face the effects of the war being fought overseas. These external forces both shatter and reconfigure their lives during the emergence of a new historical and capitalistic order. Lacking education to participate in this new order, and because the traditional values of origins, language, and religion are inoperative, all of the subjects are decentred by and caught up in historical events and forces that remain beyond their control. Families, groups, and even the nation are amputated of their men, who see the war as their only chance of salvation. The novel ends with the image of two generations of the same dismembered family, deprived of its men who have enrolled in the army, moving to better quarters, thanks to this new-found source of income, as the clouds of war loom menacingly overhead.

The postwar novel of the city establishes a new order where the notion of family is radically transformed. Traditional values continue to inform the subject and group, but they are too often menaced and threatened by new ideas, beliefs, and socio-economic factors from beyond the urban frontiers that physically circumscribe the actors. The city remains the locus of the heterogeneous, but individuals most often must conform to the pressures of the symbolic, conveyed by and through language, race, and religion, in order to prosper and to ensure the continuity and development of the family and group. If not, the subject ends up marginalized and totally isolated. To complete this study on subjectivity and identity, I have decided to include a reworked, and very abbreviated study of a seminal text that was the most popular novel written in Quebec in the 1950s, Yves Thériault's *Agaguk* (1958),[5] set in the far North in the land of the Inuit in a space hitherto very little explored and exploited in Quebec literature. Thériault's novel is the most radical questioning and deconstruction of the values that inform the literary landscape of Quebec since *La Scouine*. He depicts two individuals who cannot fulfil their aspirations under the social and cultural constraints of the tribe, and who must break with the group to found a family far away, alone on the tundra. Both young subjects, who have just attained adulthood, are equipped with all the learned skills for survival, and both overcome a series of physical and moral tests. In the process, they evolve in a manner not possible within the tribe, with its traditional beliefs, customs, values, and social order. Freed from the hierarchical strictures and structures of the group, in which individuals assume predetermined and unequal roles, Agaguk and Iriook discover their complementarity by, and through, a new body politic of sexual liberation and reciprocity. Agaguk's recognition of his spouse's legitimate desire to initiate sexual advances and practices that, by tradition, are prohibited to Inuit women leads to a new awareness by the couple, and, along with his own instinctive behaviour, is the root cause of his repudiation of the past and his acquisition of a new morality arrived at through rational thought. For the first time in Quebec literature, the eroticized body mediates the subjects' perceptual, cognitive, and passional universes, leading to a new social being and to a nuclear family freed from the shackles of tradition and the group. Indeed, the

Duplessis era, with all its inhibitions and constraints, can only be imagined, represented, and negated, with all of its contradictions, in a dreamed-of *elsewhere*, completely removed from the current and actual oppressive sociohistorical moment. To reinvent the group is first to break with it and all its symbolic structures that enfold the subject in its past. It is also to re-imagine the individual, and, more specifically in our case, the couple and the family founded on reciprocal intersubjective relations of equality where individuals, in saying "I," posit the subjectivity of the other and of his/her right to muster the potential of language, concepts that were previously repressed, prohibited, and even unthinkable. Thériault's decidedly utopian text can be considered as a desperate attempt, at the level of the imaginary, to ground subjectivity in a body politic of complementary eroticism and rationality, announcing the Quiet Revolution, that will contribute to the redefinition of interpersonal relations and a new awareness of a liberated self and other, family, group, and nation.

Parts of this volume have appeared in print but in a quite different form. Parts of chapter 1 appeared in the *Encyclopedic Dictionary of Semiotics* in a very early version in 1986 and in 1994, and have been updated and rewritten. Parts of chapter 2, published in 1989 in *New Literary History* as an 'Introduction to Greimassian Semiotics,' have been rewritten, revised, and updated. An abbreviated version of chapter 3 that appeared in Italian in 1999 in honour of Paolo Fabbri has been rewritten for this work. An abbreviated version of chapter 4 published in *Semiotica* in 1989 has been rewritten from a less technical perspective and completely revised. Parts of chapter 5 that appeared in a French version in *Fabula* in 1985 have been rewritten, revised, and updated in English. Parts of chapter 6 published in *Texte* in 2000 have also been recrafted and revised. Some of the ideas expressed in chapters 7, 8, and 11 appeared in a very abbreviated form in an introductory chapter of the book I published at the University of Toronto Press in 1996 on Yves Thériault's *Agaguk*. These chapters have been completely rewritten and considerably expanded. Very abbreviated versions of chapters 9 and 10 appeared in French, chapter 9 in honour of Henry Schogt in 1997, and chapter 10 in honour of David Hayne in 1986, and have been redrafted, expanded, and revised. Chapter 12 is a reworked, less technical, and very different version of the book I published at the University of Toronto Press in 1996. The Preface and Conclusion have not appeared in print. All of the chapters that were written as single articles or parts of an essay or book have been completely revised, recast, and integrated into a whole with a very different theoretical, methodological, and thematic slant – the elaboration of a socio-semiotic narratology focusing on the emergence of subjectivity, identity, group, and nation formation in Quebec. All have been updated incorporating recent theoretical scholarship in Saussurian semiotics and theories of enunciation.

PART I
Narratology

CHAPTER ONE

Introduction to Narratology

The purpose of this introductory chapter is to give an account of some of the major figures and key concepts that have shaped the field of narratology during the twentieth century, from both a historical and a notional perspective. The definition of narratology as 'the science of narrative' (Todorov 1969: 10) seemingly restricts the objects of study to a certain type of discourse, 'narrative,' which has been in turn defined by Ducrot and Todorov (1972: 378) as 'a referential text with represented temporality,' and then by Greimas and Courtés (1982: 203) as 'a discourse of figurative character (involving personages which accomplish actions).' Modern attempts to define narrative also frequently begin with statements concerning narratives' universality, nature, and value. For Barthes, the narratives of the world are innumerable; they cover a vast number of genres and are articulated by various means: oral, written, fixed or mobile images, gesture, painting, news items, conversation, and so on. 'Caring nothing for the division between good or bad literature: narrative is international, transhistorical and transcultural. It is simply there, like life itself' (1966: 1). For White (1980a: 5), 'to raise the question of narrative is to invite reflection on the very nature of culture and, possibly, even on the nature of humanity itself.' Whereas for Kristeva (2001), reflecting on Hannah Arendt: *'the possibility of narrating* grounds human existence in what is specific to it, in what is non-animal about it, non-physiological' (8).

Russian Formalists and the Prague Linguistic School

Historically, modern narratological theory owes much to the Russian formalists, who attempted to systematize literary criticism by elaborating an autonomous science with literature as its object of study. In his important review of the formalists' aims and achievements, as a working hypothesis Ejxenbaum (1965) stressed the primacy of theory in locating, delimiting, and understanding the systematic nature of literary facts. Moreover, the formalists clearly identified their object of study through a careful examination of what Jakobson called *literaturnost*, 'literarity,' the pertinent features of literature that distinguish it from other discourse. Their early studies compared poetic language with spoken language to consolidate this principle of specification, to illustrate methodological procedures, and to define the specificity of literary discourse. Contemporary linguistic theory enabled the group to consider relationships between wholes and parts and to investigate the structural laws and creative aspects of poetic language. Shklovsky (1929) broke new ground and extended the group's object of study when he analysed the short story and the novel using some of the concepts gleaned from what had been learned about poetry. In *O Teorii Prozy* he showed the existence of processes inherent to composition and demonstrated their link to general stylistic processes through the examination of a large number of heterogeneous texts. In this work, he related artistic form to literary history by considering it as both a permanent and a variable phenomenon. For him a work of art was not an isolated phenomenon, and its form could not be understood in and by itself but only in relationship to the forms of other works.

For the formalists, the notion of motivation was another fundamental theoretical breakthrough that played a major role in the study of the novel and short story. They identified techniques or devices that were mostly concerned with plot construction: circular construction, composition by steps or decomposition of the action into episodes, frame, and the rhetorical procedures built into this – parallelism, enumeration, oxymoron. This led them to formulate the distinction between elements in the construction of a work (*subject*) and those that make up its materials (*fable*). These new concepts of form and process, linked to that of subject as construction, laid the groundwork for Propp's (1928) seminal discovery of function in the plot analysis of folk tales, one of the crowning achievements of formalist investigation.

The Prague Linguistic School (1926–48), in which Jakobson and Trubetzkoy played leading roles, continued and developed the tradition handed down by the Russian formalists. The school greatly contributed to literary theory in general, but especially from a structuralist point of view. Mukarovsky (1934) elaborated the distinction between the existing norm (*langue*) and individual utterances (*parole*), which, according to Tynianov and Jakobson (Todorov 1965), could also be applied to literature. By integrating his theory of literature into the general framework of communication theory from a semiotic perspective, Mukarovsky provided the basis for reception theory (Jauss 1970). A major area of investigation, often ignored by Anglo-American critics, was the Prague School's linguistic approach to narrative structures. Indeed, the first anthology of the school's writings to appear in English was Garvin (1955), and it was not until 1977 that English translations of Lotman (1977) and a collection of articles by Mukarovsky (1977) were published. Doležel (1973), drawing examples from Czech literature, applied methods of structural linguistics, as developed by the school, and the modern methodology of semiotics to the study of narrative. In later works, Doležel (1979, 1990, 1998) explored the level of macro-structures (narrative worlds) by integrating the ideas of a purely formal possible world semantics into an empirical theory of literature.

Early Anglo-American Contributions

Anglo-American writings constitute a parallel intellectual trend in narratology. Concerned with the technical aspects of the art of fiction, early Anglo-American critics were not aware of the more theoretical advances made by the Russian formalists or the Prague School. In addition, the exponents of the Anglo-American tradition had in common an empirically founded conception of text and did not consider their object of study from a systematic perspective or as a system of signs governed by definable rules.[1] As a result, Henry James's prefaces (1934) dealt with 'dramatic scenes,' 'form,' 'character,' and 'first person narrative,' but from a non-formal point of view. The same can be said of Lubbock (1921) and Forster (1927), who, even though they contributed to general knowledge about the nature of narrative by suggesting concepts such as 'telling and showing,' 'voice,' and 'flat and round characters,' were not always systematic in their theoretical presentation. A second generation of critics attempted to classify literary works in terms of either 'conventions' (Frye 1957) or 'forms of plot' (Friedman 1955a) by means of taxonomies or non-formalized typologies. However, it is in the analysis of 'point-of-view' (Friedman 1955b) and 'time' (Mendilow 1952), or 'temporal distance and point-of-view' (Booth 1961a) that the Anglo-Americans' contribution to narrative theory is greatest, a contribution crowned by Booth's monumental *The Rhetoric of Fiction* (1961b).

French Narrative Semiotics

French narrative semiotics can be viewed as an extension and development of Russian formalism and Prague structuralism. This heritage was transmitted through Jakobson and Lévi-Strauss during their common period of exile in New York in the early years of the Second World War. Lévi-Strauss perceived a formal relationship between anthropology and linguistics and advocated that the social sciences use methods and concepts similar to those employed in linguistics. In his analysis of myth, Lévi-Strauss set forth the following principles:

> First, structural linguistics shifts from the study of *conscious* linguistic phenomena to the study of their unconscious infrastructure; second, it does not treat *terms* as independent entities, taking instead as its basis of analysis the relations between terms; third, it introduces the concept of *system* ... finally, structural linguistics aims at discovering *general laws*, either by induction or ... by logical deduction, which would give them an absolute character. (1963: 62, 71, 33)

The Structural Analysis of Narrative

In a special issue of *Communications* devoted to the analysis of narrative structures, Barthes (1966), in recalling the establishment of what has been labelled the Paris School of Semiotics, acknowledges a debt to Lévi-Strauss and to Émile Benveniste.[2] Narrative analysis must be based on deductive procedures and construct a hypothetical model of description patterned on structural linguistics. Level of description is a fundamental concept also borrowed from linguistics that permits the classification of a great number of elements making up narratives. Each level bears a hierarchical relationship to other levels, and narrative elements have both a distributional relationship (if the relations are situated on the same level) and an integrative relationship (when situated on different levels). In turn, levels are defined as operations or systems of symbols and rules. Barthes then distinguishes three levels of description – 'functions,' 'actions,' and 'narration' – linked together in a progressively integrated mode. A function has meaning only within the field of action in an actant, and action is meaningful only when narrated by discourse having its own code.

Functional units are further divided into two classes. Functions *per se* are considered as units of content and, at a distributional level, correspond to Propp's definition of the term. Indices, a second class of functional units, are integrative, that is, in order to understand them one must proceed to another level of description (actions of characters, or narration). Moreover, functions can be subdivided further into *cardinal functions* (or kernels) and *catalysts* (or secondary functions). Syntax, or rules of a logical nature, is then developed to describe the relations between the various functions that combine to make up sequences of actions. Sequences, logical successions of kernels linked together by presupposition, have at one and the same time an internal syntax and a syntax organizing their various relationships. The analysis of the narrative syntagm must be complemented by the description of a second level – actions – where primary units take on meaning. Whether labelled dramatis personae or actants, characters constitute a level of description rendering 'actions' intelligible. These *agents* are described by theoreticians not in terms of what they are but by what they do. In other words, characters are defined by their participation in a limited number of classifiable spheres of action inasmuch as they participate in three major semantic axes: communication, desire (quest), and test. In addition, participation is arranged in pairs, and the vast number of characters is reduced to a paradigmatic structure (Subject/Object, Addresser/Addressee, Helper/Opponent) projected along the entire narrative. However, since these categories are defined at the level of discourse, characters, as units of the actantial level, become meaningful only when integrated into the third level of description – narration. The narrative as an object of communication is dependent upon an Addresser (narrator) and Addressee (narratee), and formal marks of both narrator and narratee (Prince 1973) are considered as being immanent to the text.

Text Grammars

Contemporary semiotic literary theory of narrative owes much to Barthes's programmatic introduction, which attempts to set up a global structural model of analysis. Todorov (1969) founded his text grammar on the hypothesis that there exists a universal grammar that can be used to account formally for narrative. He utilizes three primary categories: the proper name, corresponding to the agent; the adjective, corresponding to the qualification of the agent (adjectives are divided into three groups – *state*, *property*, and *status*); and the verb, representing the predicate of an action. He also distinguishes three types of verbal functions: actions that modify a situation, actions of a reprehensible nature, and actions that entail punitive activity. This level of description is concerned primarily with the internal organization of propositions and with the number of propositions constituting a sequence. Bremond (1973) maintains Propp's notion of function but restructures his concept of sequence so that actions are analysable in terms of elementary sequences and complex sequences. Within the framework of general text grammars, van Dijk (1972) adopts a generative transformational text grammar to construct formal models for the study of literary texts. He begins by sketching the general rules of literary text grammar characteristic of both textual and sentential structures – that is, of phonology, morphology, and syntax. He then elaborates the abstract deep structures defining their macrocoherence, and, finally, proposes a pragmatic component to this global theory of text.

Narrative Models

Like Todorov (1969), Genette (1972) distinguishes three levels of textual analysis: the story (*histoire*) – signified or narrative content; the narrative (*récit*) – the signifier or utterance; and narration (*narration*) – the real or imaginary situation in which it takes place. He then suggests as the objects of narratology the study of the relationship between the signifier (*récit*) and signified (*histoire*), narration and signified, and narration and signifier. (For a critique of Genette's use of the notion of level see Bal 1985.) Time and mood are analysed successively at the level of the relationship between narration and signified, narration and signifier. In the study of time, Genette establishes the categories of order, duration, and frequency. Under mood he links point of view and distance (showing and telling), whereas under voice not only the status of the narrator but also the problems of the time of narration and the various narrative levels are examined. Despite fluctuations in terminology that have lessened its impact, Genette's contribution to narratology is theoretically innovative and has been widely accepted.

Segre (1979) refines and develops some of the preceding notions by setting up a twofold theory of time: time within the text, that of the process of the succession of its narrative and poetic moments; and external time, that of the process of reading or recreating the text itself.

Eco (1979) innovates when he works out a complex theory of the reader as an active principle of interpretation in the generative process of text. He starts with the standard communication model (Addresser – Message – Addressee) and rewrites it to give a more complete account of the semantic-pragmatic processes at play within texts. He examines the various codes and subcodes – the variety of sociocultural circumstances in which a message is emitted and by which an author organizes a text to make it communicative to his reader. His hypothesis is that an author must form a model of a possible reader and assume that the ensemble of codes he relies upon is the same as that shared by his reader. Even though only literary texts are studied, the model established concerns narrative texts in general. This important development in narratology introduces operative notions such as model reader, closed and open texts, and semantic disclosures, and also integrates standard theory on discursive structures, narrative structures, topics, isotopies, textual levels, and intertextual competence (see chapter 2). In his pioneering studies, Eco (1979, 1986) attempts to overcome some of the dramatic oppositions that exist between the Saussurian (Hjelmslevian-Greimassian) and Peircean theories of narratological semiotics originating from very different epistemological contexts and traditions (see Parret 1989 and Perron 1989b); see also three special issues of *Poetics Today* [1980 and 1981] devoted specifically to literary semiotics, and three additional volumes, entitled *Narratology Revisited I, II, III* [1990 and 1991].

Beyond Literature

The domain of narratology has been extended progressively to include not only literary but also historical, biblical, and philosophical texts. White (1980b), applying narratological models to the examination of historical discourse, suggests that sequences of real events do not necessarily possess the formal attributes of the stories told about imaginary events. Moreover, he underscores that the fiction of a world that displays itself as a form of story could be indispensable for the establishment of a moral authority, without which the notion of a specifically social reality would be unthinkable. Rastier (1972) utilizes procedures worked out with Greimas (1966b) to analyse Destutt de Tracy's *Eléments d'idéologie*. McKnight (1978) weds hermeneutical and structural traditions to construct a methodology for New Testament narratives. Borrowing from van Dijk, Bremond, and Greimas, he develops a grammar of narrative articulating the deep and surface structures that determine the generation of New Testament narrative. Patte (1976, 1978, 1987, 1990) and the Entrevernes Group (1978) also pursue the exploration offered by semiological and structural methods for biblical exegesis.

Difficulties encountered within the field of narratology arise not only from the fact that definitions of the object of study – 'narrative' – have been conflated with those of text and discourse (Greimas and Courtés 1982: 203), but also from the fact that the object of study itself encompasses a great number of extralinguistic phenomena. Metz (1966, 1971, 1977), influenced by semiotics, made the felicitous connection between text grammar and film, and outlined a program of film analysis with far-reaching repercussions. His primary intuition was that the 'grande syntagmatique,' or fundamental syntagm of narrative film – within which he distinguished six major autonomous segments: scene, sequence, alternative, redundant, descriptive syntagma, and autonomous plane – corresponded to elements of diegesis. Chatman (1978, 1980) synthesizes the most powerful insights of the Russian, French, and Anglo-American theorists in the study of the narratological structures of film and literature, and Gaudreault (1988) and Gaudreault and Jost (1990) examine the narrative in film, especially from the perspective of focalization, all the while increasing our understanding of the multiple ways in which films actually function.

The fields of musicology and art criticism are also areas of investigation that make use of some principles discovered by modern narratology. Lidov (1980, 2000) presents a unified theory of the structure and meaning of music by revising music's structural theory, and provides a foundation for the conception of music as a discourse that has its own characteristic modes of reference and makes sense of what it represents. Tarasti (1996) explores the structures and mechanisms that, in general, make the apparition of narrativity in music possible. He studies in detail what exactly narrativity in music is, and how one can affirm that music is narrative even if it has no apparent connection with the verbal, gestural, or pictorial language that would provide it with a readymade plot. The Montreal Research Group in Musical Semiotics directed by Nattiez (1976, 1987, 1993, 1999) sets out to investigate the paradigmatic technique of analysis as proposed by Ruwet (1972) in relation to the principles of Jakobson and Lévi-Strauss's structuralism. They then explore the problem of going from a paradigmatic to a stylistic analysis of music. Goodman (1980) undertakes the study of the relationships between the order of occurrence and the order of telling in literary narratives and, by examining paintings and bronze castings from oriental and occidental cultures, relates this analysis to the problems encountered when translating the spatial relationships of pictures into temporal ones.

The Saussurian–Hjelmslevian Legacy

Since the fundamental contributions by the Russian formalists and the Prague School in the first half of the twentieth century, French theoreticians have made major contributions to the field of narratology. In France, two dominant tendencies in narratology can be traced that stem from the intellectual activity of the mid-1960s. The first tendency is founded on the Saussurian–Hjelmslevian legacy that is best represented by work done by Greimas and, what has become known as the Paris School of Semiotics. This school, which concentrates more on syntactic and semantic domains of the discipline, adopts an immanentist attitude to texts, as pointed out by Parret (1989). (For an overview of Greimas's theory of narrativity see Greimas [1987a], Schleifer [1987], Perron [1989a], Patte [1990], and Broden [1995]). It is within the context of the Paris School that Greimas (1987a), who greatly extended the application of narrative analysis to other fields, makes the strongest claim for narratology. His initial hypothesis is that meaning (*sens*) is apprehensible only if it is articulated or narrativized. Secondly, for him narrative structures can be perceived in other systems not necessarily dependent upon natural languages. This then leads him to posit the fundamental distinction between two levels of representation and analysis: an apparent level of narrative and an immanent level, which form a sort of common structural trunk where narrativity is situated and organized prior to its manifestation. The signification of a phenomenon does not therefore depend on the mode of its manifestation. Because it originates in this fundamental model, signification, so to speak, cuts through all forms of linguistic and non-linguistic manifestation (sociological, economic, literary, philosophical, and mathematical narratives; cinematographic, sculptural, and architectural discourses). Thus, this model eliminates the necessity of setting up theoretical mediations when passing from one particular type of manifestation or expression to another. Further, this general theory of narrative attempts to account for the articulation and manifestation of the semantic universe as a totality of meaning, whether it happens to be of a cultural or a personal nature. The main difficulty encountered is in constructing the actual instances of the generation of signification where semantic substance is first articulated and constituted into a signifying form, and then setting up the intermediate or mediating stages that transform the semantic substance into the last instances where signification is manifested. It is within this framework that Greimas constructs his general semiotic system and fundamental grammar. This theory of narrative has been revised by him and his followers and tested on various forms of extralinguistic texts such as non-figurative painting (Thürlemann 1979), figurative painting (Thürlemann 1981), space (Hammad 1973, 1977, 1983), and architecture (Lévy 1979).

In two of his more recent books (1987b and 1993, the latter co-authored with Fontanille), Greimas explored the possibility of constructing a discursive syntax based on aspectualities, after having set in place a modal syntax in his prior works. This final stage, which built on the actional and cognitive dimensions of analysis worked out over the last twenty-five years, attempted to establish a narratological foundation and give a semio-narrative interpretation to traditional theories of emotions and passions. In so doing, Greimas and Fontanille sought to establish a coherent methodology that articulates the relationship between semio-narrative theory and philosophy and also endeavoured to rethink semio-narrative theory in general (with its focus on action and cognition) by the introduction of the concept of passion. The study of the passional dimension of numerous literary texts was accompanied by a disengagement from Peirce's semiotic and an engagement with phenomenology and catastrophe theory, notably as represented by Merleau-Ponty (proprioception) and René Thom (perception, saliency/pregnanz).

Beyond Structuralist Narratology

The second tendency is represented by the large number of works that draw their inspiration from a radical questioning of the principles defining structuralist narratology. Kristeva (1969, 1970) and especially Barthes (1970) were instrumental in this respect. Indeed, the latter began his study of *S/Z* by challenging the very possibility of structural analysis to account for the specificity and/or individuality of any text. He then shifted the problematic from that of science and ideology to the practice of writing and rewriting – in short, to a theory of addressers and addressees, of signs and interpreters. In so doing, he also substituted a narratology of codes for one of signs and processes and, without structuring or hierarchizing them, determined five codes under which all the textual signifiers can be grouped: the hermeneutic (enigma); the semic; the symbolic; the proairetic (actions); and the cultural (references to a science or body of knowledge).

Scholes (1982), whose work deals with particular texts and ways in which they may be read and interpreted, does not concentrate on the syntactic or semantic dimension of narrative as such but adopts an approach based on the study of codes. He shows how the literary work, far from being a closed system 'free of authorial intention, free of historical necessity, and free of the reader's projection of value and meaning' (15), as New Criticism would have us believe, is, on the contrary, an open text linked to history, to cultural, semantic, and literary codes, and to other texts. Other critics, such as Culler (1981) and Eagleton (1983), have offered both a critique and discussion on the limits and/or boundaries of narratology. Barry (1999), in an innovative and seminal work, examines how the perception of the artistic form can contribute to the emergence of meaning. From Saussure to Hjelmslev, to Greimas, to Peirce, to the latest developments in cognitive or 'brain' sciences, Barry explores how the form of art, its signifier, literally helps 'make' meaning. The originality of this work is to propose a semiotics founded on a semantics of the form of expression that extends from verbal modalities to music and to painting.

Most of the narratological studies on the novel have concentrated on synchronic, semio-narrative structures: for example, Bremond (1973), who examines the logic of possibilities; Chatman (1978); Le Huenen and Perron (1980), who explore in detail the semiotics of character in Balzac's *Eugénie Grandet*; Prince (1982, 1987); Rimmon-Kenan (1983); and Coste (1989), who give us an overview of narrative structures. Perron (1996) distinguishes the multiple signs in the Quebec novel *Agaguk* and establishes a narrative grammar, based on an actional, cognitive, and passional semiotic theory, that can be applied to a text as complex as a novel. For this purpose he redefines the concept of the sign and introduces a semiotics of passions that conditions the characters' actions. None the less, little has been written on the diachronic structuration and the dialectical process of production of narrative texts, and Krysinski (1981) seeks to fill this void. Attempting to understand the novel as a historically motivated semio-narrative process, Krysinski not only strives to work out a general semio-narrative theory but also focuses his analysis on modern texts from Dostoevsky to Roa Bastos, including Henry James, André Gide, Thomas Mann, John Dos Passos, Claude Simon, and Hubert Aquin. Broden (1999b), in his analysis of *Yeux bleus cheveux noirs* by Marguerite Duras, examines body movements and the sense of touch, deriving from them other principles that inform the syntagmatic organization of discourse. He studies how modulations of pace, time, tempo, and tensivity articulate the unfolding of the narrative.

Feminist Criticism

Recent feminist criticism by De Lauretis (1984, 1988), Bal (1986), and Silverman (1983, 1984, 1988) extends narratology into other domains. De Lauretis problematizes the earlier structural models that consider desire as a type of thematic investment and re-examines the relation of narratives to genres and to epistemological frameworks. She shows how the productivity of the text engages the reader as subject in and for its process and places the reader in certain positions of plot space. Narrative is considered as obeying an Oedipal logic that constrains and defines each reader within the position of a sexual difference conceived as follows: male-hero-human as the subject; and female-obstacle-boundary-space as the other. Bal (1986), inspired by Genette (1972), extends her earlier study of a more 'scientific' and structuralist nature and works out a feminist narratology that ascribes to the gender of the narrator the same theoretical status as narrative point of view, for instance. The critique of post-structuralist narratology is furthered by Silverman (1988), who maintains the centrality of psychoanalysis and emphasizes 'sexual difference as an organizing principle not only of the symbolic order and its "contents" (signification, discourse, subjectivity), but of the semiotic account of those things' (viii). These important studies extend the theoretical boundaries of narratology into the domain of socio-semiotics and contribute to the redefinition of an important area of cultural studies focusing on current feminist theory and practice.

Theories of Reading and the Literary Sign

A number of studies have been written in an attempt to focus and refocus narratology on the literary work in general and its apprehension through the reading process (for an overview see McHale and Ronan, 1990). Two major areas of investigation are being explored, the first related to working out theories of reading, and the second examining the mediating function of the literary sign between symbolic forms and the materiality of the world. It should be noted that, although these two areas deal with what Morris (1938) identified as the pragmatic dimension of semiosis, or the relation of signs to their interpreters, both build on prior theoretical work carried out by numerous narratologists. Relying on a pluridisciplinary approach, Gervais (1990, 1993, 1998) focuses on the activity of reading, or what he calls the 'reading contract.' In so doing, he studies the structural features of the conceptual network of actions and their reception from the theoretical perspective of semiotics, logic of actions, artificial intelligence, and the cognitive sciences. By isolating the discursive representation of action and considering it as a nodal component both of the narrative and of reading – and, hence, by instituting a cognitive level of reading – Gervais frees narratological theory and analysis from the narrow confines of the structuralist paradigm, opening up a very promising area of further inquiry. From a more theoretical perspective, Perron and Danesi (1993) critically examine Greimas's narratological semiotics as a theory of cognition – notably, its specific implications for the study of mind. To this end they extract several narratological fibres from the Greimassian theoretical fabric that are woven into a frame of reference for viewing how humans might generate and understand signifying structures.

The Social Function of Narrative

Ricœur (1980) sketches a general theory of narrative discourse from a philosophical perspective and considers three areas of investigation. The first concerns the place and role of narrative in historical understanding and in historiography. The second deals with the place and role of narrative in literature, and the third with the truth claims of both historiography and literature. In a much more radical mode, however, Ricœur (1984, 1985, 1988) situates narrative at the very core of social existence. He proposes a phenomenological and hermeneutic theory of narrative whereby external time becomes human time (temporality) only when it is articulated through narrative, and, as a corollary, where narrative is meaningful only in so far as it configures human experience. Narrativity is hence the cornerstone of Ricœur's theory, and on this point his position is similar to that of Greimas, for whom signification cannot exist without narrativity. As Ricœur (1989: 551) notes (in contrast to linguists who often deal with objects having no social or institutional existence), narratives 'already have their social functions, and they are understood in a certain way in social intercourse among writers, narrators, readers and speakers, for example.' In short, Ricœur's integrated theory of narrative as temporalized actional, cognitive, and passional structures attempts to account for the organization of a subject's experiential existence, the configuration of the experiential in narratives, and the rules that govern an individual's understanding in general.

Saussure and Peirce

The need to break out from the immanentist theoretical assumptions of structuralism that restricted and enfolded narratological structures in the text has also spawned a great deal of work of a Peircean nature that could possibly be termed post-narratological. Numerous theoreticians are re-examining Peircean theory and demonstrating its heuristic value in the study of literary texts. Pinto's semantico-semiotic approach to the reading of time (1989) is such an attempt to develop an approach that goes beyond structuralism, which concentrated on how time was organized in a text. Pinto sets out to study the reader's behaviour with respect to temporal relations and to explain reading strategies within semantic and semiotic theory. He adapts Peirce's categories of firstness, secondness, and thirdness, and equates them with perception, apprehension, and interpretation of the reading process, before applying the model to the study of a play by Harold Pinter and a novel by Lèdo Ivo.

Sheriff (1989) also proposes a radical critique of narratological studies stemming from Saussurian or structuralist theory that can describe a literary work only as a closed formal network (Morris's syntatics and semantics), thereby negating its signification (e.g., the relation of the text to its interpreters, to being and possibility). Sheriff then re-examines Peirce's trichotomic theory of signs and studies what he considers to be the three aspects of a literary text: the text not actualized through the act of reading is seen as a virtual signifier, corresponding to the eighth category of legisigns (rheme). The act of reading actualizes meaning by giving an interpretation related to the lived experience; here the text corresponds to the ninth category of legisigns (dicisign). The text as sign of autorepresentation, the most abstract level, corresponds to the tenth category (argument).

Most of the semioticians currently working in the Peircean paradigm adhere to some degree to Sheriff's critique of the limits of narratological theory of Saussurian or structuralist inspiration and recognize the need to open up the study of text to the social environment. As Fisette (1991:

184) notes, these works, which raise important epistemological questions about the concept of texts, their mode of existence in a given culture, and also their contribution to the issue of symbolic productions in general, could herald a renewal of textual studies 'which, this time, would be free of all the canons inherited from structuralism.'

In spite of the above critique of narratological theory based on a certain reading of the Saussurian–Hjelmslevian paradigm of so-called structuralist origin, in this work I have attempted to reconceptualize the theory and methodology that have informed much of European narratological analysis since it has sought out the nature of its object of study and has developed a coherent and heuristic methodology. Benveniste's reflections on subjectivity and enunciation have enabled me to rethink some of the major contributions from the Paris School and rework them in terms of a more global theory of production and reception by taking into account the pragmatic dimension of discourse. I have also attempted to reconceptualize both the Paris School and Benveniste in terms of Paul Ricœur's *Time and Narrative I, II, III*, introducing an ontological dimension to the analysis of narrative. In so doing, I have concentrated especially on the enunciative strategies and mechanisms in a text that position, cognitively manipulate, and move the enunciatee-reader. In short, what I have set out to do is to integrate in the global model of narrative analysis, through recourse to phenomenology, the perceived, thought, and felt semantic universe, by and through the body.

CHAPTER TWO

A.J. Greimas and Narratology

The intention of this chapter is neither to retrace the development of semiotics in Europe nor to situate in every detail all of Algirdas Julien Greimas's works within the intellectual tradition of his times. J.C. Coquet, in his lengthy and informative introductory chapter in *Sémiotique – L'École de Paris* (1982) and his 'Éléments de bio-bibliographie' (1985), provides us with a detailed overview of the fundamental role played by Greimas in the history of semiotics as well as an up-to-date bibliography of his seminal works. In addition, Herman Parret and Hans George Ruprecht in their perceptive introduction to *Recueil d'hommages pour / Essays in honor of Algirdas Julien Greimas* (1985) not only discuss some of the salient features of the theory but also sketch the intellectual horizon in which it was elaborated. Also, Schleifer (1987) and Broden (1995), in his commemorative essay, inform us about the intellectual climate that fostered the evolution and the development of Greimas's theory. In addition, Broden, in his Foreword (2000) to the critical edition of *Algirdas Julien Greimas. La Mode en 1830*, gives an incisive and illuminating analysis of the European intellectual tradition that informed Greimas's early work predating his reading of Saussure, beginning with a historical and social study of French vocabulary, followed by his encounter with historicist structuralism, and leading to structural semantics. In this chapter, I give an account of the development of the main features of Greimas's theory and methodology as they evolved over the years, since his many contributions to the study of narrative inform a good deal of the analysis undertaken in the next ten chapters of this book. In evaluating his work, I shall also take into account some of the dominant theories of narrative in the twentieth century.

The first essay appearing in *Du sens* (1970), which opens with the cursory remark 'It is extremely difficult to speak about meaning and to say something meaningful about it' (7), explores and puts in place the first two phases of Greimassian narrative semiotics. In 1956, in *Le Français moderne*, Greimas published a programmatic article entitled 'L'Actualité du saussurisme' in which he examined works by Merleau-Ponty and Lévi-Strauss and concluded that the 'Saussurian postulate of a structured world apprehensible in its significations' (193) can, in fact, contribute to the elaboration of a unified methodology in the human sciences.[1] At this time, Greimas became aware that, although structuralism in its many forms focused mainly on problems of language from a linguistic perspective (e.g., Lévi-Strauss and Dumézil in anthropology, Barthes in literature, and Lacan in psychoanalysis, to name but a few of the dominant figures who revolutionized their respective disciplines), no structural linguists were attempting to do the same in their own field. In France, according to Greimas, the latest word in linguistics was Bloomfield's distributionalism.[2] None the less, it was apparent to him that, through the extrapolation of concepts borrowed from Saussure and Hjelmslev and the forging of new methods of investigation, great strides were being made in various areas of the human sciences.

Beginnings

'Comparative Mythology,'[3] written in 1962, owes a great deal to Lévi-Strauss and Jakobson with respect to its methodological and theoretical underpinnings. Greimas's point of departure was that the investigation of meaning is by definition a metalinguistic activity that paraphrases and translates words and utterances by means of other words and utterances. For him it therefore followed that the first step in describing signification resided in the transposition of one level of language into another level, of one language into another language. Since meaning could be described as this very possibility of transcoding, it was necessary for him to develop a new terminology and construct an adequate metalanguage that could account for the object in question. Thus, to uncover the 'mythological signified,' Greimas endeavoured to work out a rigorous methodology based on objective criteria of analysis partially adopted from structural linguistics, which had, at the time, more or less abandoned research in the area of semantics. Dumézil's work on myth, considered as the translation of mythological language into ideological language, was 'overanalyzed' in much the same way that Lévi-Strauss overanalysed the Oedipus myth. In short, a new formulation of Dumézil's analysis was proposed by which the study of myth and the structural methodology borrowed from the social sciences were used to examine the superstructures of social ideologies. This was indeed a major development from a semiotic point of view, since in Hjelmslev's terms a 'connotative semiotics' was transformed into a 'denotative semiotics' that, for him, was a precondition for an adequate description of a text.

With the problem of meaning reduced to its minimal dimensions, that is to say, to the transcoding of significations, 'scientific' activity in this domain consisted in establishing techniques of transposition.[4] The main feature in the analysis of Dumézil's work can be found in the conversion of the syntagmatic manifestation of myth into paradigmatic relations, or, in other words, in the setting up of correlations between a limited number of units of the mythic signified distributed throughout the narrative. As a first important methodological step, a relevant level was defined and a discourse, based on the principle of interdefinition, was constructed on the mythological object. However, it should be noted that this new formulation of Dumézil's text does not correspond *stricto sensu* to formalization as defined, for example, by logicians in formal theory. From the outset, semiotics was not considered a formal language as such, but rather an intermediary stage towards explanation, towards giving a more 'scientific' account of meaning.

Yet in spite of the real gains made in adopting the preceding methodological perspective, the conclusions of this study clearly point to the insufficiencies of Lévi-Strauss's paradigmatic definition of myth. This he considered as a correlation of two pairs of units of the signified that are in significant opposition to each other and that exclude any syntagmatic relation. Indeed, Greimas did use methodological procedures borrowed from structural anthropology, and even refined major constituent units by breaking them down into distinctive features called semes,[5] or semic categories and archilexemes (sets of semic categories constituting pairs of lexemic oppositions making up the elementary structures of myth). Yet he also made a case for the need to investigate, in addition to the Lévi-Straussian paradigmatic structures, syntagmatic structures that could be grounded in discourse analysis.

Structural Semantics

Sémantique structurale (1966b), which sketched out the initial model of the elementary structure of signification, was the first important monograph published by Greimas. For the first time, he presented a syntactic and semantic (actantial) theory of discourse. (For a detailed account of this seminal work, see Jameson, *The Prison House of Language* [1972] and Schleifer's 'Introduction' to *Structural Semantics* [1983].) In this book, he elaborated the elementary structure of signification, the notion of semantic axes, and that of semic articulation, and defined semes in relationship to lexemes, along with the notion of isotopy. In the description of signification, he established the categories of predicate and actant, logical syntax and semantics, all the while stressing the modal character of the actantial categories. He worked out the actantial model, comprised of a Sender and a Receiver, a Subject and an Object, aided or hindered by a Helper or an Opponent, and ended up by giving a detailed example of the description, focusing on the semantic universe of Georges Bernanos.

'Toward a Semiotics of the Natural World,' written in 1968, raised further questions of a metasemiotic and theoretical nature by exploring the possibilities of the description, or the apprehension of signification in systems not dependent on natural languages. Paraphrasing Hjelmslev, Greimas (1970) defined semiotics as 'a hierarchy that can be subjected to analysis and the elements of which can be determined by reciprocal relations (and by commutation)' (22). In other words, a semiotics exists only as a possibility of description, and the system of relations described does not depend on the nature of the sign by which the external or internal world is manifested. Description was thus thought of as the construction of a network of relations by the identification and naming of both the observed relations and their points of intersection or disjunction.

Gesture

This investigation of the gestural domain of the natural world through the description of relevant features at the level of content that are at the same time distinctive and significant brings to the fore the anthropological dimension of Greimas's narrative semiotics. 'Comparative Mythology,' as I noted, focused on the paradigmatic organization of text. In contrast, 'Toward a Semiotics of the Natural World' investigated the syntagmatic dimension of gesture, considered both as a 'discursive structure,' because it appears within the context of the subject/object relation, and as an 'utterance' constructed by the human subject and deciphered by another subject, within the context of a program of enunciation that is at the very origins of intersubjective relations. The semiotic status of gestural signs, which were defined in terms of the semiotic relation between expression and content, was studied in conjunction with the fundamental problem of identifying what actually constitutes gestural units. Human beings, as bodies, were first of all viewed as figures of the world and then as complex mechanisms that, through mobility, produce differential (positional) gaps at the level of the signifier by which signification can take place at the level of the signified. Gestural activity was explored within the framework of the project defining it. Consequently, a programmed gestural project can be said to constitute the signified of gestural activity, whereas the gestural sequence can be equated with its signifier. This enabled Greimas to define the semiosis of a gestural program as the relation between a sequence of gestural figures taken as the signifier and the gesture project considered as the signified. Yet when all is said and done, the analysis of gesturality raises problems as to the functional nature of gestural semiotics.[6] Greimas here identified the need to work out a level of analysis that would deal specifically with the organization of content and be part of a general functional semiotics also encompassing the semantic dimension of natural languages; he also hinted at the possible form it could take.

Propp and Lévi-Strauss

'The Interaction of Semiotic Constraints' (1968), co-authored with François Rastier, and 'Elements of a Narrative Grammar' (1969) laid the groundwork for what became the cornerstone of Greimas's narrative semiotics. These two works openly acknowledged a debt both to Propp (1928), who provided the syntactic component for the deep semio-narrative grammar, and to Lévi-Strauss (1963), who furnished the idea of the semantic component. Propp's thirty-one functions (designating syntagmatic units that remain constant despite the diversity of narratives, and whose ordered sequence makes up the structure of folk-tale) were redefined in terms of a limited number of actants. It then became possible to conceive of a principle of organization underlying whole classes of narratives. Deep structures were thus posited as being the principle of organization, not only of figurative discourses, but also of abstract discourses (philosophical, political, scientific, etc.), as well as of other semiotic systems not necessarily expressed through natural languages (cinema, figurative painting, architecture, advertising, gesture, etc.). Moreover, following Petitot-Cocorda (1985), I suggest that these structures are lived existentially in human passions, ideology, actions, and dreams and that semio-narrative structures, to borrow a phrase from Gilbert Durand (1963), can be thought of as 'the anthropological structures of the imaginary.'[7] It then became of utmost importance for Greimas to work out a means, or a grammar, that could account for such structures. Indeed, the semio-narrative grammar he elaborated established a specific relation between syntax and semantics that Petitot-Cocorda (1985) described as 'the projection of the paradigmatic axis onto the syntagmatic axis, the understanding of which constitutes one of the central problems of structuralism, perhaps even its most central problem' (48–9).

The Semantic Universe

According to this theory, the semantic universe, defined as the set of the systems of values, can be apprehended as meaningful only if it is articulated or narrativized. Thus, any discourse presupposes a semantic universe hypothetically made up of the totality of significations, postulated as such prior to its articulation, and which it actualizes in part. This partial realization, or microsemantic universe, at the fundamental level, articulates elementary axiological structures such as life/death (individual universe) and nature/culture (collective universe). These basic structures situated at the deep semantic level are considered as ad hoc universals that serve as starting points for the analysis of semantic universes, be they individual or collective. Their meaning is never apprehensible as such, but rather only when they are manifested in the form of an articulated signification, or in other words, when they are converted into actantial structures. Petitot-Cocorda (1985) clearly perceived the theoretical import of Greimas's semiotics when he situated the semio-narrative structures within an anthropological framework:

> The deep semantic categories are universals of the imaginary. We are not conscious of them, and they exist only because they are axiologized and ideologically invested in objects of value, the quest for which governs the actions (narrative programs in Greimassian terminology) of the subject actants. It is only through the circulation of object-values governed by actantial syntax that they can be apprehended. In other words, they cannot

be subjectivized as such but instead only by means of a logic of actions. The role of actantial syntax is therefore to convert into a narrative doing the fundamental semantics that constitute the message of narrative and determine its anthropological function. This syntax enables one to grasp, through the simulacrum of a 'scene' that dramatizes them, the unconscious crystallising processes of subjectivity. (50–1; my translation)

The Generative Trajectory

'The Interaction of Semiotic Constraints' suggests the possibility of a generative trajectory, beginning with a fundamental semiotic level that is then converted into an actantial syntax before ultimately being manifested through discourse, but focuses especially on the first domain of the global trajectory. The main object of the theory of the semiotic square is to articulate the substance of the content (in Hjelmslev's terms) and therein constitute the form of content. This elementary structure should be considered 'on the one hand, as a concept uniting the minimal conditions for the apprehension and/or the production of signification, and, on the other, as a model containing the minimal definition of any language (or, more generally, of any semiotic system or process) and of any semiotic unit' (Greimas and Courtés 1982: 314). Prior to any semantic investment whatsoever, the elementary structure appears as a complex binary semic category that correlates two contrary semes by means of a relation of junction (conjunction/disjunction) and by a relation of reciprocal presupposition. Yet, as Petitot-Cocorda (1985) remarks, 'As a simple logical form formalized in terms of Boolean elementary set logic, the semiotic square is trivial, and of little interest, since it only reformulates logical squares going back to Aristotle. But if we see it as a structure in the strong sense of the term, then everything changes, since it becomes an "organic" and "self-regulating" system of interdependent and founding relations that do not define terms. But rather, in much the same way as in a phonological paradigm, they are positional values, places that are defined in a purely relational fashion.' The constituent relations of contrariety and contradiction of the semiotic square, it is argued, are not logical in nature, but in the Jakobsonian sense are 'qualitative oppositions and privative oppositions and must be treated as such.' The formal characteristics of the semiotic square are founded on a dynamic topology of places and connections and not upon a static logic of terms and connections (51–2).

Narrative Grammar

'Elements of a Narrative Grammar,' puts in place the various components and the interrelationships of the first two levels of the theory of narrativity, represented graphically in their entirety under the heading of 'Generative Trajectory' in Greimas and Courtés (1982: 134). The semio-narrative structures, constituting the most abstract level or starting point of the generative trajectory, are present in the form of a semiotic and narrative grammar. These grammars contain two components – syntactic and semantic – and two levels of depth, a fundamental syntax and fundamental semantics on the deep level, and a narrative syntax and narrative semantics on the surface level. Finally, the discursive structures, less deep than the other two, take up the surface semiotic structures and set them into discourse. At this level, a discursive syntax is identified comprising the subcomponents of actorialization, temporalization, and spatialization. The semantic component, or discursive semantics, is made up of the subcomponents of thematization and figurativization.

Conversion

The main theoretical problem arising from this model of narrativity concerns the passage (conversion) on the one hand from a taxonomic morphology, or paradigmatic relation, to an operative syntax, or syntagmatic relation, and on the other, the passage (conversion) from a fundamental abstract syntax to a narrative anthropomorphic surface-syntax, and ultimately to a discursive-figurative syntax. It should be noted, however, that there exist in the theory two types of conversions: 'vertical' conversions (having to do with the relations between levels) and 'horizontal' conversions (dealing with the relations between the syntactic and semantic components of each level). At the deep level, horizontal conversion, or the passage from the elementary morphology constituted by fundamental relations to an operative syntax, is ensured by the introduction of an actant subject. 'Signification, to the extent that one seeks to find in it an object, appears as an articulation of stable fundamental relations; it can also be represented dynamically, if one considers it as an apprehension of the production of meaning by a subject' (Petitot-Cocorda 1982: 5). In short, equivalencies are established between the fundamental constituent relations of the taxonomic model and the projections of the same relations or operations by means of a horizontal anthropomorphic conversion at the deep level. And, thus, the relation of contradiction at the taxonomic level as a contradictory operation at the syntactic level will negate one of the terms and at the same time affirm its contradictory term.

In this transpositional model, the problem of vertical conversion, or the passage from the fundamental syntax to the surface anthropomorphic narrative syntax, is resolved by the setting up of procedures that establish equivalencies between these two levels. I would like to stress, though, that the equivalencies posited here do not correspond to identity but rather are founded on the presupposition that 'two or more syntactic forms (or two or more semantic formulations) can be referred to a constant topic' (Greimas and Courtés 1982: 62). In addition, insofar as meaning is transformed into signification when articulated, each new articulation is an enrichment or increase in meaning. Hence, in proceeding from the deep level to the surface levels, we must regard the surface as richer than the deep level: 'Consequently any conversion must be viewed as equivalence and as a surplus of signification' (ibid. 62). As Greimas stated in an interview with Ruprecht (1984), conversion is homotopic and heteromorphic: 'the forms pass from the deep structures (where operations take place on the semiotic square) to the semio-narrative level (where there exists a surface narrative grammar). Both of these levels are concerned with the same thing but in a different way' (14).

The conversion of the deep level into the surface level is ensured by the establishment of equivalencies between syntactic operations at the fundamental level and those occurring at the surface level. Thus, syntactic activity, having been converted from syntactic operation that was itself converted from taxic relations, provides the necessary mediation for the generation of a narrative utterance that is the major component of narrative grammar. The utterance $NU = F(A)$ is seen as a process that is composed of a function, in the Proppian sense, and an actant. Conversion thus rests on the equivalence between the syntactic operation and syntactic activity, on the one hand, and between syntactic activity and an elementary utterance of actantial activity, on the other.

Greimas always claimed, and rightly so, that semiotics was not a science but rather a scientific project, still incomplete, and that what he attempted to do was to establish theoretical principles that needed to be completed and transformed. However, we should not minimize the import of the theoretical problems related to the issue of conversion already alluded to in this chapter. These are due to the generative conceptualization of the model according to which various components are linked together along a trajectory that proceeds from the simplest to the most complex, from the most abstract to the most concrete. The problem of conversion and equivalencies is raised on numerous occasions by Greimas himself, beginning with 'Elements of a Narrative Grammar.' In an interview with Frédéric Nef (1976), the author admits that 'A theoretical construct, no matter how satisfying it appears at first view, runs the risk of remaining hypothetical as long as the problem of equivalencies between different levels of depth is not clearly posed, as long as the procedures of conversion from one level to another have not been worked out' (24). Again, in a special issue of *Le Bulletin* (1981) devoted to the semiotic square, Greimas once more stated that one of the urgent tasks facing semioticians is to undertake research on conversion. It is necessary to conceive of and construct procedures for passing from the deep level of semantic categorizations to the more surface ones of anthropomorphic narrative syntax and of its investments (45–6). The same awareness of the possible weak point in the theory is demonstrated in Greimas and Courtés (1982): 'As can be expected, the elaboration of conversion rules will be one of the fundamental tests of the coherence of semiotic theory.' (62)

It is especially on this very issue of conversion and equivalencies within the framework of the narrative grammar we have just sketched that Paul Ricœur (1984) puts forth reservations about the actual coherence of the theory. Ricœur basically takes issue with the model on three counts. The first concerns the conversion of contradiction at the deep level into polemic at the surface level; that is to say, polemical negativity cannot be derived either from the taxonomic relations of contradiction–contrariety or from the syntactic operation of negation. The second is related to the fact that there exist syntagmatic supplements at the surface level that cannot be obtained from the conversion of the fundamental grammar to the surface grammar. The third is that the praxic–pathic dimension of narrative sets into play a semantics of action that activates a syntax the very intelligibility of which is mixed, since it is both phenomenological and linguistic. In his work on the morphogenesis of meaning, Petitot-Cocorda (1985) argues that for Ricœur's critique to be truly pertinent, the implicit phenomenology of the praxic–pathic semantics of action would have to be formalized so that it could be integrated into a formal model. He concludes that the hypothesis of a syntagmatic supplement that is irreducible to the paradigmatic is tenable only if one forces Greimas's thought and views conversion as a simple equivalence between metalanguages, and this is far from being the case (268). In the final analysis, the real problem in the theory that must be addressed is the one Greimas himself has raised all along, namely, the need to establish the actual procedures of conversion.

The Subject

The anthropomorphic actantial dimension mentioned above establishes relations between subjects and objects, subjects and anti-subjects, and subjects and senders and receivers. The first relation, founded on the institution of the subject as a wanting subject and the object as an object of value, can be described in terms of modal utterances. Wanting is the first of a series of determined semantic restrictions that specify actants as virtual operators of an act; the second is having. Other semantic restrictions, the introduction of the modalities of being able and knowing, constitute the being or the activity of the actant subject. The relation of subject and object furthermore can be described syntactically in terms of utterances of state that are junctive in nature. The second relation, between subject and anti-subject, is considered as the conversion of the paradigmatic relation.

The third relation, between subject and sender or subject and receiver, is reformulated in terms of a general structure of exchange. The attribution of an object of value is here seen as a disjunctive operation (privation) and a conjunctive one (attribution). This reformulation made it possible to represent the previous operations as places of transfers of objects of value from one location to another. A topological syntax of objective values can therefore be established that, since it follows the logical operations at the level of deep grammar, organizes narration as a process creating values. However, by changing focus and examining the relation between operators – subject and sender or receiver – we can see that topological syntax governs the transfer both of the subject's capacity to do and of the values. Also, by manipulating subjects and endowing them with the virtuality of doing, the topological syntax governs the institution of syntactic operators. In a later, more complete version of the theory, the subject and sender are characterized by a dual contractual relation, since not only will the subject actant have a contractual relation with the manipulating operator actant (sender) that institutes it as an operator subject, but performance is also sanctioned by a final sender, whose absolute competence is presupposed.

The Object

In surface narrative grammar, the object is one of the terms of the elementary utterance that, when inscribed in a junctive relation with the subject, guarantees the latter's semiotic existence. However, the object, while remaining unknowable in itself, exists semiotically as a locus of fixation, a locus of circumstantial clustering of the value determinations. Values invested in the object can be accounted for only syntactically, and it is in this syntagmatic unfolding that syntax joins semantics. Moreover, it is only when they are converted from semantic into syntactic structures that values can be apprehended as signification. Subsequently, conversion makes it possible both to define narrativization as the syntagmatic emplacement of values and to perceive it as a discursive organization that manipulates the constitutive elements of the elementary utterance. Moreover, two broad categories of values – descriptive (consumable or storable objects, states, and feelings) and modal (wanting, being-able-to, knowing-how-and-having-to-be/to-do) – can be distinguished. In turn, descriptive values can be divided further into subjective (essential values) and objective (accidental values), and in narrative programs base values can be distinguished from instrumental ones (see Greimas and Courtés 1982: 365).[8]

Object and Value

Since narrative, at the surface level, was defined as the transformation of a series of utterances of state (junctive utterances) by a metasubject operator (utterance of doing), this syntactic organization makes it possible to represent narrative as a series of virtualizations and actualizations of values. Values inscribed within a given axiological universe circulate in two ways. In the case of constant values between subjects in an isotopic and closed universe, they circulate as conflictual–polemic confrontation, whereas in the case of exchange, the presence of two objects of value is required, and this structure constitutes a new virtualization and a new actualization. Simple exchange can then be considered as a complex mode of value transfer at the level of surface syntax. None the less, for such an operation to take place in the case where exchange values are not identical requires their preliminary identification by subjects who, by fixing the exchange value of the said objects of value, establish a fiduciary contract between themselves. When the objects of value are objects of knowing, or messages being communicated, and when the subjects in question are competent but unequally modalized, then the polemic-contractual, which is one of the fundamental organizing structures of narrative grammar, is transposed into the very core of intersubjectivity. This is where, as Greimas (1983a) notes, 'It seems to be able to account for the fiduciary, troubling and groping, but, at the same time, cunning and dominating nature of communication' (11).

In participatory communication, the contractual dimension of exchange, within a closed universe, is ensured by a sender who guarantees the circulation of values. The sender corresponds to a mediating domain between an immanent universe and a transcendent universe that are manifested through the presence of actants at the level of surface syntax. The sender, who is the source of the contract in discourse, is the disengaged representative of the paradigmatic system of the invested contents, or the values that are the taxonomic constituents of the fundamental grammar (Courtés 1976: 99). From this it follows that the internalization of the conversion of the paradigmatic dimension in the narrative is constituted by the relation between the contractual sequence and the performance sequence. If the contractual sequence is accepted as a narrative program by the subject-receiver, it is transformed into a performing subject if, and only if, it acquires a modal competence that ensures the mediation between system and process, and realizes virtual values.

Actants

Insofar as it guarantees the semiotic existence of actants, the narrative organization of values continues to be the foundation of narrativity. The object of value, which is one of the terms of the elementary utterance previously defined as a semiotic simulacrum, representing our relation to the world in the form of a scene, is also a syntactic concept. The distinction between actants (considered initially as simple supports and then progressively invested by values through junctive relations) and actors (that can syncretize several actants) enables us to explore the relations between elementary narrative structures and discursive structures.

As an actant progresses through its narrative trajectory it can assume a certain number of narrative states or actantial roles that are defined by its position within the narrative trajectory (syntactic definition) and its modal investment (morphological definition). As a necessary step towards performance, the subject actant will be endowed successively with the modalities of competence, and in this case the subject assumes those actantial roles that manifest the subject in terms of wanting, the subject in terms of knowing, the subject in terms of being-able-to-do, and the subject in terms of having-to-do, and that then indicate the four states in the acquisition of its modal competence. Actantial roles, because they are defined morphologically by their modal content and syntactically by the position of actant in the narrative trajectory, are situated within narrative syntax. However, when associated with 'thematic roles (which structure the semantic component of the discourse), they allow for the construction of actors as loci where narrative and discursive structures converge and are invested' (Greimas and Courtés 1982: 6).

Actors

What first of all distinguishes an actantial role from an actor is that, at the level of discourse, 'an actor's semantic content is defined by the presence of the semes that are (1) figurative entity (anthropomorphic, zoomorphic order), (2) animated, and (3) subject to individuation. At the same level, the actantial role is "manifested," as a qualification, as an attribute of the actor. From a semantic point of view, this qualification is no more than the denomination subsuming a field of functions (that is to say behaviors actually noted in the narrative, or simply implied). Consequently, the minimal semantic content of role is identical to the concept of actor, despite the exception of a seme of individuation, which the former does not possess. The role is an animated figurative entity, albeit anonymous and social. In turn, the actor is an individual integrating and assuming one or several roles' (Greimas 1970: 255–6). From this it follows that there are three distinct levels of narrative interplay: roles, which are elementary actantial units corresponding to coherent functional domains, are related to actants (elements of the narrative) and to actors (units of discourse) (ibid. 256).

The actor is thus seen as the point of investment of both syntactic and semantic components. To be designed as an actor, a lexeme must have both an actantial and a thematic role. And thematic roles, in turn, 'in order to realize their virtualities, call into play the lexematic level of language and are manifested in the form of figures that are extended into discursive configurations.' Thus the figurative level of discourse, which is the final domain of the narrative trajectory, is characterized by the investment of themes and values in figures. Figures, defined as 'figures of content that correspond to the figures of the expression plane of the natural semiotic system' (Greimas and Courtés 1982: 120), when strung over sequences, constitute their discursive configurations. The procedures of figurativization, the first of which can be described as figuration and the second as iconization, invest these figures with specificities that produce a referential illusion. And one of the basic components of figurativization is the onomastic one. Figurativization specifies and particularizes abstract discourse 'insofar as it is grasped in its deep structures and by the introduction of anthroponyms (corresponding respectively, on the plane of discursive syntax, to the three procedures constitutive of discursivization, actorialization, spatialization, and temporalization) that can be inventoried as going from the generic ("king," "forest," "winter") to the specific (proper nouns, spatiotemporal indices, dates, etc.)' (ibid. 119).

Beyond Propp and Lévi-Strauss

A further phase of Greimas's semiotic project, while he continued to evolve a theory of narrativity, focused on constructing a semio-narrative grammar developed as a modal and aspectual grammar. Sensing the need to construct a better-articulated elementary syntax, he abandoned the Proppian formulation of narrative in order to free the theory from concepts that remained too close to the manifest level of discourse. The first step consisted in reformulating surface narrative syntax in terms of modalities. Starting with the definition of modality as 'that which modalizes a predicate of an utterance,' he then considered modalization as the production of a 'modal utterance which over determines a descriptive utterance' (Greimas and Courtés 1982: 193). Defined in terms of the structure of the elementary utterance whose end terms are actants, utterances of doing or utterances of state can be considered as the transformation of a junctive state. However, a reformulation of the act as that which causes to be permits its redefinition as a structure combining competence and performance, with performance presupposing competence, but not vice versa.

Transitive relations defining the descriptive predicate between the subject and the utterance of doing are distinguished both from veridictory relations established by a subject and an utterance produced by another subject, and from factitive relations between the subject and object that are already an utterance of doing. These last two relations, which occur between two hierarchical, distinct subjects – a cognitive subject and a pragmatic subject – constitute the simple modal structure. The advantage of reformulating the act in these terms is that a theory of performance can be developed in three directions: a semiotics of manipulation (the manipulation of the subject by the sender), a semiotics of action (the acquisition of competence by the subject), and a semiotics of sanction (judgments on oneself and on other subjects).

I noted when defining the Subject that, when considered at the level of the organization of pragmatic competence, it had four fundamental modalities: the modalities of having and wanting, which virtualize the process, and the modalities of being able and knowing, which actualize it. Because this canonical representation of competence does not always correspond to what happens at the level of manifestation, it was necessary to construct a model that could account for the fundamental modal structure by subsuming its diverse articulations through a series of interdefinitions. 'The criteria of interdefinition and classification of modalities should be simultaneously syntagmatic and paradigmatic; each modality would be defined on the one hand as a hypotactic modal structure and, on the other hand, as a category which could be represented on the semiotic square' (Greimas and Courtés 1982: 195).

The Epistemic Act

Another area of investigation mapped out within the confines of a theory of modalities is related to procedures leading to the epistemic act. When situated at the level of surface narrative (manipulation, action, sanction), both persuasive and interpretive activity (doing) are defined as cognitive procedures that, in the first case, end up as causing-to-believe and, in the second, as an act of believing, that is, as an epistemic act. The epistemic act is then defined as a transformation that, when articulated on the semiotic square (to affirm, to refuse, to admit, to doubt), at the level of surface syntax is manifested as a series of hierarchically linked narrative programs. Epistemic modalizations can also be represented as modalities and junctive operations, and, before becoming act, or operation (which is of the order of doing), a modal competence or the being of the doing is presupposed on the part of the subject. A further step is taken after noting that, since transactions engage the subjects in a fiduciary contract, communication can be defined in terms of contract propositions, a definition that in fact is a presupposition to communication. Situated within a semiotics of manipulation and sanction, cognitive space becomes the locus for a manipulation according to knowing, in which a subject transforms another into a convinced subject, and submits it to judging epistemic activity on the part of a final subject.

However, since the initial definition of the epistemic act converted the elements of the square onto the surface syntax not as contradictions but as linear gradations, Coquet (1985) notes that 'this type of semiotic square represents an important development of "syntagmatic rationality"' (lxxxii). Technical thinking of an algorithmic nature 'founded on objective modal necessity (= on a /not-being-able-to-not-be/),' is opposed to practical thinking, "of a stereotypical nature [which] depends on the co-occurrence, in temporal contiguity, of acts – or the utterances that describe them – whose successivity can be considered predictable and therefore plausible or even necessary ("subjectively," according to the mode of /having-to-be/)' (lxxxii). At the surface level of discourse, causal reason, or syntagmatic rationality, is further defined in terms of technical thinking and practical thinking. Yet parallel thinking leads us to discover a bi-isotopic[9] nature of discourse based on the seeming of the implicit characterizing figurative discourses that, when dereferentialized, create a new referent or thematic level. Parallel discourse, by projecting a double reference (one that moves deeper and creates a more abstract thematic isotopy, and one that moves laterally and develops a new parallel figurative isotopy), constitutes an original type of syntagmatic articulation. Figurative models such as parables, allusive in nature, are given as an example of figurative reasoning. These models, projected by the sender, fiduciary by definition, and of the order of subjective /having-to-be/, are opposed to homological thinking, which 'introduces mathematical proportion into the evaluation of the relations between isotopies that are presumed to be parallel' (lxxxii). Greimas (1987a) further refined the theoretical foundations of modal grammar when he studied the relations between the fiduciary and the logical within a cognitive universe. He defined this universe as a network of formal semiotic relations from among which the 'epistemic subject selects equivalencies it needs in order to receive veridictory discourses' and thereby demonstrates that believing and knowing 'are part of the same cognitive universe' (179).

From Actions to Passions

After having analysed the modality of doing, Greimas turned to the modality of being. As Coquet (1985) notes, this analysis completes the study of the actions of the subject (modal competence) and prepares the way for the study of their passions (modal existence) within the context of a modal grammar reformulated along the lines of surface narrative syntax (lxxviii). Thymic space, which at the deep level represents the elementary manifestations of a living being in relation to its environment (animated), at the surface level is converted into modal space appearing as an overarticulation of the thymic (human) category. Yet, in any utterance, the subject's semiotic existence is determined by its relation to the object of value and the modalizing of being considered as the 'modifications of the status of the object of value' (lxxviii). The modalities affecting the object (or rather the value invested therein) are said to be constituents of the subject of state's modal existence. A taxonomic network for modal syntax is elaborated by projecting the modal utterances onto the semiotic square (wanting-to-be [desirable for the subject of state], having-to-be [indispensable], being-able-to-be [possible], knowing-how-to-be [genuine]). The same interrelations discovered when analysing the modalization of doing are encountered here, and a syntax of modalized values is worked out, based on elementary narrative syntax.

It has been shown that thymic values are converted from the deep level when invested with syntactic objects defined by junctive relations with subjects. As Parret and Ruprecht (1985) perceptively remark, this conversion profoundly affects value by placing it under subjectivity and its intentionality. As a theoretical consequence of this, the possibility for the pragmatization of Greimas's semiotics by the introduction of tensivity and graduality in the deep structures themselves is opened up. And the theory is freed 'from the notion that at the deep level values are economical (in the Saussurian sense) and at the surface level they are graduated and tensive' (xlvii). In this way, the introduction of modality theory and the working out of conversion procedures constitute decisive steps towards an integrated theory of narrativity.

I did suggest that the problematic of passions is linked to the study of the modal existence of the subject and, more precisely, to the modal component of the actantial structures. Whether the object of investigation happens to be a lexeme-passion such as anger – considered as a virtual narrative trajectory – or, on the contrary, passional stories that are realized narrative syntagms, as Landowski (1979) notes, the exploration of the 'passional field' closely involves 'all of the levels of the articulations of the theory of narrativity. This includes not only the semio-narrative structures proper (instances of passions being identifiable by their underlying modal and actantial structures), not only the discursive structures (aspectualization, actorialization, semanticization of the underlying syntagma), but also the deep level abstract structures' (8).

In contradistinction to action, which can be defined as a syntagmatic organization of acts (Greimas and Courtés 1982: 6), passions can be considered as the syntagmatic organization of states of feeling, or the discursive aspect of the modalized being of narrative subjects (Greimas and Courtés 1986: 162–5). Passions, which are either simple or complex (a syntagmatic intertwining of states and of doing), are expressed through actors and, along with actions, determine the roles (actantial and thematic) they realize. Thus, the opposition between action and passion represents the 'conversion on the discursive level of the deeper and more abstract opposition between being and doing, or more specifically between modalized being and modalized doing' (162).

The subject's being, whether, for example, in simple or in fiduciary expectation, is first of all modalized by the modality of wanting, which actualizes (wanting-to-be-conjoined) in order then to be realized (i.e., to be conjoined with the object of value). It is this very conjunction that guarantees the subject's semiotic existence. Whether at the semiotic or at the discursive level, the notion of value, which we also saw with regard to the doing of the subject, is at the very heart of the theory. Thus, parallel to the trajectory of the subject of doing, made up of the acquisition of competence and the accomplishment of performances, there exists a comparable trajectory of the subject of state, presented as successions of 'feeling states' made up of highs and lows. Consequently, the modalization of the subject's being has an essential role in the constitution of the competence of syntactic subjects, and the concept of passion is closely linked to that of actor. Passion thus becomes 'one of the elements that contribute to actorial individuation, able to offer denominations for recognizable thematic roles ("the miser," "the quick-tempered," "the unconcerned," etc.)' (Greimas and Courtés 1986: 162–3). Moreover, the linking of passions to actors and the investigation of relations between thematic roles and actantial roles have opened up a new domain of research into passional typologies.

Conclusion

In concluding and summarizing this chapter, I would like to stress, once again, that Greimas found the inspiration and the sources of his work in two of the great twentieth-century scholars of anthropology and folklore. Lévi-Strauss provided him with the paradigmatic cover of the theory and Propp with the syntagmatic, or syntactic, one. After working out the necessary theoretical mediations, he linked two complementary models and constructed a theory that could be generalized in terms of a general narrative semantics. He then freed the theory from Propp's formula of the tale as a means of analysing narrative, and an elementary syntax that could organize any types of discourse was developed. Propp's model was broken down into three successive sequences, which correspond to the syntagmatic unfolding of the actantial model (paradigmatically articulated in a quest sequence [subject → object] and a communication sequence [sender → object → receiver]), in which two sequences of communication frame an action sequence. The mandate sequence and the evaluation sequence bracket the action sequence that transforms the states. From this a semiotics of manipulation was established – how the sender manipulates the subject – followed by a semiotics of action – how competence is acquired to carry out performance – and, finally, by a semiotics of evaluation or sanction.

As I noted above, over this period of time attempts were made to construct a model of meaningful actions in an intersubjective frame. Greimas first constructed a model of actions before introducing notions such as modalities and aspectualities that overdetermine the actants. Four fundamental modalities (two virtual ones and two actualizing ones), as well as three aspectualities (inchoativity, durativity, and terminativity), were posited and interdefined. Then, as folk-tales were considered as an intersection between two conflictual and contractual actions in progress, Greimas was able to transform the Proppian model into an interactional one. Instead of a subject, an object, and an opponent, two modally competent interacting subjects were posited. Each subject, with its own modal organization, was situated in a polemico-contractual relation with the other. Strategy became more important than rules. Moreover, in addition to the system of being-able, the actantial model was able to define the construction and transmission of meaning. Thanks to the work of Marcel Mauss and Lévi-Strauss, communication was rethought in terms of exchange and challenge, and the concept was extended from the circulation of objects and messages to the exchange of modal values within the framework of a fiduciary contract that must be maintained actively during interaction.

The opening of the fiduciary dimension introduced the subject matter of belief and adhesion in the cognitive dimension, a matter that raises at least two orders of questions: on the one hand, the relevance of the figurative component and, on the other, that of the passional. Through the mediation of the enunciative instance, the virtual structures of action are realized and figurativized differently according to the categories of the natural world employed as forms of expression. As far as the passional dimension is concerned, it became possible to give an operational account of the emotional systems and processes. In other words, the transformation of the states of feeling of the subject with respect to the actions that incite them and the actions they lead to (see Greimas [1987a] 'On Anger,' and [1990] 'The Challenge' and 'On Nostalgia'). When dealing with figurativity, we encounter the problem of the typology of signs, especially non-linguistic and non-arbitrary signs, and their efficacy. When dealing with passions, we are basically concerned with the stringing of modalities, tensitivity, and thymism, and, in general, with the dimension of bodily propioceptivity.

Throughout this chapter, in which I have traced the salient features of Greimas's semiotic from a developmental perspective, I have attempted to highlight the constructed and hypothetico-deductive aspect of a theory in which concepts are interdefined and hierarchically ordered. I have also emphasized the anthropomorphic dimension of the global theory, conceived of as an ongoing scientific project founded on internal coherence as a precondition to formalization. Further, I have identified three major phases: formulation, narrative grammar, and modal and aspectual grammar, as well as the manner in which research began on deep structures, and have explored semio-narrative structures, before concentrating on surface (discursive and figurative) structures. However, we should not conclude that the transpositional semiotic theory presented here is in any way a fully completed theory, since research is currently being carried out on the pathemic, ethical, and aesthetic dimensions of discourse. This should contribute to the construction of the semio-narrative grammar, and further work on aspectualities should lead to the development of an integrated and complementary discourse grammar.

PART II

Discovery, Conversion, and Colonization

CHAPTER THREE

First Encounters and Myth Making: Jacques Cartier's *Voyages* to New France

Jacques Cartier's *Voyages* are considered by modern-day historians and ethnohistorians as the most reliable and accurate account of the northern coast and the St Lawrence region of North America written in the sixteenth century.[1] Indeed, his *Voyages* of 1534, 1535, and 1541, but especially the first two, can be considered as the founding texts of all subsequent historiographical narratives on the French presence in the northernmost regions of this part of the New World. The *Voyages* of 1534 and 1535 give complete accounts of the beginning of the quest, the various discoveries and obstacles or tests encountered along the way, the fear and trembling, the surprise and horror, the awe and loathing of the discoverer and the discovered. They relate the positive or negative resolutions of conflict or negotiation, the return of the heroes, and their public sanction by the lords of the realm, and even by the king himself. However, Cartier's third voyage did not survive in the original and came down to us in an English translation that was recapitulatory, incomplete, and truncated.[2] It is barely nine pages in length and ends with an account of Cartier and his expedition enclosed in a fortress on the St Lawrence River, attempting to understand why the inhabitants, who now mistrusted and feared them, no longer wanted to bring them any fish.[3] This questioning of the motives of the indigenous people by Cartier and the members of his expedition is, in fact, a reversal and a revelation. The Europeans, after initially cognitively manipulating the original inhabitants of New France, making them believe (is not what appears), realize that the latter have discovered the nature of their motives and have begun to distrust them for having erected a fortress in their country (is what appears). They simply transcribe to the other, and project on them, the implicit awareness of their own ambitions and desires, and this interrogative reversal of motives functions as the suspended closure of the narrative.

As I suggested in the preceding paragraph, Cartier's two initial *Voyages* can be considered as the Ur narratives of a long line of New France discovery texts. The French explorers, missionaries, and colonizers who borrowed from his works, as well as the numerous translators of his *Voyages* who came after him, owe much to his observations, descriptions, and reflections on the fauna, flora, and peoples of the new world.[4] But it is at the beginning of the seventeenth century, when the French intensified their exploration of North America, that Cartier's *Voyages* became the point of reference and discussion of all the authors who subsequently wrote about this part of the continent. Marc Lescarbot, in his *Histoire de la Nouvelle France*, 1609, includes the first two voyages and is aware of the existence of the third. He also takes the earlier explorer to task on a number of issues, as do Samuel de Champlain in his various writings[5] and Gabriel Sagard in his *Le Grand Voyage du pays des Hurons*, 1632, and his *Histoire du Canada*, 1636. Paul Le Jeune in his *Relations de ce qui s'est passé en la Nouvelle France en l'année 1633*,[6] Charlevoix in his *Histoire et description générale de la Nouvelle France*, 1744, and François-Xavier Garneau, the first major French-Canadian historian, in his *Histoire du Canada*, 1845–52, along with all other authors dealing with the origins of the European presence in Canada, all relied heavily on Cartier's accounts. A textual lineage therefore begins with Cartier. None the less, what links each of the texts mentioned above is Cartier's *Voyages*, which – because of their stylistic qualities, their exactness, and their articulation through the setting up of objectifying strategies, notably related to focalization, as well as the conditions or enunciative contract[7] laid out between the enunciator and his enunciatees – can be considered as foundational texts of observed phenomena that have been effaced and that have disappeared. In brief, Cartier's texts are notable in giving us one of the few, written, firsthand accounts of the initial European contact with this region of North America. As Cook (1993) remarks, they are the product of their period, and they provide us with the image of a person who was both an honest observer and had the preoccupations of a shrewd Breton navigator who interpreted what he saw through the lenses of his times. In his descriptions of the people who inhabited the St Lawrence region, Cartier, like all informants, organized and framed events to conform to his education, his beliefs, his understanding, and his point of view (x). It should be noted, however, that the enunciator's knowledge, will, duty, and power, or the modalities that constitute his competence permitting his performance of narrating these *Voyages*, are shared by the enunciatees of his time and, in part, by those of other generations.

Without entering into a prolonged discussion about the actual author of the *Voyages*, it should be stated immediately that they are signed 'Cartier,' and that even when the narrator designates himself in the third person, the texts are all assumed and guaranteed by him. He is the observer through whose eyes all events and descriptions are refracted, projected, and then interpreted. Instead of critiquing Cartier for being Eurocentric, which he undeniably is, I explore the relationship among the events he witnessed, the text written that relates them, and the roles assumed by the enunciator who narrates it and the enunciatee, or its implied reader. The enunciator and enunciatee's roles are established and governed by specific rules (which can be called the preconstructed) and by variable ones (the presupposed).[8] We can define the preconstructed as the symbolic structuration of language – that is to say, as a sign system that interfaces with the events and mediates them for both the enunciating observer and the potential reader, all the while transforming them. The presupposed is governed by variable rules belonging to cultural and social codes – ideologies, for example. These rules, which vary among individuals and communities, can be defined, according to Clifford Geertz (quoted by Ricœur 1984, I: 57), 'As the set of conventions, beliefs, institutions that make up the symbolic framework of a culture' (58). The preconstructed that is of the order of language is relatively stable and evolves very slowly; the presupposed, however, is readily transformed over time. In brief, the presupposed is of the order of discourse and articulated by means of discursive rhetorical forms, and the presuppositions are defined by their mobility, by style, by periodicity, by genre codes, by aesthetic codes, by customs, and so on. In this chapter, I examine more specifically the representation of other and otherness in Cartier's *Voyages* in order to lay the groundwork for a better understanding of the specificity of early exploration and discovery literature at the origin of New World historiography.

Exploration narratives of the Americas, and, in our case, particularly those focusing on the period of French colonization, are generally characterized by an agent who assumes at one and the same time the roles of observer, man of action, and writer. To give credibiliy to and to legitimize his mission, he first receives his mandate from a powerful sender (political, religious, commercial) to explore or to colonize a territory, to set up an administrative and commercial structure, or to convert the Native people,[9] after which he and the members of the party swear allegiance to the mandator. Conforming to this convention, the opening page of the first *Voyage* clearly identifies the role of the all-powerful mandating sender and the taking of the oath by all members of the expedition: 'Après que messire Charles de Mouy, chevalier, seigneur de La Milleraye, et vice-amiral de France, eût reçu les serments et fait jurer les capitaines, maîtres et compagnons des dits navires de bien loyalement se porter au service du roi sous la charge dudit Cartier, partîmes du havre et port de Saint-Malo, avec lesdits deux navires, du port d'environ soixante tonneaux chacun ...' (39) (When Sir Charles de Mouy, Knight, Lord of La Meilleraye and Vice-Admiral of France, had received the oaths of the captains, masters, and sailors of the vessels, and had made them swear to conduct themselves well and loyally in the King's service, under the command of the said Cartier, we set forth from the harbour and port of St Malo with two ships of about sixty tons' burden ...) (3). This mandate is made even more explicit in the very first lines describing the next expedition: 'Seconde navigation faite par le commandement et vouloir du Très-Chrétien Roi François, premier de son nom, au parachèvement de la découverte des terres occidentales ... suivant votre royal commandement ... n'ayant pas eu autant de crainte que [les philosophes] de courir l'aventure de ces périls et dangers ...' (75) (The second voyage undertaken by the command and wish of the Most Christian King of France, Francis the First of that name, for the completion of the discovery of the western lands ... not being so afraid at your royal command to run the risk of those perils and dangers, as were the ancients ...) (35–6). Moreover, not only is the mandating role of the sender clearly defined, but also his role as defender of the faith. The sender has previously been institutionally and religiously sanctioned by the church and therefore by God (presupposed: Cook, 36). The geopolitical stakes are clearly delimited and their ideological underpinnings expressly defined. The aims of Christianity and its belief in conquering and converting the world – aims that are common knowledge and shared duty and will between the enunciator and the enunciatee and that guarantee their adhesion to the enunciated programs – are expressed without any ambiguity whatsoever. These modalities defining the competence of the sending and receiving subjects and constituting the minimal conditions for the enunciative pact between them will be consolidated by the enunciator's ability or power to organize convincingly what he has observed, along with the enunciatee's capacity to comprehend and adhere to what is narrated:

Je pense ... qu'il plût à Dieu, par sa divine bonté, que toutes créatures humaines, étant et habitant sur le globe de la terre, ainsi qu'elles voient et connaissent ce soleil, elles ont eu et auront pour le temps à venir connaissance et croyance de notre sainte foi. Car premièrement notre sainte foi a été semée et plantée en Terre Sainte qui est en Asie, à l'Orient de notre Europe, et depuis, par la succession du temps, apportée et divulguée jusqu'à nous; et finalement à l'occident de notre dite Europe, à l'exemple dudit soleil, portant sa clarté et chaleur d'orient en occident, comme il est dit. (76)

(I ... am of the opinion that it pleases God in His divine goodness that all human beings inhabiting the surface of the globe, just as they have sight and knowledge of the sun, have had and are to have in time to come knowledge and belief in our holy faith. For first our most holy faith was sown and planted in the Holy Land, which is in Asia to the east of our Europe, and afterwards by succession of time it has been carried and proclaimed to us, and at length to the west of our Europe, just like the sun, carrying its light and its heat from east to west, as already set forth.) (37)

The origins of Christianity are spelled out and its past, present, and future struggles indicated; the roles of the sender, object, and receiver are defined, and their shared belief in the church's manifest destiny is declared. This extremely complex and long mandate, sequence concludes with the enunciator/actor interpreting his mandate for his implied reader, all the while fixing its goal: the conversion of the Native people and the settling of this land by the French – colonization: 'Lesquelles choses donnent à ceux qui les ont vues, certaines espérances de l'augmentation future de notre dite très sainte foi, et de vos seigneuries et nom très chrétien, ainsi qu'il vous plaira de voir par ce présent petit livre, dans lequel sont amplement contenues toutes les choses dignes de mémoire que nous avons vues et qui nous sont arrivées, tant en faisant ladite navigation que lorsque nous étions et séjournions en vos dits pays et terres, les routes, dangers et situations de ces terres.' (77) (These things fill those who have seen them with the sure hope of a future increase of our most holy faith and of your possessions and most Christian name, as you may be pleased to see in this present booklet, wherein is fully set forth everything worthy of note that we saw or that happened to us both in the course of the above voyage and also during our stay in those lands and territories of yours, as well as the routes, dangers, and situation of those lands) (38).

The mandate sequences, justifying the two voyages and sanctioning the role of the observer/actor/explorer/narrator, are interspersed with, and complemented by, sequences establishing a relationship instituting an enunciative contract between the enunciator and enunciatee, the virtual reading public that he hopes to instruct about the geography, the fauna and flora, and the customs of the indigenous peoples of the continent. 'Et maintenant en la présente navigation, faite par votre royal commandement, à la découverte des terres occidentales ... vous pourrez voir et savoir la bonté et fertilité de celle[s]-ci, l'innombrable quantité des peuples y habitant, la bonté et paisibilité de ceux-ci, et pareillement la fécondité du grand fleuve ...' (77) (And now through the present expedition taken at your royal command for the discovery of lands ... you will learn and hear of their fertility and richness, of the immense number of peoples living there, of their kindness and peacefulness, and likewise of the richness of the great river ...) (37–8). Here, the enunciator clearly articulates, through this micro-narrative in recapitulatory form, the narrative to come. This enunciative contract fixes not only the status of the enunciator, who assumes both the role of narrator and that of actor, but also that of the enunciatee, who, in the end, passes judgment, through the coherence and credibility of the unravelling of the tale, whether or not the pact has been respected. The enunciator will also attempt to interest the reader through suspense, by relating a story of venturing into the unknown. In spite of a lack of common referents, the enunciator in the *Voyages* can more or less account for the exotic, the unfamiliar, the strange, the new, or the unforeseen by using comparative parataxe[10] that positions the enunciatee as the descriptions unfold in the land of the known. See, for example, Cartier's descriptions of creatures, such as the penguin and the walrus, that are unknown to his readers: 'Une partie de ces oiseaux sont *grands comme des oies*, noires et blanches, et ont *le bec comme celui d'un corbeau. Et ils sont toujours dans la mer, sans jamais pouvoir voler en l'air parce qu'ils ont de petites ailes, comme la moitié d'une main* ...' (40) (Some of these birds are *as large as geese*, being black and white *with a beak like a crow's*. They are always in the water, not being able to fly in the air, inasmuch as they have *small wings about the size of half one's hand* ...) (4); 'Il y a autour de cette île, plusieurs grandes bêtes, *comme des grands bœufs* qui ont deux dents dans la gueule *comme des dents d'éléphant*, qui vont en mer' (49) (Round about this island are many great beasts, *like large oxen*, which have two tusks in their jaw *like elephant's tusks* and swim about in the water) (14).[11] These descriptions not only evoke the shared knowledge and beliefs, instituting a commonplace, a common ground, a common referential universe between narrator and narratee, but also set in place a temporal arc of past experience that, at the present of the moment of reading, is projected into an uncertain future of expectation.

I should also point out that Cartier's narratives are characterized by the fact that they simulate intersubjective exchange between a present observer-subject and absent reading subjects who cannot appropriate *in praesentia* all the resources of language, and hence must overcome temporal and spatial distance separating enunciator and enunciatee. The poles, or deixes situating the interlocutors, that can be polyvalent and invested in variable ways during the decoding of the narrative, are not simply neutral or cognitive positions but are invested differently according to the varying passional dispositions of the enunciator and virtual enunciatee, and their presuppositions. In describing the fauna and flora, the narrator marvels and expresses admiration, surprise, and satisfaction, positioning his narratee to share the same feelings of the extraordinary, and hence assigning her/him an actantial role that must be assumed but need not necessarily be invested, depending on the pragmatic force of the description: 'des oiseaux, desquels il y a si grand nombre, que c'est une chose incroyable pour qui ne le voit ... Et ces oiseaux sont si gras que c'est une chose merveilleuse ...' (40) (whose [birds] numbers are so great as to be incredible, unless one has seen them ... And these birds are so fat that it is marvelous ...) (4). After the opening of the narrative, the enunciator passes from *we* to *I* through the act of naming, but the singular personal pronoun *I* appears on the backdrop of an undifferentiated and anonymous *us* that is articulated not by means of the past tense but by the gnomic[12] tense of the eternal present. Here, deixization is not of the order of the positional *stricto sensu* but actually abolishes time and space by instituting an indisputable absolute – *there is*: 'Partant de la pointe de Dégrat en entrant en ladite baie, pointant vers l'ouest, un quart du nord-ouest, l'on double deux îles, qui se trouvent à babord ... Je nommai celle-ci, Île Sainte-Catherine' (42) (Leaving Point Dégrat and entering the said bay, heading west, one quarter northwest, one doubles two islands which are left of port ... I named this island St Catherine's Island) (7). The *I* is absorbed into a *there is*, a formula that recurs in the two following pages of the narrative; but it will, in turn, become a *we*: 'Le dixième jour dudit mois de juin, entrâmes dans ledit havre du Brest avec nos navires pour avoir des eaux et du bois' (43) (On June 10 we entered Brest Harbour with our ships to get wood and water) (8).

However, the non-persons, the spoken about, the excluded in the intersubjective act of communication, the other, the *he/she/them* and their representation in the original New France discovery narrative should not be forgotten. How does Cartier relate his initial and subsequent contacts with the Native people in his three *Voyages*? How does he ascribe to them believable roles? First, to travel is to 'encounter' the other, to encounter with the gaze. I have remarked that Cartier classes, names, counts, describes, grids, maps, and transposes on a symbolic plane what he sees and hears from those whom he considers to be reliable witnesses,[13] and for those whom he posits as reliable readers. Moreover, the system of naming functions through metonymy, metaphor, and transposition, the Gregorian calendar not only serving as the system of reference but also providing the names of saints as signposts for these hitherto 'unnamed' places, assigning an actantial role to his enunciatee by conjuring up the same presuppositions that organize their respective semantic universes. In addition, he assigns names of real or existing persons of the realm to some of these 'unknown' places (i.e., Cartier's own, that of the Duc d'Orléans, etc.).[14] In brief, to name is, here, to appropriate in a system of reference consisting of commonplaces shared by the enunciator and the enunciatee. The act of naming, in effect, reduces the unknown to the known by means of a presupposed system of beliefs and knowledge common to those occupying the sending and the receiving poles of this intersubjective communication.

But how does the enunciator's gaze account for this strange, unknown land, or, again, for the body of the other, encountered – first fleetingly, then massively – during the enunciator's wanderings? Initially, the other appears suddenly on the material and framed backdrop of a barren and sterile country unsuited for cultivation by eventual settlers: 'mais [la terre] ne devrait pas se nommer Terre-Neuve, étant composée de pierres et rochers effroyables et mal rabottés ...' (45) (but the land should not be called the New Land, being composed of stones and horrible rugged rocks ...) (10). The explorer's gaze scans, searches, examines, and analyses: 'car en toute ladite côte du nord, je n'y vis une charretée de terre ... il n'y a que de la mousse et de petits bois avortés' (45) (for on the whole of the north shore I did not see one cart-load of earth ... there is nothing but moss and short, stunted shrubs) (10). Seeing, which here is the differential trait of knowing, leads to an assimilation of the seen into a common biblical frame of reference that defines sender and receiver, all the while accentuating the ultimate purpose of the expedition: colonization and cultivation. 'Enfin, j'estime mieux qu'autrement que c'est la terre que Dieu donna à Caïn' (45) (In fine, I am led to believe that this is the land God gave to Cain) (10).[15] Immediately after the biblical evaluative frame, there is a description of the very first impression of the Native people, one that is both physical and moral, because of the presuppositions civilized–observer/barbaric–observed, and that is organized from the general to the particular: 'Il y a des gens à ladite terre, qui sont d'assez belle corpulence, mais ils sont farouches et sauvages' (45) (There are some people on this coast whose bodies are fairly well formed, but they are wild and savage folk) (10). The portrait follows a specific spatial order, from top to bottom,[16] beginning with head-dress: 'Ils ont leurs cheveux liés sur leur tête, à la façon d'une poignée de foin tressé, et un clou passé parmi, ou autre chose; et ils y lient des plumes d'oiseaux' (45) (They wear their hair tied up on the top of their heads like a handful of twisted hay, with a nail or something of the sort passed through the middle, and into it they weave a few bird's feathers) (10).[17] Their clothing is also inscribed within the same series of presuppositions (woven/skins; processed/unprocessed; life/death, etc.): 'Ils se vêtent de peaux de bêtes, tant hommes que femmes; mais les femmes sont plus closes et serrées en leurs dites peaux et ceinturées par la taille' (45) (They clothe themselves with the skins of animals, both men as well as women, but the women are wrapped up more closely and snugly in their skins, and have a belt at their waists) (10). The portrait finishes with the reinforced opposition of civilized–make-up/barbaric–tattoo: 'Ils se peignent de certaines couleurs tannées' (45) (They paint themselves with certain tan colours) (10). This is how the first description of the Native people, taken as a group but still differentiated according to sex, comes to a close. The narrative is followed by a description of their principal hunting and fishing activities. This first portrait of the collective subject ends with the establishment of a link between seeing and knowing where a re-evaluation and rectification of the description occurs after the fact, because of new information brought by a presupposed reliable informant/interpreter: 'Après les avoir vus, j'ai su que là n'est pas leur demeurance, et qu'ils viennent des terres plus chaudes, pour prendre desdits loups-marins, et autres choses pour leur subsistance' (45) (Since seeing them, I have been informed that their home is not at this place but that they come from warmer countries to catch these seals and get other food for their sustenance) (10). Here the seeing, the observer, is qualified, rectified by a supplement of information derived elsewhere that enables the witness to interpret the scene. This corresponds to the establishment by himself of the modal competencies of the enunciator/ observer, who not only tells what he sees but can also interpret by means of supplementary knowledge transmitted by someone considered to be worthy of confidence. In short, this descriptive strategy basically confirms the cognitive dimension of the observer/focalizer who auto-sanctions his own observations and descriptions, all the while creating for the enunciatee what could be called not a Barthesian 'reality' effect but, rather, what I would call a 'truth' effect.

In the second encounter, two weeks later at the end of the month of June, the visual framing of the other occurs by means of the collective actant, *we*, inscribing the *I* in the belief systems common to all who witnessed the event and to those for whom it is intended: 'vîmes des barques de sauvages, qui traversaient ladite rivière' (51) (we caught sight of some savages in their canoes who were crossing the river) (17). The activity of the observed is noted, but, as on the first occasion, no interpersonal relations take place. A next unexpected meeting happens when the French are pursued by a lone Native, who gesticulates and – when they do the same in response – flees: 'À ce cap, nous vint un homme, qui courait après nos barques, le long de la côte, qui nous faisait plusieurs signes, de revenir vers ledit cap. Et nous, voyant de tels signes, commençâmes à ramer vers lui, voyant que nous retournions, commença à fuir, et à se sauver devant nous' (51) (At this cape a man came in sight who ran after our longboats along the coast, making frequent signs to us to return towards the said point. And seeing these signs we began to row towards him, but when he saw that we were returning he started to run away and to flee before us) (17). For the observer there is no doubt as to the intentions of the other; he wants them to return to the cape, and when they do he bolts off. The signs he makes are considered as being totally transparent and immediately comprehensible to the European explorers, since it never occurs to them that this is not what is meant or that they could be mistaken, even when the other does the contrary of what is expected. The fourth occurrence happens towards the middle of July, but this time the other does not flee when approached, and the body, instead of shying away from the gaze of the foreigner, exhibits itself to the explorer. However, in displaying itself, the body once more eludes the foreign observer. The voyager, indeed, perceives only an active gesticulation of this body in movement. The voyager sights 'deux bandes de barques de sauvages ...; et dont l'une desdites bandes de barques arrivait à ladite pointe, dont ils sautèrent et descendirent à terre en grand nombre, ceux-ci faisaient un grand bruit' (54) (two fleets of savage canoes that were crossing from one side to the other ... Upon one of the fleets reaching this point, there sprang out and landed a large number of people, who set up a great clamour) (20). Motion is immediately transformed into gestures and then signs. They made 'plusieurs signes d'aller à terre, nous montrant des peaux sur des bâtons ... et vinrent jusqu'après notredite barque, dansant et faisant plusieurs signes de joie et manifestant le désir de vouloir notre amitié' (54) (frequent signs to us to come on shore, holding up to us some skins on sticks ... and all came after our longboat, dancing and showing many signs of joy, and of their desire to be friends) (20). The perception and interpretation of the gestural precedes that of the verbal. Although Cartier and his men do not understand the Micmac language, they still interpret it for their intended readers within a vast semiotic system whose gestural and verbal signs they themselves semiotize and re-semiotize situationally without taking into account the presuppositions of the other: 'nous disant dans leur langage: *Napou tout daman asurtat*' (54) ('saying to us in their language: *Napou tou daman asurtat*) (20).[18] The first words spoken by the other are inscribed in an intersubjective relation of fiducia, exchange, and confidence, but their exact meaning ironically remains problematic, for the explorer immediately adds: 'et autres paroles que n'entendions' (54) (and other words we did not understand) (20).

Yet these signs are perceived and interpreted as being hostile, insofar as the French had only a single boat whereas the others had several. This minority relation is construed as menacing: 'Et parce que nous n'avions, comme on l'a déjà dit, qu'une de nos barques, nous ne voulûmes pas nous fier à leurs signes' (54) (But for the reason already stated, that we had only one of our longboats, we did not care to trust their signs) (20). Here we note that, although Cartier and his men think that they can read the others' signs, according to them reciprocity does not exist in this communication since the others cannot, or will not, read theirs: 'Nous leur fîmes signe qu'ils se retirassent; ce qu'ils ne voulurent pas ... Et voyant que malgré les signes que nous leur faisions, ils ne voulaient pas se retirer, nous leur tirâmes deux coups de passe-volants par dessus eux' (54) (We waved to them to go back, which they would not do ... And seeing that no matter how much we signed to them, they would not go back, we shot over their heads two small cannons) (20). This first cannonade does not succeed in dispersing them: 'Et alors, ils se mirent à retourner vers ladite pointe, et firent un bruit merveilleusement grand' (54) (On this they began to return towards the point, and set up a marvelously loud shout) (20); the explorers fire a second round that scatters them. The next day, within the context of exchange and barter, sign-gestures are immediately decoded by both collective subjects: 'Et dès qu'ils nous aperçurent, ils se mirent à fuir, nous faisant signes qu'ils étaient venus pour trafiquer avec nous ... Nous leur fîmes pareillement signe que nous ne leur voulions nul mal' (55) (As soon as they saw us they began to run away, making signs to us that they had come to barter with us ... We likewise made signs to them that we wished them no harm) (21). The inhabitants exchange goods with the explorers, who do not recognize the comparable value of the objects in question: 'des peaux de peu de valeur, desquelles ils se vêtent' (55) (some skins of small value with which they clothe themselves) (21) for some knives and iron goods, and a red cap for their chief. During the bartering ceremony they show: 'une grande et merveilleuse joie d'avoir et d'obtenir desdits objets de fer et autres choses, dansant et faisant plusieurs cérémonies ...' (55) (a marvelously great pleasure in possessing and obtaining these iron wares and other commodities, dancing and going through many ceremonies ...) (21). They literally strip and dispossess themselves of all their clothing in bartering 'tout ce qu'ils avaient tellement qu'ils s'en retournèrent tout nus, sans rien avoir sur eux; et nous firent signe, que le lendemain, reviendraient avec d'autres peaux' (55) (all they had to such an extent that all went back naked without anything on them; and they made signs to us that they would return on the morrow with more skins) (21). The observer/focalizer describes the next day's trading session in the same terms as the previous one, except for the fact that this time, in addition to the dancing, the women sang, 'en faisant plusieurs signes de joie' (56) (exhibiting many signs of joy) (22). Once more they exchange all their possessions and clothing for European goods and 'nous donnèrent tout ce qu'ils avaient, qui est chose de peu de valeur' (56) (offered us everything they owned, which was, all told of little value) (22).

Upon better familiarization with the trading practices of the indigenous people in the name of all the explorers present, the observer will describe their activities by introducing a second series of qualifications that had begun to emerge at the time of the previous bartering session. During their sixth encounter, the next day, when they begin to trade, 'une partie de leurs femmes, qui ne traversèrent point, dansaient et chantaient, étant dans la mer jusqu'aux genoux' (56) (some of their women, who did not come over, danced and sang, standing in the water up to their knees) (22). At each successive encounter, men and women are described indifferently as expressing great joy, singing, and dancing while they trade with the explorers: 'Nous leur donnâmes des couteaux, des patenôtres de verre, des peignes, et autres objets de peu de valeur, pour lesquels ils faisaient plusieurs signes de joie, levant les mains au ciel, en chantant et dansant dans leurs dites barques' (58) (We gave them knives, glass beads, combs, and other trinkets of small value, at which they showed many signs of joy, lifting up their hands to heaven and singing and dancing in their canoes) (24); 'De quoi ils démontrèrent beaucoup de joie, et tous les hommes se mirent à chanter et à danser, en deux ou trois bandes, faisant de grands signes de joie à notre venue' (58) (At this they showed great joy, and the men all began to sing and to dance in two or three groups, exhibiting signs of great pleasure at our coming) (25). Champlain in his *Voyages* of 1603 and 1605, Lescarbot in his *Histoire de la Nouvelle France* of 1609, and Sagard in his *Grand Voyage* of 1632 will all characterize the indigenous people with these traits.

What can one retain from the observation of this newly discovered population?[19] First, sign-gestures, just like verbal signs, are transparent for the observer/focalizer and his narratee, who share the same system of beliefs and who, without knowing the language, or without an interpreter, can decode a/the meaning by projecting their own presuppositions on the other's semiotic system. Second, as Gomez-Géraud (1995) notes, early explorers, and in our case Cartier, perceive the other in terms of ceremonies and gestures that constitute a stereotype of the Native peoples, reducing them to a series of clichés and commonplaces that will be repeated by most authors writing on New France from Cartier to the beginning of the twentieth century. The indigenous people, or 'Barbarians,' dance, sing, cry, and yell in a barbaric, unpredictable, and uncontrolled way, which again contrasts markedly with the choreographed, civilized, and controlled behaviour presupposed both in the enunciatee and the mandating sender (nobility, church, court, etc.). Not only is this motif reiterated throughout the three *Voyages*, but it also occurs in most exploratory literature, therefore becoming the foundational element in the construction of the textual and imaginary Amerindian.[20]

Finally, though, after having described the last scene of the natives divesting themselves of their last shreds of clothing for European goods, the enunciator evaluates the exchange sequence based on perceived fiducia, estimates the relative value of the objects traded, and inscribes the entire process into the presupposed teleology of the mandating sender. The objects are certainly not considered to be of equal value, for the other, who trusts the enunciating subject ('so much at ease did they feel in our presence'), has only objects that are 'all told of little value' when compared with imported, fabricated goods. The ease with which the other is devalued – cognitively and emotionally manipulated – brings about a thematic change in the sanctioning subject. An act of barter founded on an act of faith enables the enunciator to shift to belief values based this time on the verb, on the word. Divesting these others of their valueless clothing in exchange for valued objects prefigures divesting them of their valueless beliefs in exchange for valued beliefs: 'Nous reconnûmes que ce sont des gens qui seraient faciles à convertir' (56) (We perceived that they are people who would be easy to convert) (22). Moreover, just like their relation to their own clothing, which they shed at the will of the traders, they have only a tenuous relation to this land since they neither occupy nor till it, as they: 'vont d'un lieu à l'autre, vivant et prenant du poisson, au temps de la pêche, pour vivre' (56) (go from place to place maintaining themselves and catching fish in the fishing-season for food) (22). So, too, they are seen by the explorers as willing to shed the land that, in a European economy of settlement, is interpreted as being valueless to them, and this part of the narrative ends with an eschatological vision of cultivation. This is the opposite of the land of Cain mentioned at the beginning of Cartier's account, since the discovery of the *Voyage* actually projects it as the land of bounty and riches that already in the wild partially fulfils its great potential. It is first absorbed into the European countryside: 'Leur terre est au point de vue chaleur, plus tempérée que la terre d'Espagne, et la plus belle qu'il soit possible de voir, et aussi unie d'un étang' (56–7) (Their country is more temperate than Spain and the finest it is possible to see, and as level as the surface of a pond) (22). What initially was described as *Terra Incognita*, through textualization has been converted into *Terra Nullius*, in which the inhabitants are first disenfranchised and effaced, while nature is transformed into culture through metaphor and simile, then domesticated by European agricultural practices: 'Et n'y a aucun petit lieu, vide de bois, et même sur le sable, qui ne soit plein de blé sauvage, dont l'épi est comme seigle, et le grain comme avoine; et des pois, aussi gros que si on les avait semés et labourés; groseilliers, blancs et rouges, fraises, framboises, et roses rouges et blanches, et autres herbes' (57)

(There is not the smallest plot of bare wood, and even on sandy soil, but is full of wild wheat, that has an ear like barley and the grain of oats, as well as pease, as thick as if they had been sown and hoed, of white and red currant-bushes, of strawberries, of raspberries, of white and red roses and of other plants of a strong and pleasant odour) (22–3). This domestication of the wilderness, the unknown by the known, through nomination and assimilation to Old World cultivated species, along with the substitution and effacement of indigenous practices with European ones by the enunciator/observer/focalizer, for his enunciatee/ reader, is embedded in, and enclosed by, a final conversion sequence, this time with a first person singular deixis: 'J'estime mieux qu'autrement, que les gens seraient faciles à convertir à notre sainte foi' (57) (I am more than ever of the opinion that these people would be easy to convert to our holy faith' (23), as compared to 'Nous reconnûmes que ce sont des gens qui seraient faciles à convertir' (56) 'We perceived that they are people who would be easy to convert ...) (22). We have travelled full circle, and the finality of the text is brought back to the very reasons at its origins, those of colonization and conversion, which will also be the motivating factors of the other subsequent exploration narratives dealing with New France.

The events described by Cartier are obviously no more since they have been set into discourse, a discourse generating meaning, although certain descriptions can be verified even today.[21] Nevertheless, all readers of the *Voyages*, along with Cartier himself, must be bound by the same preconstructed, which belongs to the order of the sentence, of textualization. What differentiates different readings of these texts is related to the presupposed or argumentation, since, for example, readers could always substitute the Micmac's lunar calendar for Cartier's liturgical calendar, or even substitute their own evaluative discourse for Cartier's – a substitution that would surely change the reading of the text. However, they can never substitute their actual witnessing for Cartier's and state, for instance, that he did not see what he reports having seen. If they were to do so, they would have to find inconsistencies in his narrative, or contradictions, or actual errors that would discredit him as a reliable witness and/or observer. Yet, as I have shown, Cartier's discourse is selective and programmed by the particular teleology described above, and therefore it can be demonstrated that he did not narrate all that he had seen and observed. What any reader can put into question are the presupposeds of the reconstitution of the textualization of the events. From this perspective, it is clear that the reader of this exploration narrative does not have the power of unlimited interpretation, since the founding text is the ultimate reference, and the number of substitutions at the level of the presupposed remains limited. Reading Cartier's founding narrative, therefore, corresponds to correlating the preconstructeds that are quasi-identical, and interfacing the presupposeds, that, as we saw, vary according to societies, cultures, and ideologies.

CHAPTER FOUR

Settlement and Conversion: Jean de Brébeuf's *Jesuit Relations* of 1635 and 1636

In the next three chapters I turn to a different series of texts than those of first encounters or discovery narratives such as Cartier's *Voyages*. I have chosen to examine three facets of ethnohistorical discourse as exemplified in the *Jesuit Relations*, the most detailed and complete texts available to us regarding the social, religious, political, and cultural organization of Amerindian society as it existed in seventeenth-century New France. Although the *Relations* deal mainly with Jesuit missionary attempts to convert the indigenous people, they abound in descriptions, comparisons, and commentaries on the life of the early inhabitants of the New World. Paul Le Jeune, who was Superior of the Jesuits in Quebec from 1632 to 1639, as well as a missionary in Quebec, Sillery, Tadoussac, Trois Rivières, and Montreal from 1639 to 1649, before becoming responsible for the entire mission in Canada (1649–62), was the first compiler of the *Jesuit Relations* of New France. Published annually from 1632 to 1673, and almost exclusively by the editor Cramoisy in Paris (the *Relation* of 1637, printed in Rouen by Jean Le Boullenger, is the only volume not published by Cramoisy), the corpus of the *Relations* is made up of annual reports sent by the mission heads to the Superior in Quebec, who, for the most part, is responsible for composing them and who, in turn, transmits them to the Provincial in Paris. They are most often compiled during the month of August, the text covering as much as possible information relating to the current year. The *Relations*, sent to France in the fall on one of the last ships leaving New France, receive the imprimatur from the Father Superior in Paris, and the king, shortly after their arrival. They are generally published early during the next spring, are widely distributed and read, and, indeed, can be considered as 'best sellers.' Their intent is to attract sympathy and spiritual and financial aid for the missions in New France (Pouliot 1966: 466), while their ultimate aim is to instruct and move readers to make them contribute to the objectives of the Jesuit missionaries.

It should be noted that before the Jesuits arrived in New France, the missions were the sole responsibility of the Recollet order, invited by Champlain at the beginning of the seventeenth century to send missionaries to the colony. The Huron mission was manned by several members of this order from 1615, when Father Joseph le Caron, one of the first Europeans to set eyes on Lake Huron, arrived on the banks of Georgian Bay 150 kilometres north of the current city of Toronto. The Recollet Gabriel Sagard, 'the first historian of Canada' (see Warwick 1978: 296–9) also sojourned in Huronia for one year between the summer of 1623 and the end of the spring of 1624. After leaving Quebec (during this period there were only about fifty French people in New France), he undertook his great voyage to the country of the Huron, a trip of some 1300 kilometres, by canoe, following the path taken by other missionaries and traders en route to Huronia. During the period prior to Sagard's arrival – for example, between 1615 and 1621 – there were never more than four Recollets in all of New France. The members of this order were not successful in their attempts to convert the Huron, and were unable to overcome the opposition of the merchants engaged in the fur trade (the brothers de Caën, Huguenots, were the dominant economic force in Quebec at this time). Subsequently, the Recollets called upon an order more powerful and better established in France than theirs, one with superior financial means. They invited the Jesuits to provide missionaries to New France in 1625, and the order responded by sending three of its members – Charles Lalemant, Enemond Masse, and Jean de Brébeuf – who spent the first winter sharing the life of a band of Montagnais hunters en route to their winter quarters. All the missionaries survived the rigours of winter, and Brébeuf, according to Besterman (1957), returned to Quebec 'riche d'une expérience et d'une connaissance inestimables des Indiens, de leurs habitudes, de leur façon de penser, de la nature de leur langage. Mais surtout, il s'était fait aimer des Peaux-Rouges, ce qui ne fut point aisé, car l'homme blanc qu'il était eut souvent de la peine à atteindre au degré d'hospitalité, de loyauté, de bonne camaraderie et de mutuelle bienveillance qui était généralement de règle chez les Indiens' (rich in his invaluable experience and knowledge of the natives, their habits, their ways of thinking, and their language. But especially, he made himself liked by them, which is no easy task, for the white man that he was often had difficulty in attaining the degree of camaraderie and mutual good will that was generally the rule with the Indians) (xiii).

At the end of July 1626, Brébeuf and his companions travelled to Huronia from Quebec and, when they arrived, benefited from Étienne Brulé's knowledge of the Huron language and culture. Brébeuf set up the mission at the village of Toanché with the tribe of the Bear. He stayed three years and learned their language but was not successful in converting the Huron. He returned to Quebec in 1629 and left for England with most of the French in Canada after the fall of the city that same year to the English, led by the Kirkes. The Kirkes, who had left England while their country and France were still at war, were unaware when Quebec fell in the summer of 1629 that the two countries had already signed a treaty. Champlain took three years to make the rulers of the two nations recognize that Quebec had been conquered during peacetime, reducing the Kirkes' capture to an act of piracy. Though theoretically the Recollets were the only order officially having permission to return to the colony, the Jesuits took over the missions, returning to New France after the Treaty of Saint Germain-en-Laye, in 1632, which retroceded the territory to France. As a countermeasure, to make the missionary work of the Recollets better known, and at the same time to lay claim to their right to return to New France, Sagard published *Le Grand Voyage du pays des Hurons* during the summer of 1632. After publication of this volume, the Recollets obtained permission to return to New France, but they were not ready to leave immediately, and when they attempted to do so in 1635 they were not given authorization. Again, Sagard reacted by publishing in 1636 his *Histoire du Canada et voyages que les frères mineurs Récollets ont fait pour la conversion des infidèles*, a plea for the order to take up once again its work in the missions that had been interrupted since the fall of Quebec. This had no immediate effect as, from that time on, the Jesuits were solely in charge of the missions in Canada.

On 7 July 1634, Jean de Brébeuf embarked with Antoine Daniel and a hired man, Baron, for the Huron country, giving instructions that if other parties followed they were to meet at the village of Ihonatiria. One week later, Father Davost and two others left for the same village, while the remainder of the party followed shortly afterward (*Relation* 1635: 24–5). Brébeuf, who had previously travelled to Huronia, had an uneventful though extremely tiring and even exhausting one-month trip, having to paddle and to carry heavy loads over numerous portages.

Father Davost was ill-treated by his guides, many of the supplies he carried were stolen, and he was forced to leave behind almost all the books and most of the paper he was bringing to the village for all the missionaries. Finally, he was abandoned on an island with the Algonquin, though he eventually made his way to the Huron village, arriving despondent, dejected, and in ill health. The others fared no better: all faced extreme hardship, were badly treated, put up with harsh conditions, and were in constant danger (*Relation* 1635: 26). As Superior of the mission in Huronia in 1635 and 1636, Brébeuf was mandated to compose the yearly account of the missionary activity and send it on to the Quebec Superior, Paul Le Jeune.

It is mainly Le Jeune, though, who must be credited with having created the extraordinary instrument of propaganda that the *Relations* turned out to be. 'Mais je ne prétends pas décrire tout ce qui se fait en ce pays, mais seulement ce qui tend au bien de la foi et de la Religion' (I do not pretend to describe all that occurs in the country but only what concerns the welfare of faith and religion) (*Relation* 1635: 4).[1] Unstable at the beginning, the form of the *Relations* will, as Rigault and Ouellet (1978: 641) state, become more fixed with

> [t]he *Relation* of 1634 that, after regrouping subjects into chapters, closes with a 'Journal of things that could not be included in the previous chapters.' In subsequent *Relations* these will generally fall under the rubric of 'Grouping of various things in the form of a Journal' that enables them to narrate what the thematic order of the chapters did not permit, and to augment the *Relation* 'every day until the ships leave by writing about the most remarkable things that could happen.' (*Relation* 1634: 57)

Le Jeune comments perceptively on the structure of the first *Relations*: 'Ce que j'écris dans ce journal n'a point d'autre suite, que la suite du temps: voilà pourquoi je passerai souvent du coq à l'âne, comme on dit, c'est-à-dire que quittant une remarque je passerai à une autre qui ne lui a point de rapport, le temps seul servant de liaison à mon discours' (What I write in this Journal has no other order, except that of time: which is why, as we say, I leap from one topic to another, that is in finishing an observation I pass on to another one not connected to it. Time alone is what links the various parts of my narrative) (*Relation* 1634: 63).

Jean de Brébeuf's *Relations* are of particular import in terms of the accuracy of the information they contain, as he was very knowledgable with respect to Huron customs, governance, and political structures and had a good command of their language, which he spoke fluently and even wrote. After Samuel de Champlain (in 1615) and Gabriel Sagard (in 1623), Brébeuf was the first missionary to live with the Huron, and the third person to write about their customs. The *Relations* of 1635 and 1636 cover his second voyage to the country of the Huron and the first two difficult and critical years of the mission after the return of the French to Canada.

> Mon R. Père,
> C'est pour vous rendre compte de notre voyage en ce Pays des Hurons, lequel a été rempli de plus de fatigues, de pertes et de coûts que l'autre, mais aussi qui a été suivi et le sera, Dieu aidant, de plus de bénédictions du Ciel.
>
> (Reverend Father,
> This is to give you an account of our voyage to the land of the Huron, during which we encountered more fatigue, losses and pains than our last trip, but also which was followed and will be, God willing, by more benedictions from Heaven.) (1635: 23)

This is how Jean de Brébeuf begins his *Relation* of 1635, dated 27 May of that same year, 'jour auquel le S. Esprit descendit visiblement sur les Apôtres' (the day on which the Holy Spirit visibly descended upon the Apostles) (1635: 41). This account is much shorter than the one written the next year (the latter is approximately four times longer), its brevity due, in part, to the scarcity of necessary supplies and to the difficulty of establishing the mission after such a long absence: 'le peu de papier et de loisir que nous avons, m'oblige à vous dire en peu de mots ce qui pourrait faire un juste volume' (the little paper and the lack of time we have forces me to say in a few words what could actually take a volume to say) (1635: 33). 'Tous les Français qui sont ici s'y sont ardemment portés, ramenant l'ancien usage d'écrire sur des écorces de bouleau faute de papier' (All the French here, have ardently committed themselves to this; reverting to ancient ways of writing on birch bark for lack of paper) (1635: 37).

None the less, these two texts written by Brébeuf, in spite of their unequal length, illustrate in an exemplary fashion the very conditions of the existence of the *Relations* in general, as well as the process of representation by which one establishes a situation of communication.[2]

Each of the *Relations* written by Brébeuf – or for that matter by any other Jesuit – assumes the form of a long letter sent to the priest in charge of the mission in Quebec (in this particular case, Paul Le Jeune). Their titles are, respectively, *Relation of What Occurred in the Land of the Huron in 1635* and *Relation of What Occurred in the Country of the Huron in 1636*. If one considers its form of expression, the previous *Relation*, at first sight, is of a heterogeneous or composite nature. On the one hand, it articulates the discontinuous and mixed nature of the genre; on the other, it simulates, in its semiotic function, a process of enunciation. The first part of the text unravels as a retrospective travel narrative enfolding the particular events described in a causal and temporal order. The arrival at Trois Rivières on 5 July 1634; the discussions with the Bissirian and the Huron; the intervention of the admiral of the fleet, Sir du Plessis Bochart; the departure with the Native people; the dangers encountered, and so on, are each described in turn:

> Ajoutez à ces difficultés, qu'il faut coucher sur la terre nue, ou sur quelque dure roche, faute de trouver dix ou douze pieds de terre en carré pour placer une chétive cabane; qu'il faut sentir incessamment la puanteur de Sauvages recrus, marcher dans les eaux, dans les fanges, dans l'obscurité et l'embarras des forêts, où les piqûres d'une multitude infinie de mousquilles et cousins vous importunent fort. Je laisse à part un long et ennuyeux silence où l'on est réduit, j'entends pour les nouveaux qui n'ont parfois en leur compagnie personne de leur langue, et ne savent celle des Sauvages.

> (Add to these difficulties that we have to sleep on the bare ground, or on some hard stones, because we are unable to find a plot of land ten by ten or twelve by twelve on which to build a flimsy cabin. That we have to put up constantly with the stench of the Indians we recruited. We have to walk in water, in muck, in the darkness, hindered by the forests, where we are greatly bothered by the bites of an infinite multitude of flies and their relatives. I leave aside the long and tedious silences to which we are reduced, especially the newcomers who sometimes have no one who can speak their language with them and who do not know that of the Indians.) (25).

Finally, the arrival in the country of the Huron 'le cinquième d'août, jour de notre Dame des Neiges, ayant demeuré trente jours par les chemins, en continuel travail' (August 5, day of Our Lady of the Snows;

having spent thirty days on the way, and continually working) (1635: 26). He then describes the greetings of the Huron, the first dealings with the personalities of the village of Teandeouihara, and the strategic reasons for staying with a particular person:

> Je me logeai chez un nommé *Aouandoïé*, lequel est, ou au moins a été un des plus riches des Hurons. Ce que je fis à dessein, par ce qu'un autre moins fort eût pû être incommodé du grand nombre de Français que j'attendais et qu'il fallait nourrir jusqu'à ce que nous fussions tous assemblés et que notre cabane fût faite. Vous pouvez vous loger où vous voulez, car cette Nation, entre toutes les autres, est fort hospitalière envers toute sorte de personnes, même envers les Étrangers.
>
> (I moved in with someone named *Aouandoié*, who is or who has been one of the richest of all the Huron. I did this deliberately, because someone less well off could have been put in an awkward situation by the great number of French that I was expecting, and who would have to be fed until we could all move in together when our cabin is finished. You can live with whomever you want, for this Nation among all others, is extremely hospitable with Strangers.) (1635: 29).

This is immediately followed by observations on the population of the villages and the geography of the country, and on the language and beliefs of the inhabitants. Here the chronological organization gives way to a topical description of the daily activity of the Huron.

However, when it is a question of accounting for the mission itself, the chronological frame of the Gregorian calendar becomes the principle organizing the events narrated:

> Après cela, nous nous sommes employés à la visite, sollicitation et instruction des malades ... ç'a été dans ce pieux exercice que nous avons acquis des âmes à notre Seigneur, jusqu'au nombre de treize ... Ce fut le six septembre 1634 ... Le 26 du même mois, je baptisai Marie *Oquiaendis*, mère du Capitaine de ce village ... Le 20 octobre, je partis pour aller à la Nation du Pétun. En ce voyage Dieu me fit la faveur de baptiser et envoyer au Ciel trois petits enfants ... Le vingt-et-un octobre, fut baptisé Joseph *Sondaarouhané* ... Le vingt-sept novembre, Martin *Tsicok* ... Le dix-neuf janvier ... Finalement le vingt avril, je baptisai à *Oënrio* une femme fort vieille. Elle décéda le vingt-quatre ... Ce sont là les fruits que nous avons recueillis de nos visites et instructions particulières.

(After that, we devoted ourselves to visiting, soliciting and instructing the sick ... it was during this pious exercise that we gained souls for Our Lord, actually there were thirteen ... His was on September 6, 1634 ... The 26, of the same month, I baptized Marie *Oquiaendis* the mother of the Captain of that village ... October 20, I left for the Nation of the Petun: during this trip God gave me the honour of baptizing and sending three children to heaven ... The twenty-first of October Joseph *Sondaarouharmé* was baptized ... The twenty-seventh of November Martin *Tsicok* ... the nineteenth of January ... Finally the twentieth of April, I baptized in *Oënrio* a very old woman. She passed away on the twenty-fourth ... These are the fruits we gathered from our visits and particular instructions.) (1635: 37–9)

Moreover, the text is punctuated with metanarrative comments – on the selective aspect of writing: 'À propos de leurs admirations, j'en pourrais ici coucher plusieurs faits ...' (Regarding their admirations, I could mention several things ...) (1635: 33); on the regulatory mechanism used to organize it: 'Reste maintenant à dire quelque chose du pays, des mœurs et coutumes des Hurons, de la disposition qu'ils ont à la Foi, et de nos petits travaux' (I now must say something about the country, the manners and customs of the Huron, on their predisposition to the Faith, and on our minor works) (1635: 34); and on the inscription of the fragmentary within the virtual totality: 'C'est ainsi, pour finir ce discours, qui serait trop long si je voulais tout dire' (Hence, to end this discourse, which would be too long, if I wanted to say everything) (1635: 36). In fact, between the moment the *Relation* is finished on 27 May and its voyage to Quebec by canoe, a last, brief, one-page fragment was attached that could not be melded into the main narrative.

Within the framework of functional logic, as a genre the 1635 *Relation* does not succeed in integrating a series of events within the unity of a single action. Assembled from fragments, these texts unfold in a fragmented way and, to cite Barthes (1966), their internal economy is regulated by a structure of a stemmatic nature.[3] Instead of being systematically incorporated into a system of events organized according to the twofold causal and temporal principle of the traditional narrative, the *Relation* takes on meaning especially through its metonymic *rela*tionship of contiguity with the whole. This very mechanism also regulates Brébeuf's *Relation* of 1636, which is divided into two parts of unequal length. The first is composed of four chapters, the initial one of which gives a synoptic overview of the state of the mission. The second, which has the heading 'Chapter II, Containing in Chronological Order the Other Remarkable Things That Happened This Year,' subordinates events to a chronological frame but ends with a metanarrative statement about the need to regulate this discourse of persuasion and belief for an uninformed reader. 'J'eusse pû ajouter ici beaucoup de choses qui se sont passées cette année, et dont nous avons été témoins oculaires; mais j'ai jugé plus à propos de les reserver à la seconde partie de cette *Relation*; j'espère que j'éviterai par ce moyen plus aisément la confusion, et contenterai à mon avis davantage tous ceux qui sont curieux de savoir les mœurs et les coutumes de ces Peuples' (I could have added here many things that occurred this year and of which we were eyewitnesses. But I thought it more proper to reserve them for the second part of this *Relation*. I hope by this that I will avoid confusing the reader, and in my opinion, this will satisfy better everyone who is curious to learn about the habits and customs of these People) (1636: 76). The second part, composed of nine chapters, focuses on the language of the Huron, their beliefs – in particular regarding the immortality of the soul – their divinity, their superstitions, their government, and their funeral ceremonials and rites. It ends with the description of the 'Solemn Feast of the Dead,' the most famous ceremony of the Huron Nation.

The two parts of the *Relation* of 1636 are composed in such a way as to favour *relata* of contiguity. They also stand out because of the heterogeneous character of the disparate materials, which are not integrated within the unity of a single action. I would like to mention here that, at the functional level, the *Relations* overturn the fictional regime by subrogating the distributional functions to indexical units that refer to a 'higher level,' finding their domain of sanction in the ultimate paradigm of the truth of religious belief.[4] An exemplary micronarrative embedded literally and figuratively in the *Relation* of 1635 illustrates most eloquently the process just described. The narrative in question is produced by a mechanism of enunciation that functions as a *mise en abyme* characteristic of the entire forty-one volumes published by the Jesuits on New France between 1632 and 1673.

> En ce voyage, passant par *Onnentissati*, j'allai voir un nommé *Oukhahitoüa*, qui avait l'an passé embarqué un de nos hommes; le trouvant à l'extremité, je l'instruisis; il crut, il détesta sa vie passée, il fut baptisé sous le nom de François, et deux jours après quitta ce monde pour s'envoler au Ciel.

66   Part II. Discovery, Conversion, and Colonization

> (During this voyage, passing through *Onnentissati*, I went and visited someone named *Oukhahitoua*, who last year had embarked one of our men. Finding him close to death, I instructed him, he believed, he detested his past life. He was baptized and given the name François, and two days later he left this world to fly off to Heaven.) (1635: 39).

We can recognize here the barest, most minimalist narrative recapturing the totality of the *Relations* that basically can be considered, both as the iteration and concatenation of this primitive nucleus of conversion, and as subordinating the syntagmatic functions to the same indexical paradigmatic expansion. An *I*, who assumes the dual role in the narrative of the manipulating agent who persuades a manipulated subject *he*, will rule on the success and value of the latter's conversion and final state of belief. The acting agent, Jesuit, has himself been subjected to a prior intellectual and spiritual manipulation by various religious and educational institutions that have sanctioned him in the name of the ultimate Sender and Receiver, God, who, in this narrative, is always presupposed. He puts in place a program of 'conversion' that consists in persuading or making someone – in this instance, the Huron who is the Receiver-Subject – believe in his own system of beliefs. To carry out this program of conversion, the agent must undertake a journey (spatio-temporal disjunction-conjunction) to encounter the other: 'During this voyage ... I went and visited someone called *Oukhahitoua*.' He then institutes a program of persuasion, or making someone believe – 'I instructed him' – that corresponds in the Huron to the acquisition both of the modal values (having-to, wanting-to, knowing-how, and being-able-to) and of the object of value, belief: 'he believed.' The success of the operation, or the passage from making-someone-believe to his actually believing, is doubly sanctioned. First, by the word, or the interpretive activity of the Enunciator-Sender, and second by the witnessing of the Huron, who, in turn, repudiates his former ancestral beliefs, along with the customs of his Nation ('He detested his past life'). The sequence of repudiation – the principal test undergone by the Huron that corresponds to a belief act – undeniably confirms the authenticity of the conversion (manipulation of the belief system) and the importance of the new modal values acquired. It is followed by a dual sanction that posits the true situation of the final state of the Receiver-Subject. The glorifying test 'he was baptized' confirms the fact that the operation of 'believing' has been successful. This can be seen as the acquisition of the value 'belief' as well as a confirmation both of the true knowledge of the Jesuit and the Huron, and also of the exact nature of the object of value. Moreover, this program is immediately assumed by the ultimate Receiver, 'God,' who remains unnamed but who is omnipresent and presupposed from the very beginning ('two days later he left this world to fly off to Heaven').

Obviously, the *Relations* do not produce only narrative programs of 'conversion' confirmed by the Jesuit missionary, since there are many anti-programs of resistance or 'repudiation' that call into question and oppose the desired result. In the above case, the success of the conversion is crowned and is confirmed at the onomastic level by the avatars of the Huron's name and by its remotivation. 'Someone called *Oukhahitoua,*' after having detested his past life, will be 'baptized and given the name François,' before 'flying off to Heaven.' Yet, though the failure of the conversion can sometimes be attributed to a lack of knowledge, the enunciator/missionary never expresses any doubts about the ultimate consecration of the legitimating instance of the Original Sender, God, through the sociopolitical and religious institutions, the church and the crown, its temporal representatives. This emblematic micronarrative produces a final utterance that defines positively the relation between subject and object. The possession of 'belief,' at the manifest level, is of the order of truth, whereas the state of 'non-believing,' defined negatively on each of the two planes, is of the order of falsehood. Hence, the axiology /Life-Death/ that is configured by the actors of the narrative at the practical and pragmatic level is cognitively invested by the Sender-Narrator at the mythical level,[5] so that life and its figure 'Heaven' (above) are the real Receiver of the Huron, whereas death and its figure 'Earth' (below) are their Anti-sender. This particular narrative, which unfolds solely on the axis of truth and does not configure the positions of the Anti-sender and Non-sender implicitly presupposed as constituting the axis of falsehood, none the less confirms the domains of being and appearance, of immanence and manifestation. In brief, if for the subject of 'believing' to say is to do, the sanction uttered by the narrator, the cognitive subject of the enunciation, underpins the very reason for any further pragmatic intervention. He sets out as first principle that the infidel Huron is dead in life (appearance), whereas, brought to the true faith by his legitimate Sender, he will be living in death (being), and will join the promised Paradise by leaving 'this world to fly off to Heaven.'

Aussi des philosophes, dont l'autorité dans le domaine de la littérature et de la culture est immense, ont-ils placé dans leur définition de l'homme le 'phonétique,' comme s'il semblait que la voix fût la propriété exclusive de l'homme. Théophile Protospatharius, dans une dissertation très docte et très élégante sur la structure du corps humain, écrit: l'homme 'est un animal logique, phonétique et dialectique,' où, on le voit, il donne à l'homme le nom 'd'être doué de voix,' parce qu'ayant été doué de raison, il a pour privilège d'exprimer par la voix les pensées intimes de son esprit.

(And so philosophers, whose authority in the domain of literature and culture is immense, have placed in their definition of man the 'phonetic,' as though it seemed that the voice was the exclusive property of man. Theophile Protospatharius, in a very learned and elegant dissertation on the structure of the human body, writes: 'Man is a logical, phonetic and dialectic animal.' We can see, that he gives man the name 'being endowed with voice,' because being endowed with reason he has the privilege of expressing through voice the intimate thoughts of his mind.) (Father Lois de Cressolles, 1620: 175).

One cannot confuse a situation of communication, in particular the actual process of enunciation that is polylogical and polyphonological, with its configuration and dramatization in the *Relations*, which allegorize and put in place the actual mechanisms of representation. In contrast 'to oral communication that postulates the trace of the successive appropriation of language by interlocutors, their mutual co-presence and the spatio-temporal context where dialogue is exchanged, however, in its structural economy the written message must restore and reiterate the existence of the spatial and temporal distance that separates the act of emission from its reception and its response' (Le Huenen and Perron, 1984b: 36). As with the functional level described above, one also finds in the *Relation* of 1635 a *mise en abyme* of the elaboration of a signifying place of 'voice' emblematizing the construction of the space of desired discourse that governs the entire *Jesuit Relations* from beginning to end. Brébeuf notes in detail the reactions of the Huron to a number of unfamiliar European-manufactured objects that the Jesuits and their hired men have transported to this part of the country, and notably dwells at great length on the clock that chimes.

Pour ce qui est de l'horloge, il y aurait mille choses à dire: ils croient tous que c'est quelque chose vivante, car ils ne se peuvent imaginer comment elle sonne d'elle même, et quand elle vient à sonner, ils regardent si nous sommes tous là, et s'il n'y a pas quelqu'un de caché pour lui donner le branle.

Ils ont pensé qu'elle entendait, principalement quand, pour rire, quelqu'un de nos Français s'écriait au dernier coup de marteau, c'est assez sonné, et que tout aussitôt elle se taisait. Ils l'appellent le Capitaine du jour. Quand elle sonne, ils disent qu'elle parle, et demandent, quand ils nous viennent voir, combien de fois le Capitaine a déjà parlé. Ils nous interrogent de son manger. Ils demeurent des heures entières, et quelquefois plusieurs, afin de la pouvoir ouïr parler. Ils demandaient au commencement ce qu'elle disait; on leur répondit deux choses, qu'ils ont fort bien retenues: l'une, que quand elle sonnait à quatre heures du soir pendant l'hiver, elle disait: Sortez, allez-vous-en, afin que nous fermions la porte; car aussitôt ils lèvent le siège, et s'en vont; l'autre, qu'à midi elle disait, *yo eiouahaoua*, c'est-à-dire, sus dressons la chaudière, et ils ont encore mieux retenu ce langage: car il y a ces écornifleurs, qui ne manquent point de venir à cette heure-là, pour participer à notre Sagamité. Ils mangent à toutes heures, quand ils ont dequoi; cependant d'ordinaire ils ne font que manger deux chaudières par jour, sauvoir est, au matin et au soir: partant ils sont bien aises pendant le jour de prendre part à la nôtre.

(As for the clock, there would be a thousand things to say about it. They all believe that it is something living, for they cannot imagine how it chimes by itself. And when it happens to ring they look to see if we are there, and if there is not someone hidden to set it off.

They thought that it could hear, especially when in jest one of our Frenchmen cried out at the last chime of the bell, 'that's enough ringing,' and immediately afterwards it stopped ringing. They call it the Captain of the day. When it rings they say it speaks and ask, when they come to see us, how many times the Captain has already spoken. They question us about its food. They remain before it for hours on end, and sometimes a number of them, to hear it speak. They asked at the beginning what it said. We answered two things that they retained very well. One that when it rang at four o'clock in the afternoon in the winter it said 'Leave, get out' so that we could close the door. They immediately get up and leave. The other is that at noon it said '*yo eiouahaoua*,' that is to say, let us put on the kettle. They retained these words even more. For a number of these scroungers, come at this time expressly to share our Sagamite.[6] They eat at all hours, when they have the where-with-all. However, normally they only eat two kettles a day, morning and evening. They are more than willing during the day to share ours.) (1635: 33)

I have noted that the minimal narrative of 'conversion' analysed above put in place a narrator-actant *I*, who had a composite role since he was both enunciator and agent in the narrative. However, in the 'Clock' sequence, the narrator-actant, though still concerned with a virtual narratee having a modal competence that is clearly specified throughout the narrative,[7] is also clearly part of the collective actant: 'We,' 'our Frenchmen.' Indeed, the Receiver, or collective actant, 'They,' 'these scroungers,' will once again be manipulated to carry out a program both pragmatic and cognitive, that will be sanctioned by the collective Sender. None the less, we are not dealing, as in the first case, with the establishment of a unique narrative program, confirming the modal competence of the Sender enunciator, but rather with an actual setting into discourse of the central figure of the 'Clock' presented in the first sentence of the text. In fact, what the narrator – configured by an *I* appearing in the last sentence that ends the previous section dealing with another invention imported by *us* into this land: 'Je crois que c'est à cause que le moulin fait la farine trop fine' (I think it is because the mill grinds the flour too fine) (1635: 32–3) – proposes to do is to describe this 'Clock,' about which 'there would be a thousand things to say.' It should be noted, though, that as very often occurs throughout the *Relations*, the impulse to enunciate in the first person subsides, shifting into the collective mode and making the doxological voice ring out and resonate aloud.[8]

At the textual level, the dissolution of the individual into the collective, of the *I* into the *not-I*, reproduces the 'split,' to cite Greimas and Courtés (1982),[9] between empirical subject and discourse, insofar as, at least formally, the narrative implements discontinuity and simulates disengagement with respect to the enunciating subject that corresponds to the constitution of the automatization of discourse. Whereas the initial disengagement of enunciation projects, at the actorial level, the *not-I* actors, the 'Captain of the day' extract reproduces the articulation *I–not-I*, in the form of a 'We'/'Clock'/(*I*)–'They'/'Clock'/(*not-I*). That is to say, the enunciator establishes two clearly defined classes of actors. The first consists of the collective Sender-actant, the legitimate possessor of the machine to measure time and the holder of theoretical and practical knowledge that can assure its upkeep and its function. The second is made up of the destitute collective Receiver-actant who does not master the knowledge necessary to make it work, to regulate it, or again to use it.

In this particular case, to narrate the 'Clock,' to set it into discourse, is, first of all to select among all the relations 'We'/'Clock'–'They'/ 'Clock' directly observed or reported by eyewitnesses (narrator-actor, or other actors of the utterance).[10] 'There would be a thousand things to say about it.' Second, it is to semanticize these relations by establishing a value system based on difference: 'these scroungers, come at this time.' Moreover, this setting into discourse presupposes a specific actorialization and temporalization. If, in the first sentence, temporalization creates a disengagement effect, *not-now*, in contrast the second sentence, by setting in parentheses the opposition between the categories of time (past-present), creates the effect of a return to enunciation: 'there would be' versus 'They all believe.' The fourth sentence, 'They thought that it could hear ... it stopped ringing,' re-actualizes the original temporal operation *not-now*, re-instituting disengagement; whereas the fifth, 'They call it the Captain of the day,' constitutes a negation of *not-now*, and simulates an effect of enunciation or an engagement, tending to create an illusion of enunciation that aims at both situating and positioning the enunciator and the enunciatee. This alternating process of homo-categorical temporal disengagement and engagement, characteristic of Jean de Brébeuf's *Relations*, occurs clearly in the following sentence – 'They asked in the beginning what it said. We answered ... that it said "Leave, get out" ... They immediately get up and leave' – alternately reproducing a referentialization and a de-referentialization of the utterance. This interplay of temporal assertion (*not-now*) and negation (*now*), along with the spatial (*not-here–here*) and actantial assertions (*not-I–I*), actually generates the referential and enunciative illusions in all the *Jesuit Relations*. The shifting in and out of disengagement ('the effect of which is to referentialize the domain where its operation begins'), and of engagement ('that produces a de-referentialization of the utterance that it concerns')[11] ends up, at the moment of disengagement, by positing the difference and the strangeness of the event and the described (*not-I, not-here, not-now*). This shifting in and out immediately after the engagement attempts in vain to dissolve otherness and alterity in the infinite paradigm founding the domain of the Enunciation of Origins, '*In principio erat verbum*.' The *Relations* of 1635 and 1636, in their structural organization, reiterate, by showcasing it, the second-degree enunciative mechanisms, playing out the troubling scenario of the verb, which, as soon as it appears, is estranged, and which, feverishly, must return to its impossible original domain.

This is certainly the case with the curious internal second-degree disengagement that signals the beginnings of the pseudo-dialogues in Brébeuf's narrative when, on three separate occasions, the anonymous actant, having the status of the non-individualized collective actant, speaks out to develop a sequence about the 'Clock' that talks. It is the case, though, with respect to the structure of this pseudo-dialogue, that the internal disengagement that can be linked with 'direct discourse' always originates in the same class of interlocutors, *us*: 'one of our Frenchmen cried out at the last chime of the bell, "that's enough ringing" ... we answered two things ... it said "Leave, get out" ... it said "*yo eiouahaoua.*"' In contrast, the addressees, who always appear as a collective, undifferentiated 'They,' will never gain the status of speaking subject since they cannot appropriate all the resources of language and enter into an authentic *inter*locutory relationship with the addresser. The questions, answers, and replies of the other – a non-person – which in a *dia*logical situation would occur in the form of disengagement, here are reported, resumed, even translated, and therefore recuperated by the enunciator who construes and constructs the enunciatee. The logos is inflected and subsumed in the form of indirect discourse: 'They all believe ... When it rings they say it speaks ... They question us ... They asked at the beginning what it said ...' The language of desire is, by this very gesture, transferred, transported to the reassuring locus of the maternal tongue, and deviated from its legitimate holder. It is then appropriated in the form of the citational – 'it said "*yo eiouahaoua,*"' – before being translated into the common web of explanation – 'that is to say, let us put on the kettle' – thereby producing the iterated simulacrum of the enunciative illusion. This shuttling to and fro between direct and indirect discourse constitutes a second-degree formal echo of the procedures of disengagement and engagement set up by the enunciator of the *Relations*, who attempts to articulate the troubling alterity and difference founding his discourse (referentialization). He also seeks by every possible means to resorb them in ultimate similarity and sameness (de-referentialization), which, in final analysis, appears as the mute and final justifying instance and the unspoken guarantor of all discourse.

The specific temporalization of this extract enables us both to situate the actual position of the 'We' in relationship to the 'Clock' and to define its axiological competence with respect to that of the 'They.' The procedures of actorialization establish a situation where 'We' becomes the secondary interpreter of a first interpretation of the 'Clock.' At the level of manifestation this extract is almost entirely devoted to the establishment of a recurring structure by which the 'Clock' is interpreted as 'something living.' Whereas on a second level – which is relatively implicit here, but much more explicit in the ensemble of Brébeuf's *Relations* – this explanation is, in turn, evaluated by a 'We.' The first process gives a paradigmatic interpretation of the figure in the form of an expansion for a class of actants, 'They,' of the *isotopy*[12] 'Life.' For 'They,' the 'Clock' is above all 'something living'; perhaps there is 'someone hidden to set it off'; moreover, this 'someone' undoubtedly can 'hear.' In addition 'it speaks,' it 'eats,' and so on. However, for the other class of actants, 'We' (our Frenchmen), this figure is inscribed in the isotopy 'Death,' and is indeed part of the class of animate objects: 'They all believe ... they cannot imagine how it chimes by itself. And when it happens to ring they look to see if we are all there ... when in jest one of our Frenchmen cried ...'

Insofar as elements belonging to the class of 'something living' or to the presupposed class of 'something dead' can be substituted for the figure 'Clock' in this discourse, the 'Clock' takes on the status of a sign. But since the 'Clock' appears as an 'animated being' for the 'They,' but as a 'mechanical thing' for the 'We,' it will fall to the narrator, who is included in the category of the collective actant, to assign to each a position on the chequer-board of veridiction. The outcome is fixed beforehand; the dice in the game of truth are loaded from the start, since the collective actant that negotiates the figures, attributes points, dictates the rules, and assigns the respective roles to the players is at one and the same time the main player.

The first dimension, where the 'We'/'Clock'–'They'/'Clock' relations are developed and defined, corresponds to the evaluative and consequently to the cognitive dimension. But another dimension is elaborated where the figure of the 'Clock' plays the role of actor. For the class to which the narrator belongs both announces, or rather says, the hours (*Hora legein*) and also gives the proper measure of time, whereas for the others, 'it speaks' but 'they do not know what it says.' Although its actorial situation remains stable, as an actor the 'Clock,' in the first trajectory, is correlated with the figures belonging to 'something living,' while in the second this figure is linked to the indisputable evidence of the 'inanimate mechanical.' Compared with figures of the second trajectory, those that belong to the first are much more varied and for the most part mythical figures. This setting into discourse of the 'Clock,' in most cases, links both trajectories in the same syntagm, so that the text appears as a concatenation of practical and mythical figures: ('someone hidden' versus 'ring'; 'it could hear' versus 'that's enough ringing'; 'it speaks' versus 'it rings'; 'The Captain has already spoken,' 'its food,' 'hear it speak,' 'it said' versus 'four o'clock in the afternoon,' 'at noon'). The mythical figures take on the status of values that can order about the 'They,' and in this context the 'Clock,' interpreted as a thematic operator, manipulates the values of 'something living' for the subjects 'They.' But if the thematic operator 'Clock' 'manipulates the values of the figures, it carries out an operation analogous to the one normally reserved for the domain of enunciation which, in the setting into discourse, sets out values for figures' (Panier 1983: 67).

Although the first sentence of the extract proposed to 'say' a certain number of things about the 'thousand things to say about' the 'Clock,' the latter has, in a way, itself spoken up by articulating the thematic values at the expense of the figures. 'Phonetic,' having the gift of speech, the 'Clock' captures and fixes the attention of its addressees, provokes a situation of expectation, of demand setting off a quest for meaning – a dialectic that ends up in the reciprocity of ambiguous speech. This ultimate mechanism of third-degree disengagement–engagement, by dramatizing and playing out the staging of the troubling *mise en abyme* of the domain of enunciation, succeeds in contesting it and denouncing it as a simple simulacrum. The relationships between the interlocutors, although by necessity interdependent, none the less are not situated at the same level. For if the 'Clock' expresses itself through its own voice, in contrast, as we have seen, the addressee's voice is always taken up, resumed, or, again, deviated from its source by the intermediary of indirect discourse. At the enunciative level, the interlocutors actualize clearly defined roles. In the first instance when the 'Clock' engages (*I, here, now*) the Huron 'cannot imagine how it chimes by itself' and, suspecting the creation of a simulacrum, they immediately mime a disengagement (*not-I, not-here, not-now*) when they look to see 'if we are *all here*.' Moreover, 'They' doubt that it has the capacity to constitute itself, as an autonomous subject of enunciation since 'They' imagine that there is 'someone hidden to set it off.' But once convinced that the 'Clock' is an animated being and that it 'rings' by itself, not only are 'They' taken in by this interplay of enunciation but 'They' also referentialize this 'living' mechanical being by endowing it with actorialization, spatialization, and temporalization. And this endowment at one and the same time simulates the domain of enunciation and modalizes the subject of enunciation. The phonetic activated the quest for the etymon, since the 'Clock' harbours the principle of understanding along with an internal logic, founded on its capacity to decipher speech: 'They thought it could hear when ... one of our Frenchmen cried out ... it stopped ringing.' 'A phonetic, logical and dialectical animal,' the Captain of the day (head, chief 'endowed with reason'), much in the same manner as Theophile Protospatharius's man, is not only gifted with a hunger for speech ('When it rings they say it speaks'), but also with a real hunger ('They question us about its food'). They are trapped by their own construction – the referential illusion consolidated at the moment when the projected voice, the simulacrum's tongue, is realized as an actual speech act: '"Leave, get out" ... They immediately get up and leave.' The engagement succeeds, speech has acted, the domain of enunciation has finally been reconstituted. The 'Clock's' voice has been authenticated.

Not quite, though. It would be a mistake to stop here, for on closer inspection the text rectifies this position *in extremis* by a final effect of disengagement – *trompe l'œil*, in fact. We were dealing with a case of misunderstanding that resulted on the one hand from the murmur of the original tongue of the 'Clock' and on the other from a simple trick of ventriloquy. For if the 'Clock' now speaks from its stomach – 'It said "*yo eiouahaoua*," that is to say, let us put on the kettle' – it also speaks only about the other's stomach – 'at noon ... these scroungers come at this time ... they are more than willing to share ours (kettle).' *Not-here, not-now, not-I* – the subject of enunciation is uprooted, decentred, and, by foundering in the frozen syntagm of the utterance, is again inextricably anchored in the discourse of the other. We have come full circle; the illusion is destroyed since, whether or not the voice happens to be 'something living,' speech, discourse that defines the relationship to the other, appears, when all is said and done, as the 'discourse of the other,' to cite Bakhtin.[13] The product of interdiscourse, the 'Clock' also appears as a mechanism that both produces and denounces the illusion of the subject who would be at the origin of his own discourse: 'where he is only the medium and the effect.'[14] Endless interplay of mirrors: the 'Clock' that is at first constituted as enunciating subject through reciprocal complicity not only serves as the interdiscursive mediator and seems to assume the role of object of value for the manipulating subject 'We' in the final conversion of the other 'They'; it also functions as an autonomous system that regulates all the daily activity of the 'We' by modelling it on the liturgical rule. If the logos of the hour is not the same for all the interlocutors, what is certain is that it is not where one thinks it is.

Chime-talk, as figure the 'Clock,' as I noted above, takes on the status of the sign, insofar as its value is determined by the place it occupies in the two 'practical' and 'mythical' configurations. But in the narrative trajectory, the 'Clock' is also modalized concurrently by the collective actants 'They' and 'We.' For the first class of actants who, in fact, 'engage' it, the figure of the 'Clock' is invested and constructed by means of a cataphoric process, so that the configuration that founds it, by forbidding all recourse to a referent, unfolds only in the realm of the empire of signs. By contrast, if for 'They' there exist only signs behind or beyond signs, for the collective actant-Sender 'We' who disengages this same figure, the universe of signs is organized by the Grand Rhetoric that carries them elsewhere towards the one and only meaning of the privileged trope of metaphor. In final analysis, the project of conversion can be reduced to the careful elaboration of procedures of rhetoric and eloquence – a simple translation of tropes – for in the *Relations*, to make someone believe, when all is said and done, is to invest through the other's speech the domain disengaged by cataphor and displace it through the effect engaged by metaphor. A simple modulation of voice, then, converts, 'turns' the other 'towards,' the absolute origin of speech.[15]

CHAPTER FIVE

Founding Nations: Jesuit–Huron Relations in Seventeenth-Century New France

Toute notre force est au bout de la langue, et en la monstre et production de nos livres et Écritures, dont ils ne cessent tous les jours d'admirer les effets; ce qui nous sert uniquement envers ces peuples ...

(Our entire strength resides at the tips of our tongues, and in the manifestation and showing of our books and Scriptures, whose effects, daily, they increasingly admire. These are the sole grounds for the credibility we have with these people ...)

(*Relations*, 1639: 82)

[L]a grande tentation des Sauvages, est que le Baptême et la prière les font mourir. Un certain appellé François *Kok8eribabougouz*, voyant un de nos Pères entrer dans sa cabane, l'attaque et lui demande s'il ne sait pas enfin la cause pourquoi ils meurent ainsi tous, depuis quelques années qu'on leur a parlé de notre foi.

([T]he great temptation for these Indians is that Baptism and prayer make them die. A certain François *Kok8eribabougouz*,[1] seeing one of our Fathers enter his cabin, confronts him and asks him if he does not know finally why they have all been dying over the last few years since we have been speaking to them about our faith.)

(*Relations*, 1643: 13)

The above quotations illustrate, in an exemplary fashion, both the problems encountered by the French missionaries in their attempts to convert the Huron Nation to Christianity, and the ensuing disarray and hostility experienced by the latter after coming into contact with European cultural values and objects. On the one hand, spoken and written languages are identified by the first narrator (Jérôme Lalemant) as the primary means of communicating with others, and subsequently of influencing them. Yet, in order to do so, it is necessary to learn the Huron language in all its subtleties, so that imported religious books and Scriptures can be not only shown to the inhabitants but also explained to them. Admiration, recognition of the value of the message, and the sender's credibility seem to be directly proportional to the subject's demonstrated linguistic competence. From the point of view of the narrator of the first citation, conversion is a rather straightforward procedure that implies a sender who has access to the receiver's language, masters its code, and then translates a different world-view into a translucent language that is decoded and accepted by a passive subject.

On the other hand, the second narrator (Barthélemy Vimont) introduces tension into this unitary vision by stressing the context and what could be called the polemico-conflictual dimension of communication. Exogenous religious ceremonies, transmitted by foreigners manipulating the Huron language, are linked to disruptive forces within the stable cultural order. Baptism and prayer bring death to the Huron people. The destabilizing effect of the entire process actually can be observed materially at the onomastic level where both Christian (François) and indigenous (*Kok8eribabougouz*) names meet, clash, and remain in antithetical relationship without being reabsorbed into a unified whole. Neither language succeeds in overcoming the duality inherent in the nominative syntagm, and the bipolarity (figuratively manifested in the narrator's discourse by the juxtaposition of two irreconcilable signifiers of disparate origins to designate one and the same person) accentuates the tension existing between irreducible axiological systems. In brief, this mixed system of nomination, emblematic of the twenty volumes of the *Jesuit Relations* (1634–54) dealing with the conversion and destruction of the Huron Nation, articulates a paradigmatic relationship between two systems of values that the narrative attempts to synthesize syntagmatically into a harmonious unity by erasing all indigenous signifiers as they are translated into the mother tongue. The conflicting themes, life in death (implicit-Jesuit) and death in life (explicit-Huron), are clearly manifested in the text when the divided subject refuses to accept passively the sender's message, transmitted in his own native tongue. Instead, the receiver, through questioning the very nature of the sender's system of values, constitutes himself as a thinking, critical, anti-subject with his own system of values, thereby instituting communication not as a simple transmission of messages but as a confrontation between two contractual and/or polemical subjects, each with his own competence and his own belief system.

The difficulties encountered by French missionaries who came into contact with the Huron Nation must be attributed not only to their conception of conversion as the simple transmission of their own value system by means of a foreign language but also to their fundamental belief that the inhabitants are basically incompetent to learn any other tongue. Commenting upon the missionaries' efforts to influence the Huron, Jean de Brébeuf writes to the Father Superior in Quebec, 'Le P. Antoine Daniel et les autres Pères vont tous les jours par toutes les Cabanes enseigner aux enfants, soit baptisés ou non, la doctrine chrétienne, savoir est le signe de la Croix, le *Pater*, l'*Ave*, le *Credo*, les Commandements de Dieu, l'Oraison à l'Ange Gardien, et autres brèves prières; le tout en leur langue, parce que ces Peuples ont une ineptitude naturelle d'en apprendre une autre' (Every day Father Antoine Daniel and the other Fathers visit the cabins to teach their children, whether they are baptized or not, the Christian doctrine, that is to say the sign of the Cross, the *Pater*, the *Ave*, the *Credo*, God's commandments, the Prayer to the Guardian Angel, and other short prayers; all of this in their language, since these People are naturally inept at learning another) (*Relations*, 1636: 79). Such a basic premise, which, in fact, differentiated 'civilized' from 'barbaric' nations, was held not only by the missionaries but also by the French in general, whether involved in colonizing or in trading. This belief began with Samuel de Champlain who, as we noted, starting a long tradition after his visit to Huronia in 1615, sealed an alliance with the Nations by entrusting the youth Étienne Brulé to a Huron chief so that he might master their tongue and serve as interpreter for the French.

The difficulty of learning and codifying the Huron language for Europeans coming into contact with this people was first stressed by Gabriel Sagard, a Recollet missionary, who spent one year (from the summer of 1623 to the spring of 1624) in Huronia and wrote his *Dictionnaire de la langue Huronne* 'for the convenience and use of those who have to travel to this land and do not understand the said language, for I know how difficult it is to deal with a people and not to understand them' (Sagard 1632: 5). In his introduction, Sagard raises questions about the specificity and uniqueness of the Huron language and about variations in pronunciation from one speaker to another inhabiting different villages or even the very same cabin. 'For example, to say raisins one will pronounce *Ochahenna*, and another will say *Ochahenda*; and to say, that is well, that is correct, one will say *Onguinné* and another will say *Onguiendé*' (1632: 6). He also points out that several words can signify the same thing; that verb tenses, gender, and number are extremely difficult to master; that context has a determining function in the composition of words; and that the language is in a constant state of flux: 'Their language is so unstable and they change their words so often, that over time ancient Huron is almost totally different from present-day language) (1632: 9). In contradistinction to other First Nations languages, where one can establish 'declensions and conjugations and quite readily observe tenses, gender, and number,' in the Huron language 'everything is so imperfect, as I said before, that only practice and extended use can make competent those who are negligent or not very studious' (1632: 11).

Sagard's dictionary is not, strictly speaking, organized alphabetically; rather, it is arranged conceptually, with French headwords and phrases and their Huron equivalents. See, for example, entries such as '*Couper* [to cut] – cut this fish, *Tisiaykiaye*; cut off a head, *Onontsiskia*; to cut off a finger, *Aondia*; cut off a finger, *Seindia*; severed nose, *Acoindiaye*; we will cut off, we have cut off N's head in the village, *Onontsiskiaye N andata*' (1632: 40–1). '*Desrober* [to steal] – give me N that you have stolen from our cabin, *Tanonte N issa squaquanraye chénon chianon*; the French do not steal from the cabins of the H., *Dánstan téhataton agnonhaq H. onadaon*' (1632: 50). '*Image, figure, pourtrait* [Image, figure, portrait] – *Eathra*; Is this your portrait? *Issa chiahra*' (1632: 72). '*Lire* [to read] – I read, I will read, *Aquaanton*; read, *Saquaanne*; he reads, *Onquaanton*; he does not know how to read, *Téayeinhouy ondaquaanton*' (1632: 76). '*Manger* [to eat] – give me something to eat, *Taetsenten Saataésenten*; do you want to eat me? *K. Dyoutsenten*; do you eat any N? *N. Trscoiche Tiscoiche*' (1632: 79–82). '*Parentage et consanguinité* [Kinship and blood relations] – the creator, *Yoscaha*; His grandmother, *Ataeinstic*; the French are related to the H., *Fr. Aesquanehon H*' (1632: 104–7).

Our purpose here is not to explore the inventory of the lexical items contained in the *Dictionnaire*, nor to give an account of the semantic fields covered (which in itself could lead to important socio- or ethnolinguistic conclusions), but simply to point out that Sagard gives culturally determined lexical and sentence equivalents in the target language that correspond to the working functional vocabulary he deemed necessary for the French to converse with and to convert the Huron.

Though the Jesuits were acquainted with Sagard's dictionary, it does not seem to have been considered of much use to them because, on returning to Huronia after a six-year absence, they set about writing their own almost as soon as they arrived.[2] Describing Huronia in general terms, Brébeuf alludes to Sagard's work and questions the latter's knowledge of the language: 'Il y a vingt Bourgades, qui disent environ trente mille âmes, sous une même langue, et encore assez facile à qui a quelque maître. Elle a distinction de genres, de nombre, de temps, de personnes, de mœuds, et en un mot très parfaite et très accomplie, contre la pensée de plusieurs' (There are twenty villages with roughly thirty thousand souls speaking the same language, which is quite easy to learn if one has a teacher. It has the distinction of having gender, number, tense, person, mood, and in a word it is a very perfect and very accomplished language, in spite of what others have said) (1635: 33).[3] Yet, despite Brébeuf's affirmation that Huron is quite easy to learn, the subsequent *Relations* are strewn with remarks to the contrary about its difficulty and complexity. Newcomers who do not know the language are exposed to mockery and teasing by the young, who make light of their ignorance and naïvety. Learning Huron entails coming to grips with a 'diversité de ses mots composés, [qui] est quasi infinie. Tous les Français qui sont ici s'y sont ardemment portés, ramenant l'ancien usage d'écrire sur des écorces de bouleau faute de papier' (diversity of compound words that is almost infinite. All the French at the mission are eagerly at work on the language, resorting to the ancient custom of writing on birch bark for want of paper) (1635: 37). Brébeuf is able to understand much of what the inhabitants say, and even to explain some of the mysteries of his faith to them, but for most missionaries 'la langue Huronne sera votre saint Thomas et votre Aristote, et tout habile homme que vous êtes, et bien disant parmi des personnes doctes et capables, il vous faut résoudre d'être assez longtemps muet parmi des Barbares; ce sera beaucoup pour vous, quand vous commencerez à begayer au bout de quelque temps' (the Huron language will be your Saint Thomas and your Aristotle, and no matter how clever you happen to be, or how able you are to express yourself in front of learned and capable persons, you will have to accept remaining mute for a long time amongst these Barbarians; you will have accomplished much when you begin to stammer after a while) (1636: 94).

Throughout the early *Relations*, constant references are made to the preparation of dictionaries, grammars, and texts that are indispensable for training new missionaries who can go out into the field to convert the inhabitants:

> Après nos exercices, nous fîmes un mémorial confus des mots que nous avions remarqués depuis notre arrivée, et puis nous ébauchâmes un dictionnaire de la langue des Hurons, qui sera très profitable. On y verra les diverses significations, on y reconnaîtra aisément la différence des mots par ensemble, qui ne consiste quelquefois qu'en une seule lettre, ou même en un accent. Finalement nous nous occupâmes à réformer, ou plutôt à ranger une Grammaire. Je crains qu'il ne nous faille faire souvent de semblables réformes, car tous les jours nous allons découvrant de nouveaux secrets en cette science; ce qui nous empêche d'envoyer rien à imprimer pour le présent.

> (After our exercises we made random lists of the words noted since our arrival, and then we drafted a Dictionary of the Huron language, which will be very useful. You will find the different meanings, you will easily recognize the difference of the words as a whole; which sometimes consists in a simple letter, or even in an accent. Finally we spent our time in reviewing, or rather in organizing a grammar. I fear that we will have to review it often, because every day we discover new secrets in this science, which for the time being prevents us from sending anything to the printer.) (1636: 86)

The study of the language is a daily preoccupation, and they make ready progress, thanks to a recent convert who then explains to others in Huron the mysteries of the faith.[4] 'Il le faisait avec grâce, et montrait qu'il les comprenait et possédait très bien. Ah! que je souhaiterais parler en Huron aussi bien que lui: car il est vrai qu'en comparaison je ne fais que bégayer, et cependant la façon de dire donne toute une autre face' (He did this with such grace and showed that he had understood them so well: Ah! Would that I spoke Huron as well as he, for it is true that in comparison I only stammer, and yet the way of expressing things gives them a completely different appearance) (1636: 86). With the help of Louys de Sainte Foy,[5] the missionaries translate prayers into Huron that are then read to the assembly (1639: 89–90). The work undertaken on the Huron language is considered so crucial for the success of the enterprise that when the missionaries fear for their lives they confide their most sacred treasures to a recent convert for safekeeping: 'J'ai été d'avis que nos Pères et nos domestiques se retirent chez ceux qu'ils croiront être leurs meilleurs amis: j'ai donné charge qu'on porte chez Pierre notre premier Chrétien tout ce qui est de la Sacristie, sur tout qu'on ait un soin particulier de mettre en lieu d'assurance le Dictionnaire; et tout ce que nous avons de langue' (I advised our Fathers and our domestics to take refuge with those they believe to be their best friends: I ordered that everything in our Sacristy be brought to Pierre our first Christian, and particularly that special care be taken to put the Dictionary and all that we know about the language in a safe place) (Besterman 1957: 199).

The dictionary gives access to the lexical items of the semantic universe in question, and the study of grammar opens into an understanding of the modes of existence and the functioning of language and, more generally, of the semiotic systems that must be mastered before the Huron can be brought to the 'true faith.' In the broadest sense, Brébeuf organizes his study of language into morphology (dealing with words and word classes) and syntax (concerned with sentence articulation). In one of the few fragments of the period that have survived to this day, in the form of a brief introduction to some aspects of the language, grammatical and linguistic discussion is accompanied by evaluative comments of an ethnocentric nature:

> Ils ne connaissent point de B. F. L. M. P. X. Z. ... La plus part de leurs mots sont composés de voyelles. Toutes les lettres labiales leur manquent; c'est volontiers la cause qu'ils ont tous les lèvres ouvertes de si mauvaise grâce. Comme ils n'ont presque ni vertu, ni Religion, ni science aucune, ou police, aussi n'ont-ils aucuns mots simples, propres à signifier tout ce qui en est. De là est que nous demeurons courts à leur expliquer plusieurs belles choses tirées de ces connaissances.
>
> (B, F, L, M, P, X, Z are unknown to them ... most of their words are composed of vowels. All the labial letters are missing; and this is actually the reason why they all speak with open lips, which is so unsightly. As they are lacking in almost all Virtue, Religion, or Science or Police, they hardly have any simple words to designate them. And so it is difficult for us to explain some of the important things that can be gleaned from this knowledge.) (1636: 89)[6]

In the same passage he notes that composite words are the key to unlocking the secret of the Huron language and that their nouns are universally conjugated: 'for example *Assé*, it is cool, *assé chen*, it was cool, *gaon*, old, *agaon*, he is old, *agaone*, he was old, *agaonha*, he will become old.' Yet the fact that 'relative nouns' always take on the meaning of one of the three possessive pronouns raises problems regarding Christian dogma: 'Suivant cela nous nous trouvons empêchés de leur faire dire proprement en leur Langue, *Au nom du Père, et du Fils, et du saint Esprit*. Jugeriez-vous à propos, en attendant mieux, de substituer au lieu, *Au nom de notre Pere, et de son Fils, et de leur saint Esprit?*' (We can therefore not make them say in our language *'In the name of the Father, and of the Son, and of the Holy Spirit.'* Do you think that it is proper, for the time being, to substitute instead *'In the name of our Father, and of his Son, and of their Holy Spirit?'*) Brébeuf then asks the Father Superior for permission to make the necessary linguistic adjustments to take into account the Huron semantic universe until 'La langue Huronne soit enrichie, ou l'esprit des Hurons ouvert à d'autres langues' (The Huron language becomes enriched, or the minds of the Huron open up to other languages) (1636: 89). The *'Our Father who art in Heaven'* also creates difficulties, since to pronounce this in front of those whose beloved parents are dead is to insult them. The same holds true for the *'Honour thy Father and thy Mother.'*

This dual project of enriching the Huron language and of opening up their minds to other languages is followed by considerations on the conjugation of verbs. On the one hand, these resemble 'nos conjugaisons latine et française' (our Latin and French conjugations); on the other, the action signified by the verb always has a morpheme referring to a person or a thing. Curiously, though, the example given is the verb *ahiaton*, to write,[7] which refers to a signified that did not exist as such prior to the arrival of the French in Huronia: '*ichiaton*, I write, *chiehiantonc*, you write, *ihiahiatonc*, he writes, *seõahiatonc*,[8] you (plural) write, *authiatonc*, they write.' In addition, Brébeuf notes that there is a feminine conjugation in both the singular and the plural: '*ihaton*, he says, *iõatan*, she says; *ihonton*, they say, *ionton* (feminine) they say.' He concludes that the principal distinction of this feminine conjugation from the masculine is that the letter H is missing: 'peut-être pour donner à entendre aux femmes, qu'il ne doit y avoir rien d'âpre ni de sévère en leurs paroles et en leurs mœurs, mais que la grâce et la loi de clémence doivent être posées sur leurs langues' (perhaps to make women understand that their words and behaviour must be neither harsh nor severe but that grace and the law of clemency must flow from the tips of their tongues) (1636: 100).

From a semio-narrative perspective, the above examples of contextualized and/or 'applied' linguistics have in common the setting into discourse of a subject who, on the one hand, undertakes to acquire modal competence by studying the lexicon and the grammar and, on the other, tests his competence by attempting to manipulate others at the cognitive level, causing-them-to-believe.[9] In the above case, the Jesuit is unsuccessful, since the other is not converted, or does not immediately believe. Nevertheless, these examples are significant for several reasons, since the non-realization of the projected program leads to a re-evaluation of the Jesuits' competence and to revelations about the very nature of conversion. First, causing-to-believe can be considered as an attempt by a subject to communicate to the other a certain vision of human experience that is accepted as fundamental and true. Moreover, the fundamental conviction to be transmitted through the appropriation of the other's language raises a problem related not to specific convictions as such but rather to value systems and/or the compatibility (or incompatibility) of divergent axiologies. In brief, Brébeuf's texts raise the issue of the actual possibility of communicating, in their native tongue, a radically different system of beliefs to a people who do not share the same semantic universe. This dilemma is manifest at the thematic level when the narrator posits the quasi-absence in Huronia of what he considers to be positive values such as 'Virtue, Religion, Science and Police,' as well as a paucity of simple words to designate them. In addition, the choice of *ahiaton*, to write, to illustrate the conjugation of verbs is not without interest, for it demonstrates how the other's tongue is used to try to translate a foreign, even non-existent, signified into a target language. As such, the translation is unsuccessful, since the problem remains of rendering the sign operative for the other by making it a meaningful part of daily signifying practice. The mastery of the conjugated verb, though theoretically a first step towards converting the other, in this specific instance corresponds to the creation of an empty Huron signifier that neither brings the two semantic universes into contact nor makes them overlap.

The second example, related to the translation of the prayer '*In the name of the Father and of the Son ...*' by '*In the name of our Father and of his Son ...*' seemingly achieves a partial solution to the problem of conversion by negotiating a common ground, a common place, where these two antagonistic value systems can come together. Yet when the narrator is forced to adapt his semantic universe to that of the other by adopting the only existing linguistic forms to render his prayer ('relative nouns' such as Father, Son, Master, etc., always take on the meaning of one of the three persons of the possessive pronouns), a real fear is expressed concerning the possible unfaithfulness of the rendition. The use of this non-French language shifts the translator inexorably back into the domain of non-orthodox Christian dogma, since these grammatical forms articulate kinship and social relations that organize the Huron semantic universe. This is also the case regarding the *'Our Father who art in Heaven'* and formulaic utterances such as *'Honour thy Father and thy Mother,'* where, to communicate, the translator is obliged to take into account the other's system of beliefs, and thus (paradoxically) to shift the common ground back to the Huron semantic universe. The only solution to this problem of translation lies in radically modifying the rules and literally translating (*trans latio*) the common place to new non-Huron beliefs and languages, either by 'la langue Huronne soit enrichie, ou l'esprit des Hurons ouvert à d'autres langues' (enriching the Huron languages or opening up the Huron mind to other languages) (1636: 89).

From the point of view of fundamental semantics, Brébeuf's study of grammar posits two microsemantic universes articulated by means of two distinct languages in a relation of reciprocal presupposition.[10] To convert the Huron is ultimately to put in place narrative programs that will bring the Huron to accept the system of beliefs inherent in the French language. However, since the Huron are deemed 'Barbarians,' and thus incapable of learning any language other than their own, the missionaries must attempt to become competent modal subjects by learning the other's language and finding a topos of overlap common to both systems of belief. Yet to learn the Huron language as such is to accept $\overline{S1}$'s vision of human experience and to assume the position of non-French language and beliefs, since S1 and $\overline{S1}$ are in a relation of contradiction. It is also, potentially, to assume the position of S2, since $\overline{S1}$ and S2 are in a relation of complementarity. At the figurative level this occurs when Étienne Brulé adopts the Huron language and beliefs and thereby negates his antecedents, a reversal that, as far as the missionaries are concerned, remains a scandal even after his death.[11] Again at the figurative level, consider the example of the woman whose mother had recently died, and who, after hearing *'Honour thy Father and thy Mother'* (a literal translation of the French), refuses baptism. For this subject, the formula sets up an impossible situation, as it maintains both S1 and $\overline{S1}$ simultaneously. Since for her this type of utterance is contradictory in nature, and therefore incomprehensible and non-meaningful as such, she refuses to be baptized and reverts back to $\overline{S1}$ then S2, non-contradictory and meaningful deixes which are in a relation of complementarity. It therefore follows that, for the converting subject, the only possible solution is to master the existing Huron language and then 'enrich' it or 'open up the Huron mind to other languages' so that programs of cognitive manipulation can be put in place that will make them occupy $\overline{S2}$, which is in a complementary relation to S1.[12] The fundamental semantics of the narrative posits this relation as the positive deixis the Huron must be brought to accept; from an axiological perspective, the acquisition of this new enriched language corresponds to the acquisition by the manipulated subjects of non-Huron language and beliefs.[13]

Although the study of the Huron lexicon and grammar gives initial access to the other's semantic universe, only a thorough knowledge of the rhetorical organization of the other's discourse can enable one to cause-to-believe and to persuade. To convert, as was suggested, is to bring about a shift in beliefs by finding a common place, a commonality of experience; in other words, to recognize a fundamental sameness in difference. Thus the narrator, when he prays for rain and performs ceremonies that the Huron repeat, identifies in their linguistic and gestural readiness to imitate a 'natural Rhetoric,' which, because of the Creator, is common to all of humanity. 'Nous faisons quelque prière; puis j'adorai et baisai la Croix, pour leur montrer comme ils devaient faire; ils me suivirent les uns après les autres, apostrophant notre Seigneur crucifié par des prières que la Rhétorique naturelle et la necessité du temps leur suggerait' (We said some prayers, then I adored and kissed the Cross to show them what they should do, they followed me one after the other, addressing our Crucified Lord with prayers that natural Rhetoric and the specific situation suggested to them.) He then observes that the Huron were so good that on that very day 'Dieu leur donna de la pluie, et enfin une très heureuse récolte, avec une très grande admiration de la Puissance divine' (God gave them rain and, in the end, a very fruitful harvest, with a great admiration for divine Power) (1636: 85).

However, in spite of what was said earlier, the narrator admits that, though not perfectly civilized like the Chinese and Japanese, the condition of the Huron is not, as others have maintained, akin to that of animals, because they actually have some sort of civil and political life. Most are affable and gentle, 'quasi incroyable pour des Sauvages' (which is almost unbelievable for Indians). Most also have quite good minds, which 's'éveillent et se façonnent merveilleusement; de sorte qu'il n'y en a quasi point qui ne soit capable d'entretien, et ne raisonne fort bien et en bons termes sur les choses dont il a la connaissance' (can be awakened and marvellously moulded, so that there are hardly any with whom one cannot converse and who do not reason well on things they know). He remarks that these 'Peuples ne sont pas tout à fait si rudes et mal polis que quelqu'un se pourrait bien figurer' (people are not as unrefined and crude as some could think) and suggests that, since 'les lois sont comme la maîtresse roue qui règle les Communautés, ou pour mieux dire l'âme des Républiques' (laws are the main wheel which governs communities, or better yet, they are the Soul of Republics), one cannot say that they are without government. They punish murderers, thieves, traitors, and sorcerers, but murderers are not punished by death; 'le peu de désordre qu'il y a en ce point, me fait juger que leur procédure n'est guère moins efficace qu'est ailleurs le supplice de la mort' (the small amount of social disorders resulting from this makes me think that their procedure is not less efficient than the death penalty is elsewhere) (1636: 118–19).

This brief inventory of common places, manifested through and by the Huron tongue, provides a storehouse in language for the missionary, both of the principal discursive themes and of the most general configurations that constitute the main '*topoi*' of a fundamental taxonomy that is the basis for communication. To understand how others structure the main features of their semantic universe, it therefore becomes necessary to examine the Huron language and its syntagmatic organization in action. The displacement of the study of language from grammar and dictionary to the organization of discourse, a change that can take place only after the missionaries have been involved in all aspects of the life of the Nation, shifts the problematic back to the domain of rhetoric – not unfamiliar ground to Jesuit missionaries.

Recognizing the importance of the councils held in the villages on a regular basis as a means not only of learning about how the other's discourse functions but also of exercising one's linguistic competence, the missionaries participate in these meetings as often as they can. Commenting upon a talk given by a 'Captain,' Brébeuf remarks: 'Il a employé toute sa Rhétorique pour nous faire dire le mot, et obtenir tout à fait notre consentement ... Il me fit ce discours; mais je lui ferai tort de le mettre ici, car je ne lui donnerai pas la grâce qu'il avait en la bouche de ce Capitaine; n'importe on verra toujours ses pensées, que j'ai rangées à mon avis à peu prés dans leur ordre' (He employed all of his rhetoric to make us say the word, to obtain our full consent ... He made the following speech: but I would not do him justice by setting it down here, for I will not transcribe the elegance with which the Captain pronounced it; never mind, you can always appreciate his thoughts which, in my opinion, I set down more or less in the proper order) (1636: 122). After transcribing the speech in his own words, the narrator concludes on its powers of persuasion. 'Voilà la harangue de ce Capitaine, qui passerait, à mon avis, au jugement de plusieurs pour une de celles de Tite Live, si le sujet le portait' (That is the Captain's speech, which in my opinion, many would identify with Livy if the subject could so lend itself) (1636: 125). Noting that during their councils individuals uplift their style and attempt to speak well – 'quelques-uns semblent être nés à l'éloquence' (some of them seem to be born with the gift of eloquence) – the manipulating subject turns to his own ends the rhetorical skills and conventions of the participants who 'ratiocinent fort bien, et ne bronchent point en leurs discours' (reason well and do not hesitate when they speak) (1636: 127). During their deliberations, after someone expresses an opinion, the chief of the council repeats what is said, or asks someone else to do so. Turning this custom to his own ends, when participating in a council meeting, Brébeuf offered a gift and accompanied the gesture with a speech exhorting them to take the road to Heaven: 'un des Capitaines répéta fort heureusement tout ce que j'avais dit, et le dilata et amplifia mieux que je n'avais fait, et en meilleurs termes: car en effet dans le peu de connaissance que nous avons de cette Langue, nous ne disons pas ce que nous voulons, mais ce que nous pouvons' (fortunately one of the Captains repeated everything that I had said, expanded and amplified it in much better terms than I had; for because of our limited knowledge of this language we do not say what we want to, but what we can) (1636: 128).

At first glance, it would seem that the manipulative subject, by taking advantage of how council debate functions and then using the other's rhetorical competence to communicate a foreign system of beliefs, overcomes his own discursive incompetence and actually brings about a program of conversion. Yet on closer examination it can be seen that, as the narrator defines rhetoric as the art of speaking well and of persuading, it is basically considered as a single class of discourse, argumentative in nature. However, conversion (or causing-to-believe) is an attempt to make a non-believer share one's vision of human experience, and as such deals primarily with convictions or beliefs – not with rational argument, which assumes that speakers and hearers always share the same semantic universe. All Brébeuf succeeds in doing here is creating an empty argumentative simulacrum that cannot be implemented in concrete action, or causing-to-do, since the hearers do not yet believe.[14]

However, the study of rhetoric reveals a second dimension of the other's semantic universe, axiological in nature, which both *dispositio* and *inventio* fail to reveal. Initially, the narrator notes that rhetorical figures are of fundamental importance in their public discourses. 'Les métaphores sont grandement en usage parmi ces Peuples; si vous ne vous y faites, vous n'entendez rien dans leurs conseils, où ils ne parlent quasi que par métaphores' (Metaphors are widely used by these people; if you are not used to this then you will understand nothing in their Councils, where they speak almost entirely in metaphors) (1636: 119). This might be seen as a simple concession to *elocutio* by which the narrator, because of his classical training, identifies the various tropes that ornament Huron discourses. Yet on further examination, we note that, rather than being purely stylistic components the dimensions of which are those of the sentence and word, rhetorical figures (and in this instance metaphors) are the organizing principle by which the fundamental semantics (axiology) is figurativized (actorialized, temporalized, and spatialized) and set into discourse. This 'rhetoric,' or metaphorical organization, structures every aspect of Huron existence and articulates the Huron relationship not only to the cosmos:

> Ils s'addressent à la Terre, aux Rivières, aux Lacs, aux Rochers dangereux, mais surtout au Ciel, et croient que tout cela est animé, et qu'il y réside quelque puissant Démon ... Ils croient encore que le ciel est courroucé, quand quelqu'un se noie ou meurt de froid; il faut un sacrifice pour l'appaiser.

> (They address the Earth, Rivers, Lakes, dangerous Rocks, but especially the Sky, and believe everything is animated and that there lives within these a powerful Demon ... They also believe that the Sky is angered when someone drowns, or freezes to death: a sacrifice is needed to appease it.) (1636: 107–8)

... or their daily activity:

> Ils tiennent les poissons raisonnables, comme aussi les Cerfs et Orignaux; c'est ce qui fait qu'ils ne jettent aux Chiens ni les os de ceux-ci, quand ils

sont à la chasse, ni les arêtes de ceux-là tandis qu'ils pêchent; autrement sur l'avis que les autres en auraient, ils se cacheraient et ne se laisseraient point prendre ... Les poissons, disent-ils, n'aiment point les morts, et là-dessus ils s'abstiennent d'aller à la pêche quand quelqu'un leur est mort.

(They think that Fish are rational, as well as Deer and Moose, so that they neither give the bones of the latter to their dogs when they are hunting, nor the bones of fish when they are fishing: otherwise their prey, being warned, would hide and would refuse to be caught ... Fish, they say, do not like the dead and so they abstain from fishing when one of them dies.) (1636: 100)

... or the world of dreams:

Le songe est l'oracle que tous ces pauvres Peuples consultent et écoutent, le Prophète qui leur prédit les choses futures ... en un mot le songe fait ici tout, et est à vrai dire comme le principal Dieu des Hurons.

(The Dream is the oracle that these poor people consult and listen to, the Prophet who predicts future things ... in short the dream does everything here, and is, so to speak, like the principal god of the Huron.) (1636: 109–10)

... or political life:

Il est vrai que leurs discours sont d'abord difficiles à entendre, à cause d'une infinité de Métaphores, de plusieurs circonlocutions et autres façons figurées: par exemple, parlant de la Nation des Ours, ils diront, l'Ours a dit, a fait cela; l'Ours est fin, est méchant; les mains de l'Ours sont dangereuses.

(It is true that their speeches are first of all difficult to understand because of an infinite number of Metaphors, and several circumlocutions and other figures; for example, speaking about the Bear Nation, they will say the Bear has said, has done this; the Bear is crafty, is spiteful, the hands of the Bear are dangerous.) (1636: 127)

... but also to all facets of their daily lives:

Vous diriez que toutes leurs sueurs, leurs travaux et leurs traites ne se rapportent quasi qu'à amasser de quoi honorer les Morts.

92   Part II. Discovery, Conversion, and Colonization

(You would think that all of their sweat, their work, their bartering are only undertaken in order to gather together the wherewithal to honour the Dead.) (1636: 128)

The metaphoric organization of discursive structures articulating the fundamental belief system of the Huron semantic universe, which is clearly at odds with the narrator's, is most apparent in Brébeuf's description of how the Nation speaks about all aspects related to the 'Solemn Feast of the Dead,' the most famous feast of the country, which takes place every twelve years.

> Cette fête est toute pleine de cérémonies, mais vous diriez que la principale est celle de la chaudière, cette-ci étouffe toutes les autres, et on ne parle quasi de la fête des Morts, même dans les Consils les plus sérieux, que sous le nom de Chaudière: ils y approprient tous les termes de cuisine, de sorte que pour dire avancer ou retarder la fête des Morts, ils diront détiser ou attiser le feu dessous la chaudière, et quand on est sur ces termes, qui dirait, la chaudière est renversée, ce serait à dire, il n'y aura point de fête des Morts.

> (This feast abounds in ceremonies, but you might say that the principal ceremony is that of the kettle; this latter overshadows all the rest, and the feast of the Dead is hardly mentioned, even in the most important Councils except under the name of 'the Kettle.' They appropriate to it all the terms of cookery, so that, in speaking of advancing or of delaying the feast of the Dead, they will speak of scattering or of stirring up the fire beneath the kettle; and, employing this way of speaking, one who would say 'the kettle is overturned,' would mean that there would be no feast of the Dead.) (1636: 131)

In this last and longest chapter of the 1636 *Relation*, the narrator observes that the entire ceremony is described by the Huron in terms of figures belonging to the alimentary code that ensure the translation between the continuous and discontinuous, the here and there, life and death. In his description Brébeuf, in order to demonstrate his in-depth knowledge and his real mastery of the alimentary code that cuts through all the activities of the Nation, and that mediates and organizes the relationships between 'nature' and 'culture,' pursues his relation of the struggles for the control of Huronia: 'Or il n'y a d'ordinaire qu'une seule fête dans chaque Nation; tous les corps se mettent en une même fosse: je dis d'ordinaire, car cette année que s'est faite la fête des Morts, la chaudière a été divisée ...' (Now usually there is only a single feast in each Nation: all the bodies are placed in a common pit. I say usually, for this year, that happened to be the time for the Feast of the Dead, the kettle was divided ...) (1636: 131).

The remainder of the chapter deals with the different phases of the numerous ceremonies linked to the manipulation of the 'bodies,' 'bones,' 'souls' (the removal of the flesh from the bodies, the preparation of the bones by the families of the dead, their displacement in the villages of the Nation, the suspension and exposition of the packages of 'bones,' 'souls,' in predetermined longhouses belonging to the same clan, and, finally, their burial in a common pit). What occurs at the level of the practical dimension is the passage from the poly-tope to the mono-tope – the bodies from all the cemeteries are transferred into a common pit – whereas at the level of the mythical, that is, the passage from the mono-deme to the poly-deme, the opposite happens – the bodies are first venerated by a single family before being venerated by the entire Nation. This passage is articulated by means of the alimentary code, and events are always described in culinary terms linked to fire, to cooking (the raw, the rotten, the cooked, the smoked, the roasted, the boiled). In short, the 'name kettle,' given to the 'Solemn Feast of the Dead,' for which they 'use all the terms of cooking,' designates not only this important ceremony but also other varied cultural domains, such as fishing and hunting, the social, and the political: 'Pour lors la chaudière n'était pas encore divisée ... Quelque temps après la chaudière fut divisée ... Au Printemps il se fit une Assemblée générale des Notables de tout le Pays, pour aviser à tout ce qui concernait cette fête, et pour tâcher d'ôter ce schisme, et réunir la chaudière ... On me fit instance sur la division de la chaudière, et me demandèrent, puisqu'il y avait deux chaudières, c'est-à-dire deux fosses, de quel côté je désirais que fût notre fosse particulière' (At that time the kettle was not yet divided ... some time afterwards the kettle was divided ... In the Springtime a general assembly of all the Notables of the land gathered, to decide on this feast and to attempt to heal this schism, and gather together the kettle ... They told me about the division of the kettle, and asked me that since there were two kettles, that is to say two pits, which one did I want as our own) (1636: 137).

Knowledge of the rhetorical and metaphoric structures by which 'primitive thought' is organized and figurativized at the level of discourse gives access to the rational processes that govern the other's world vision. Nevertheless, an understanding of this 'foreign' tongue, which 'est autant différente de nos langues Européenes, qu'est le Ciel de la terre' (is as different from our European languages as is Heaven from earth) (1636: 86), cannot by itself lead to conversion, since all it reveals is the workings of the holders' underlying system of convictions. The problem remains of eliciting a response by which the narrator's vision of human experience imposes itself upon the non-believer. The daily experience of the failure of their project, founded on argumentation, leads the missionaries to search for parallel solutions by incorporating in their programs other integrated semiotic systems that stimulate emotional responses. Having remarked that 'ces Peuples sont grands admirateurs et font état des personnes qui ont quelque chose de relevé par dessus le commun; à cette occasion ils les appellent, *oki*, du même nom qu'ils donnent aux démons' (these People are great admirers and esteem persons who have qualities which set them above the common: they call such persons *oki*, the same name they give demons), the narrator concludes that, if one of the missionaries possessed extraordinary power and performed wonders that would reorganize the Huron's ambient environment, then their conversion would be ensured: 'S'il y avait ici quelqu'un doué du don de miracles, ainsi qu'étaient les premiers qui ont annoncé l'Évangile au monde, il convertirait à mon avis sans difficulté tous ces Barbares' (If there were someone endowed with the gift of miracles, as were those who first proclaimed the Gospel to the world, then, in my opinion, he could easily convert all of these Barbarians) (1636: 85). Since, by definition, they radically modify the other's experiential field, miracles as perceptible signs offer a potential solution to conversion that argumentative discourse cannot. They ostensibly decentre the other and, by visibly attesting to the truthfulness of the miracle maker's belief system, materially sanction it. Such power to restructure the other's vision of the world would constitute a syncretic language capable of eliciting admiration and the corresponding emotional response. Within this context, argumentation solicits an oral 'rational' response to verbal signs, whereas conversion, or making someone believe, evokes a passionate response to the various processes that break up, supplant, and rearticulate the existing semiotic systems.

From the point of view of the manipulating subject, no actor is endowed with the gift of miracles, though the possibility of performing such wonders reveals the very nature of conversion. In essence, to convert others is literally to turn them towards and make them admire those who wield powerful new sign systems that confirm the 'Grand

Rhetoric' sanctioning them. These signs of a semi-symbolic nature,[15] which are in a syncretic relation to the subject's primary linguistic system, are multiform and can be either gestural or material. In addition, from a hierarchical perspective such signs are considered by the Jesuits to be secondary phenomena that facilitate manipulation: 'Nous leur enseignerions la façon de le prier. Cette Nation est fort docile, et sous la considération des biens temporels vous les fléchissez où vous voulez' (We teach them to pray. This Nation is extremely docile and with temporal goods you can sway them any way you want) (1636: 83).

Soon after the Jesuits' arrival in Huronia, Brébeuf describes the collective actant as demonstrating sound judgment and approbation when contemplating the wondrous spectacle unravelling before them. The Huron show admiration not only for French know-how – 'bien que ce ne soit pas grand chose, les Sauvages ne laissent de la venir voir, et la voyant de l'admirer' (although it [the cabin] is not much, the Indians continuously come and visit it, and seeing it admire it) – but also for objects fabricated by European technology – 'Cependant, comme j'ai dit, on ne laisse pas de nous venir visiter par admiration, principalement depuis que nous avons eu deux portes de menuiserie, et que notre moulin et notre horloge ont commencé à jouer. On ne saurait dire les étonnements de ces bonnes gens, et combien ils admirent l'esprit des Français' (Yet, as I said, they continue to come and visit through admiration; especially since we installed two wooden doors and since our mill and our clock have begun to work. It is impossible to describe the astonishment of these good people and how they admire French ingenuity) (1636: 32). The narrator goes on to list the objects brought with them to this country (magnetic stone, magnifying glass, globe, grinding mill, clock, paper, ink, tools, arms, clothing, food, sacramental wine, religious costumes, sacred images, crucifixes, bells), and then evaluates and judges the Huron reactions in terms of astonishment and admiration as they contemplate and handle them. For Brébeuf such objects constitute a complementary semiotic system that, in conjunction with oral language, can be used to attain the desired ends.

The narrator, as I noted in the previous chapter, gives two privileged examples of know-how that he interprets as being especially worthy of admiration: the clock and writing. Although both of these examples illustrate, within a semiotics of manipulation, how 'tout cela sert pour gagner leurs affections, et les rendre plus dociles, quand il est question des admirables et incompréhensibles mystères de notre Foi' (all of this is used to win their affection and to make them more docile with respect to the admirable and incomprehensible mysteries of our faith) (1635: 33) and constitute a simulacrum of the process of enunciation,[16] they also have the virtue of showing how signs are invested and take on meaning within two different value systems that come into contact with one another. On the one hand, certain signs are uncritically assumed to be an integral part of a value system positing the supremacy of reason, technology, and Christian faith, a value system sanctioned by the ultimate sender 'God' (presupposed), who founds and justifies the manipulating subject. On the other hand, the same signs, accompanying the 'foreign' subjects, initially denote 'power' (demon – *ondati*) and are semioticized through their integration in the Huron vision of human experience. This process of semiosis, which semanticizes and resemanticizes signs according to their position in the system, all the while investing them with positive animate qualities, is interpreted by the manipulating subject as an immutable symbolic process that fixes the value of the sign once and for all and confirms the unquestionable validity of his own system of beliefs. 'Mais ils ont tout dit, quand ils ont dit qu'ils sont *ondaki*, c'est-à-dire des Démons; et nous relevons bien ce mot à leur profit, quand nous leur disons: Or ça mes frères, vous avez vu cela et l'avez admiré, et vous pensez avoir raison, voyant quelque chose d'extraordinaire, de dire *ondaki*' (But they have said everything, when they have said that they [objects] are *ondati*, that is Demons: and we then turn this to our advantage, when we say to them, well my brothers, you have seen this, and you have admired and you think that you are right, when seeing something extraordinary, you call it *ondati*) (1635: 32).

Other, more sacred objects are integrated within a global program of conversion to provoke admiration and convert the non-believer. First, all of the inhabitants of the village are called to the missionaries' chapel by the sound of the bell. Then 'Je me sers du surplis et du bonnet carré, pour donner plus de majesté' (I wear my surplice and square bonnet to give greater majesty) (1636: 39). The altar is adorned with tapestries, and sacred vessels are placed upon it; the crucifix and holy images are hung for all to see. Prayers are chanted; first a priest sings a couplet and the congregation is asked to follow. When everyone is seated, 'Je me lève et fais faire le signe de la Croix à tous, puis ayant récapitulé ce que j'ai dit la dernière fois, j'explique quelque chose de nouveau' (I stand and ask them all to make the sign of the cross, then having recapitulated what I said the last time I explain something new). Afterwards, young children and young girls are questioned, and a small prize is given to those who have answered correctly: 'Les parents sont fort aises de voir leurs enfants bien dire et remporter quelque petit prix' (Their parents are happy to see their children answer properly and leave with a prize). Then, to reinforce the process, 'nous faisons reprendre chaque leçon, par nos deux petits garçons Français, qui s'entr'interrogent l'un l'autre; ce qui ravit les Sauvages en admiration' (we make one or two little French boys question each other, repeat each lesson. This fills the Indians with admiration). The baptismal ceremony, performed when the Huron are on the point of death, is also accompanied by instruction, the sign of the cross, and gifts. 'Ayant apporté pour nous quelques petits rafraîchissements, nous leur donnions, à l'un un peu de prunes, à l'autre un peu de raisins; aux autres quelque autre chose' (Having brought with us some food, we give them either a few prunes, or raisins, or something else) (1636: 40).

My purpose here is not to attempt even to sketch a simple semiotic framework for the analysis of such complex ceremonies, which integrate visual, gestural, and oral languages to manipulate a perceived passive subject's belief system (mimogesturality, oral repetition, material sanction, second-degree representation – the two young French boys), but only to point out that these complex and integrated semiotic systems, which at the outset designate only otherness, are used to provoke an emotional response within a specific context. The initial reactions of astonishment and admiration for exogenous non-verbal signs representing French ingenuity and power are progressively transformed by a radical modification of the contextual situation. Whereas the manipulating subject maintains the immutability and eternal truth of his belief system, which posits life in death, the manipulated subject associates death in life with all of its figurativized representations. Because none of the French die during the epidemics that decimate the Huron nation between 1635 and 1640,[17] they are considered evil sorcerers sent by terrifying temporal powers and gods, whose mission is not to convert but to destroy. Whether sacred or profane, the signs and symbols that form the language of conversion are caught up in an ongoing process of semiosis, desemanticized and resemanticized by the anti-subject. When actualized through discourse, the same linguistic structures, rather than stimulating a positive emotional response, have the opposite effect and provoke fear, terror, and hate in the non-believer.

Investing most of the signs used to figurativize the missionaries' belief system with death and resisting all attempts to communicate with them in their own spoken language, which has been dislocated by its hierarchical subordination to foreign signs and symbols, the Huron assume the role of anti-subject, and not only counter the other's discourse but also engage in open conflict and polemic. Both as symbol and gestural sign, the cross is associated with death, and the Huron ask the French to take it down from the front of their chapel. Most of them disappear and hide their children when they hear the bell calling them to worship or announcing a visit for instruction. They refuse to pray and, as baptism is generally administered when they are on their deathbed, 'la grande tentation des Sauvages, est que le Baptême et la prière les font mourir' (the great temptation for the Indians is that baptism and prayers make them die) (1643: 13). Certain objects are considered dangerous, and they no longer accept gifts such as sugar, 'la neige de France, c'est ainsi qu'ils appellent le sucre, et a persuadé à quelques-uns que c'était comme un espèce de poison ... Le diable sait assez bien combien ces petites douceurs nous ont déjà servi, pour lui tirer des mains tant d'âmes qu'il tenait captives' (called snow from France and they are persuaded that it is a sort of poison ... The devil knows very well how these small treats were useful to us in saving from his clutches the souls he held captive' (1637: 167). The 'Captain of the day' is kept under wraps, since the Huron believe that it is the demon who kills, and so are the images that for them represent only what happens to those who are sick. Breviaries, writing instruments, and writing itself are thought to be magical objects that bring death, and most Christian ceremonies are regarded with suspicion: 'Si nous voulions ou nous mettre à genoux, ou dire notre Office à la lueur de cinq ou six charbons, c'étaient justement là ces magies noires dont nous les faisions tous mourir. Demandions-nous le nom de quelqu'un pour l'écrire dans le régistre de nos baptisés, et n'en pas perdre la mémoire, c'était, nous disaient-ils, pour le piquer secrètement, et déchirant par après ce nom écrit, faire mourir d'un même coup celui ou celle qui portait ce nom-là' (If we wished either to kneel or to say our Office in the light of five or six coals, this was said to be the black magic that made them die. If we asked someone's name to write down in our baptismal registry, in order not to forget, this was, they said, to secretly prick him, and afterwards tearing up the written name, to make the person die at the same time) (1640: 62).

None the less, certain icons – notably, life-sized printed pictures – are continuously resemanticized by those contemplating them:[18] 'Il arriva justement qu'une femme de cette bourgade nous vint visiter ce jour là;

elle fut merveilleusement surprise à l'entrée de notre cabane: elle s'arrêta quelque temps, n'osant s'avancer et passer outre. Ce fut un plaisir de la voir dans ce combat: car d'un côté elle se sentait puissamment attirée par la nouveauté de cet objet; d'un autre côté la crainte qu'elle avait, qu'approchant de plus près nos tableaux elle ne fût incontinent saisie du mal, la faisait reculer en arrière. Néanmoins apres avoir bien disputé, la curiosité l'emporta: Ça, dit-elle, il n'y a remède, *Iariscon*, il faut que je m'hazarde, il faut que je voie, quand il m'en devrait couter la vie' (A woman from this village just happened to visit us on that day; she was marvellously surprised on entering our cabin: she stopped for a time, and did not advance. It was a pleasure to see her in this struggle; on the one hand, the fear she had, that on approaching nearer to our pictures she would immediately fall ill, made her retreat. None the less, after having struggled, curiosity overcame her fears: There is no remedy for this, *Iarisiou*, I have to take a chance, I have to see even if it costs me my life) (1637: 176). Fascination for this object of representation is the first step towards conversion; yet other images have contrary dissuasive effects.

> Le jour du baptême de Pierre *Tsiouendaentaha*, nous avions exposé une fort belle image du jugement, où les damnés sont dépeints, les uns avec des couleuvres et des dragons qui leur déchirent les entrailles, et la plupart avec quelque espèce d'instrument de leurs supplices. Plusieurs tirèrent quelque profit de cette vue; néanmoins quelques-uns se sont persuadés que cette multitude d'hommes désespérés et entassés les uns sur les autres, était tous ceux que nous avions fait mourir cet Hiver; que ces flammes représentaient les ardeurs de cette fièvre pestilentielle, et ces dragons et ces serpents, les bêtes vénimeuses dont nous nous étions servis pour les empoisonner.

> (The day of Pierre *Tsiouendaentaha*'s baptism, we had exposed an excellent image of the last judgment, where the damned are depicted, some with serpents and dragons tearing out their entrails, and most with some sort of instrument of torture. Some profited from this sight; nevertheless, others were persuaded that this mass of desperate men piled up one on top of the other were all those we had made die this winter; that the flames represented the ravages of the pestilent fever, and the venomous beasts were used to poison them.) (1637: 177)

Life-sized images produce the greatest effect on the beholder: 'nous avions de la peine à leur faire croire, que ce ne fût que de plates peintures, aussi les pièces sont-elles de grandeur naturelle, car les petites figures ne font que fort peu d'impression sur leurs esprits' (we had difficulty in making them believe that these were only flat paintings, and these pictures are life-sized, for small figures make very little impression on their minds) (1638: 33). Further mention is made of pictures whose eyes seem to move and follow onlookers no matter where they happen to position themselves, which, according to the context, can be interpreted negatively or positively. These semi-symbolic signs, used by the missionaries to move others, take on meaning independent of the system producing them as they undergo contextual semanticization when integrated into different semiotic systems.

Resistance to missionary discourse, as was suggested, is not uniform, since a small minority, because of the power and knowledge of the converting subject, resemanticize the signs in a light that is deemed positive. Noting that none of the French die during the epidemic, some Huron seek baptism to regain their health or to live longer. In constant danger, the missionaries make use not only of their knowledge of technology but also of their knowledge of astronomy – to predict the lunar eclipses of 1636, 1638, and 1639, and subsequently to use their ability to read 'natural' signs as proof of the truth of their beliefs. 'Car, leur disions nous, vous avez vu comme la Lune s'est éclipsée le même jour et au même moment que nous avions prédit; au reste, nous n'eussions pas voulu mourir pour vous maintenir cette vérité, comme nous sommes prêts de faire, pour vous maintenir que Dieu vous brûlera éternellement, si vous ne croyez en lui' (For we said to them, you have seen how the moon eclipsed the same day and at the same time that we had predicted; moreover, we did not wish to die so that we could confirm this truth, as we are already to do so, that God will burn you for eternity, if you do not believe in him) (1638: 58). On rare occasions, though, some of the gravely ill recover after 'l'usage et application du Crucifix et eau bénite' (the use and application of the crucifix and holy water) (1640: 62). Unable to expel or eliminate the missionaries, whose discourse in all its complexities is sanctioned by temporal power, the Huron are caught up in a double bind, since they have formed an alliance with the French against their traditional enemies, the Iroquois, and also depend on their allies for the fur trade.[19] Unable to act to eradicate the bearers of death, they can only wait and accept their fate. 'Monsieur de Champlain et Monsieur le Général du Plessis Bochart nous obligèrent grandement l'année passée, exhortant les Hurons en plein conseil à embrasser la Religion Chrétienne, et leur disant que c'était là l'unique moyen non seulement d'être un jour véritablement heureux dans le Ciel, mais aussi de lier à l'avenir une très étroite amitié avec les Français, lesquels en ce faisant viendraient volontiers en leur Pays, se marieraient à leurs filles, leurs apprendraient divers arts et métiers, et les assisteraient contre leurs ennemis' (Monsieur de Champlain and Monsieur le général du Plessis Bochart greatly aided us last year, exhorting the Huron during their Council to embrace the Christian Faith, and telling them this was the unique means not only to be one day truly happy in Heaven, but also in the future to consolidate a very close friendship with the French, who would happily come and live in their Country, marry their daughters, teach them various crafts and skills, and assist them against their enemies) (1636: 80).

But of all the sign systems defining communication in the *Relations*, the body acquires and becomes a language in its own right; as such, it is at the origin of proprioceptive experience and is the most outspoken advocate of axiology. Father François Bressani, an Italian Jesuit attempting to reach Huronia in 1642, was taken prisoner and tortured by the Iroquois before making his way back to Europe. When he returned to New France and to Huronia in 1645, although he did not know the language, he began proselytizing and was immediately considered the most successful preacher in the mission. 'S'il n'eût point été pris captif des Iroquois en son premier voyage, il saurait déjà la langue Huronne et serait un ouvrier formé; mais il faut avouer que les providences de Dieu sont aimables. Les cruautés que lui ont vu souffrir aux Iroquois quelques Hurons qui en sont échappés, et ses mains mutilées, ses doigts coupés l'ont rendu meilleur Prédicateur que nous ne sommes, dès le point de son arrivée, et ont servi plus que toutes nos langues, à faire concevoir plus que jamais à nos Chrétiens Hurons les vérités de notre foi' (Had he not been captured by the Iroquois during his first voyage, he would already know the Huron language, but we have to admit that God's providence is kind. The cruelties that several Huron who escaped saw him suffer because of the Iroquois, his mutilated hands, his severed fingers, immediately made him a better preacher than we are, and they were more successful than all of our tongues in making our Christian Huron understand the truths of our faith) (1646: 73). All Bressani has to do is to show his wounds and, in the words of the Huron, 'elles nous disent plus efficacement que tu ne pourras faire quand tu sauras entièrement parler de notre langue, que nous devons servir et adorer celui dont tu attends un jour qu'il te rendra et la vie que tu as exposée si franchement pour lui, et les doigts qu'on t'a brûlés si cruellement, en venant ici pour son service' (they tell us more efficiently than you could when you know how to speak our language fluently, that we serve and adore him whom you are awaiting who will one day render both the life you have so candidly exposed for him, and your fingers that were so cruelly burned in coming here in his service) (1646: 73). An incorporated sign system, the mutilated body expresses both the converting subjects' belief system and the values that inform the converts' semantic universe. As such, the altered body, manifested as the resultant figure of a fragile proprioceptive system of convictions, moves and provokes emotional responses in non-believers just as it consolidates new believers' shared semantic universe. Yet the acquisition and communication of this incarnated language of conviction, which re-actorializes, re-spatializes, and re-temporalizes the daily lives of believers, is simply an intermediate stage along a predetermined trajectory that returns the body to its eternal origin. And thus, the martyred, massacred bodies of a converted people, dismembered by the hand of the Iroquois in 1649, become the final expression of the flesh made word as the Huron Nation is attacked, dispersed, and totally destroyed, leaving behind only fragmentary written traces of its language and culture, recorded in the annals of the *Relations*.

CHAPTER SIX

Narrating and Reading the Body: The Martyrdom of Isaac Jogues

Isaac Jogues was one of eight Jesuit missionaries, beatified in 1925 and canonized in 1930, who lost their lives during the Iroquois–Huron wars of 1642–9.[1] Accounts of their execution, along with their biographies, are related in print for the first time in the *Jesuit Relations*, where each death, beginning with René Goupil's, is narrated by the Jesuit in charge of the mission in Huronia or in Quebec City, in the *Relation* covering the year in which it occurs. Yet the account of Isaac Jogues's capture, torture, hiding, release, and escape to France; his return to New France one and a half years later; and finally his capture and assassination by the Iroquois in October 1646 is the most interesting by far, from the point of view of its composition and of its relation to the rest of the narrative enfolding it. Jogues's narrative, a founding text, is the most intricate and fascinating of all, since it is constructed in several stages and spans several *Relations*. It is also dialogical in the extreme, as it has a number of different narrators and narratees who cite and constantly refer to one another. As well, it incorporates and integrates numerous sources of different origins and different times, both written and oral, in constructing the persona 'Jogues.' Indeed, even before Jogues says *I* in his own narrative of 1643, he emerges as the complex intersection of the directly and indirectly reported and transcribed past and present voices of all the speaking and writing subjects of New France (both Christian and non-Christian) and the Motherland inscribed in previous *Relations*. Polyglotic and temporalized, the subject *I* speaks by and through the polyphonic and historialized *we*.

The introduction to the *Relation* of 1642, dated 4 October and written by Barthélemy Vimont, the Superior of the Mission of Quebec, as well as chapter 11 of the same *Relation*, composed by Paul Le Jeune, are the first mentions of Isaac Jogues's captivity by the Iroquois. Vimont simply notes that, if the priest is still alive, he is a prisoner of the enemy, along with two French servants and twenty-three Christian Huron captives. However, Le Jeune's short narrative of the missionary's capture is preceded by a long description of the Iroquois wars against the Algonquin and the subsequent campaign against the French. Le Jeune quotes another missionary, Jacques Buteux, who was told about the cruelty of the Iroquois by one of two Algonquin women who were captured with Jogues but who subsequently escaped. Most of the tale is directly narrated by Buteux, who adopts the perspective and point of view of the captured woman – indirect discourse – as he recounts the events that occurred the year before. On occasion, however, the actual witness is allowed to speak on her own, but only for a brief moment, by addressing the missionary directly. She shifts the scene into the present tense as though it were actually unravelling before Buteux, or any other listener/reader. She begins her story at the moment she is about to go to bed, with a premonitory statement in the present: 'C'est fait de nous, les Iroquois nous tuent' (We are done for, the Iroquois are killing us) (1642: 45). The narrator-missionary immediately appropriates her scene, displaces the witness by speaking in her stead, substituting in the evaluative mode, and in the past tense, his voice, his vision, for hers: 'Je ne sais par quel instinct elle proféra ces paroles' (I do not know what instinct pushed her to pronounce these words). He then shifts back into the present: 'quoi que c'en soit, à même temps ces tigres entrent les armes à la main dans leur cabane, en saisissent quelques-uns par les cheveux, d'autres par le milieu du corps' (be that as it may, at the same time she says this, these armed tigers enter the cabin, seizing some of the inhabitants by the hair, others by the waist) (1642: 46). The narrator describes the massacre, always in the present, as though observing it at first hand. He becomes the centre of focalization, the eyewitness, investing the text with his previously confirmed missionary sentiments and beliefs. Though he substitutes his voice for hers, he does not assume total responsibility for the narrative, in the end leaving it with the woman who lived the event, saw it with her own eyes, and therefore can be considered a reliable witness.[2] The aggressors gather wood, fetch water, and get the large cauldrons boiling. The narrator substitutes his voice for hers in the present, before shifting back to the past: 'La boucherie n'est pas loin. Ils démembrent ceux qu'ils viennent de massacrer, les mettent en pièces et les jettent pieds et jambes, bras et têtes dans la marmite, qu'ils font bouillir avec autant de joie, que les pauvres captifs qui restaient en vie, avaient de crève-cœur voyant que leurs compatriotes servaient de curée à ces Loups-garoux' (The slaughter is not long. They dismember those they have just massacred. They cut them in pieces, and throw the feet and the hands, the arms and the legs into the cauldron, which they boil with such great joy, that the poor captives who were still alive, were heart broken seeing their companions served as spoils to these Werewolves) (1642: 46).[3]

The Iroquois are presented as an undifferentiated mass, appearing suddenly in the night and, much like the plagues of old, bringing death and destruction to the French, their Christian allies, and all of their enemies. Like the demons of Christian lore, these agents of fire torture and cook their victims, even devour them. Moreover, these instruments of hell attack and destroy the social unit of Christianity *par excellence*, the family. 'Les femmes et les enfants pleuraient amèrement, et ces demi-Démons prenaient plaisir à ces chansons lugubres' (Women and children wept bitterly as those half-Demons took pleasure in hearing their gloomy songs) (1642: 46). A further motif is developed, that of the passive flock, which in turn evokes the pastor to come (the Lamb of God who takes away the sins of the world). 'Le souper étant cuit, ces loups dévorent leur proie; qui se jette sur une cuisse, qui sur la poitrine. Les uns sucent la moelle des os, les autres ouvrent une tête pour en tirer la cervelle' (Their supper being cooked, these wolves devoured their prey, one attacks a thigh, another a breast. Some suck the marrow from the bones, others split open a head to extract the brain).[4] The inhumanity of the other is stressed when the narrator states, 'En un mot ils mangent les hommes avec autant d'appétit et plus de joie que les chasseurs ne mangent un Sanglier ou un Cerf' (In short, they eat men with such appetite and with more joy than hunters eat wild boar or deer) (1642: 46). The Iroquois are subsequently characterized as 'wolves,'[5] who devour children: 'Ils prirent nos petits enfants, les attachèrent à une broche, les présentèrent au feu et les firent rôtir tout vifs devant nos yeux' (They took our little children, they tied them to a spit, put them over a fire and roasted them alive before our eyes). When the aggressors bring their captives to the village they are depicted in diabolical terms: 'Quelques Démons y attendaient les prisonniers ... Entrant dans cet Enfer ... comme les Démons font des âmes damnées ... une danse au milieu des Démons ... ces tigres ... *Homo homini lupus*; l'homme devient un loup envers un homme, quand il se laisse gouverner aux Démons ... La fureur de ces lions' (Some Demons awaited the prisoners ... Entering this hell ... Like Demons with the souls of the damned ... dance in the midst of these Demons ... these tigers ... these Demons ... *Homo homini lupus*; man becomes a wolf for a man when he is governed by Demons ... the fury of these lions) (1642: 47–8).[6] The diabolical and predator–prey imagery used to qualify the actants constitutes a common lore between narrator and narratee, founded on shared experience and knowledge of the same Christian texts and motifs, be they biblical or taken from the writings of the Fathers of the church. This overdetermination of common imagery and motifs constitutes a representation for the reader of past knowledge and belief, an activation of a temporal arc, a *memoria* of past/present/future, inscribing, in the here and now of reading, the gruesome scenes that occurred in another time, another place, calling for an inexorable conclusion, an end to come.

Immediately after announcing that man is a wolf for man, without naming the main protagonist, Lalemant refers directly to the tale he is about to narrate. 'Hélas! serait-il bien possible, que le Père et les Français, dont je vais bientôt parler, fussent traités de la sorte par ces Barbares, qui les ont pris et emmenés depuis peu en leur pays!' (Alas! Is it truly possible that the Father and the Frenchmen, about whom I shall soon speak, have been treated this way by these Barbarians, who captured and recently took them to their country) (1642: 48).[7] This constitutes the minimal narrative of the priest's capture, and it is followed by four paragraphs describing the activities of the enemy in the spring, before once again turning to the events leading to the battle and narrating those that follow in the past tense.[8] On the second of August, twelve Huron canoes were returning home to Ste Marie bringing with them Isaac Jogues when 'furent attaqués et défaits d'une troupe d'Iroquois, armés par les Hollandais de bonnes arquebuses, desquelles il se servent aussi bien que nos Européens' (they were attacked and defeated by a band of Iroquois, armed by the Dutch with arquebuses that they can use as well as our[9] Europeans) (1642: 49). He was captured, along with two young Frenchmen, and carried off to their village. Continuing the metaphor of the wolf/dog pack, he notes that these barbarians 'en feront peut-être une curée plus sanglante que les chiens ne font d'un cerf' (might make him a more bloody quarry than hounds do to a stag) (1642: 49). He further comments on the courage God has given to Jogues and the two French captives, all the while speculating on their fate: 'si ces tigres les brûlent, s'ils les rôtissent, s'ils les font bouillir, s'ils les mangent, ils leurs procureront de plus doux rafraîchissements en la maison du grand Dieu, pour l'amour duquel ils s'exposaient à ces dangers' (if these tigers burn them, if they roast them, if they boil them, they will procure for them the greatest refreshments in the house of the great Lord, for they expose themselves to these dangers for those they love) (1642: 49). This potential torture and sacrifice is then assimilated to that of the Saviour and his apostles and their disciples: 'Voilà le prix et la monnaie avec laquelle Jésus-Christ a acheté le salut des Grecs et des Barbares: c'est avec la même monnaie qu'il leur faut procurer l'application de son sang' (This is the price and the coin with which Jesus Christ has bought the salvation of the Greeks and the Barbarians: it is with the same coin that the application of his blood must be procured for them) (1642: 49).

Chapter 12 of the *Relation* of 1643, again edited by Barthélemy Vimont, covers the Iroquois wars during that period. When the Iroquois returned to the St Lawrence valley, they had with them three or four Huron prisoners captured the previous year, along with Isaac Jogues and the French. Two of them escaped, met with Jean de Brébeuf in Trois Rivières, and let him know that the captives were still alive when they left them. Again we have embedded narratives, where the Huron relate to Brébeuf, who relates to Vimont, who relates to Filleau ... Here, we learn what happened to Jogues, Goupil, and Couture after their capture. This section of the text fills in a gap between the now of narration and the past of the event, and serves to overwrite the text of 1642.[10] It describes Jogues's refusal to escape in order not to abandon the captive Huron, his baptism of prisoners, the beatings of the French by the Iroquois, who tore out their beards and nails, burned their fingers, sectioned Jogues's left thumb, and bit off his middle finger. It recounts, in turn, Goupil's assassination by an irate warrior who had just learned about the death of some of his kin, Couture's refusal to flee during battle in order not to be separated from Jogues, the attempt by the two Dutchmen to buy the priest from the Iroquois, who refuse, and finally, the long letter the missionary gives to a Huron warrior to bring to the French (1643: 66–7). This chapter also contains the letter in question, the only surviving one of four sent by Jogues to the governor of New France. The document, dated 30 June 1643 and cited *in extenso*, relays information about some of the other captives (Couture and Henry), their treatment, their living conditions, the number of Iroquois warriors and the quantity of their arms, the intertribal wars and campaigns, the Iroquois strategy to eliminate as many important Algonquin and Huron leaders as possible in order to create a united nation, and, finally, Jogues's missionary activities.

108 Part II. Discovery, Conversion, and Colonization

Lalemant intervenes once more in his tale, addressing his readers directly and inviting them to share his appreciation of the captive's text: 'Cette lettre a plus de suc que de paroles; la tissure en est excellente, quoique la main qui en a formé les caractères soit toute déchirée; elle est composée d'un style plus sublime que celui qui sort des plus pompeuses écoles de la Rhétorique' (This letter has more substance than words; its weft is excellent, although the hand that formed the characters is all torn to pieces; it is composed in a more sublime style than that which emanates from the most pompous schools of Rhetoric) (1643: 67). The narrator uses this occasion to revisit Jogues's capture on 2 August 1642, and dwells on the cruel treatment he received in the village afterwards, as told to him by two Huron who had escaped from the Iroquois. As before, the primary narrator becomes the centre of focalization, organizing the tale as though he himself had directly observed the scene. His torture (beating with ropes and sticks, tearing out of his hair and beard) by a group of villagers is related in the past, but as soon as the narrator focuses on his hands the scenes are slowed down, elaborated, and presentified. It is as though both the narrator and the narratee were actually present, witnessing the slow unfolding of this gruesome spectacle.[11] The scene is briefly commented upon in the past tense, followed, in the very same sentence, by a return to the present: 'ce n'est pas tout, ces Barbares lui arrachent sa soutane, ils le dépouillent, et pour couvrir sa nudité, lui jettent un bout d'une vieille peau, chargée de saleté et de puanteur' (this is not all, these Barbarians tear off his cassock, strip him, and to cover his nakedness, throw him a piece of a stinky old skin, covered with filth) (1643: 68). Afterwards, the narrator evokes Jogues's general treatment by the Iroquois and their hatred for and torment of the French and the Christian Huron. Although not present at the time it allegedly occurred, though presumably witnessed by the Huron who had escaped, he conjures up a reported scene where one of the warriors taunts the missionary: 'Prends courage, mon neveu, lui dira un Capitaine en se gaussant, ne t'afflige point, tu verras bientôt ici quelques-uns de tes frères qui te viendront tenir compagnie. Nos guerriers ont envie de manger de la chair des Français, tu en pourras goûter avec nous' (Take courage, my nephew, one of the Captains said mocking him, you will soon see some of your brothers who will come and keep you company. Our warriors feel like eating some French flesh, you will be able to taste some with us) (1643: 68). The narrator adds: 'Voilà comme on nous a dépeint ce Martyr vivant, ce Confesseur souffrant, cet homme riche dans l'extrême pauvreté, joyeux et content dans le pays des douleurs et de la tristesse, en un mot ce Jésuite vêtu à la Sauvage, ou plutôt à la saint Jean Baptiste' (This is how this living Martyr was depicted, this suffering Confessor, this man rich in extreme poverty, joyful and content in this land of sorrow and sadness, in a word, this Jesuit, clothed like a Savage, or rather as Saint John the Baptist) (1643: 68). The motif of the martyr is evoked twice in the *Relation* of 1643 – three years before Jogues's actual death – thus fixing in the present memory of the reader both an evaluation of the past events and the ready interpretation of a potential future outcome. The missionary is depicted as being persecuted and taunted for spreading the true faith, and when he is finally executed in 1646 during the Iroquois–Huron–French wars, the reader will have been prepared to accept this particular reading of the causes of his death.[12] Lalemant quotes a number of Jogues's phrases (direct discourse) as though he had actually been present, even though they had, in fact, been reported to him by the Huron informants who witnessed them. These phrases conjure up Jogues's resignation to God's will, his acceptance of his likely death, his faith in Jesus Christ, his desire to stay and bring solace to the French and Native captives, some of whom are Christians, and his wish to baptize the young Iroquois children who are dying. Finally, the scenario of Guillaume Couture, who refuses to abandon Jogues, and who 'veux mourir avec le Père ... pour l'amour de Jésus-Christ' (wishes to die with the Father ... for the love of Jesus Christ) (1643: 68), is played out once more.

The *Relation* of 1644, covering what occurred in Huronia from June 1642 to June 1643, was recomposed by Jérôme Lalemant and sent to Quebec. In fact, when this *Relation* was sent down to Quebec for the first time in September 1643, it was intercepted by the Iroquois. The 1644 text includes another abbreviated account of Jogues's capture and treatment by the Iroquois narrated by Lalemant, who learned of it from one of the Christian captives, Joseph *Taondechoren*, who, in turn, had escaped from his enemies. Most of the events concerning Jogues's capture, torture, and missionary activity in the village are narrated in the past tense, with evaluative comments by the narrator in the present. There are two scenes of reported direct discourse, one attributed to Jogues, who refuses to abandon his flock, and the other to a sworn enemy of the French,[13] who is a token representative of all those who hate them. However, the narrator is omnipresent in his text, commenting upon and reacting to some of the scenes he is describing, hence collapsing the historic past into the eternal present of the moment of writing and reading. Following the magician's tirade, Lalemant dwells on the cruelty of the spectacle[14] as though he were actually there, suffering with the victim: 'mais j'ai horreur de parcourir tous ces tourments, quoiqu'ils soient plus horribles à souffrir que non pas à écrire' (but I loathe going over all these tortures, though they are much more horrible to suffer than to describe) (1644: 73). He succeeds in including the reader in his own reaction to the horror of the scene by use of the first-person-plural *we*: 'Il suffit pour nous consoler, de savoir que Dieu anima tellement le Père d'un courage tout à fait héroïque ...' (we can console ourselves by knowing God gave the Father such heroic courage that ...) (1644: 73). It should be noted that the term 'martyr' does not appear a single time in this particular narrative.

The *Relation* of 1645 mentions only that Fathers Isaac Jogues and François Bressani, when they returned to New France, embraced as friends: 'ceux qui ont déchiré leurs corps, arraché leurs ongles et coupé leurs doigts, en un mot ceux qui les ont traités en tigres' (those who had torn their bodies to pieces, ripped out their nails and cut off their fingers, in a word, those who had treated them as tigers would) (1645: 2). A peace treaty is reached between the French, their allies, and the Iroquois that will hold for a year. The *Relation* of 1646, signed by Jérôme Lalemant, begins by referring to the above-mentioned treaty and is followed by an account of the deaths of Fathers Anne de Noüe and Enemond Masse. Both of these deaths are placed under the sign of martyrdom, though the former died from exposure to the elements and the latter of natural causes. After mentioning their deaths, Lalemant unequivocally states that 'L'une des grandes faveurs que Dieu ait faite aux saints Apôtres et aux saints Martyrs, a été de les jeter dans les occasions, et comme dans une heureuse nécessité d'agir et de souffrir fortement pour leur Maître; les deux Pères dont je vais parler semblent avoir participé à cette bénédiction' (One of the great favours that God bestowed on the Holy Apostles and the Holy Martyrs, was to give them the opportunity and, as it were, a happy necessity, to act and suffer deeply for their Master: the two Fathers of whom I will speak seem to have shared this benediction) (1646: 9). On 30 January 1646, Anne de Noüe set out from Trois Rivières accompanied by two Frenchmen and a Huron to administer the sacraments of Penance and the Eucharist in Fort Richelieu, twelve leagues away. In one day they covered only six leagues because of the snow and the exhausted state of the three people accompanying the priest. Father Noüe decided to set out alone at two in the morning the next day to get help, but died frozen to death in a kneeling position: 'Cette charité lui a ôté la vie: heureux martyre de mourir des mains de la charité' (This charity cost him his life: blessed martyrdom to die at the hands of charity) (1646: 9). This scene is followed by a brief biography of each of the protagonists, demonstrating that Anne de Noüe and Enemond Masse led exemplary missionary lives.

In the next chapter, entitled 'Of the Mission of the Martyrs Begun in the Land of the Iroquois,' Lalemant again places all deaths of the French missionaries under the sign of martyrdom:

> Quand je parle d'une Mission Iroquoise, il me semble que je parle d'un songe, et néanmoins c'est une vérité; c'est à bon droit qu'on lui fait porter le nom des Martyrs: car outre les cruautés que ces Barbares ont déjà fait souffrir à quelques personnes amoureuses du salut des âmes, outre les peines et les fatigues que ceux qui sont destinés à cette Mission doivent encourir, nous pouvons dire avec vérité qu'elle a déjà été empourprée du sang d'un Martyr, car le Français qui fut tué aux pieds du Père Isaac Jogues, perdit la vie pour avoir fait exprimer le signe de notre créance à quelques petits enfants Iroquois.

> (When I speak of a Mission among the Iroquois, it seems to me that I speak of a dream, but nevertheless it is true, and we are right in giving it the name of the Martyrs; for in addition to the cruelty with which these Barbarians treated some persons impassioned for the salvation of souls, in addition to the sorrows and fatigues that those destined for this Mission are bound to incur, we can say in truth that it has already been turned crimson by the blood of a Martyr, for the Frenchman who was killed at the feet of Father Isaac Jogues, lost his life for having expressed the sign of our creed to some little Iroquois children.) (1646: 14)

Throughout the period of the French–Huron–Iroquois wars (1642–9), the motif of martyrdom permeates the discourse of conversion, with the Iroquois assuming the role of Satan, the sworn enemy of the true church. In fact, at this time the mission attained the state when conversion was considered possible if, and only if, the missionaries were persecuted and executed for their faith by the hellhounds of Satan. 'Il est croyable (si cette entreprise réussit) que les desseins que nous avons contre l'empire de Satan pour le salut de ces peuples, ne porteront point leurs fruits qu'ils ne soient arrosés du sang de quelques autres Martyrs' (It is credible [if this endeavour succeeds] that the plans we have against Satan's empire for the salvation of these people will only bear fruit if they are soaked with the blood of some other Martyrs) (1646: 14).[15]

The *Relation* of 1647, composed by Jérôme Lalemant and sent from Quebec to Paris on 20 October 1647, is much different from the previous ones dealing with Isaac Jogues and Jean de La Lande. It begins with a brief mention of their deaths in the dedication to Étienne Charlet, the Provincial of the Jesuit order, and for the most part it will expand on the elementary narrative program of the life and death of these two missionaries. However, in contrast to all the earlier segments concerning them both,[16] a specific end, a teleological finality of martyrdom, organizes and gives meaning to all the events of their lives.[17] Yet, much as in the previous *Relations*, this is a composite and complex text in which Lalemant, as editor, integrates, melds, and weaves together various written as well as a large number of verbal narratives that are, at first glance, difficult to disentangle. The initial chapter opens with the departure on 24 September 1646 of Isaac Jogues from Trois Rivières, returning to the land of the Iroquois to evangelize them. The Iroquois turn on the French, accusing them of spreading illness and causing death with their prayers and ceremonies, and put both of them to death.[18] This signals the end of the peace treaty and the beginning of new eruptions of violence. The narrator then shifts to the state of general warfare throughout the colony, describing in chronological order the havoc and terror wrought on the French and their Native allies. The next two chapters evoke a number of episodes related to individual acts of prowess, escapes, or reprisals by the allies of the French. The third ends with an exhortation of a metanarrative nature to all virtual readers, inviting them directly, and associating them through the inclusionary usage of the first-person-plural *us* and the second-person-plural *you*, to imagine, observe, and sympathize with the scenes that are to follow: 'Mais entrons, s'il vous plaît, dans des croix bien plus saintes, dans des souffrances ardemment désirées et dans une mort plus aimable que la vie même ... Commençons, s'il vous plaît, par sa première entrée au pays de ses amertumes et de ses douceurs, de ses mépris et de sa gloire' (But let us enter, if you will, into crosses that are much holier, into ardently desired sufferings and into a death that is more lovable than life itself ... Let us begin, if you will, by his first visit to the land of bitterness, and by his gentleness, by his disregard and his glory) (1647: 17).[19]

The fourth chapter opens abruptly with a micronarrative nine lines long, describing Jogues's origins in Orleans, France, his arrival in New

France, his six years in Huronia, and his death, that recapitulates, or mirrors, in an extremely condensed form, the story that is about to unravel. However, before focusing on the main topic, the narrator makes a series of comments of a metatextual nature regarding the origins of the tale he is about to relate and the reliability of all the information contained therein: 'Ce qu'on a dit de ses travaux dans les *Relations* précédentes provenait pour la plupart de quelques Sauvages, compagnons de ses peines. Mais ce que je vais coucher est sorti de sa plume et de sa propre bouche, il a fallu user d'autorité de Supérieur, et d'une douce industrie dans les conversations plus particulières pour découvrir ce que l'estime très basse qu'il faisait de soi-même tenait caché dans un profond silence' (What was said about his [Jogues's] labours in the earlier *Relations* came for the most part from a few Indians, who were fellow sufferers. But what I am about to write came from his own pen and from his own mouth. I had to use the authority as his Superior, and gentle persuasion in more intimate conversations, to discover that the low self-esteem he had of himself was kept hidden under a profound silence) (1647: 17).[20] Here, Lalemant grounds truth in the visual and corporeal experience of the person who lived the event, Jogues, who becomes the ultimate guarantor of what is described. In so doing, the narrator depreciates and plays down the witnessing and oral reporting of the indigenous people who saw what happened and spoke about it to the missionary but could not write about it. From this perspective, to *say* is to have *seen* and *experienced* for oneself. Yet, in Lalemant's narrative, the fact that Jogues assumes the roles of embedded narrator, actant, and scriptor guarantees the truth of what occurred.[21] Lalemant and Jogues tend to become one and the same since they share the same presuppositions about both the potential of language to reconstitute the event and also its ultimate meaning in terms of a shared and unquestioned eschatology. This melding of voices is borne out when the focus of the narrative abruptly shifts from Lalemant to Jogues himself, with no punctuation marks except a period indicating the change: 'Écoutons-le parler sur ce sujet, et sur la suite de son voyage. L'obéissance m'ayant fait une simple proposition, et non pas un commandement de descendre à Québec, je m'offris de tout mon cœur ...' (Let us hear him speak on this subject, and on the outcome of his journey. Obedience having proposed to me and not ordered me to go down to Quebec, I offered wholeheartedly to do so ...) (1647: 17–18). The shifting of focalization, from Lalemant to Jogues, is relayed by other European witnesses who *saw* and fixed in *writing* what they had *perceived*.[22] Here, seeing is the differential trait of knowing and, in contrast to the voice of Native informants, writing establishes events as having occurred – as truth.

The five following chapters, which give the most complete and final account of the life and death of Isaac Jogues, can be considered as the founding narrative of his martyrdom, one that led not only to his canonization, but also to that of the seven other missionaries. It became the model of the genre in the *Relations*, and the form of its content and expression generated the accounts of the seven other 'Martyrs' who lost their lives during this troubled and violent period in the history of the mission. It is, in fact, composed – that is, put together and structured – by Lalemant in terms of an indisputable finality and shared eschatology, and it is the ultimate rewriting of all the events of Jogues's existence that are deemed significant in establishing his hagiography.[23] Although the oral witnessing of Native informants is said to be unreliable, Lalemant's narrative, established from other written accounts, in the main covers the same ground as theirs. Rather than attempt to give a linear commentary of these chapters I propose a more semio-narrative analysis of them as sketched in the preceding pages.

We are dealing here with embedded narratives at the level of enunciation where the primary enunciator, Lalemant, conjoins the role not only of scriptor/witness, but also, from time to time, of actor, since he both tells the story and, at various moments, intervenes as an actual character in the fable. He, in turn, is relayed by Jogues, who also has the role of enunciator and primary actor, a role he shares with other enunciator/actors who knew the victim and gave evidence of the degree of their knowledge through their writings (Buteux, the Dutch, etc.). All of these enunciators, who must be defined by and through intersubjective relations of communication (real or virtual), confirm their narrative competence by the simple performance, or act, of narrating. Yet their narrative competence is founded on a certain number of presuppositions or variable rules belonging to the cultural and social codes, the ideologies, defining them as Europeans. As I noted in chapter 4, such conventions, beliefs, and institutions constitute the symbolic network of culture that is shared by individuals and that assigns them a specific place[24] in the symbolic order and hierarchy. Each enunciator and enunciatee is defined by a common base of theoretical knowledge (writing, measure, time, etc.); a passion – actual or by proxy – to convert the heathen; and the physical, mental, and moral power (and duty) to impose the true faith. These modalities, which constitute their competence, are organized in ordered series with obligation or duty (to God's dictates) commanding, in sequence, the will, knowledge, and power of all the actants concerned.[25] What differentiates each narrating trustworthy actor is the degree and intensity – rather than the order – of the modalities that motivate his competence. Moreover, it is presupposed that all of these modalities enabling narrative to come into being in the form of writing and reading have been sanctioned by a large number of social and religious institutions of obvious European origin.[26] Each and every enunciator and enunciatee has in turn been destined by the Sender, God, and simply carries out his order to write, read, believe, and live for the true Receiver, God, who has mandated him/her to undertake this divine project.[27]

None the less, this *Relation*, like all the others, is organized in terms of descriptions, scenes, and dialogues where personae interact physically, emotionally, intellectually, and spiritually. The discursive construct, Jogues, the main subject (S1) of this narrative, is depicted by Lalemant, progressively and in stages, as the prototypical and exemplary missionary who will attain God's will through suffering, sacrifice, and dying for the faith. At the most elementary level of analysis, the subject (S1) who has been mandated by God, and whose competence has been sanctioned by the social, cultural, intellectual, and religious institutions (presupposed),[28] will undertake a journey, or quest, into the unknown. The missionary will undergo a series of qualifying tests, reported and evaluated by a series of representatives of the temporal and spiritual orders, before being legislated into the eternity of sainthood by the final sanctioning body of the church. In turn, each test in the series can be considered as the transformation of one state ($s1$) of the Subject (S1) into another state ($s2$), and the entire sequence, making up the narrative, can be transcribed as: $s1(S1)$ tr. $s2(S1)$ tr. $s3(S1)$ tr. ... $sn(S1)$, where sn represents the end point. It should be noted, however, that the transforming agent, or catalyst, necessary to bring (S1) to the penultimate end point of martyrdom, and to the end point of canonization, is none other than the collective Anti-subject (S2), the Iroquois.

At the discursive level, Lalemant figurativizes the actor Jogues according to the precepts of classical rhetoric[29] that prescribe two levels of description when composing the portrait of a persona. The first level is a description that has as its object the face, the body, the features, the physical qualities, the bearing, and the movement of a person, whereas the second deals with the person's mores, character, vices, or good and bad moral qualities.[30] Each successive test faced by Jogues is described on both levels, and attests to his exemplary physical, moral, and spiritual qualities, which can be revealed only under incredible, life-threatening adversity and duress. In each of these qualifying tests, which progressively increase in difficulty and horror, the Subject (S1) successfully overcomes the taunts and tortures of the Anti-subject (S2), who, as we saw, was depicted as Satan's hellhound.

The originality of Lalemant's narrative, though, must be attributed to the textualization of the episodes, to the rhythm and intensity of their staging, to the complex interplay and changes in focalization, to the enunciative strategies set in place, and to the impact created by the overlay of recurring characters and events. For the reader or scriptor of the *Relation* of 1647, the name 'Jogues' is not an empty signifier, nor is it a simple potential waiting to signify through the creation of a temporalized actional intrigue. The signifier, Jogues, has an anaphoric function[31] that sets in motion in the reader a *memoria*, a temporal arc (past-present-future), reaching at one and the same time back, to all the intratextual and intertextual references to his prior deeds and actions, and forward, projecting his inevitable future in death and martyrdom. The signifier, Jogues, evokes a body that has previously been tortured and mutilated, a body in action, an acting body, a body being acted upon. It is by and through the description of the body in action that the hero's physical, moral, and spiritual qualities are revealed. Yet the complete story of his life and death must be told and iterated a final time, in large part by himself, before being frozen in timeless legend.

Whether the enunciator happens to be Lalemant, or Jogues, or Buteux, the body is always a focus of fixation. Jogues, who has the option of fleeing after being captured in 1642, decides not to: 'La fuite me semblait horrible: Il faut, disais-je en mon cœur, que mon corps souffre le feu de la terre, pour délivrer ces pauvres âmes des flammes de l'Enfer, il faut qu'il meure d'une mort passagère, pour leur procurer une vie éternelle' (Fleeing seemed horrible to me. I said in my heart, my body must suffer the fire of earth, to deliver these poor souls from the flames of Hell. It must die a temporary death, to procure eternal life for them) (1647: 18–19). His own body is thus inscribed in a virtual narrative program of sacrifice (man being spiritually dead in life and spiritually alive in death), with a clearly defined finality (giving up life on earth so that the other can attain eternal life). The body is a transitory home for the eternal soul, and the flesh must be racked and sacrificed for the self and the other to enter into the kingdom of heaven.

In narrating his own capture, Jogues organizes events for the most part by using the past-definite tense, which, as I remarked,[32] is the time of historical discourse that maintains a temporal distance between the time of narration and the time of the event. The first sequence of torture, related in the past-definite tense, is framed by two sequences of ministration, narrated in a mixture of present and past tenses: 'j'appelle l'un des Iroquois ... Il s'advance, et m'ayant saisi il me mit au nombre de ceux que la terre appelle misérables ... Ce bon jeune homme confessa sur l'heure. Lui ayant donné l'absolution, j'aborde les Hurons, je les instruis et les baptise ...' (I call one of the Iroquois guards ... he approaches, and having seized me he put me with those that are called the miserable of this world ... This good young man confessed immediately. Having given him absolution, I approach the Huron, I instruct and baptize them ...) (1647: 19); 'je recherchai aussi mon partage, je visite tous les captifs, je baptise ceux qui ne l'étaient pas encore, j'encourage ces pauvres misérables à souffrir ... je reconnus en cette visite que nous étions vingt-deux captifs' (I was also seeking my share, I visit all the captives, I baptize those who were not yet baptized, I encourage these poor wretches to suffer ... I learned during this visit that we were twenty-two captives) (1647: 19–20). This shifting in and out of historical time into the present imposes another temporal rhythm on the reader, that of distancing and presentifying the events made flesh as they are conjured up in the act of reading. The historically temporalized action of the body is folded into the timelessness of the gesture of ritual. Yet the violence with which his captors torment him is described in the past-definite tense: 'Ils se jetèrent sur moi d'une furie enragée, ils me chargèrent de coups de poings, de coups de bâtons et de coups de masses d'armes, me ruant par terre à demi mort. Comme je commençais à respirer, ceux qui ne m'avaient point frappé s'approchant, m'arrachèrent à belles dents les ongles des doigts, et puis me mordant les uns après les autres, l'extrémité des deux index dépouillés de leurs ongles, me causaient une douleur très sensible, les broyant et les écrasant comme entre deux pierres, jusqu'à en faire sortir des esquilles ou de petits os' (They fell upon me with an enraged fury. They beat me with their fists, with sticks and with their weapons, flinging me to the ground half-dead. As I was beginning to breathe, those who had not struck me, approaching, tore off the nails of my fingers with their teeth. And then biting one after the other the ends of my two forefingers stripped of their nails, causing me extreme pain, crushing them and grinding them as if between two stones, until splinters and small bones emerged) (1647: 19). Although the racked body is described in the past, the images unravel both with violence and uncommon slowness, as the use of the gerundive – 'flinging,' 'approaching,' 'biting,' 'causing,' 'crushing,' 'grinding' – stretches out the tormented and mutilated body in time, creating in the reader, through intensified durativity, reactions of attraction and repulsion, identification and horror. His mutilated, festering, and suffering body in movement is depicted in all its horror during the thirteen-day trip from the place of capture to the Iroquois village: 'la faim, la chaleur très ardente, les menaces et la haine de ces Léopards, la douleur de nos plaies, qui pour n'être point pansées se pourrissaient jusqu'à produire des vers, nous causaient à la vérité beaucoup de douleur' (hunger, the burning heat, threats and the hatred of these Leopards, the pain of our wounds, which were not bandaged and were rotting to the extent that they produced worms, caused us, in truth, great suffering) (1647: 20). Eight days into this trip, the party meets up with another band of Iroquois on the warpath, and the captives are made to run the gauntlet. Blows hail down on them; Jogues falls once more to the ground and passes out, near death:

> Ils me voulaient mener tout vif en leur pays, ils m'embrassent donc, et me portent tout sanglant sur ce théâtre preparé; étant revenu à moi, ils me font descendre, ils me donnent mille et mille injures, ils me font le jouet et le but de leurs opprobres, ils recommencent leur batterie, déchargeant sur ma tête et sur mon col et sur tout mon corps une autre grêle de coups de bâtons. Je serais trop long si je voulais coucher par écrit toute la rigueur de mes souffrances, ils me brûlèrent un doigt, ils m'écrasèrent l'autre avec leurs dents, et ceux qui étaient déjà déchirés ils les pressaient et les tordaient avec une rage de Démons, ils égratignaient mes plaies avec les ongles, et quand les forces me manquaient ils m'appliquaient du feu aux bras et aux cuisses.

> (They wanted to bring me back alive to their country, they gather me in their arms, and carry me covered in blood to this stage. Having revived me, they make me come down. They cast a thousand insults at me. They make me the sport and object of their reviling. They begin to beat me again, raining down on my head, and on my neck and on my entire body a hail of blows with their sticks. It would be too long for me to write down the full extent of my suffering. They burned one of my fingers, they crushed another with their teeth, and they continued to press and twist with the rage of Demons those that were already torn. They tore at my wounds again and again with their nails, and whenever my strength failed me they applied fire to my hands and my thighs.) (1647: 21)

The manipulated and punished body is once more depicted graphically as it is caught up in a whirligig of changes of tenses from the past-definite tense to the present, back to the past-definite tense, and then to the imperfect. This shifting in and out not only positions the reader before what is happening, but also creates rhythm and tension in the description. The assailed, sensitized, passive body is projected out of the horror of the historical into the abhorrence of the vivid timeless now ('they gather me,' 'carry me covered in blood,' 'make me come down,' 'they cast,' 'they make me the sport ...'). The tormented body is seized, struck, and dismembered by violent sudden gestures in the past-definite tense that reduce the moment to a single point in time, inscribing it in a causal chain, maintaining ambiguity between temporality and causality, and calling for a development, an unravelling, an end of tribulation[33] ('they burned,' 'they crushed'). Finally, the tortured body, subjected to the throes of lasting, recurring, and agonizing suffering, is enfolded in the imperfect tense, stretching and reiterating the activity, over time, imposing a tempo of haunting and excruciating durativity, iterativity and tensitivity ('they begin to beat me again,' 'they continued to press and twist,' 'they tore at my wounds, again and again,' 'whenever I lost ... they applied') that not only engages the intellectual attention of the reader but also provokes intense feelings of identification, empathy, torment, and repulsion. Indeed, if, through and by Jogues's experience, the flesh is made word, by his narrative the word is also made flesh for the reader, who, in turn, experiences Jogues's travails in the past and present imagined and lived depths of her/his own body.

The tortures continue, and Jogues gives isolated examples both of scenes that include other individual protagonists, and also of dialogue between them. They go on to the village, and the missionary lives a real Calvary along the way as he bears his cross, describing events that occurred as either singular, durative, or iterative.[34] The captives meet up with another party in the wilderness before being paraded from one village to another and tortured again and again.[35] They are once more made to run the gauntlet and flagellated, then exposed on a platform. The priest is further mutilated,[36] then stretched out and tied to the stake, all the while offering up his sufferings to the Lord.[37] These tortures, with variations, are repeated in two other villages, each repetition spanning a three-day period.[38] Jogues is sentenced to death with some Huron captives and prepares for the end: 'Mon âme à ces paroles est très contente; mais mon Dieu ne l'était pas encore, il voulut prolonger mon martyre. Ces Barbares se ravisèrent, s'écriant qu'il fallait donner la vie au Français' (My soul is very pleased on hearing these words; but God himself was not, he wished to prolong my martyrdom. These Barbarians changed their minds and said the Frenchmen had to be kept alive) (1647: 24). After Jogues witnesses Goupil's assassination, the narrative switches back to Lalemant: 'Ce jeune homme ou ce saint martyre, étant ainsi massacré, le Père s'en retourne en sa cabane; ses gens lui portent la main sur la poitrine pour sentir si la peur n'agitait point son cœur' (This young man or this holy Martyr, having been slain in this way, the Father returns to his cabin; one of his captors holds a hand to his chest to feel whether fear did not make his heart beat) (1647: 26). It should be noted that the description of the body is never a completed portrait so that, in the end, the reader's memory cannot conjure up an actual image of the man Jogues. The description isolates, focuses on, and re-depicts parts of the body that are amputated, bludgeoned, burned, scratched, cut, torn out. The more gruesome the details described, the more the totality is dissolved and diffused. The greater the specificity, the greater the reader's difficulty in imagining the overall effect. Though the parts bear a metonymic relation to the whole, they do not evoke an individualized physical portrait; rather, they function indexically, since they conjure up heroic moral and spiritual strength under the adversity of suffering and persecution.

Jogues spends the year in captivity in the Iroquois village. He has dreams and visions, like the patriarchs of old,[39] and his life is in constant danger. Once an angry warrior enters the priest's hut and bludgeons him over the head twice, leaving him half-dead (1647: 32). Lalemant narrates Jogues's flight to freedom, triggered when he learns that the Iroquois are awaiting his return to the village to kill him. In doing so, he comments on the composition of his work and its intratextual links with other *Relations*: 'Cette nouvelle fut l'occasion de sa délivrance, de laquelle ayant suffisamment parlé en la Relation l'an 1642 et 1643 au chap. 14 je ne rapporterai ici que quelques particularités dont on n'a fait que peu ou point de mention' (This news was the occasion for his deliverance, of which, having sufficiently mentioned in the *Relations* of 1642 and 1643 in chapter 14, I will only relate here a few particulars that were either barely, or not touched on at all) (1647: 33). In escaping from his captors, Jogues is once more mutilated, this time by a guard dog. His wounds are treated before he boards a ship for England, where, on arrival, he is robbed of his cassock and hat. He then makes his way to France.[40] The rest of Jogues's adventure, as he heads to meet his fate, is told at an extremely accelerated pace compared with the account of his capture and torture at the hands of the Iroquois, an account that takes up the major portion of the narrative though it covers a much briefer period of time.[41] This structural amplitude of variations, 282 lines for several hours dealing with his capture and first torture, compared with 9 lines for his one-and-a-half-year stay in France, is accompanied by an acceleration of the rhythm of the tale as it winds to a conclusion. The end is marked by an increasing number of summaries and ellipses, whereas the beginning – recounting the capture, torture, and constant threat of death at the hands of the Iroquois – is marked by long-drawn-out scenes.

In the tale of Jogues, the Iroquois are reduced to a horrifying presence and are never described physically. Indeed, as I noted, for the narrators and narratees they are an ominous, demonic, discarnate, evil presence, reduced to the sudden violent inhuman gestures they carry out on their enemies' bodies. They are the menacing absent signifieds in the intersubjective communication between Christians and potential Christians that can appear at any moment and wreak havoc on the colony and the missions. Yet they are always there, and felt in the hearts, the souls, and the very bodies of the individuals who fear them. I intimated in the previous chapter that the body was the most omnipresent, complex, and expressive of all of the sign systems making up interpersonal relations in the *Jesuit Relations*. This is not only because those who convert are different from the indigenous people in their dress and grooming (European clothing and beards are considered unsightly by the Iroquois and the Huron); nor is it because the body subjects itself to constraints that attest to difference (chastity, ceremonial) or reacts to the harshness of the environment in a marked way; nor is it even because the body reacts to torture in a controlled way. Rather, it is because the body is the most elaborate and expressive semiotic system – one that generates and incorporates all others. As such, the body in action – the tormented, mutilated, and sacrificed body – is at the origin of all the experience of the senses and of the mind, and is the most outspoken advocate of the true faith. When Jogues was waiting for a boat in which to escape from the Dutch settlement, a young man came up to him, took him aside, and 'se jeta à ses pieds, lui prenant les mains pour les baiser, en s'écriant: Martyr, Martyr de Jésus-Christ; il l'interrogea et connut que c'était un Luthérien qu'il ne pût aider pour n'avoir pas connaissance de sa langue, c'était un Polonais' (threw himself at his feet, taking up his hands to kiss them, and crying out: 'Martyr, Martyr of Jesus Christ.' He interrogated him and found out he was Lutheran. He could not help him as he did not know his language, he was Polish) (1647: 34).[42] When he was in Paris, 'la Reine ayant ouï parler de ses souffrances, dit tout haut: On feint des Romans, en voilà un véritable entremêlé de grandes aventures. Elle le voulut voir, ses yeux furent touchés de compassion à la vue de la cruauté des Iroquois' (the Queen having heard of his sufferings, says out loud: 'Romances are feigned, but here is a genuine combination of great adventures.' She wished to see him, her eyes were touched with compassion at the sight of the cruelty of the Iroquois) (1647: 36–7). As I noted in the previous chapter, the tortured and scarred body, the incarnation of the flesh made word, is the most eloquent and convincing of all languages, since it actualizes in its expressive materiality to the ultimate degree the values that inform the believers' semantic universe. Marked and mutilated by the hereditary temporal representatives of the negative values that threaten the very existence of the missions and the Huron Nation, the disfigured body, through semiosis, constitutes an ultimate semiotic system that articulates the material and spiritual values of human experience. The recurring and iterated drawn-out descriptions of the torn and tortured body move and provoke emotional responses from all actual and potential believers, all the while consolidating their shared semantic universes and their value and belief systems.

In the second part of chapter 8, dealing with the sequel to Jogues's death, Lalemant evaluates and interprets the events that occurred over the missionary's lifetime. Unlike the other segments of the Jogues narrative (especially those relating to his capture and torture, which are overwritten and amplified in successive *Relations*, so that what occurred once is narrated on numerous occasions – repetition and iteration creating an effect of intensity, horror, and truth),[43] this segment fills in some minor gaps in the narrative but also serves to give a final orientation and reading to the text. Once more, Jogues is evoked as a martyr by all those who came into contact with or heard of him. Public opinion, or the doxa, is unanimous about the ultimate meaning of the life and death of the missionary, and Lalemant articulates their voices in the final segment of his hagiography.[44] He begins by stating that all the missionaries in New France, the collective *We*, continue to speak as one: 'Nous avons respecté cette mort comme la mort d'un Martyr, et quoique nous fussions en divers endroits, plusieurs de nos Pères, sans savoir rien les uns des autres pour la distance des lieux, ne se sont pû résoudre de célébrer pour lui la Messe des trépassés ...' (We have honoured this death as the death of a Martyr, and though we were in different places, several of our Fathers, without knowing anything about the others because of the distance, could not reconcile themselves to celebrate for him the Mass of the Dead ...) (1647: 38). The secular clergy and religious orders voice this same opinion, and 'ont respecté cette mort, se sentant plutôt portés d'invoquer le Père que de prier pour son âme' (honoured this death, feeling rather more inclined to invoke the Father than to pray for his soul) (1647: 38). This is re-echoed as a logically constructed argument by 'Plusieurs hommes doctes, et cette pensée est plus que raisonnable que celui-là est vraiment martyr devant Dieu ... cette mort est la mort d'un martyr devant les Anges ... Nous sommes persécutés de ce que par notre doctrine qui n'est autre que celle de Jésus-Christ, nous dépeuplons à ce qu'ils disent leurs contrées, et c'est pour cette doctrine qu'ils ont tué le Père, et par conséquent on le peut tenir pour martyr devant Dieu' (Several learned men, and this idea is more than reasonable that he is truly a martyr before God ... This death is the death of a martyr before the Angels ... We are persecuted for our doctrine that is none other than Jesus Christ's, according to them we depopulate their lands, and it is for this doctrine that they killed the Father, and consequently we can consider him as a martyr before God) (1647: 38–9).

The tale closes with an injunction and an invitation to the reader to re-examine, with the narrator, over Jogues's entire lifetime, his moral and spiritual qualities: 'Disons deux mots des vertus de notre Martyr' (Let us say a few words about the virtues of our Martyr).[45] This can be considered as the final *ethopeia* or argument that integrates the reader in the eulogy, through the use of the possessive pronoun *our*, convincing her/him that we are, in fact, dealing with an indisputable case of martyrdom. This section, analeptic in nature, sweeps back over Jogues's early years, organizing all the events of his life in terms of the 'end [that] is there, transforming everything.'[46] This apologia is tautological and simply states that already in France the young Jogues was what he will become since he demonstrated *there* all the qualities that he will reveal *here* in New France. Most of the sequences, related in the imperfect, are durative and iterative, and they simply reiterate the implied fundamental proposition, which we can state as follows: 'What he repeatedly did, before and after his capture and death, prepared him for martyrdom. Hence he is a Martyr.' The amplitude of all of these iterative flashbacks, both internal and external, bring a repeated temporal consistency that subordinates the *past* to the *now* of enunciation, to the description of Jogues's moral and spiritual portrait. 'Il était doué de ... Il approuvait dès sa jeunesse ceux qui le châtiaient ... Il était une grande partie du jour devant le saint Sacrement ... il était d'un naturel assez appréhensif ... quoiqu'il fût d'un naturel prompt et sec ... plus de cent fois ils lui ont dit' (He was endowed with ... he approved in his early years those who chastized him ... he spent a large part of the day before the holy Sacrament ... he was naturally apprehensive ... although he was of a hasty and quick temper ... more than a hundred times over they said to him) (1647: 38–41). The other flashbacks, which are singulative, relating once events that occurred once, are vivid illustrations of the identified qualities that all martyrs must possess and demonstrate.

Lalemant also constructs his conclusion in the ironic mode since, on the one hand, Jogues is systematically presented as interpreting at one level all that he does, thinks, feels, and believes, while, on the other, everyone who comes into contact with him is said to have a different opinion. The parallelism of these two iterated points of view constitutes a limited number of semantic series (or isotopies) that ensure great cohesion and give great impact to this final plea. He has a low opinion of himself (he considers himself unworthy of all that befalls him, and lets those about him know this), whereas everyone who comes into contact with him holds and voices a contrary point of view: 'Il était doué d'une humilité toute rare ... C'était l'affliger que de lui témoigner tant soit peu l'estime de ce qu'il avait enduré pour Jésus-Christ ... La Reine ayant désiré de le voir, il ne pouvait se persuader qu'elle en eût véritablement envie ... C'était le tourmenter que de lui demander à voir ses mains toutes déchirées' (He was endowed with a rare humility ... He was distressed when he was shown any esteem for what he had endured for Jesus Christ ... When the Queen wished to see him he could not persuade himself that she truly wanted to ... He was tormented when she asked to see his hands that were all torn) (1647: 39–40). Cruelty/forgiveness and hate/love make up another series of isotopies: 'Jamais il n'eut au milieu de ses souffrances, ni dans les plus grandes cruautés de ces perfides, aucune aversion contre eux; il les regardait d'un œil de compassion comme une mère regarde un sien enfant ...' (Never in the midst of his suffering, or during the greatest cruelties of these treacherous people, did he feel any loathing for them; he considered them with the eye of compassion a mother holds for a child of hers ...) (1647: 40). Purity/sin and cowardliness/courage are two other series: 'On ne saurait exprimer le soin qu'il avait de conserver son cœur dans la pureté ... lui faisait dire qu'il n'était qu'un poltron, et cependant les Supérieurs qui le connaissaient, s'appuyaient dessus lui aussi fermement que sur un Rocher' (One cannot express the care he took to keep his heart pure ... made him say that he was only a coward, and yet the Superiors who knew him, depended on him as firmly as a rock) (1647: 40); as are indulgence/abstinence and humility/arrogance: 'J'ai déjà remarqué qu'il aima mieux se passer d'un peu d'eau et de farine d'Inde ... que de manger de la viande qu'il savait être immolée au Démon ... quoiqu'il fût d'un naturel prompt et sec, il savait néanmoins si bien se soumettre lorsque l'humilité Chrétienne et la charité le demandaient' (I already remarked that he would rather content himself with a little water and corn flour ... than eat meat that he knew was sacrificed to the Devil ... Although he was of a hasty and quick temper, he nevertheless knew so well to submit when Christian humility and charity required it) (1647: 41). Child/adult is the final pair: 'Le Père qui était avec lui la dernière année de sa vie à Montréal, reconnut bien que Dieu le disposait pour le Ciel, lui donnant des sentiments d'un enfant, il recherchait tous les plis et replis de sa conscience, depuis le premier usage de sa raison jusqu'à lors, les déclarant avec une humilité et une candeur d'un petit enfant' (The Father who was with him during the last year of his life in Montreal did recognize that God was preparing him for Heaven. Having given him the sentiments of a child, he examined all the folds and recesses of his conscience, from the first use of his reason to then, revealing them with the humility and candour of a child) (1647: 40). Here the child is literally and figuratively father of the man, predestined and prepared for his final end.[47]

A singular, exemplary incident encapsulates the interplay between the seemingly contradictory constitutive isotopies of Jogues's moral and spiritual portrait. During his captivity, an Iroquois who had fallen ill dreamed that, in order for him to be healed, a dance and other ceremonies had to be held with the missionary present, his prayer book in hand. Some Iroquois came and told the missionary that he held the key to the recovery of the suffering warrior. He, in turn, 'rebukes the vanity of their dreams' and refuses to come with them. Other messengers are sent, and when he continues to rebuff them they decide to carry him off against his will: 'Mais comme il était agile et fort adroit et bien peu chargé de graisse, il esquive de leurs mains, gagna au pied. Ils le poursuivent à toute force, ils trouvèrent qu'il avait des jambes de Cerf, et que s'il se fût voulu sauver qu'il l'eût fait, puisqu'il devançait les meilleurs coureurs du pays' (But as he was agile and very deft and very little burdened with flesh, he evades them and takes to his heels. They pursue him with all their might. They find that he had the legs of a stag, and that if he had wished to escape he could have done so, since he outstripped the best runners of the country) (1647: 41). And Lalemant continues, giving unequivocal meaning to the scene: 'En effet la seule charité le retint parmi les Iroquois, préférant le salut des captifs à sa vie et à sa liberté. Pour conclusion, il retourna à la bourgade avec résolution de mourir plutôt que de conniver tant soit peu dans leurs superstitions. Notre Seigneur voulut qu'on ne lui en parlât plus' (In fact charity alone kept him among the Iroquois, for he preferred the salvation of the captives to his life and liberty. In conclusion, he returned to the village resolving to die rather than in any way to associate with their superstitions. Our Lord desired that they spoke not more of this with him) (1647: 41). This scene demonstrates to one and all that Jogues is not what he is perceived to be for his tormentors; rather, he is what he appears to be for the narrator, all those who knew him, and the reader – a heroic and exemplary figure who, in living out his role, predestined and motivated by God, willingly abnegates his own will and intelligence, his tendencies and flesh, placing them entirely in the service of the Lord. Lalemant brings closure to the composition of the life and death of the martyr by framing Jogues's decision to abandon the Iroquois in 1643 with the help of the Dutch with an anticipatory vision he had of his own fate. He would not have escaped 's'il n'eût vu que c'était fait de sa vie, et qu'il ne pourrait plus secourir ces pauvres Barbares s'il ne se sauvait pour les venir retrouver une autre fois, jamais il ne les aurait pû abandonner: mais notre Seigneur lui prolongea la vie pour lui venir présenter une autre fois en holocauste au lieu où il avait déjà commencé son sacrifice' (if he had not seen that his life was over and that he could no longer help these poor Barbarians. If he did not know he would return and find them once more he could never have abandoned them: but our Lord prolonged his life so that he could once again present it as a burnt-offering in the land where he had already began his sacrifice) (1647: 42). The signification of Jogues's desire to flee from the dangers he faced during his captivity is recuperated by the fate he met at the hands of the Iroquois three years later. The last image left with the reader is that of the convergence of all the events witnessed and experienced into the grand adventure of martyrdom, the written testimonial of which will call out and beckon the other seven martyrs to be inscribed with him in the pantheon of French-Canadian sainthood.

For the next two hundred years, the narrative of the massacre of these Jesuit martyrs was not widely diffused in New France except through a limited number of images, notably reproductions of Huret's painting, and orally. The *Jesuit Relations* on New France, *per se*, ceased to be published by the order in 1673 because their content no longer corresponded to the sensitivities or served the politics of metropolitan France. In addition, with Racine replacing Corneille as the king's playwright in Versailles, a change that corresponded to different, emerging concepts of the hero and heroic behaviour, the *Relations* lost their purpose, and their audience. The Corneillian hero, who incarnated duty, abnegation of the self, and stoicism in suffering, was supplanted by the Racinian hero, who was much more problematic since passion, or overwhelming love, was always in conflict with duty, or reason: 'The heart has its reasons that reason ignores.' It was only with the return of the Jesuits to Canada in 1842, along with the birth of French-Canadian historiography and the emergence of French-Canadian literature, that the cult of the hero of New France became widespread in French Canada. The father of French-Canadian historiography, François-Xavier Garneau, certainly initiated this when he narrated the death of the Jesuit martyrs at the hands of the Iroquois in his ground-breaking *Histoire du Canada*, in which all the episodes are directly taken from the *Jesuit Relations*, the main source he cites. As Denis Martin (1988: 2) notes, the spreading of the cult of the hero in nineteenth-century French-Canadian society was mainly due to the clergy, who controlled the quasi-totality of historical production. During this period, most of the historians defined the nation by evoking and creating a glorious past between the time of discovery and the Conquest of 1759. As Guy Rocher remarks, 'It is generally in its past, in its history, through its former social organization that the colonized society will seek the values in which it will take refuge. Historical action finding no future in which to construct itself is concerned with elaborating a past that is more and more mythical.'[48] This vision of the past quickly spread to the general public, and the cult of the martyrs and great Christian figures of the Ancien Régime helped to define an imaginary historical space where the French-Canadian inhabitants could establish their national origins and unity in a common language, race, and religion.

PART III

Historiography and the Novel:
Nation and Identity

CHAPTER SEVEN

Before and after the Fall – The Historical Novel: *Les Anciens Canadiens* (*The Canadians of Old*)

Part two of this volume has been devoted to the elaboration of a semio-narratological theory and methodology that permits us to analyse the discovery texts – Cartier's *Voyages* – and parts of a vast corpus of writings on colonization – the *Jesuit Relations* – that provide some of the major themes of historiographical and literary production in nineteenth- and twentieth-century Quebec. In that section, I stressed that these narratives are founding texts which set the parameters and established the discursive representations of encounters between the Old World and the New. I attempted to show that Cartier's *Voyages* are, indeed, symbolical appropriations of New France through mapping, gridding, and naming that at one and the same time describe the land in terms of future colonization and conversion and construct the others, the encountered, within a stereotypical and socio-economic network that has been used over the years to justify their spoliation and exploitation. The same presuppositions inform the *Jesuit Relations* regarding the conversion of the Huron and future colonization. But, in addition to establishing strongly motivated stereotypes of the inhabitants of the New World, these narratives demonize the opponents of the faith and create a dangerous, cruel universe in which missionaries and the French are constantly menaced and persecuted by heathens. The missionaries, their domestics, and their Huron converts are depicted in this hostile environment, while a number of exemplary lives are traced of those who were actually executed during the wars with the Iroquois. Their tortures and deaths are delineated in gruesome detail, and the descriptions of tormented and torn bodies of these 'Martyrs' move readers in France to contribute financially to the well-being of the missions.

Such models of heroic behaviour, examples of great physical and moral strength, had a real effect on the population of the homeland until the last quarter of the seventeenth century, when their publication ceased. It was not until almost a century after the fall of Quebec in 1759 that these heroes – explorers and missionaries alike – along with the social, historical, and geographical environment of New France, were rehabilitated and proposed to the population by the historical and literary establishment as founding their collective identity as the French-Canadian nation, a people with a common origin, language, and faith. In this last section, I study the emergence of the novel in French Canada, all the while working out a historico-narratological theory that can account for the complex relationships that tie the imaginary individual to the family, to the group, to the nation, and to his or her lived environment.

However, like all other artefacts, novels do not appear in a void, but rather bear traces of complex interrelations with other texts and objects belonging to various cultural and institutional series. They are, therefore, written both for and against other narratives, and are considered as spinning intricate intertextual webs with diverse texts that take on disparate forms. My purpose in this chapter is to attempt to map schematically, from an elementary historico-narratological perspective, the various options open to writers from 1837 onwards, when the first novel, *L'Influence d'un livre*, by Philippe Aubert de Gaspé, *fils*,[1] appeared in Quebec, all the while concentrating upon the historical novel. Although the literary essay and the short story flourished in the nineteenth century in ever-increasing numbers,[2] the novel as a literary genre was not prominent. No author in Quebec actually published an *œuvre* of note during this century,[3] and most brought out only a single volume in their lifetime.

Numerous reasons can be cited to account for the ambiguous and precarious status of the novel during this period:[4] the lack of a publishing and distribution infrastructure, including the paucity of lending libraries or book dealers; the prohibitive cost of producing bound volumes; the difficulty and expense of putting out fascicules and distributing them to a highly dispersed population of potential readers;[5] competition from imported novels or translations from France, especially from 1850 onwards; or even the lack of literary journals that could legitimize writing in the province. Nevertheless, as Hayne (1977: 39) notes, it was in 1853 that G.H. Cherrier in his '*Avis de l'éditeur de Charles Guérin*' launched the publishing of literary texts in French Canada: 'Dans l'état actuel des choses, nous croyons donc avoir fait un acte de courage et de bon exemple, en achetant les premiers une œuvre littéraire, en offrant à un de nos écrivains une rémunération assurée, si mince qu'elle soit, pour son travail, en lui épargnant les risques et les ennuis de la publication qu'il était du reste bien décidé à ne plus supporter' (In the actual state of affairs, we believe we have committed an act of courage and given a good example. We are the first to buy a literary work, to offer one of our writers a guaranteed fee, no matter how small, for his work, thus sparing him the risks and worries of publication that he had in fact decided not to undertake).[6]

Other reasons given for the failure of the novel to emerge as a dominant genre within the community of readers until after the mid-nineteenth century are mainly of an institutional or ideological nature. Much as in France, the novel was considered a frivolous genre not consecrated by classicism.[7] Its authors had not yet succeeded in creating their own class of readers, nor had they theoretized the novel and their own creative activity in competition with other genres.[8] Their works could succeed in occupying the symbolic field only by establishing or appropriaating their own institutional instruments of legitimation, be they editorial (journals, newspapers, independent publishers, etc.), or academic (collèges classiques, lending libraries, etc.). In addition to being decried because of its so-called lack of seriousness,[9] the genre was also evaluated and gauged within the framework of traditional values coupled with an emerging nationalism.

On the one hand, the novel in general was condemned as a waste of time and a distraction from more useful activities that could better advance the social good. Imported from France, or translated into French from other literatures, novels were seen as depicting either societies radically different from the French-Canadian community of the times or imaginary worlds that the inhabitants could not identify with. As Etienne Parent declared in 1846, for example, in a speech given at the Institut Canadien,

> Ainsi, quel est le jeune Canadien qui, en prenant pour le lire un des romans du jour, puisse, la main sur la conscience se dire qu'il ne saurait plus utilement employer son temps et pour lui et pour son pays? En effet, qu'y apprendra-t-il? qu'y verra-t-il? des leçons de morale, en supposant qu'il y en ait? Son catéchisme lui a tout dit là-dessus, et bien mieux que ne sauraient le faire Eugène Sue et Alexandre Dumas. Des peintures de mœurs? lorsqu'il s'en rencontrera de fidèles, elles ne pourront que fausser ses idées dans les applications qu'il voudrait en fair, et ce sera un grand

mal. Mais la plupart du temps, il sera transporté dans un monde fantastique, où tout sera exagéré, chargé, caricaturé de telle sorte, que le lecteur européen lui-même ne s'y pourrait reconnaître.

(Hence, when picking up a recent novel, which young Canadian can say with a clear conscience that his time could not be put to better use, both for himself and for his country? Indeed, what can he learn from this? What can he see in this? Moral lessons, supposing they exist? His Catechism has already told him everything he needs to know, and much better than either Eugène Sue or Alexandre Dumas could. Descriptions of social mores? When he comes across those that are faithfully depicted, they will refer to a state of society so different from ours, that his ideas will simply be falsified when he attempts to put them in practice, and that would be very wrong. But most of the time he will be carried off in a world of fancy, where everything is exaggerated, overdone, caricatured, so much so that even a European reader would not be able to recognize himself in it.)[10]

On the other hand, an equally strong current of opinion attempted to legitimize the novel within the community of developing French-Canadian nationalists by stressing its didactic and moralistic virtues. As Aurèle Plamondon noted in 1844, in launching *Le Ménestrel*:

Dans ce tableau du cœur humain le lecteur intelligent peut trouver l'image de ce qu'il doit être; il y apprend ce qu'il doit à la patrie, ce qu'il doit à ceux qui l'entourent, ce qu'il doit à lui-même. Au récit d'une action héroïque, son cœur s'enflamme et bat d'une noble émotion, tandis que le crime et la lâcheté ne lui inspirent qu'horreur et dégoût; la peinture du bonheur domestique adoucit ses mœurs en offrant à son admiration la vie de l'homme simple et juste, présentée sous les couleurs les plus tendres ... les effets de la littérature sont donc d'insinuer dans le cœur les préceptes de morale dont la sévérité disparaît sous le prisme de la poésie.

(In this painting of the human heart, the intelligent reader can find the image of what he is and of what he should be. He learns what he owes to the homeland, what he owes to those surrounding him, what he owes to himself. At the tale of a heroic action his heart becomes impassioned and beats with noble emotion. While crime and cowardice inspire in him only horror and disgust; the painting of domestic bliss tempers his manners in offering up to his imagination the life of a simple and just man, presented under the most delicate of colours ... The effects of literature are therefore to instil in the heart moral precepts the harshness of which disappear under the prism of poetry.) (1–2)

In the same year, Joseph Doutre, in the preface to his novel *Les Fiancés de 1812. Essai de littérature canadienne*, makes an identical case while referring to one of the novels decried by Parent two years later. For Doutre, society must be transformed to become more just, social progress must rest on moral progress, and literature can contribute to such transformations and progress: 'Serions-nous d'ailleurs à une époque assez dépravée pour que le spectacle de la vertu et les horreurs du vice fussent pour rien dans les efforts et les progrès de la civilisation? Nous défions aucun homme public de produire autant de bien que l'a fait Eugène Sue par son admirable roman [referring to *Les Mystères de Paris*]' (Are we in an age so depraved that the spectacle of virtue and the horrors of vice happen to be for naught in the efforts and the progress of civilization? We defy any public person to produce as much good as has Eugène Sue with his admirable novel) (Doutre, 26).

Yet the novel genre would progressively impose itself, partially in serial form through newspapers and journals, partially in bound volumes, partially by slowly building up its readership, or again through literary criticism. In fact, journals, notably *Les Veillées canadiennes* and *La Ruche littéraire* in Montreal, and *Soirées canadiennes* and *Le Foyer canadien* in Quebec city, as well as literary societies such as the Club des Anciens, which met in Charles Hamel's bookstore from 1850 to 1860, and the École de Québec, which met at the Crémazie bookstore from 1860 onward, played an important role, not only in diffusing the genre but also in determining its form and content. During this period, a movement was launched by one of founders of the *Soirées canadiennes* and *Le Foyer canadien*, Abbé Casgrain, that was crucial in making the novel an agent of patriotic and religious action. As Hayne (1977) notes, the novelist was to serve the national cause by reviving the glories of the past: 'C'était sonner le glas du roman de mœurs contemporaines, et inaugurer le règne de la grande légende, du roman historique et du roman à thèse' (This was to sound the knell of the contemporary novel of manners, and inaugurate the reign of the grand legend, of the historical novel and of the 'roman à thèse') (67).

The historical and social conditions that shaped the Quebec novel of the nineteenth century also had a profound and prolonged impact on its literary criticism. Robidoux and Renaud (1966) begin their study on the twentieth-century Quebec novel by stating forthrightly that French-

Canadian literature is born from history and borne by history. In this seminal work, in which the authors examine the origins of the Quebec novel, they conclude that the novels produced during the first half of the nineteenth century are considered as mixing fiction with history by means of a conventional love plot that links historical episodes to descriptions of social customs and habits. For those with even a cursory knowledge of the history of French Canada, it is not surprising that the emergence of the novel is linked to events that shaped the aspirations and the imagination of successive generations. Until 1944, with the publication of Roger Lemelin's *Au pied de la pente douce*, followed in 1945 by Gabrielle Roy's internationally acclaimed *Bonheur d'occasion* (*The Tin Flute*), when the novel emigrated to the city, nationalistic and patriotic aspirations, by which characters were defined, measured, and valorized, were presented primarily through works with historical and agricultural backgrounds. However, in French Canada more than in other societies, the rise of the novel is closely linked to the advent of historiography. It is noteworthy that no histories of the province appeared from the time of the Conquest in 1759 until shortly after the Durham Report of 1839. None the less, the monumental *Histoire du Canada* by François-Xavier Garneau, published in four volumes in 1845, 1846, 1848, and 1852, can be considered as a partial response to Lord Durham's famous definition of French Canadians as a 'people without a history and without a literature.' Following Garneau, over the next forty years, seventeen other histories dealing with topics such as New France before the Conquest, Canada under English domination, famous French families of Canada, parishes, famous New France religious personages, First Nations people, institutions, law, and even popular history were published in an attempt to define the specific human, geographic, and historical identity of French Canadians before and after the Conquest. This quest for origins and identity was closely mirrored in literary works produced during the same period.

Of the fifty-three novels published in Quebec in the nineteenth century, twenty-six can be defined as historical novels, dealing mainly with subjects such as New France before the Conquest, the Conquest, the Canada–U.S. War of 1812, the Rebellions of 1837 and 1838, and the Acadian diaspora. This period saw the consolidation and propagation of an imaginary French-Canadian subject who anchored and constructed his or her origins in historicity, thereby creating personae rooted in the era of the Ancien Régime, with its codes of behaviour, valour, and honour predating the Conquest. Such subjects periodically confirmed their lineage at critical historical moments by reincarnating, reenacting, reliving, and redramatizing the codes in question, thereby systematically projecting a cultural heritage that defined the nation at the level of the imaginary.[11] Although the percentage of historical novels among works published in the twentieth century diminished progressively, their actual number still remained relatively high. From a thematic perspective, the historical novel massively inscribes imaginary personae who are dependent on a generally accepted and widely recognized referential code, situating their thoughts, actions, and passions in reconstituted topoi that supposedly existed in the past, thereby creating a 'historical' effect.

Although not the first historical novel written in Quebec, Philippe Aubert de Gaspé's *Les Anciens Canadiens*, which appeared in 1863, constituted a radical break from previous novels and was by far the most popular and widely read novel in nineteenth-century French Canada.[12] In fact, the first edition of 1000 volumes was sold out in a few months, and a second edition of 5000 volumes was published the following year in 1864, along with a translation into English, by Mrs G.M. Pennée, entitled *The Canadians of Old*.[13] Further editions and translations appeared throughout the nineteenth and twentieth centuries, contributing substantially to the lustre of the author's reputation.[14] The success of this novel is all the more remarkable given that popular education was not extensive and literacy was still largely confined to the élite segments of the population.

Philippe Aubert de Gaspé, who published this text, his very first novel, at the age of seventy-six, takes an active part in the relation of his tale of before and after the fall of Quebec city to the English in 1759, so that it is often difficult to distinguish him from the narrator. In his opening chapter, Aubert de Gaspé establishes the protocol for a rudimentary poetics and aesthetics of the novel. He first of all informs his readers, whom he addresses directly, that he has no intention of composing a classical work, and then narrates how he came to write this book at his advanced age: 'Ceux qui me connaissent seront sans doute surpris de me voir commencer le métier d'auteur à soixante et seize ans; je leur dois une explication' (Those who know me will undoubtedly be surprised to see me begin the profession of author at the age of seventy-six; I owe them an explanation) (15). He openly acknowledges that his work is not perfect; nor is it a work of art: 'J'admettrai franchement qu'il y a mille défauts dans ce livre, et que je les connais' (I will frankly admit that there are a thousand imperfections in this book and I am aware of them) (16). He then attempts to disarm his potential critic: 'Je n'ai pas assez d'amour-propre pour tenir le moins du monde à mes productions littéraires. Consigner quelques épisodes du bon vieux temnps, quelques souvenirs d'une jeunesse, hélas! bien éloignée, voilà toute mon ambition' (I do not have enough pride to take seriously in the least my literary productions. To describe some episodes of the good old times, some memories of my youth, alas, long gone, that is my foremost ambition) (16). He goes on, continuing to protect himself from malevolent criticism by shifting the responsibility for undertaking this work to others: 'Plusieurs anecdotes paraîtront, sans doute, insignifiantes et puériles à bien des lecteurs: qu'ils jettent le blâme sur quelques-uns de nos meilleurs littérateurs, qui m'ont prié de ne rien omettre sur les mœurs des anciens Canadiens' (Several anecdotes will undoubtedly appear insignificant and childish to many a reader: let them throw the blame on some of our best authors, who asked me to omit nothing of the morals and the customs of the Canadians of old) (16–17).

Finally, the real import of his narrative becomes clear. He owes the truth to the past, to the dead, for his task will be to restore the memory of the collective group, to reconstitute the temporal arc – past-present-future – of a people before the Conquest, and to show that though it did not, as Lord Durham suggested, possess either a written literature or a written history, it still had an extremely rich oral tradition, handed down from generation to generation, founded in its own history in the seigneurial system as it existed in New France. Aubert de Gaspé is also aware of what the activity of the novelist should be for a specific class of readers under British rule: 'ce livre ne sera ni trop bête, ni trop spirituel. Trop bête! certes, un auteur doit se respecter tant soit peu. Trop spirituel! il ne serait apprécié que des personnes qui ont beaucoup d'esprit, et, sous un gouvernement constitutionnel, le candidat préfère la quantité à la qualité' (this book will be neither too foolish, nor too witty. Too foolish! Of course, an author must have the minimum of self-respect. Too witty! He would be appreciated only by people who have a great deal of wit, and, under a constitutional government, political candidates prefer quantity over quality) (17). His text, which he would like to be: 'entirely Canadian with respect to style,' will be original and independent of modern-day literary fads, as he '[entend] bien avoir, aussi, [s]es coudées franches, et ne [s]'assujjétir à aucunes règles prescrites, – qu'[il] conna[ît] d'ailleurs, – dans un ouvrage comme celui qu'[il] publie. Que les puristes, les littérateurs émérites, choqués de ces défauts, l'appellent roman, mémoire, chronique, salmigondis, pot-pourri: peu

The Historical Novel: *Les Anciens Canadiens* 139

[l]'importe' (expects to have free reign, and be exempt from any prescribed rules – which [he] happen(s) to know – in a work such as the one [he is] publishing. Let the purists, the most highly skilled literary hacks, shocked by these faults, call it novel, memoirs, chronicle, hodgepodge, pot-pourri, no matter!) (17). His narrative is especially addressed to the class of readers he is targeting and writing for, that is to say, those true patriots whose language, race, and religion, in spite of the Conquest, are rooted in the distant past of the origins of New France: 'Ce qui paraîtra insignifiant et puéril aux yeux des étrangers, me disaient-ils, ne laissera pas d'intéresser les vrais Canadiens, dans la chronique d'un septuagénaire né vingt-huit ans seulement après la conquête de la Nouvelle-France' (What will appear insignificant and childish in the eyes of foreigners, they told me, will without a doubt interest true Canadians, in the chronicle of a seventy-year-old born twenty-eight years after the conquest of New France) (17).

Though *Les Anciens Canadiens* is not a sophisticated text from an aesthetic perspective, nevertheless it remains a complex work from two points of view. First, the initial section of the novel, which narrates the habits and customs of New France in the form of a voyage through the province, is somewhat different in tone and theme from the second section, which is directly related to the fall of Quebec and the aftermath of the battle of the Plains of Abraham. The novel only very loosely integrates the various series of events into the unity of a single action.[15] Moreover, even though its form remains fundamentally hybrid, since it hesitates between being an actual historical document and a work of fiction, one could possibly argue that its so-called unity is ensured by the author's addition of seventy-five pages of notes and explanations at the end of the tale. None the less, the tension between its mixed and contradictory aims, to tell the truth (history), and to give aesthetic pleasure in telling a tale (fiction), creates both a 'reality' and a 'historical' effect, where the suspension of belief is systematically brought back to the cognitive dimension of the recognition of a common past shared by author and reader.

Second, Aubert de Gaspé's narrator is highly involved in his tale and identifies with the main protagonists of the novel. The enunciator often interrupts the flow of his story of yesteryear with the now of the gnomic (neither past time nor past space), thereby collapsing or shading the past into the eternal present of the reader's each and every actualized reading, thus instituting collective durativity and permanence. But the enunciator is not simply a passive recorder of former times; he is, in fact, massively present in his novel. He takes sides, evaluates, makes positive and negative comments; he is ironic, judgmental, impassioned, and emotional. His modesty and good humour are infectious. He is extremely fond of his characters, who are truly part of his inner life and being, and he makes them come alive before our eyes. The conclusion of the novel is emblematic of the narrator's skill as an extremely effective storyteller, his empathy for the universe he has created, and his belief in the authenticity of his narrative.

As a matter of fact, there are two endings to the story. The narrator brings closure to his tale in the past tense by relating Jules's ongoing fidelity to the memory and customs of his parents under the Ancien Régime in Quebec before the Conquest. Then, without transition, the role of narrator is suddenly assumed by the author himself, who speaks in his own name and in the present tense: 'L'auteur a tant d'affection pour les principaux personnages de cette véridique histoire, qu'il lui en coûte de les faire disparaître de la scène: on s'attache naturellement aux fruits de ses œuvres. Il craindrait aussi d'affliger ceux des lecteurs qui partagent son attachement pour ses héros, en les tuant d'un coup de plume ...' (The author is so fond of his principal characters of this true story, that it pains him to make them disappear from the scene; one becomes naturally attached to the fruits of one's labours. He also fears afflicting those of his readers who share his attachment for his heroes, by killing them off with a stroke of the pen ...) (280). Still in the present, the author continues by evoking a typical recurring scene, with the entire family, composed of Jules, his nameless spouse, and his son and daughter, gathered by the fireside, while Blanche and Archibald play a game of chess. Young Arché d'Haberville[16] is both following the game and contemplating the blazing fire in the hearth when his father asks him what he is thinking about. The son replies: 'J'ai suivi avec un intérêt toujours croissant un petit groupe d'hommes, de femmes, d'enfants qui marchaient, sautaient, montaient, descendaient; et puis tout a disparu' (I have followed with an ever-increasing interest a small group of men, women, and children who were walking, dancing, jumping, climbing, descending; then everything disappeared) (281). Like a retrospective poetics of the very act of writing and reading, the author, blending, folding, and fading the 'imaginary' into the 'real,' fiction into reality, the past into the present, directly addresses all of his future and potential readers: 'Semblables à ces figures fantastiques que regardait le jeune d'Haberville, mes personnages, cher lecteur, se sont agités pendant quelque temps devant vos yeux, pour disparaître tout à coup

The Historical Novel: *Les Anciens Canadiens* 141

peut-être pour toujours, avec celui qui les faisait mouvoir. Adieu donc aussi, cher lecteur, avant que ma main, plus froide que nos hivers du Canada, refuse de tracer mes pensées' (Like those figures of fantasy that young d'Haberville was looking at, my characters, Dear Reader, bustled about for some time before your eyes, and disappeared suddenly, perhaps forever, with him who animated them. Farewell too, Dear Reader, before my hand, colder than our Canadian winters, refuses to continue to trace my thoughts) (281).

The value systems, or axiology, this work develops and displays, served as models for subsequent historical novels, especially with respect to the construction of the imaginary French-Canadian subject. The plot is rather straightforward. The novel opens with two friends, Jules d'Haberville and Archibald Cameron of Locheill, leaving school in Quebec city in the spring of 1757, the former to serve in the French army, the latter in the English army. Archibald visits Jules's family manor, and the first part of the novel deals with the seigneurial system in New France, and the mores and customs of the inhabitants. The second section of the novel opens in the spring of 1759 with the British invasion of New France, during which Jules and Archibald oppose one another in battle. Jules is wounded, the d'Haberville family is ruined, and Archibald, victorious, is promoted to the rank of major. Unknown to the d'Habervilles, he helps the family by ingratiating himself with General Murray. After the fall, both he and Jules leave Canada: the former goes back to England, and the latter to France. They both return to Canada seven years later, Jules having married a nameless English woman and sworn allegiance to the crown. In contrast, Archibald, who was in love with Jules's sister, Blanche, finds his love unrequited, as Blanche wishes to remain faithful to the old order, the only way she can prove her patriotism and fidelity to the past. Both Blanche and Archibald swear not to marry anyone else, and the Scotsman settles on land next to the d'Haberville's. The end of the novel shows Archibald helping to raise Jules's family, while he himself remains unwed.

Within a semio-narrative framework, where subjects are defined in a conjunctive or disjunctive relation with an object of value desired by other subjects, one could rewrite the previous script in the following way. Initially, before the British invasion, the masculine subjects evolve in an ordered world that articulates the values of the seigneurial system. Intersubjective relationships are predicated on the existence of a contractual universe, whether those contracts link the seigneur to the clergy or to the 'habitants' or even to other members of the seigneurial class. Again, if one assumes that, for a subject to be able to perform, it must be competent to do so, then the question arises as to the nature of the competence of the performing subject in this universe. As I have noted in previous chapters, however, a simple solution to the problem of working out a semiotics of the subject is to posit the existence of a limited number of modalities that inform the performing agent. When examining the actions of all the agents or subjects in the universe of *Les Anciens Canadiens* in terms of the modalities, it can be seen that all subjects of European origin have different types of knowledge (habitant versus seigneur versus clergy, for example) that coexist in harmony. However, all of this knowledge is rooted in long-standing tradition handed down from France and adapted to Canada. The same holds true for wanting-to, or desire, where each agent possesses different desires that are all determined and regulated by a specific social and cultural order. As for being-able-to or ability, individuals are differentiated according to physical characteristics linked to genetics and/or race. Both Archibald and Jules are constructed in terms of clichés: the former, of British origin, is tall, blond, blue-eyed, freckled, with a prominent chin, extremely strong and calm; the latter, of Latin blood, is slight, short, dark, black-eyed, lively, agitated, and quick. The women also have similar traits, thus corresponding to recognizable nationalistic commonplaces and stereotypes.

Yet what defines each and every agent is his or her having-to-do or having-to-be. In *Les Anciens Canadiens*, this deontic modality governs all the others in the series – that is, for a subject to do or to be, it has to do or be in the mode of duty, whether from a social, religious, educational, political, or ethical point of view. Hence, duty permits the subject or agent to perform, or to be. From this perspective, one can see that all interacting subjects, be they polemical or contractual, are governed by a deontic modality anchored in a universe of traditional values that ensure the cohesion of the group. There is no room here for agents whose behaviour or performance is regulated by the modality of desire. In this universe, the energized subject is never an individual erotic subject but must act according to pre-established patterns handed down from the past. Tradition and fidelity to language, race, and religion motivate behaviour and guarantee the survival, and even prosperity, of a conquered homogeneous nation. In short, this imaginary universe sets in play an agent that we can call a collective subject, since it can only reproduce and realize the perceived values of the group.[17] No individual agent can want or desire for itself and by itself. Nor can two subjects reciprocally desire each other and actualize this desire outside the norms of wedlock and family, sanctioned by the group through its social, cultural, and religious institutions. Here the subject, or *I*, is, in fact, another, or *we*.

Les Anciens Canadiens, much like all other historical novels written in nineteenth-century Quebec, puts in place and explores complex spatial structures that are positively or negatively invested as the narrative unfolds. The historical novel, the novel of change and complicity, understanding and collaboration, nostalgia and loss, establishes, by superimposing them, two specific domains and two distinct temporal moments where subjects realize their aspirations in the mode of conflict, defeat, and resignation.[18] The historical novel, by definition, will articulate a tri-dimensional temporal structure, in which an absolutely valorized past (time and place) has been violently eradicated and fundamentally transformed by a singular cataclysmic event that imposes a degraded future necessity.[19] From this perspective, the past becomes a locus of dream and regret, the present an instance of the enunciation of loss, and the future a projected faded discontinuity.

The opening chapter of *Les Anciens Canadiens* is emblematic of the spatio-temporal organization of the nineteenth-century historical novel. The 'first narrative' opens immediately after the author's remarks in his preface with a brief, original poem, which functions as an epigraph, consisting of three quatrains written in alexandrine verse.[20] This poem, to Quebec city of old, is descriptive and refers back to the beginnings of the colony before the Conquest, establishing ancient roots and glory in the era of the Ancien Régime. The first stanza, in which the animated and living city dominates the St Lawrence, sings the praise of former glory and relations to French monarchy. The second establishes the joyful and glorious links of state and church, and the latter's omnipresence and happy acceptance by the population. The third evokes the passage of 'wilderness' to 'culture,' and the bloody 'Canadien'–Iroquois[21] wars during the period of colonization. Yet this poem, which encapsulates the first 150 years of the French presence in Quebec without any reference to the present of enunciation, is immediately followed by a description that recapitulates both the state of the country before the Conquest and the state of affairs after it. I suggest, contrary to what is generally assumed by the traditional distinction made in literary theory between description and story, that, from my theoretical perspective, description is neither a static system of spatialization that sets the coordinates and conditions for action, nor a means for the reader to 'imagine' the universe in which agents evolve. Rather, what a text sets in play is not simply a description in the narrative, but a narrative in the description, where value systems and states of affairs are transformed into states of feelings and meanings.

In fact, this initial prose description functions as an embryonic, virtual recapitulation, an actual *'mise en abyme,'* or micronarrative, announcing the events that will radically transform and alter the French presence in Canada. The narrator begins by inviting his reader to go back in time to the period before the fall of Québec: 'Que ceux qui connaissent notre bonne cité de Québec se transportent, en corps ou en esprit, sur le marché de la haute ville, ne serait-ce que pour juger des changements survenus dans cette localité depuis l'an grâce 1757, époque à laquelle commence cette histoire' (Let those who know our good city of Quebec return in body or soul to the market of the upper town, if only to judge the changes that have occurred here since the year 1757, the date when this story begins) (17–18). He then describes the same cathedral as the one in the poem by comparing it to the cathedral of today, changed by the addition of a modern tower. The Jesuit college of former times has now become a military barracks, but:

> Qu'est devenue l'église construite jadis à la place des halles actuelles? Où est le bocage d'arbres séculaires, derrière ce temple, qui ornaient la cour maintenant si nue, si déserte, de cette maison consacrée à l'éducation de la jeunesse canadienne? La hache et le temps, hélas! ont fait leur œuvre de destruction. Aux joyeux ébats, aux saillies spirituelles des jeunes élèves, aux pas graves des professeurs qui s'y promenaient pour se délasser d'études profondes, aux entretiens de haute philosophie, ont succéder le cliquetis des armes, les propos de corps de garde, souvent libres et saugrenus!

> (What has become of the church formerly built on the spot of the current market? Where is the grove of century-old trees behind this temple, which embellished the yard, now so empty, so deserted, of this establishment dedicated to the education of Canadian youth? The axe and time have wrought their work of destruction. The joyous frolics, the witty comments of young students, the solemn steps of professors who walked to relax from scholarly work or philosophical discussions have been replaced by the clatter of arms, and guardroom banter that is often unrestrained and ludicrous.) (18)

The description of the past and present continues, accentuating the glorious, animated, intellectual, and homogenous state of the city, *there*, where all lived in peace, calm, and harmony and where now the opposite is true. Moreover, in former times no foreign presence disrupted the link between fatherland and country, but now the joys of intellectual and spiritual life have been eradicated and replaced by occupying forces from *elsewhere* that impose another order, another system of governance and social interaction.

The young d'Haberville befriends Archibald of Locheill, a Scots Catholic who is perfectly bilingual, and the two become inseparable friends. They spend ten years in college together and, after graduation, Jules's father, a seigneur, invites the young man to spend time in his manor with his son before they both leave for Europe in 1757, Jules to serve in the French army, and Archibald in the British. During their long trip to the manor house, where, on arrival, the foreigner is adopted by the family and then becomes enamoured of Blanche, the daughter, they discover and talk about the habits and customs of yesteryear. Moreover, they also experience the physical and moral dangers of the *wilderness*, when Archibald saves a family worker from certain drowning by plunging into the river at ice break-up and swimming to safety. In the course of their journey, they also learn about the indigenous people, as well as the phantoms, criminals, and werewolves that are omnipresent in the forest. When they arrive at the manor house, *here*, they are greeted with great warmth and love. *Here* begins the idyllic narration of the customs and religious celebrations under the protection of the seigneur: the Feast of May, that of Saint John the Baptist, evening dances, dinners, and story telling about legends and deeds of the past.

War erupts, and the conflict, *elsewhere*, is played out in Quebec with the two soul brothers fighting for opposing armies. The British forces destroy and burn all in their wake: countryside and manor are torched. The French also revert to guerrilla warfare, using their Native allies to try to stem the tide of destruction. In fact, the person saved from drowning by Archibald rescues him from torture and certain death at the hands of a group of Native warriors, after he is taken prisoner by them. As a result of the fall, *here* is now but a shadow of its former glory. The family has lost most of its fortune and influence, and a small and impoverished manor has been built to replace the splendours of the past. *There*, has also been transformed fundamentally by the massive intrusion of the new order from *elsewhere*, and the *beyond* of the wilderness is no more, since the French no longer can form alliances with the Native people to counter the British presence in New France. The die has been cast, and the changing age imposes a break with the past, a space and time of discontinuity and new beginnings with which subjects will have to renegotiate their futures and identities. It should be noted, though, that these new horizons do not, in fact, correspond to a complete break with the past, but rather are presented as forms of possible negotiations of continuity in change. And from this perspective, the numerous interventions of the narrator in the novel, as well as the notes and explanations at the end of it, can be considered as promptings and formulae to incite and help his readers to come to grips, as he himself has done, with the past and the future, the past in the future.

Les Anciens Canadiens at both the diegetic and the narrative levels figurativizes and thematizes the emergence of a new awareness of state and identity.[22] At the thematic and figurative levels, three generations of characters are involved in an effort to come to grips with and offer solutions to the problem of nationality that is played out. In this novel, before the Conquest, at the thematic level, nationality is defined by means of the French language, the Catholic faith, and the customs, traditions, laws, and institutions of the transplanted inhabitants of New France. The members of the oldest generation, made up of Jules d'Haberville's parents and extended family, are not active participants in the struggle between the French and the English for the control of North America. Hence, Jules's father and uncle, who were born in France and have strong family and social connections there, and whose sworn enemies are the English, accept the defeat of France and the emergence of a new subject with a dual identity. Jules's father pardons Archibald Cameron of Locheill (who has led an English company during the war of 1759) for following Montgomery's orders to burn down the manor house. After receiving a letter from his son, who is convalescing in France, in a conversation with the other members of the family he strongly expresses the opinion that Jules should return to Canada, since

> Ses plus chers intérêts sont ici où il est né. Le Canada est sa patrie naturelle; et il ne peut avoir le même attachement pour celle de ses ancêtres. Sa position, d'ailleurs, est bien différente de la mienne: ce qui serait lâcheté chez moi, sur le bord de la tombe, n'est qu'un acte de devoir pour lui qui commence à peine la vie ... Le nouveau gouverneur est déjà bien disposé

The Historical Novel: *Les Anciens Canadiens* 147

en notre faveur ... il a exprimé, en maintes occasions, combien il compatissait aux malheurs de braves officiers qu'il avait rencontrés face à face sur le champ de bataille, et que la fortune, et non le courage, avait trahis ... Qu'il prête serment de fidélité à la couronne d'Angleterre; et mes dernières paroles dans nos adieux suprêmes seront: 'Sers ton souverain anglais avec autant de zèle, de dévouement, de loyauté, que j'ai servi le monarque français, et reçois ma bénédiction.'

([H]is dearest interests are here where he was born. Canada is his natural country; and he cannot have the same attachment here as for the land of his ancestors. His situation, moreover, is very different from mine: what would be cowardly for me, at the edge of my grave, is simply an act of duty for him who is barely beginning in life ... The new governor is already very positively disposed in our favour ... he has expressed on numerous occasions how much he sympathized with the misfortune suffered by the courageous officers that he met face to face on the battleground, and who had been betrayed by fate and not by lack of courage ... Let him swear allegiance to the Crown of England; and my last words in our final parting will be: 'Serve your English Sovereign with as much zeal, devotion and loyalty, as I have served my French Monarch, and receive my benediction.') (235–6)

The narrator adds in a footnote: 'Telles furent les dernières paroles du grand-père de l'auteur à son fils unique' (These were the last words the author's grandfather said to his only son) (236).

The second generation of this family is a composite one, made up of Jules and his sister, Blanche, who have been born, raised, and educated in New France. In a conversation during which Jules tries to convince Blanche to marry Cameron of Locheill, who loves her and whom she has rejected for ideological reasons, she clearly articulates the aspirations of this group: 'Si tu épousais une Anglaise, mon cher Jules, je la recevrais dans mes bras avec toute l'affection d'une sœur chérie ... Il est naturel, il est même à souhaiter que les races française et anglo-saxonne, ayant maintenant une même patrie, vivant sous les mêmes lois, après des haines, après des luttes séculaires, se rapprochent par des alliances intimes' (If you married an Englishwoman, my dear Jules, I would embrace her with open arms, with all the affection of a cherished sister ... It is natural, it is desirable that the French and Anglo-Saxon races, now occupying the same country, living under the same laws, after hating each other, after endless battles, should get closer together through intimate alliances) (267–8). In this same conversation, Blanche, who herself admits that she has not fought in the war, deems that it would be cowardly for her to marry someone from the conquering race.[23] 'Il serait indigne de moi d'en donner l'exemple après tant de désastres; on croirait, comme je l'ai dit à Arché, que le fier Breton, après avoir vaincu et ruiné le père, a acheté avec son or la pauvre fille canadienne, trop heureuse de se donner à ce prix' (It would be unworthy of me to give the example after so many disasters. People would believe, as I told Arché, that the proud Briton, after having conquered and ruined the father, had bought with his gold the poor Canadian woman, who was too happy to sell herself for this price) (268). And so, wedded to values of pre-Conquest New France, Blanche[24] does not marry Arché. They both decide to remain celibate and have no descendants in the new order.

The third generation, born in Canada of the alliance between French and English – 'Jules épousa l'année suivante la blonde fille d'Albion, qui sut bien vite gagner le cœur de tous ceux qui l'entouraient' (Jules married the following year the blond Albion woman, who quickly gained the hearts of all those around her) (275) – represents the way of the future for French Canadians who did not participate directly in the colonial wars between France and England. Jules and his nameless spouse, like his own parents, have two children, a boy named Arché, after his closest friend, and a girl not given a name in the novel, who both share all the national characteristics of the two nationalities. The boy's upbringing is entrusted to Uncle Raoul, who had been wounded in the wars and who, when his grand-nephew turns four, proudly states that: 'Le petit gaillard ... aura le bouillant courage des d'Haberville, avec la ténacité et l'indépendance des fiers insulaires dont il est issu par sa mère' (The little fellow ... will have the fiery courage of the Habervilles, and the tenacity and independence of the proud islanders on his mother's side) (276). In brief, the amalgamation has occurred, and the death-bed words of Captain Haberville to his son are an iteration of the first remarks he made before Jules returned to Canada: 'Sers ton nouveau souverain avec autant de fidélité que j'ai servi le roi de France; et que Dieu te bénisse, mon cher fils, pour la consolation que tu m'as donnée' (Serve your new sovereign with as much fidelity as I served the King of France; and God bless you, my dear son, for the consolation you have given me) (275).

The narrator, in his commentaries, footnotes, and seventy-five pages of endnotes, reiterates the same logic as his characters, linking the nation to a homeland (France) and the homeland to a country (England) and, consequently, to the political and military power of that country. Historiography has rehabilitated and heroized the conquered inhabitants of New France and their descendants. At the very beginning of the section on the Franco-British war, Aubert de Gaspé addresses himself directly to his readers: 'Honneur, cent fois honneur à notre compatriote, M. Garneau, qui a déchiré le voile qui couvrait vos exploits! Honte à nous, qui, au lieu de fouiller les anciennes chroniques si glorieuses pour notre race, nous contentions de baisser la tête sous le reproche humiliant de peuple conquis qu'on nous jetait à la face à tout propos' (Honour, honour a hundred times to our compatriot M. Garneau,[25] who has torn the veil that covered your exploits! Shame on us, who, instead of searching the ancient chronicles so glorious for our race, were content to bow our heads under the humiliating blame of a conquered people that is constantly being thrown up at us) (162). Aubert de Gaspé clearly distinguishes between the sentimental homeland, before the Conquest, which is at the root of nationality, and the real country to which one owes loyalty, by condemning what occurred in France from the middle of the eighteenth century to the end of the monarchy: 'Je suis loin de croire cependant que tout soit perdu: la cession du Canada a peut-être été, au contraire, un bienfait pour nous; la révolution de 93, avec toutes ses horreurs, n'a pas pesé sur cette heureuse colonie, protégée alors par le drapeau britannique. Nous avons cueilli de nouveaux lauriers en combattant sous les glorieuses enseignes de l'Angleterre, et deux fois la colonie a été sauvée par la vaillance de ses nouveaux sujets' (I am far from believing, however, that all is lost; the transfer of Canada was, perhaps, a good thing for us; the revolution of 1793, with all its horrors, did not weigh on this happy colony, which was protected by the British flag. We have gathered new laurels by fighting under the glorious colours of England, and twice the colony was saved through the valour of its new subjects) (163). Thankful to have escaped the excesses of the French Revolution and to be protected by the British crown from annexation by the United States, Aubert de Gaspé concludes that it is the status of colony and colonized that now guarantees nationality founded in a pre-revolutionary heroic past. 'À la tribune, au barreau, sur les champs de bataille, partout sur son petit théâtre, le Canadien a su prouver qu'il n'était inférieur à aucune race. Vous avez lutté pendant un siècle, ô mes compatriotes! pour maintenir votre nationalité, et grâce à votre persévérance, elle est encore intacte; mais l'avenir vous réserve peut-être un autre siècle de luttes et de combats pour la conserver. Courage et union, mes compatriotes!' (In the parliament, in court, on the battlefield, everywhere in its small theatre, the Canadian has proven that he was not inferior to any race. You have struggled for a century, oh my compatriots! to maintain your nationality, and thanks to your perseverance, it remains intact; but the future perhaps holds out to you another century of struggles and combats to keep it. Courage and union, my compatriots) (163). The rehabilitation of the past, firmly anchored in the homeland before the regicide that swept away social and religious values, is a necessary condition for accepting a new monarchy founded on divine right which substitutes one symbolic order for another. This, on the one hand, preserves distinctive national features and traits and, on the other, guarantees the collective interests of the country of Canada.

Aubert de Gaspé's conception of French-Canadian nationality and nation echoes for the most part the program sketched by François-Xavier Garneau in the conclusion of his monumental history of Canada when he states 'Ce people a grandi de lui-même, sans secours étranger, dans sa foi religieuse, et sa nationalité' (This people has grown up alone, without any foreign help, in its religious faith and its nationality) (715). For both Garneau and Aubert de Gaspé, this people has shown 'qu'il conserve quelque chose de la noble nation dont il tire son origine' (that it maintains something of the noble nation of its origins) (715), and that it has founded all of its politics on its own conservation. By maintaining its language and religion, it has helped England keep a foothold in America in 1775 and 1812. The English flag flying over the citadel of Quebec has forced the young republic of America to act with prudence. In contrast to Aubert de Gaspé,[26] though, who has a very different agenda of justifying his own ideological position, Garneau believes that 'Les Canadiens-Français forment un people de cultivateurs, dans un climat rude et sévère' (French Canadians are an agricultural people, in a harsh and severe climate) (716). Moreover, they both hold the view that they are also descendants of 'cette France qui se tient à la tête de la civilisation européenne depuis la chute de l'empire romain' (that France which has been in the vanguard of European civilization since the fall of the Roman Empire) (716). Their greatest wish is 'Que les Canadiens soient fidèles à eux-mêmes; qu'ils soient sages et persévérants, qu'ils ne se laissent point séduire par le brillant des nouveautés sociales et politiques!' (That the Canadians remain faithful to themselves; that they be wise and persevering, that they not let themselves be seduced by the glitter of new social and political ideas!) (717). Quebec is, and must remain, a conservative society since 'Pour nous une partie de notre force vient de nos traditions; ne nous en éloignons ou ne les changeons que graduellement' (For us, a part of our strength comes from our traditions; let us not stray from them or let us only change them gradually) (718).

CHAPTER EIGHT

Family, Group, and Nation in the Nineteenth-Century Agrarian Novel: *La Terre paternelle* (*The Paternal Farm*)

In chapter 7, I examined *Les Anciens Canadiens*, an exemplary nineteenth-century historical novel that has remained extremely popular, even until today. I now focus on a less obvious and more subtle inscription of historicity in the agrarian novel, the most widely published genre of the first century of literary production in Quebec. I begin once again by proposing a simple semio-narrative framework for the historico-narratological study of a type of text that circumscribes the subject's activity within the confines of a clearly defined homogeneous topography or territory. Positively invested agents can realize and fulfil their destiny from a social, political, ethical, and religious perspective only within a specific space. Other forms of the novel obviously existed during this period – the novel of manners and the moralistic novel, for example – but they never attained the popularity of what Bernard Proulx (1987) calls '*le roman du territoire*,' or the agrarian novel.

The first such novel, Patrice Lacombe's *La Terre paternelle* (*The Paternal Farm*), published in 1846, established a pattern that would continue for more than a hundred years. From the point of view of literary technique and popularity, though, the genre would reach its zenith with Louis Hémon's *Maria Chapdelaine* (1916) and Ringuet's *Trente arpents* (1938), and would more or less come to an end with Germaine Guèvremont's *Marie-Didace* (1947).[1] As Jean-Pierre Duquette (1982) has written, 'Avec cette œuvre de Germaine Guèvremont, c'est exactement un siècle de roman québécois traditionnel qui s'achève; roman paysan, du terroir, régionaliste, de la fidélité, nos cent premières années de création romanesque sont très largement dominées par le thème de la terre' (With the appearance of Germaine Guèvremont's work, exactly one century of the traditional Quebec novel comes to a close; the rural novel, the novel of the land, the regionalist novel, the novel of fidelity, under these various classifications, the first one hundred years of the production of the novel are greatly dominated by the theme of the land) (611).[2]

Space, the mapping of space, boundaries, and frontiers now become the topoi by and within which the subject's identity is constructed. For the sake of this analysis, I distinguish two types of agrarian novels: the novel of the paternal farm, transmitted from one generation to the other along family lines, as exemplified by *La Terre paternelle* and *Trente arpents*; and the novel of colonization, as exemplified by *Maria Chapdelaine* and *Marie-Didace*, in which the clearing of land and the demarcation of the frontier mime the original gesture of delimiting the space that delineates the agent's domains of activity. Yet, insofar as each of these novels integrates subjects within (or ejects them beyond) boundaries that are clearly identifiable though different in scope, I have decided to focus on Patrice Lacombe's *La Terre paternelle*, a seminal work that inaugurates a series of texts which offer solutions, at the level of the imaginary, to the fundamental problematic I have identified: that is, the articulation of humanized topoi in which socialized and historialized subjects can realize their potential with respect to the survival, the continuation, and the development of the group, the race, and the nation. It also establishes and elaborates a poetics and an aesthetics of the novel that is indigenous to French Canada by contrasting it to the dominant literary production of the period in metropolitan France. Indeed, it is in the conclusion of *La Terre paternelle* that Lacombe, both directly and indirectly, attempts to define what the activity and aims of the novelist should be, what the novel as a genre should be and do, and, finally, what the reader – more especially his own French-Canadian reader – should be and believe.

Lacombe begins by distinguishing two types of indigenous novels. Those of the first type, though written in Quebec, are derivative, borrowing their inspiration mainly from Gothic and Romantic models as represented by Honoré de Balzac, Victor Hugo, Eugène Sue, and other proponents of these genres. Philippe Aubert de Gaspé, *fils*, and Joseph Doutre are seen as being representative of this class of authors. These novels, with their surprises, quids pro quo, violence, and gore, are vehicles for a cosmopolitan ideology that in no way corresponds to what the moral, cultural, religious, and social aspirations of the French-Canadian reader should be. In Lacombe's view, the agrarian novel – and I would extend this to include the historical novel as well – in its own special way, is a novel of fidelity to the past. It is also an art form to be emulated, since somehow it defines what the characters in the text should be and should do. These two major forms of the Quebec novel in the nineteenth century (the historical and the agrarian) articulate the conditions of before and after the fall, before and after the Conquest. They also propose a solution to this traumatic and unthinkable moment based on the construction of an identity of a subject in terms of social, historical, cultural, and religious values founded in long-term continuity. Moreover, these two genres define themselves against the French metropolitan novel and promulgate a distinctly nationalistic program and agenda.

The conclusion of *La Terre paternelle* identifies two specific types of novels – international and national – and defines them in terms of a series of oppositions: French/Romantic/Gothic/heterogeneous/exaggerated/unbelievable/open versus Québécois/agrarian/historical/homogeneous/sober/true/closed. Initially, the novel as genre is inscribed in an ideological, sociocultural, historical context and is construed as corresponding directly to the values of the society in which it is written. Its form and content, its decor, the verisimilitude of the actions, thoughts, and passions of its protagonists, along with their intersubjective relations, are considered as reflecting directly the individuals and groups represented in the ambient society: 'Quelques-uns de nos lecteurs auraient peut-être désiré que nous eussions donné un dénouement tragique à notre histoire; ils auraient aimé à voir nos acteurs disparaître violemment de la scène, les uns après les autres, et notre récit se terminer dans le genre terrible, comme un grand nombre de romans du jour' (Some of our readers perhaps would have liked us to have given a tragic ending to our story; they would have seen our actors disappear violently from the stage, one after another, and our story end in the genre of the horrible like a large number of novels today) (117). Not only do the protagonists in the open metropolitan novel pursue vice while recognizing and approving good, but their actions are defined as a series of individualistic discontinuities and breaks with the wished-for value systems of the group. By contrast, Quebec novels of the agrarian/historical class attempt to define and establish a bucolic, controlled, moral and civil closed space, where individual subjects play out and define the values of the group they incarnate: 'Mais nous les prions de remarquer que nous écrivons dans un pays où les mœurs en général sont pures et simples, et que l'esquisse que nous avons essayé d'en faire, eût été vraisemblablement ridicule, si elle se fût terminée par des meurtres, des empoisonnements et des suicides' (But we ask them to note that we write in a country where morals are generally pure and simple, and that the sketch we have attempted to make of them, would have been unbelievable and absolutely ridiculous, had it ended in murders, poisonings, and suicides) (117–18). The discontinuity of the elsewhere is opposed to the continuity of the here. *There* is the world of excess, individuality, desire, and passion: *Here* is the world of constraint, moderation, measure, and control. The old countries are seen as unnatural, civilized spaces where personal feelings, lust, even assassination are accepted forms of behaviour, and also acceptable imaginary worlds of escape. *There* is made up of immoral open spaces of danger and conflict, polemic, self-interest, and destruction, where subjects realize themselves through struggle, violence, and domination, unlike the closed new world, which is characterized by religion, civility, and peace. *Here* is a contractual world, conducive to the actualization of potential in the form of duty, resignation, and patience: 'Laissons aux vieux pays, que la civilisation a gâtés, leurs romans ensanglantés, peignons l'enfant du sol, tel qu'il est, religieux, honnête, paisible de mœurs et de caractère, jouissant de l'aisance et de la fortune sans orgueil et sans ostentation, supportant avec résignation et patience les plus grandes adversités' (Let us leave the old countries, spoiled by civilization, their bloody novels, let us paint the child of the soil, as he is, religious, honest, with peaceful habits and character, enjoying well-being and fortune without pride and ostentation; bearing the greatest adversity with resignation and patience) (118). Born of the soil, this child of nature is a moralized subject who lives in harmony with members of the group.

In contrast to the old world, where the space of the present, life and death, are seen and experienced as a series of violent physical and moral breaks with the past, *here* continuity, harmony, and fidelity define the moral closed space where the actors evolve and prosper. *Here* life and death, desire and duty, reproduce the house of the father and are presented as the ultimate goals of the protagonists. *Herein* lies the trajectory by which the subject is realized; *here* is the enclosed space of identity, oneness – the space of unity of language, race, and religion that ensures the continuity of the family, the parish, and the nation: 'et quand il voit arriver sa dernière heure, n'ayant d'autre désir que de pouvoir mourir tranquillement sur le lit où s'est endormi son père, et d'avoir sa place près de lui au cimetière avec une modeste croix de bois, pour indiquer au passant le lieu de son repos' (and when he sees his last hour arrive, having no other desire than wanting to die peacefully in the bed where his father has passed away, and have his place next to him in the cemetery with a modest wooden cross, to indicate his place of rest to the passer-by) (118). In this universe of bipolar temporality, the events of the present and future simply reproduce those of the past, thereby instituting a wished-for enclosed universe of reproduction and myth, of continuity in change, where actors may differ but the roles and structures that define them remain the same. Profound and deep similitude with superficial and surface difference become the prototypes, the models that will generate all future agrarian novels until the middle of the next century.

As I mentioned earlier, *La Terre paternelle* is the first agrarian novel written in Quebec. Moreover, although its influence is not often acknowledged in the critical literature, this work had a profound and lasting effect on literary production for more than a century. Insofar as it produced a matrix, implicitly and explicitly approved by the dominant class, for generations of readers who were immigrating to the city, this agrarian novel can be considered as a founding text that establishes the patterns and structures that will determine the form and content of all successive novels of the genre. *La Terre paternelle* is a short work of some eighty pages, written in a spare style that is neither complex nor aesthetically sophisticated. It nevertheless set the stage for, and made possible, such extremely widely read, well-written, and popular novels as *Maria Chapdelaine*, *Trente arpents*, and *Marie-Didace*. Lacombe's text has a very simple plot line, laid out in ten brief chapters, followed by a lapidary conclusion. It opens with a laconic, bucolic description of the island of Montreal, before focusing on the paternal farm that is located there. This is followed by a flashback of great amplitude and duration that functions as a genealogy establishing origins and continuity, beginning with Jean Chauvin, the first concession holder in 1670, and ending with Jean-Baptiste Chauvin,[3] the farm's owner when the story opens. This heterogeneous flashback inscribes what is about to happen in antecedence, historicity, and long-term continuity:

> La famille qui était propriétaire de cette terre, il y a quelques années, appartenait à une des plus anciennes du pays. Jean Chauvin, sergent dans un des premiers régiments français envoyés en ce pays, après avoir obtenu son congé, en avait été le premier concessionnaire, le 20 février, 1670, comme on peut le constater par le terrier des seigneurs; puis il l'avait léguée à son fils Léonard; des mains de celui-ci, elle était passée par héritage à Gabriel Chauvin; puis à François, son fils. Enfin, Jean-Baptiste

Chauvin, au temps où commence notre histoire, en était propriétaire comme héritier de son père François, mort depuis peu de temps, chargé de travaux et d'années.

(The family that owned this land some years ago belonged to one of the most ancient families in the country. Jean Chauvin, sergeant in one of the first French regiments sent to this country, after having obtained his release, was the first concession holder, on 20 February 1670, as demonstrated from the seigneurial documents. He in turn bequeathed it to his son Leonard, who passed it on to Gabriel Chauvin, who then passed it down to François, his son. Finally, Jean-Baptiste Chauvin, at the time this story begins, was the landholder, having inherited it from his father, François, who had died a short time before, ancient in years and burdened down by labours.) (41)

The farm has been passed on from father to son for almost two centuries. Not only do events take on their meaning in terms of duration, but also in terms of repetition; repetition of the same agrarian gestures, governed by the seasons, intermittently interrupted by death, but still, none the less, reiterated by and through succeeding generations.

The time frame of the novel, after the first narrative, covers some sixteen or seventeen years, and most events are narrated in the order in which they occur, with a minimum number of explanatory flashbacks. The temporal continuity of *La Terre paternelle* – generally narrated in the past-definite and imperfect, tenses that communicate the iterative and repetitive nature of the event and thereby establish duration and cycle[4] – is interrupted periodically by narrative interventions in the present, either constituting instances of moralization, truth, or judgment, or marking the occurrence of a singular, important, and usually catastrophic event. In some cases, the narrator's interventions directly address the reader in order to modify, rectify, or adjust the plot line. Nevertheless, in most instances, the text negotiates in the imperfect iterative events that are narrated once but occur repetitively, establishing a temporal harmony of duration as the cyclical norm, while marked singular[5] events are narrated in the present. The singulative denotes disruption, a new temporal order of surprise and change that radically transforms reoccurrence into novelty, destabilizing iterated harmony through the eruption of the unexpected, the heterogeneous, chance, into the homogeneous, closed universe of the known. It thereby reinstitutes a troubling tri-dimensional temporal structure by projecting the past and the present onto a new open future. Here, open, tri-dimensional historical temporality irrupts into and threatens radically the closed, mythical, stable, bi-dimensional temporality of the eternal return, where the present simply repeats the past while the future confirms the present.

The family, made up of father, mother, two sons, and a daughter, initially live in tight harmony, but the younger son, Charles, to the sorrow of all, decides to leave the farm and sign up with the North West Company as a trader with the Native people. The father, thinking that his elder son might be tempted to do the same, and in agreement with his wife, decides to transfer the farm to him in exchange for a pension that will ensure his comfortable retirement. They appear before the notary and conclude their transactions, but disharmony and discord quickly set in. The elder son, lacking experience, does not fulfil his part of the contract, nor does he carry out his duties towards his father, making it necessary for the latter to reclaim the farm. But the father, who has become used to retirement from farming, decides to go into business – as the sanctioning and moralizing narrator will say, 'à risquer les profits toujours certains de l'agriculture contre les chances incertaines du commerce' (to risk the always certain profits of agriculture against the uncertain chances of commerce) (80).

After a brief period of prosperity in the village, and in refutation of the narrator's aphorism about 'the always certain profits of agriculture,' two years of drought and bad weather ruin the farmers, who cannot pay back the debts they owe to Jean-Baptiste Chauvin, who has advanced them credit on the expectation of future good harvests. Jean-Baptiste, in turn, lacks the requisite intellectual and commercial skills to succeed, for he borrows heavily and cannot repay his creditors. He is ruined and must sell everything he has, including the paternal farm, in order to pay off his debts. With his elder son, he is subsequently reduced to becoming a water carrier and seller in Montreal. This task is so difficult and demanding, and the weather conditions are so harsh that, after some ten years of hard labour, the son takes ill and dies suddenly in the middle of winter. Eventually, the younger son returns, finds his family destitute, and buys back the family farm. Everyone is happy and prosperous, all regain their former health, and stability and harmony reign once more. The novel ends with the marriages of both remaining children, Charles and Marguerite, and one of the last images left with the reader is that of two grandchildren jumping up and down on their grandparents' knees.[6]

La Terre paternelle, like all agrarian Quebec novels, clearly distinguishes four spaces that are positively or negatively invested during the unravelling of the tale, in light of the positive or negative transformations that take place. What distinguishes one agrarian novel from another is not necessarily the descriptive or narrative techniques at work, but rather the degree to which each of the following four very distinct spaces in the text are highlighted or accentuated, positively and negatively moralized, and phorically or dysphorically invested with values. The family, headed by the father, lives the greater part of its life within the clearly circumscribed space of the inherited paternal farm. It moves to the village, then to the city, while the younger son abandons the land and spends twelve or so years in the wilderness, before returning to claim and buy back this lost and rightful heritage. The wilderness is also initially inscribed in filigree at the opening of the tale when the origins of the concession in 1670 are evoked.

From the beginning of the novel, the paternal farm, with its complete family, is a positively invested space where actors with predetermined, hierarchical roles work collectively for the common good and attain unmitigated success. The knowledge needed to cultivate the land is temporal, practical, and handed down by tradition. The only subject with abstract knowledge is Marguerite, the daughter, who has been to school and who knows how to read, write, and count. None of the others has any theoretical knowledge transmitted over time by social institutions, and theirs is an oral society: 'Les parents, par une coupable indifférence, avaient entièrement négligé l'éducation de leurs garçons; ceux-ci n'avaient eu que les soins d'une mère tendre et vertueuse, les conseils et l'exemple d'un bon père' (Their parents, through guilty indifference, had completely neglected the education of their boys; these had only received the cares of a loving and virtuous mother, the advice and example of a good father) (41). The harmonious family raises, cultivates, and sells its produce successfully in the city. Each person is in good health, knows his or her place in the family hierarchy, respects the authority of the parents, and does his or her duty, be it physical or moral. This positively invested homogeneous social space of the farm and family, in which no outsiders intrude or are admitted, /life – closed/, can be maintained and enhanced only if duty regulates knowledge, ability, and desire. In short, *here* the *I* appears not as an individual subject but as a collective *we*: 'La paix, l'union, l'abondance régnaient donc dans cette famille; aucun souci ne venait altérer le bonheur' (Peace, unity, abundance therefore reigned in this family; no worries interfered with their happiness) (43).

Once the family becomes truncated, because of Charles's desire to leave for the wilderness, the collective subject becomes dysfunctional. It is through hearing stories in the tavern in the city – where men get drunk, smoke, disobey orders, and tell tales, interspersed with swear words, of man-to-man combats, danger, and long treks into the wilderness – that Charles becomes fascinated by these distant horizons. Most men who return to the village or the city squander their wages when they come back from *beyond*, exhausted, old before their days, and, as the moralizing narrator laconically states, 'ne rapportant avec eux que des vices grossiers contractés dans ces pays, et incapables, pour la plupart, de cultiver la terre ou de s'adonner à quelque autre métier sédentaire profitable pour eux et utile à leurs concitoyens' (bringing with them only vulgar vices contracted in that part of the world, and unable, for the most part, to cultivate the land or to learn some other sedentary trade profitable for themselves and useful to their countrymen) (51). Desire wells up in Charles, and 'l'idée d'être enfin affranchi de l'autorité paternelle et de jouir en maître de sa pleine liberté l'entraîna à la fin' (the idea of being freed from paternal authority and being master of his own liberty finally carried the day) (51). When the prodigal son returns after a long absence, he is described as a cross between a habitant and a Native with long hair. His costume is hybridized, and though he wears mainly woven European clothing (culture and city), his shoes are Indian moccasins (culture and wilderness), 'de peau d'élan artistement brodés en poil de porc-épic de diverses couleurs, et ornés de petits cylindres de métal d'où s'échappaient des touffes de poils de chevreuil teints en rouge' (made of moose hide artistically embroidered with porcupine quills of various colours, and decorated with little metal cylinders from which protruded tufts of deer hair dyed red) (107–8). *Beyond* is the domain of hybridization, where the individual, in order to survive, prosper, and be successful, must take on Native-Canadian modes of thought, action, belief, and behaviour, abandoning much of his European heritage. In the *beyond*, individual desire for freedom, for the unknown, regulates knowledge, ability, and duty. Wilderness is a mixed space, /non-death – non-closed/, mainly of dissipation and loss, where individual subjects, who express themselves in the mode of 'I want for me', can rarely change to 'I want for us,' for the common good. The nomadic wilderness of hunters, gatherers, and traders is a constant threat to the sedentary life of the farm, the village, and the cultivators, likely to absorb and dilute the collective dutiful subject and transform him into an immoral, desiring, Native-like individual.[7] Yet Charles, though he succumbs to the call of the wild, defies the odds and survives the inherent dangers of the wilderness because he must return to rehabilitate the destitute family.

But the village, too, is a negative space where the family and its fortune are dissipated. It is more unstable and heterogeneous than the farm after the father and mother hand over the land to the elder son, who, it should be noted, throughout the novel is not once called by his first name of individuation, although it is briefly mentioned at the beginning of the novel that he was named after his father (41). He does not marry and begin a family; the father, once retired, loses the habit of hard work and, after reclaiming the farm from his son, decides to rent it out and become a merchant in a village in the north district of Montreal (80). *There*, the father begins to desire for himself; his great ambition is to climb the social ladder and be considered 'jusqu'à l'heureux marchand de campagne qu'il voyait honoré, respecté, marchant à l'égal du curé, du médecin, du notaire, et constituant à eux quatre, la haute aristocratie du village' (as the happy country merchant that he saw honoured, respected, on equal footing with the priest, the doctor, the notary, all four of whom constituted the upper aristocracy of the village) (80). *There*, individual pride takes precedence over family virtues, and the father's lack of formal education or theoretical knowledge contributes to his downfall. Just as handing over to his son the paternal responsibility for maintaining the farm brings on failure, so, too, relying on his daughter, who is educated, to keep him informed about the state of his business leads to bankruptcy. The father has abrogated his role as head of the family, entirely responsible for its well-being, and his lack of the necessary knowledge of commerce and business brings on his ruin. Pride, or individual desire for social recognition, takes precedence over ability, knowledge, and duty: /non-life – non-open/.

If the village corresponds to the space of economic ruin, the loss of the farm, as well as the loss of all material goods and social recognition, the city, *elsewhere*, is the place of the final dissolution of the family. Winter in all its horrors imposes itself both in the streets and in the one room that serves as refuge for the four remaining protagonists. Furnished sparsely and poorly, its doors and windows let in the frigid winter air that a little stove cannot overcome.[8] Reduced to a bare subsistence in this room 'qui n'avait pas même le luxe d'une cheminée' (that did not even offer the luxury of a fireplace) (86), the members of the family are sickly; they have aged prematurely, they are emaciated, and they have neither fuel for heat nor enough food to eat. After ten years of this life, the elder son dies from malnutrition and exhaustion: /death – open/. The family possesses neither the knowledge, the will, the strength, nor the obligation to continue in this heterogeneous open space where theoretical and financial know-how of men and institutions, as well as desire for wealth and comfort, regulate all the other modalities, ensuring the survival of individuals to the detriment of the group.

Finally, the novel comes full circle. In the initial fertile space of the farm, the family prospered as the fundamental elementary social unit, /life – closed/. The space is rejected in favour of a number of other options in which subjects attempt to find solutions to the problem of individual identity (wilderness, /non-death – non-closed/; village, /non-life – non-open/; city, /death – open/), in lieu of that of the group. It is, finally, reaffirmed as the space where the family-nation can not only survive but also reproduce its founding values. The avatars of the collective subject that began with a single family unit are replaced in the end by an extended related group that prospers and multiplies and is projected into a promising and prolific future. The parents, headed by the patriarch, have realized their destiny, producing two more families who, in turn, await their own virtual offspring. Closure of the text is ensured by the moralizing narrator, who confirms the triumph and success of the final, positive, euphoric, stable, closed, homogeneous values of the semantic universe, /life/, and the failure of all other negative, dysphoric, unstable, open heterogeneous ones, /death/: 'Nous aimons à visiter quelquefois cette brave famille, et à entendre répéter souvent au père Chauvin, que la plus grande folie que puisse faire un cultivateur, c'est de se donner à ses enfants, d'abandonner la culture de son champ, et d'emprunter aux usuriers' (We sometimes like to visit this good family, and to hear Père Chauvin often repeat that a cultivator's greatest folly is to give himself over to his children, to abandon the cultivation of his fields, and borrow from usurers) (119).

I have said that the novel comes full circle, but this is not entirely true. At the outset, the protagonists live within the harmonious and prosperous environment of the paternal farm, but without articulating and positing their good fortune. However, after abandoning, renting, or selling the land, the subjects in question suffer, experience, and learn the hard lessons of rootlessness, dispossession, poverty, and ruin. At the beginning of the text, individuals realize themselves fully, instinctively, and blindly, following without question the path that has been dictated by family tradition. At the end, however, in the name of the father, they verbally, literally, and publicly iterate and reiterate the learned lesson of the call and the truth of the land. In brief, through their lived experience of the outside world, the protagonists evolve and are transformed from passive, dutiful, obedient subjects into active, dutiful ones, who willingly choose and proclaim the way of the paternal farm.[9]

For Lacombe, the concepts of nation or nationality are not overtly articulated in *La Terre paternelle*. They do not emerge clearly and must be reconstituted through inference. What becomes evident, though, is that the Chauvin family can be considered as a representative token of a type and the transformations it undergoes as the exploration of possible solutions to the problem of the survival and prosperity of this group of subjects. This cultural construct at the level of the imaginary does engage partially in the debate concerning nation and nationality insofar as it promulgates the notion of distinctive characteristics and interests, common religion, laws, institutions, and language, all rooted in long-term continuity and serving to unite all members of the group. From this perspective, the novel can be considered as echoing the dominant Ultramontain conservative ideology of the middle of the nineteenth century depicted in many publications of the times, such as *Le Nouveau Monde* (1867–1900), *La Gazette des Campagnes* (1861–76), and *L'Avenir* (1847–52).[10] The family, we saw, prospered even after the departure of the younger son, and was ruined only after the father made a settlement with the elder and handed over the paternal farm in exchange for goods and money that were due on a specific date every year. During the first part of the novel, agriculture is presented as the finest of all possible professions; it is also linked to a mode of religious practice, so that the spiritual ends of this way of life are integrated into sacred life. Here the traditional way of life not only ensures material prosperity[11] but also favours harmonious and devout behaviour. Once the family moves to the village and is ruined, religious practice is not mentioned, and it is only ten years later in the city of Montreal, when the elder son dies and the father tries to bury him in the middle of winter, that religion is mentioned again. In the city, spiritual practice and economic constraints are inexorably linked. The beadle refuses to bury Chauvin's son with a proper service unless he can pay a minimum fee of ten dollars for the ceremony. Having no money whatsoever, he is forced to bring the body himself to the cemetery, where it is stored in a wooden hut with other bodies of the poor and destitute until spring, when it will be buried in the pauper's plot. The mother prays[12] constantly for the return of her younger son, from whom they have not heard for more than fifteen years, and her request is finally granted. In the end, the farm is returned to its hereditary owners,[13] and agricultural practice is once again incorporated into sacred life, thereby ensuring the happiness, prosperity, well-being, and continuity of the family, group, and nation.

This agrarian novel explores a number of hypothetical solutions to the question of identity by setting out various options and ultimately proposing an 'ideal' solution for guaranteeing a national or collective distinctiveness. It contrasts to the historical novel, in this case *Les Anciens Canadiens*, which proposes a different option, of accepting the radical change brought by the Conquest and negotiating identity and survival through integration – but on its own terms.

In the agrarian novel, the village and city are forbidden, negative spaces. They are the *there*, the *elsewhere*, the contingent, the impossible, which dissolve the subject into an ego defining itself in and by its own desires. The wilderness, on the other hand, is a mixed space, the *beyond*, where most often the subject is absorbed, but can return to invigorate and even save the nuclear unit of society, the family. In the historical novel the city, the *there*, Quebec before the fall, and the manor of yesteryear, the *here*, are positive, safe, reassuring spaces, whereas the wilderness and the Anglo-Saxon world are either threatening, dangerous, or neutral spaces to be negotiated. What each genre does is to establish the boundaries within which the subject can determine itself, in terms of the collective aspirations of the group. In the agrarian novel, the farm, *here*, and to a much lesser degree the wilderness, *beyond*, are permitted, even necessary; they lead directly to the homogeneous, the family, and nationalism (unity of language, race, and religion). In the historical novel, the now, the occupied city, *there*, and the degraded manor, *here*, are the permitted and the necessary, but they lead directly to the heterogeneous, the mixed family, collaboration, and internationalism. In both cases, they are the *there*, the *here*, and the now – the necessity and possibility of the survival, continuity, and prosperity of the French-Canadian people.

The historical novel, on the one hand, attributes a specific stratified, mixed, /open/ or /non-closed/, space to the subject, while the agrarian novel, on the other, delimits a stable, unchanging /closed/, or /non-open/ space within which the individual can realize his or her aspirations in light of a common national goal of survival. What each of the two genres does, however, is to play and replay the ongoing struggle between the births of nationalism and cosmopolitanism, between those who feel identity can best be guaranteed by a policy of closure and those who think it can be maintained when opening up to the world. Yet both genres are profoundly dystopian in nature, insofar as they each construct universes of identity and propose them to readers who are already elsewhere, whose sociohistorical conditions are other. Although both novels deal with the unthinkable trauma of the bloody and violent passage from one symbolic order to another (monarchy to constitutional monarchy), they do so by proposing a nostalgic and mitigated return to the past, the disappearing, the no longer. In brief, rather than directly representing their own times, what these genres do is attempt to resolve, at the level of the imaginary, what the actual sociohistorical conditions render impossible. By a singular twist of irony, though, for many members of the emerging nation, the manor is no more, the farm is no more. They have already begun their massive immigration to the city, and to industrialization.

CHAPTER NINE

Nationalism and the Novel of Colonization: *Maria Chapdelaine*

Maria Chapdelaine was written in 1913 by Louis Hémon, a Frenchman from metropolitan France who had arrived in Quebec two years earlier. It appeared in serial form in 1914 and was subsequently published in 1916, several years after Hémon's accidental death, on 8 July 1913, in Chapleau, northern Ontario, where he was hit by a train. In this chapter, I continue to discuss some of the theoretical issues encountered in the elaboration of a socio-semiotics of the novel. In so doing I concentrate now on Hémon's text, the most important in a long line of novels dealing with colonization and the clearing of the land in isolated and unsettled areas in Quebec that have proven over the years to be marginal for farming.

In a groundbreaking work, Nicole Deschamps (1980) demonstrated that in France, from the early 1920s to the early 1950s, *Maria Chapdelaine* was read through the prism of right-wing ideologies. The novel became the symbol of the Family, the Country, Religion, the allegory of a people, ideally submissive, whose only function was to preserve the values received from the mother country. In Quebec, the novel got mixed reviews. On the one hand, and this is the most common reaction, the text was seen as a work of art, the bible for national survival, an epic of colonization. On the other, a small minority saw it as a false representation of modern Quebec and, later on, as a symbol of alienation. What is evident is that, both in Canada and in France, Hémon's novel was exploited and extensively cited in the discourse of those in power. From most quarters in Quebec, the nation was represented as the allegory of a people that thought of its future in terms of its past. The famous refrain 'au pays de Québec rien n'a changé. Rien ne changera, parce que nous sommes un témoignage' (in this land of Quebec, nothing has changed. Nor shall anything change, for we are the pledge of it) (198)[1] was used to bolster, for example, the historian and clergyman Abbé Groulx's[2] nationalist theses. He pleaded in favour of the constitutional status quo in order to privilege the ideal of peasant life, to maintain Catholic supremacy, and to promote the most traditional forms of French-Canadian culture. As all of these aspects were related to the question of national survival, it can be said that *Maria Chapdelaine*, in crystallizing a moment in the collective history of Quebec, cannot be dissociated from the debate on history itself. In short, during these thirty years, to quote Marcel Thivierge (1950), 'La passion du terroir l'emportait sur la vérité historique' (Passion for the land prevailed over historical truth) or, again, as André Laurendeau (1950) pointed out: 'Les Canadiens ont mis bien du temps à se rendre compte qu'ils devenaient un peuple urbain. Ils se voyaient eux-mêmes, ils se pensaient comme un peuple agricole. Nous en étions sentimentalement à *Maria Chapdelaine* quand déjà, pour une large partie, notre peuple vivait *Bonheur d'occasion*' (It took French Canadians a long time to understand that they were an urban people. They saw and thought of themselves as an agricultural people. We were sentimentally attached to *Maria Chapdelaine* when for the most part our people were living *Bonheur d'occasion*) (see chapter 11).[3] During the industrialization of Quebec and following the Crash of 1929, the discourse of and on *Maria Chapdelaine* was a matrix that cut across and structured much of the social and historical discourse of the time.[4] However, it progressively waned, to disappear at the moment of the Quiet Revolution. How is it, then, that a text that at first glance seems extremely remote from the historical situation can symbolically express the institutions the social group might have if its interests or beliefs did not stand in the way? Another way of putting this is to ask how the axiology (value system) and ideology (transformation of the values) elaborated in this text came to have such a long-term impact on the group in question.

In this chapter I examine *Maria Chapdelaine* as part of a distinct cultural series and attempt to outline, from a semio-narrative perspective, the relationship between this particular novel and the historical situation of the early-twentieth-century inhabitants of Quebec. This novel was a phenomenal success, as more than one and a half million copies were published in French and it was translated into over twenty languages. Moreover, several films were made of it, along with several adaptations for the theatre. The plot line is rather straightforward. At the beginning of the century, a small community of people is engaged

168　Part III. Historiography and the Novel

in clearing land for a settlement in a distant marginal territory. Their ideal, encouraged by the clergy, is to transform the forest into agricultural land and to occupy the land to ensure their cultural survival. The Chapdelaine family is seen as a microcosm of this community of land clearers, and, by extension, of the entire Quebec population of the times.

The logical and sequential structures of the plot unfold according to the rhythm of the passing seasons and the succession of difficult tasks involved in clearing land. The narrative is organized around the central character, Maria, a young woman to whom three suitors, from very distinct environments, will propose marriage at different times within the cycle of a single year. At the end of winter, after hearing Mass, Maria leaves church on a sunny day with her father and encounters by chance François Paradis, a sort of *coureur des bois*, who, after his own father's death, sold the family farm to strangers and went to work and trade in the wilderness. On seeing each other for the first time, they fall in love. Although François works in faraway camps and trades furs with the Native people from distant forests ('le bois connaît des magies pour vous faire venir' [the forest knows magic to attract you] Mme Chapdelaine tells him, 34–5), he promises to visit Maria in early spring. He arrives at the Chapdelaines' two weeks later, as they are clearing the land at the edge of the forest, and returns during the month of July to spend several days; 'Maria ... sentait pourtant qu'une magie s'était mise à l'œuvre et lui envoyait la griserie de ses philtres' (Maria ... nevertheless felt that magic had started to work, transmitting the intoxication of its spells) (64). Two other suitors are present during this evening gathering: Eutrope Gagnon, a neighbour who, like the Chapdelaines, is clearing the land, and Lorenzo Surprenant, an urban dweller from an important unnamed city in the north-eastern United States. He, like François Paradis, following his father's death, has returned to this region of Quebec to sell the family farm.

The next day, during an expedition in the forest to gather blueberries, François and Maria, far from the family, promise to marry in the spring after he comes back from the camps. He returns to the forest, and, often at night while she is baking bread, Maria dreams of him. She dreams of their feelings for one another, which she considers 'quelque chose d'unique, de solennel et pour ainsi dire d'inévitable ... Elle a toujours eu l'intuition confuse qu'il devait exister quelque chose de ce genre: quelque chose de pareil à l'exaltation des messes chantées, à l'ivresse d'une belle journée ensoleillée et venteuse, au grand contentement qu'apporte une aubaine ou la promesse sûre d'une riche moisson' (something apart – something holy and inevitable ... She had always had the confused intuition that something like this existed: something like the solemn joy of sung masses, like the intoxication of a beautiful sunny windy day, like the happiness that some unexpected good fortune brings, or the certain promise of an abundant harvest) (80). Yet this euphoric and luminous intuition is immediately contradicted by a gloomy dysphoric voice, which suddenly shifts focalization away from her to that of an external narrative source interrupting her stream of consciousness and which

> quelqu'un lui a chuchoté longtemps que le monde et la vie étaient des choses grises. La routine du travail journalier, coupée de plaisirs incomplets et passagers; les années qui s'écoulent, monotones, la rencontre d'un jeune homme tout pareil aux autres ... le mariage, et puis une longue suite d'années presque semblables aux précédentes ... C'est comme cela qu'on vit, a dit la voix. Ce n'est pas bien terrible et en tout cas il faut s'y soumettre; mais c'est uni, terne et froid comme un champ à l'automne.

> (for a long time whispered to her that the world and life were grey things. The routine of daily work, brightened by unsatisfying and fleeting pleasures; the years slipping by monotonously, the encounter of a young man who is the same as others ... marriage, and then a long series of years that are almost the same as the previous ones ... that is how one lives, the voice said. It is not too dreadful and in any case one has to accept; but it is monotonous, gloomy and cold as a field in autumn.) (80–1)

However, while attempting to rejoin Maria at Christmas time, François sets out on foot alone, gets lost in a snowstorm, and disappears forever in the forest. Time and social pressure have their way. Maria, resigned to her fate, now listens to the voices of 'reason' that stifle those of the magic of the forests beyond (obedience to the priest, the example of her parents, etc.) but feels oppressed by nature and her surroundings. After three months, Lorenzo returns from the United States, sells the family farm, visits Maria, and asks for her hand in marriage. She does not answer, but as she listens, she dreams of abandoning the frontier, attracted by 'la magie des villes' (the magic of the cities) (155). The third suitor, Eutrope Gagnon, then declares his feelings for her, but Maria again listens in silence and makes no promises.

In April, Maria's mother suddenly falls ill and dies in spite of patent medicines and visits by the doctor, the healer, and the priest. The mother's passing totally disrupts the family, and, during a deathbed vigil, Maria decides to marry Lorenzo and leave for the States. But her father praises his extraordinary wife, recounting their past life together. Then, while sitting by her sleeping father and dreaming of vast American cities, Maria, and Maria alone, hears three voices that evoke her very origins: 'La première voix vint lui rappeler, en chuchotant les cent douceurs méconnues du pays qu'elle voulait fuir ... L'apparition quasi miraculeuse de la terre au printemps, après les longs mois d'hiver' (The first, a murmur, brings to her memory a hundred forgotten charms of the land she wished to flee ... The marvel of reappearing earth in springtime after the long months of winter).[5] The second speaks of the French roots and origins of her country,[6] and the third, the voice of Quebec,[7] speaks of ancestral faith and language and invites her to stay in this land, where 'naught shall die and naught shall suffer silence.' Listening to the call of the internal voices, the language of her origins that wells up within her, Maria thus decides to stay and promises to marry Eutrope Gagnon, 'le printemps, le printemps d'après ce printemps-ci, quand les hommes reviendront du bois pour les semailles' (in the spring – the spring after this spring now – when the men come back from the woods to sow the crops) (201).

It is important to note, though, that Maria hears these voices only after the death of her mother, when it is a question of replacing her maternal role in the family constellation. Indeed, these voices can be considered both as constituting the collective memory of the group, and as harking back to its very beginnings, as the summoning of origins, of birth, of future offspring. Finally, they materialize as beckonings and hearkenings to the maternal tongue that gives meaning to birth, life, and death. It should also be stressed that the first two suitors, François and Lorenzo, by selling the paternal heritage after the death of their respective fathers, have abandoned all claims to birthright and origins as well as the possibility of rooting their families in their own ancestral soil. Hence, within the logic of this ideology of colonization, must follow the disappearance of François Paradis (betrayal of land – love), her refusal of Lorenzo Surprenant (betrayal of land – comfort and technology), and her acceptance of Eutrope Gagnon (fidelity to land – family and origins).

Obviously, there exist a large number of actional, cognitive, and passional sequences embedded in the above-mentioned sequences. However, they are included within the first sequence that, in the novel,

The Novel of Colonization: *Maria Chapdelaine* 171

corresponds to the 'first narrative,' and enables us to define all of the temporal discordances in the text, as well as the final sequence that it prefigures. What I am referring to here are both the first sentence of the novel, *'Ite missa est,'* in italics and quotation marks, and the last sentence of the novel '—Yes ... If you wish I shall marry you as you asked ...' which I shall call the implicit *'Fiat voluntas.'* Yet even a cursory examination of the narrative shows that the main plot described above unfolds in a year, beginning in the spring and ending with Maria's promise to marry Eutrope Gagnon one year later, in the following spring. Moreover, most of the events narrated occur within the framework of the four seasons, all the while following the temporal and chronological order in which they take place. As well as being punctuated by the seasons, chrononyms – such as the months of the year; morning, noon, and evening; breakfast, lunch, and dinner – in turn help to establish the temporal structure of the novel.

In addition to this cyclical temporal structure of the four seasons, there also exist a large number of temporal expansions and contractions in the form of flashbacks that situate particular events within the context of the past. For example, at the beginning of the tale, the first time the Chapdelaines' horse, 'Charles-Eugène,' is mentioned, a one-paragraph flashback explains the origins of the animal's name. Moreover, this flashback covers a period prior to the opening of the novel. It also is of great scope and duration, since it reaches back more than a hundred years and continues to affect current events. 'Plusieurs générations auparavant, un Chapdelaine avait nourri une longue querelle avec un voisin qui portait ces noms, et il les avait promptement donnés à un vieux cheval découragé et un peu boiteux qu'il avait, pour s'accorder la satisfaction de crier tous les jours, très fort, en passant devant la maison de son ennemi: "Charles-Eugène, grand malavenant! Vilaine bête mal domptée! Marche donc, Charles-Eugène!"' (Many generations ago, a Chapdelaine carried on a long feud with a neighbour who bore these names, and promptly gave them to a tired, lame horse that belonged to him, that he might give himself the satisfaction every day when passing his enemy's house of calling out loudly: 'Charles-Eugène, you wretched, nasty, badly brought-up beast! Get along, Charles-Eugène') (13). And the narrator concludes: 'Depuis un siècle la querelle était finie et oubliée; mais les Chapdelaine avaient toujours continué à appeler leur cheval Charles-Eugène' (For a whole century the quarrel had been finished and forgotten: but the Chapdelaines ever since had continued to call their horse Charles-Eugène) (13–14). This event, like so many others, is, so to speak, temporalized by its insertion in a forgotten and mute past that continues to regulate the present.

This is also the case for the many genealogies that define the characters, situating their names and surnames in relation to kinship ties that anchor and temporalize them, framing them with toponyms of French origin. Early in the novel, when Maria first appears at the entrance to the church, she is immediately described as the daughter of 'Samuel Chapdelaine, qui a une terre de l'autre bord de la rivière, au-dessus de Honfleur, dans le bois' (Samuel Chapdelaine who has a farm in the woods, on the other side of the river, above Honfleur) (6). One of the group gathered on the porch mentions that 'elle était en promenade depuis un mois à Saint-Prime, dans la famille de sa mère. Des Bouchard, parents de Wilfrid Bouchard, de Saint-Gédéon' (she has been spending a month in Saint Prime with her mother's family. They are the Bouchards, related to Wilfrid Bouchard of Saint Gédéon) (6). Each time a person is introduced into the family circle, mechanisms come into play that found belonging in terms of anteriority. At the beginning of the novel, when François Paradis meets the Chapdelaines, he is immediately situated in a family constellation that extends back in time, and is placed in a region of the country the name of which has First Nations resonances: 'voilà longtemps que je ne t'avais vu, François. Et voilà ton père mort, de même. As-tu gardé la terre? ... Tu te rappelles bien François Paradis, de Mistassini, Maria?' (I haven't seen you in a long time François. And your father is dead, too. Have you kept the farm? ... You remember François Paradis from Mistassini, Maria?) (8). In the same way, when Lorenzo Surprenant, who is unknown to the family, appears for the first time, accompanied by his uncle, the latter is quick to introduce him as follows: 'C'est mon neveu Lorenzo ... un garçon de mon frère Elzéar, qui avait marié une petite Bourglouis, de Kiskising. Vous avez dû connaître ça, vous, madame Chapdelaine?' (My nephew Lorenzo ... a son of my brother Elzéar who died last autumn ... Yes, a son of my brother Elzéar who married a young Bourglouis of Kiskising.[8] You should be able to recall that, Madame Chapdelaine?) (58). The narrator first of all comments on the habit of defining origins: 'the uncle felt obliged to establish his nephew's genealogy on both sides of the house, and to state his age, trade and the particulars of his life, following the Canadian custom' (58). He tells us, furthermore, that 'Du fond de sa mémoire la mère Chapdelaine exhuma aussitôt le souvenir de plusieurs Surprenant et d'autant de Bourglouis, et elle en récita la liste avec leurs prénoms, leurs diverses résidences successives et la nomenclature complète de leurs alliances' (From the depths of her memory Madame Chapdelaine dug up a number of Surprenants and as many Bourglouis, and recited the list with their baptismal names, successive places of residence and a full record of their alliances) (58). Along with this process of appropriation and inclusion of the other that inscribes him/her in a common social and physical space through shared knowledge and commonplaces, we are also dealing with a phenomenon of temporalization by which the name, in joining up with its distant origins, is projected into an explanatory past and delimited in a particular physical and cultural space by means of clearly defined toponyms.

Just as genealogy, through a dual process of deixization, anchors the being of the actors, their *now* in their anteriority, their *here* in a *there*, the numerous stories that are told, the songs sung, and the prayers recited during the evening gatherings also contribute to this process. But there is one fundamental difference insofar as they index a more distant past and a less circumscribed space. Whether we are dealing with Mme Chapdelaine's eternal refrain about how fortunate it is to live in the 'vieilles paroisses où la terre est défrichée et cultivée depuis longtemps, et où les maisons sont proches les unes des autres, comme à une sorte de paradis perdu' (old parishes where the land has been cleared and tilled for a long time, and where houses are near one another, like a sort of lost Paradise) (26); or with François Paradis's stories about people who live in the forest; with neighbours talking about hunting expeditions or M. Chapdelaine about life in the logging camps or married life with his wife; or finally with the oft-repeated prayers, especially the *Ave Maria* or the religious songs *'J'irai la voir un jour,' 'Dans son étable,' 'À la claire fontaine'* – all of these events function as deictics or flashbacks that reach far beyond the time of the opening of the narrative, instituting a relationship between now and yesteryear, here and there.

Furthermore, although described for the most part only once, these events occur many times. It should also be noted that there exist only two types of narrative programs in the novel, those that consolidate and those that dissipate the values of the group. I suggest that, as in all novels of the land, the sequences of consolidation or the sequences that unfold within the cycle of the seasons are anchored in longevity. They originate in other time-hallowed sequences that reiterate and reproduce their fundamental features. Events that occur during the cycle of the seasons are of an iterative nature: the *now* reproduces former times; *here* confirms the *there*; tomorrow must reiterate the past along with the *here*. As a matter of fact, the narrator's comments about the peasants' conversations – which 'sont comme une interminable mélopée, simple, pleine de redites, chacun approuvant les paroles qui viennent d'être prononcées et y ajoutant d'autre paroles qui les répètent. Et le sujet en fut tout naturellement l'éternelle lamentation canadienne: la plainte sans révolte contre le fardeau écrasant du long hiver' (are like an interminable song, simple, repetitive, each speaker agreeing with the words last uttered and adding more to the same effect. Naturally the theme was the Canadian's never-ending complaint; his protest, falling short of actual revolt, against the heavy burden of the long winter) (24–5) – are actually a thematized and figurativized *mise en abyme* of the entire process of temporalization discussed above.

Yet, the iterated having a long duration is sometimes interrupted by a break, an accident that is narrated a single time and occurs only once. Such an irruption of the singular, of the heterogeneous, introduces another time, another place, into this stable universe of recurrence and reproduction and risks provoking a mutation, a radical change. The singular event disturbs, menaces homogeneity by introducing other forms, other places, and even foreign bodies that transform and destabilize the repetitive structures. Thus, the irruption of François Paradis (who lives *beyond* the frontier, the village, and the city) into Maria's emotional world – this man from beyond, from the magic of the forests (34–5), this man of nature – triggers her individual will and desire and opens her mind to other possibilities by making her dream of love. Though she meets him only three times, he makes her aware of the potential for a different future, of intersubjective reciprocity. But *paradise* (Paradis) is not of this world, and the future dreams of true beginnings must give way to the iterative regularity founded on a distant past. François, who brings the seduction of 'un monde encore empli pour eux comme aux premiers jours de puissances occultes, mystérieuses ... le Wendigo géant ... toute la gamme des charmes et des magies' (a world still filled with dark and mysterious powers ... the giant Wendigo ... incantations and every magic art) (66), is therefore ejected from the narrative and dies alone, frozen in the endless snow. The same holds true for Lorenzo Surprenant, a singular being who also sees Maria three times, *surprises* her, and proposes the magic of over there, another place, another time: the time of the industrialized cities of the United States, the time of calculation, of technology, and production, where the future differs from the present and the past. This time of industrial advance and 'progress' perturbs the time of long duration and provokes desire, change, and dreams of mass-produced material

The Novel of Colonization: *Maria Chapdelaine* 175

goods, of short duration. Though it takes Maria by surprise, the sudden appearance of the singular and heterogeneous, the temptation of Lorenzo Surprenant, does not seduce her. For it is the voice of legitimacy, of the ancestral reiterating and regulating past, that will literally surprise and take hold of her: 'Et une autre voix s'éleva comme une réponse. Là-bas c'était l'étranger: des gens d'une autre race parlant d'autre chose dans une autre langue, chantant d'autres chansons ... Ici ...' (As though in answer another voice was raised. Over there were foreigners, people of another race speaking of other things in another tongue, singing other songs ... Here ...) (195). The third suitor, Eutrope Gagnon, a close neighbour who has not betrayed the land by selling it, but who is a land-clearer, a pioneer, and a founder, like Samuel Chapdelaine, visits Maria regularly over a period of several years. A man of fidelity to the past who wishes to reproduce the stable structures iterated in the narrative, he literally constitutes the 'good direction' to follow. Eutrope, from the Greek *'eu'* (good) and *'tropos'* (direction), inscribes Maria's future in the straight and narrow way. In short, Maria's many possible options and choices are traced in the onomastic interplay that fixes her destiny to the letter: No *Paradise*, no *Surprises*, *Hail Mary*, stay *Here* and follow the *Good Direction*, while listening to the *Voice of the Past, of the Good*.

Finally, the eruption of the singular is of a tensive and passional nature. A detailed analysis of the singular event, one that is always unexpected in this world of stability and recurrence, would show that, by instituting the passional dimension mediating intersubjective relations, it establishes the proprioceptive, which, in revealing the corporality of the other, makes the protagonist Maria discover her own body as tension and desire. The singular is marked by the aspects of the inchoate, the instantaneous or non-durational, and termination. It is in the singular that the maximum amount of tension occurs in this novel of colonization. It should be added that the mythical iterative, which is the norm in the novel of the land, is characterized by the non-inchoate, the enduring, and the recurring aspects. This tension is entirely different from that accompanying the physical efforts of the Chapdelaines when clearing land, efforts that institute a great deal of tensivity, but that signify in terms of a struggle against nature that accentuates the strength of bodies locked in a dire battle with their adversary. It is, therefore, by the sudden appearance of the singular that a tensive scale is manifested. Such a scale can be perceived at the level of aspects that, in pathemizing the body, awaken it to itself. The law of the genre dictates that the singular in its most extreme forms be eliminated and ejected from this universe and replaced by tension that is regulated by the iterative. What the narrative of the land puts in place is a regulatory mechanism that imposes the harsh law of reproduction and, through iteration, attempts to abolish the accident or chance of the singular.

At this stage in the analysis, I would like to pause for a moment and summarize my findings up until now. In contrast to the iterative, the singular gives sudden rise to desire, or to individual will, both of which regulate the other modalities that determine the competence of the subject. Hence, at the beginning of the narrative, the modal series that governs Maria's competence is regulated by passive duty (/duty/ → /knowledge/ → /power/ → /desire/). In this series, the Sender and the Receiver are identical: God, Country, Race, and Language. François Paradis's arrival instantly transforms the modal series so radically that it becomes regulated by the sentiment of love (/desire/ → /knowledge/ → /power/ → /duty/). Death rears up suddenly, cancelling this series, but Lorenzo brings about another, similar transformation, this time with the desire of material well-being governing the modal series. The voices provoke a final transformation, and the modal series is determined by active duty. The novel seems to have come full circle, but, because of the manipulation of the voices, Maria goes from passive obedience at the beginning to active obedience at the end. In this novel of colonization, the singular is simply an accident that reveals to the actant the truth of the iterative, where the spire at the end of the narrative appears as a simple echo of the one at the beginning.

If we now turn to the modalities that govern the agents' actions, it is legitimate to ask what type of knowledge, duty, power, and will (desire) enables the actants to bring about positive and negative transformations of the values in this closed semantic micro-universe? Each and every actant is endowed with various forms and degrees of knowledge that both distinguish them as individuals and identify them as belonging, or not belonging, to the group. Not surprisingly, practical knowledge of farming, land clearing, and husbandry, along with domestic knowledge and knowledge of origins (genealogy), are among the most widespread and most highly valued forms in this tale. Such knowledge, based on tradition and beliefs handed down by the French and adapted to this new country, has a temporal dimension, since it is transmitted, learned over time, and mediated by the family unit. When Tit'Bé, one of the young Chapdelaine sons, speaks up during a gathering at their home about the end of winter and letting the animals out to pasture, the narrator comments

The Novel of Colonization: *Maria Chapdelaine* 177

Il fumait et causait avec les hommes maintenant, de par ses quatorze ans, ses large épaules et sa connaissance des choses de la terre. Huit ans plut tôt il avait commencé à soigner les animaux et à rentrer chaque jour dans la maison sur son petit traîneau la provision de bois nécessaire. Un peu plus tard il avait appris à crier très fort: 'Heulle! Heulle!' derrière les vaches aux croupes maigres et 'Hue! Dia!' et 'Harrié!' derrière les chevaux au labour, à tenir la fourche à foin et à bâtir les clôtures de pieux. Depuis deux ans déjà il maniait tour à tour la hache et la faux à côté de son père, conduisait le grand traîneau à bois sur la neige dure, semait et moissonnait sans conseil; de sorte que personne ne lui contestait plus le droit d'exprimer librement son avis et de fumer incessamment le fort tabac en feuilles ... au pays de Québec les garçons sont traités en hommes dès qu'ils prennent part au travail des hommes ...

(He smoked and talked with the men now by virtue of his fourteen years, his broad shoulders, and his knowledge of farming. Eight years earlier, he had begun to care for the livestock, and every day to replenish the store of wood for the house with the aid of his little sled. Somewhat later he had learned to call *'Heulle! Heulle!'* very loudly behind the thin-flanked cows, and *'Hue! Dia! Harrié!'* when the horses were ploughing; to use a hay fork and to build a rail fence. For the last two years he had taken turn beside his father with axe and scythe, driven the big wood-sleigh over the hard snow, sown and reaped on his own, so that no one disputed any longer his right freely to express an opinion and to smoke incessantly the strong leaf-tobacco ... in the land of Quebec the boys are treated as men when they undertake men's work ...) (25–6)

Practical knowledge, which ensures the survival and prosperity of the family, is indisputably linked to physical maturation, a dominant motif in the narrative. Without belabouring the point, women's domestic knowledge is of the same order. It, too, is handed down from traditions adapted to the new frontier. It, too, is linked to physical maturation and transmitted from mother to daughter over time: 'Maria et sa mère n'eurent donc à faire que leur ouvrage habituel: la tenue de la maison, la confection des repas, la lessive et le raccommodage du linge, la traite des trois vaches et le soin des volailles, et une fois par semaine la cuisson du pain qui se prolongeait souvent tard dans la nuit' (Maria and her mother had only their usual tasks: housework, cooking, washing and mending, the milking of three cows and the care of the fowls, and once a week bread baking, which often lasted well into the night) (76).

François Paradis and Lorenzo Surprenant, however, both represent types of knowledge that are foreign to the group. Though he has knowledge of trading, hunting, and gathering that is handed down from the Native people, the beyond, François inevitably meets his death at the hands of nature, while Lorenzo's knowledge of manufacturing and commerce will not succeed in convincing Maria to follow him to the city. A brief scene in the novel contrasting local knowledge and experience with knowledge and experience from elsewhere can be considered exemplary of what can, or cannot, ensure the survival of the group. The three Frenchmen from France, who bought Lorenzo's family farm, meet with a group of peasants. 'Leur aspect eût suffi à les différencier des autres habitants du village' (Their appearance alone would have served to distinguish them from the other inhabitants of the village) (130). They are asked what trade they followed before coming to Canada. The father replies that he was a piano-tuner and his two sons were clerks. Samuel continues and asks if they earned good wages, and then immediately adds, probably not: 'Mais de même vous êtes ben instruit, vous et vos garçons; vous savez lire et écrire, et le calcul, eh? Et moi qui ne sais seulement pas lire. "Ni moi!" ajouta promptement Éphrem Surprenant. Conrad Néron et Égide Racicot firent chorus: "Ni moi!" "Ni moi!" Et tous se mirent à rire' (But anyway you're well educated, you and your sons; you can read and write and count, eh? And here I am, who cannot even read! 'Nor I!' stuck in Ephrem Surprenant. Conrad Néron and Egide Racicot also added 'Nor I!' 'Nor I!' in chorus. Then they all broke out laughing) (131). All of these individual subjects share the same basic practical knowledge and speak in unison with a common voice that binds them in a common destiny (*us*). Here, individuals' theoretical and abstract knowledge external to the collective wisdom can do nothing to ensure the group's survival and prosperity.

Other forms of knowledge circulate and take on meaning in relation to practical knowledge that they either confirm or contest. When Maria meets François and falls in love with him, she is immediately aware of it. Mythical knowledge, or love, is not transmitted through the group, and is revealed to Maria through the somatic reactions of her body. She is instantly attracted to François, and the course of her life seems to be changed as she becomes aware of herself as an independent subject who immediately begins to think and feel for and by herself. She begins to dream of another future – a future other – that has nothing to do with the continuity of the family gathered around the cultivation of land. This form of awareness of the other and the self, linked to the woman's biological maturation and the sudden manifestation of an independent thinking and feeling self, is unacceptable in the narrative and must be eradicated by making François disappear.

By contrast, spiritual knowledge sent by God and transmitted to the group by the priest is the preferred and privileged direction defined in *Maria Chapdelaine*. When giving advice to Maria after the death of François, the parish priest tells her that she should forget her beloved since she promised to marry him outside the family circle during their walk in the woods. In addition, the priest's spiritual knowledge is confirmed by the members of the family during the long and painful agony of Mme Chapdelaine's death. Theoretical and scientific knowledge are also opposed to faith and practical knowledge since they are shown to be inoperative at a critical moment in the mother's illness. Hearing that Mme Chapdelaine is not at all well, Eutrope Gagnon brings her some pills that his brother had bought after reading about them in the newspaper. This exogenous remedy from the city, from elsewhere, does not have the desired result of preventing her death. A doctor who has been trained in the city also comes to visit, and he, too, is powerless to cure her. Criticizing the ineptitude of modern medicine, the family then goes to get a bonesetter, Tit'Sèbe, who, unlike the doctor, speaks in a straightforward manner, stating simply that 'Si le bon Dieu le veut, elle va mourir' (She will die if it is God's will) (173). He then prays: 'un peu penché en avant, doux et triste, il semblait poursuivre avec son dieu un dialogue muet, disant: "Vous m'avez donné le don de guérir les os brisés, et j'ai guéri; mais vous ne m'avez pas donné le don de guérir les maux comme ceux-ci: alors je suis obligé de laisser cette femme mourir"' (leaning forward a little, his back bent, the gentle sad spirit seemed in silent communion with his maker: 'You have given me the gift of healing broken bones, and I have healed them; but you have not given me the power of healing illnesses such as these; so I must let this poor woman die') (174). The bonesetter then decides to go and bring back the priest 'Oui, c'est fort, un prêtre!' (who has strength beyond the strength of men) (177), and religious belief triumphs over all other forms of knowledge as they assist Mme Chapdelaine through prayer in her last moments. Here, knowledge is of the order of the eternity of timeless revelation. It is at the origin of power and can be transcribed as (/spiritual knowledge/ → /power/).

Yet practical knowledge is inextricably linked to physical strength or power. This is certainly the case with the Chapdelaines and Edwige Légaré, the hired man, who, in clearing the land, exerts enormous and tireless effort. The same holds true for Tit'Bé, who at the age of fourteen, as we saw, is physically mature, able to carry out all of the tasks of farming and land clearing, and hence is considered a knowledgable adult by all the members of this society of settlers. Two counter-examples of this appear in the text. When Lorenzo's uncle introduces him to the Chapdelaines as his nephew who has been in the States for many years, working in a factory, 'Chacun examina de nouveau avec une curiosité simple Lorenzo Surprenant. Il avait une figure grasse aux traits fins, des yeux tranquilles et doux, des mains blanches; la tête un peu de côté, il souriait poliment' (Everyone took another good look at Lorenzo Surprenant. His face was fleshy, with well-cut features, eyes gentle and unwavering, hands white; with his head a little to one side he smiled politely) (59). The motif of hands also occurs in the physical description of the Frenchmen from Paris who have just begun to till the soil: 'un des fils, les coudes sur ses genoux, contemplait avec une sorte d'étonnement les callosités que le dur travail des champs avait plaquées aux paumes de ses mains frêles. Tous trois avaient l'air de tourner et de retourner dans leurs esprits le bilan mélancolique d'une faillite ... ils n'avaient ni la force, ni la santé endurcie, ni la rudesse nécessaire, ni l'aptitude à toutes les besognes: agriculteurs, bûcherons, charpentiers, selon la saison et selon l'heure ... ces gens-là ne sont pas faits pour vivre sur la terre' (one of the sons, elbows on knees, stared wonderingly at his delicate hands, calloused by the hard work of the fields. All three seemed to be turning over and over in their minds the melancholy balance sheet of a failure ... lacking the strength, the toughened health, the ruggedness, the training for every task which fits the Canadian to be a farmer, woodsman, or carpenter, according to season and need ... men like these are not built for living on the land) (133–4). In this universe, power presupposes practical knowledge, which we can transcribe as (/practical knowledge/ → /power/).

In a scene emblematic of the main thrust of the novel during the same evening gathering with the Frenchmen and Lorenzo Surprenant, the latter states that he is happy to have sold and left the farm. Mme Chapdelaine vigorously defends this way of life stating categorically that 'Il n'y a pas de plus belle vie que la vie d'un habitant qui a de la santé et point de dettes, dit-elle. On est libre; on n'a point de boss; on a ses animaux; quand on travaille, c'est du profit pour soi ... Ah! C'est beau!' (There is no better life than that of the habitant who has good health and owes no debts. He is a free man, has no boss, owns his animals, works for his own benefit ... Ah, this is the finest life there is!)

(134–5). Lorenzo objects to this vision of the world and offers the following commentary, where duty regulates will:

Il n'y a pas d'homme dans le monde qui soit moins libre qu'un habitant ... La vérité, c'est que ce sont leurs animaux qui les ont ... 'Vous êtes les serviteurs de vos animaux: voilà ce que vous êtes. Vous les soignez; vous les nettoyez; vous ramassez les miettes des riches ... Vous auriez encore d'autres maîtres: l'été qui commence trop tard et qui finit trop tôt, l'hiver qui mange sept mois de l'année sans profit, la sécheresse et la pluie qui viennent toujours mal à point ... sans compter le grand froid, les mauvais chemins, et de vivre seuls, loin de tout, sans plaisirs. C'est de la misère, de la misère, de la misère du commencement à la fin.'

(There is no man in the world less free than a habitant ... The truth is that their animals own them ... 'You are their slaves; that's what you are. You look after them, you clean them, you gather up their dung as the poor do the rich man's crumbs ... still, you have other masters: the summer that begins too late and ends too soon, the winter that eats up seven months of the year and brings in nothing; drought and rain which always come at the wrong moment ... I have not even mentioned the extreme cold, the bad condition of the roads, the loneliness of being far away from everything, with no amusements. Such a life is one kind of misfortune piled on top of another from beginning to end.') (135–7)

The next day, Lorenzo has a long talk with Maria in which he describes the attractions of modern life in the city and then asks for her hand in marriage. Troubled by the vision of comfort, technology, and culture, she turns away and does not reply. In the first sequence in which Lorenzo berates life on the farm, /duty/ rather than freedom precedes and must governs will or /desire/. The second sequence proposes another solution, marriage and moving to the city, which is simply a lesser version of the one suggested by François Paradis where /desire/ or freedom governs /duty/. In this weaker version of the subject, unconditional love (I want for you, and for me) is replaced by creature comfort and desire of material goods (I want for me). The narrative explores these two trajectories, which express the possibility of the emergence of a desiring subject (/desire/ → /mythical knowledge/ → /power/ → /duty/), but, as we have seen, rejects and ejects them as undesirable. Hence, the preferred series, depicting the survival of the subject within the group: (/duty/ → /desire/). This can be read as /duty/ governs will or /desire/. Now this modal series holds equally true for all scenes and events in the novel that have to do with religion, language, race, origins, and so on, and, for that matter, for all the values that are transformed positively within this micro-universe. All the negative narrative programs of dissipation are eliminated and, when all is said and done, what we are left with are the modal series (/duty/ → /practical-knowledge/) → (/power/ → /desire/). In sum, no individual can desire for himself/herself (*I*), or even for and with the other, outside the value systems that confirm the continuation and prosperity of the family, group, and nation (*us*). All other virtual programs of the manifestation of individual will that are explored must be eliminated in favour of the consolidation of the collective being. In this universe of shared and presupposed values, there is no place for the actant *I*, who says 'I want for me,' but only for the actant who decides 'I am for *us*.'

I now turn to the various narrative programs and their figurative trajectories in the novel, and begin by examining in some detail the first chapter dealing with the end of Mass on Sunday – specifically, the exchanges of the men and women on the church steps afterwards, in which all manner of social, economic, and interpersonal transactions occur. It is striking that, although there are a large number of actors in the text who perform diverse and complex tasks, these can be rewritten in a simplified form as narrative programs of either consolidation or dispersion. The men leave the church before the women and exchange greetings and news about the weather, the arrival of spring, or the next harvest. In addition, one of the men, a sort of town crier, stands on the steps each week to give news of concern to the parish. He informs the men that government work will begin on the docks, that a surveyor will arrive next week, and that traders are here to buy furs. One of the villagers offers to sell his pigs, and everyone makes fun of him.[9] When the women come out, many eyes turn towards Maria, who arrives with her father. Comments are made about her by some of the younger men before François Paradis speaks to her and her father. They exchange information about their respective families, and this is where, before the gathering is dispersed, François reveals that, following his father's death, he has sold the family farm.

In this chapter, as in those that follow, one can reduce the multiple activities of the various actors to a series of operations whereby they are in a relationship of either conjunction or disjunction with various objects of value, be they figurative or abstract. Whether attempting to exchange news, or goods, or information about their desires, the actants enter into actional, cognitive, or passional contractual intersubjective relations of manipulation with each other. And from this perspective, the text unravels as a series of junctive operations that attempt to maintain the subject in either a conjunctive or a disjunctive relation with the object of value. Such operations can be defined as narrative programs (NP),[10] and interpreted as a change of state effected by any subject (S1) affecting any subject (S2). Each narrative program NP is actualized in a number of figurative trajectories and, on the basis of the utterance of state of the NP considered as a consequence, figures such as gift, et cetera, can be reconstituted on the discursive level. For example, the NP1 (Consolidation) has the following figurative trajectories: 'parish relations'; 'economic relations'; 'religious relations'; 'linguistic relations'; 'family relations'; 'historical relations'; 'domestic relations'; 'duty.' Whereas the figurative trajectories of the NP2 (Dispersal) are as follows: 'couple relations' – love – comfort; 'trade relations'; 'foreign relations'; 'scientific relations'; 'commercial relations'; 'technological relations'; 'desire.'

In this narrative, one finds a dominance of Consolidation Narrative Programs that is sanctioned by the closure of the text. Examining NP1 and NP2 from the point of view of their final states, one notes that the NP1 sets in place a positive (euphoric) state while, in contrast, NP2 is negative or dysphoric. In NP2, disjunction from the object of value is figurativized by the loss of land or the loss of the historical and cultural past, or death, whereas in NP1, positive values are linked with the clearing and maintenance of land, or life. These actions are all undertaken by the different actors, who are seeking to acquire specific objects of value. The priest, the healer, individuals acquiring objects of value through commerce or exchange, the clearing of land, the care of domestic animals – all are performances that transmit knowledge about the state of man and family, man and country, man and race, and man and language. These positive actors are opposed to negative ones who are bearers of death – exemplified by theoretical or scientific knowledge, knowledge of the city, knowledge of the wilds, love-passion, and so on.

In turn, the figurative trajectories can be reduced to actantial roles or thematic roles. I suggest that the text puts in place four distinct topoi in which the subject operators function and acquire or lose the object of value: the Frontier, the Wilderness, the Village, and the City are overdetermined and governed by the predicate *having-to-be*.[11] In *Maria*

Chapdelaine, taking into account all the transformations at the actantial level that occur throughout the novel and arriving at the end of the trajectory of all the actants, we note that the *frontier* has to be (*necessity*) and is in a relationship of contradiction with the *city*, which does not have to be (*contingency*), whereas the *wilderness* (*impossibility*), which has not to be is in the same relationship to the *village* (*possibility*), which does not have not to be.

If we now take into account all the modal transformations of the actant Maria, and confront will /wanting-to-do/ with duty /having-to-do/, then we note that the initial state of the subject until the penultimate chapter of the *Voices* is one of *passive obedience* /having to do/, and that /not wanting not to do/ is in a relationship of contrariety with *passive will* /having not to do/ and /not wanting to do/ and of contradiction with *active obedience* /not having to do/ and /wanting not to do/, as well as of complementarity with *active will* /not having not to do/ and /wanting to do/. In contrast, *passive will* /having not to do/ and /not wanting to do/ is in a relationship of contradiction with *active will* /not having not to do/ and /wanting to do/.[12] In the very last chapter, Maria listens to the voices of origins and the ancestral past. She therefore decides to stay in Quebec and marry Eutrope Gagnon and, consequently, is transformed from a subject who initially followed passive obedience, to a subject awakened to individuality and desire by her experience with François Paradis, before finally becoming a consenting active obedient subject: '*Fiat voluntas.*'[13]

Until now I have focused mainly on the relationships between thematic roles and figurative trajectories and between narrative programs and actantial roles. These results now allow us to elaborate the network of minimal units and operations on the values. An examination of the figurative trajectories permits us to deduce the following series of oppositions:

/inside/	versus	/outside/
/collective/	versus	/individual/
/closed/	versus	/open/
/stable/	versus	/unstable/
/homogeneous/	versus	/heterogeneous/
/continuous/	versus	/discontinuous/

These constitute semiological isotopies of the /relational/: family, friendship, love, social, religious, linguistic, economic, historical, somatic. All the figurative trajectories have the /racial/, /religious/, and /linguistic/ isotopies in common. To attempt to establish the semantic isotopy is to put in place that which assures the compatibility of the many figurative trajectories and thus the link between the semiological isotopies. I would propose to retain as the indicator of the semantic isotopy the opposition

/closed/   versus   /open/

This operation seems to represent the starting point of the others. The classemes /open/ and /closed/ on the semantic level are taken up by the nuclear semes (relational, social, religious, linguistic, economic, historical, somatic) on the semiological level, where they are organized by the figurative trajectory.[14] Each narrative program of consolidation and dispersal gives rise to figures of /doing/ that signify on each of the semiological isotopies.

1 /closed/ → /open/
   This passage corresponds to the narrative operations of 'departure' by François, after his father's death and to the selling of the farm.
2 /closed/ → /non-open/
   This trajectory corresponds to Mme Chapdelaine's desire, her impossible dream of moving back to the village. Its closure is assured by her death and by the priest and the voices.
3 /closed/ → /non-open/
   This passage corresponds to the narrative operations of 'departure' by Lorenzo, the second suitor, after the death of his father and the selling of the farm. This is the second axis of impossible desire and is constituted by the promise of buying gifts and giving creature comforts to Maria through 'consumer society' in the United States (virtual program of 'temptation' and 'illusion').
4 /open/ → /closed/
   This trajectory cannot occur, since after selling the paternal farm François meets his end when attempting to return for a third time, in the dead of winter, to see Maria.
5 /open/ → /non-open/
   This, too, is impossible – that is, the terms are in a relationship of contradiction, and the non-actualization of the trajectory is ensured by François's death after he has already negated the village and started trading with the Native people in the wilds.

186 Part III. Historiography and the Novel

6 /open/ → /non-closed/
   This is ensured by François, who trades for furs in the wilderness beyond. This corresponds to the introduction of furs into city manufacturing. In fact, this is mainly the unsaid, the unspoken, as the text adumbrates all cultural exchanges and any impact of the Native people on the North American inhabitants of European descent.
7 /non-open/ → /open/
   This corresponds to the young men, like François, who work in the lumber camps in the forests and trade for furs.
8 /non-open/ → /closed/
   This corresponds to the villagers, including the priest, the doctor, and the healer who visit the Chapdelaines from time to time.
9 /non-open/ → /non-closed/
   This is, again, the unspoken in the text since it corresponds to immigration to the city and eventual loss of identity, against which the novel was written.
10 /non-closed/ → /non-open/
   This, too, is of the order of the presuppositions since it corresponds to those who incarnate theoretical knowledge that has no impact on the survival of the group/family. It also corresponds to the introduction of goods manufactured elsewhere, outside this closed universe.
11 /non-closed/ → /closed/
   This corresponds to the same trajectories as in (10) above, but also to the recent immigrants from France, who know how to read and write and have worked at their trades in Paris but who, because of lack of practical knowledge and physical strength, are totally unsuited to survive on the frontier.
12 /non-closed/ → /open/
   This again is of the order of the presupposed but corresponds to the introduction, through barter, of tools and manufactured goods from the city into the wilderness.

As I indicated above, four distinct spaces are clearly delineated in this novel, defining the spheres where specific subjects can or cannot interact: frontier, wilderness, village, and city. Moreover, whereas Maria's three suitors occupy three of these spaces – wilderness, city, and frontier – her mother symbolically occupies the fourth, the village, insofar as she constantly refers to her early years spent there within the confines of the parish and church. Initially, Maria is portrayed as belonging to the class of agents whose modalities are governed by duty to church, family, language, and origins. Her knowledge, like that of the other members of her group, is practical, domestic, non-theoretical, handed down from family tradition, and essential for her to be able to function either on the frontier or in the village. The same holds true for her father, mother, brothers, the hired hand, and Eutrope Gagnon. Her being-able-to, or power, is attributable to her genetic make-up, as is that of the other individuals of her group. For any subject to function successfully in this imaginary universe, its modal series must be governed by having-to or duty, *we*.

I mentioned earlier that, when Maria falls in love with François Paradis (betrayal of the paternal farm – wilderness), the modal series informing her actions are governed by wanting, or desire. To marry François Paradis would mean to choose the *wilderness*, the /open/ nomadic space of hunting, trading, and gathering, the *beyond* of 'individual activity' (desire and love), the world of the tribe, superstition, the tent, and the open fire, instead of the *frontier*, the /closed/ sedentary space of husbandry and land clearing, the *here* of 'family activity' (duty), the world of daily prayer, the house, and the stove. She again begins to assert herself as an individual desiring subject when she is tempted by Lorenzo Surprenant (betrayal of the paternal farm – comfort and technology) to emigrate and accept the material comfort of city life in the United States. To marry Lorenzo would mean to reject the *frontier* and choose the *city*, the /non-closed/ space of manufacturing and science, the *elsewhere* of 'city life' (desire and comfort), the world of idolatry, of buildings, factories, and electricity. In marrying Eutrope Gagnon (fidelity and creation of the farm – family and origins), not only would Maria occupy the central space of the *frontier*, *here*, but she would also have access to the *village*, the /non-open/ space of gardening and commerce, the *there* of 'communal activity' (duty and parish), the world of faith and prayer, home and hearth.

In terms of the value system, or axiology, at play in the text, four spaces are established in which the subject operators function and acquire or lose the object of value: the frontier (*necessity*), the wilderness (*impossibility*), the village (*possibility*), and the city (*contingency*). Despite the third voice that Maria hears at the end of the novel – 'au pays de Québec rien n'a changé ... Au pays de Québec rien ne doit mourir et rien ne doit changer ...' (in this land of Quebec nothing has changed ... In this land of Quebec naught must die and naught must change ...) (198) – one subject, the main protagonist, undergoes radical modal transformations. To remain true to historical, social, cultural, and religious values, Maria must not cross the limits of the frontier or house, /closed/, and the village, /non-open/, which guarantee the identity of a self grounded in the shared and undisputed values of a homogeneous group rooted in history. To cross over into the magical universe of the /open/ or the technological one of the /non-closed/ inevitably leads to loss of identity and the dissolution of the collective subject. Although *Maria Chapdelaine* explores a number of hypothetical solutions to the question of identity by setting out various options, it ultimately proposes an 'ideal' solution for guaranteeing a collective or national distinctiveness. Both the wilderness and the city are dangerous and forbidden spaces, leading, on the one hand, to tribalism and sexuality and, on the other, to cosmopolitanism and the couple. They are the *beyond*, the *elsewhere*, the *contingent*, and the *impossible* that dissolve the subject into an ego defining itself in and by its own desire. What the novel does is to establish the boundaries within which the subject can determine itself in terms of the collective aspirations of the group. The frontier and the village are permitted, even necessary. They lead directly to the family and nationalism. They are the *here* and the *there*, the *necessity* and the *possibility* of the survival, continuity, and prosperity of the French-Canadian nation.

A more detailed analysis of this text would have to take into account the thymic categories – contentedness, happiness, sorrow, pain, suffering, joy, indifference, and so on – that positively or negatively invest each of the terms (/closed/–/open/–/non-closed/–/non-open/) of the elementary structure of signification. Two exemplary figures, though – the 'stove,' which is the bearer of life on the cosmological level, and of faith and language on the noological one, and the 'little window' of the house through which Maria tries to see but cannot always[15] – will serve to illustrate the thymic investment at play in the novel. These two figures are most often linked in the same scene to Maria's actions and sentiments. The 'stove' is not only located in the centre of the house but is also the centre of all the family activity at all times of the year. When Maria returns home in the second chapter after visiting her relatives she sees her mother stirring 'le feu dans le grand poêle de fonte ... Le grand poêle à trois ponts occupait le milieu de la maison; un tuyau de tôle en sortait, qui après une montée verticale de quelques pieds décrivait un angle droit et se prolongeait horizontalement jusqu'à l'extérieur, afin que rien de la précieuse chaleur ne se perdît' (the fire in the big cast-iron stove ... The three-decked stove stood in the centre of the house; the sheet-metal pipe, after going vertically up for some feet, turned at a right angle and was carried through the house to the outside, so that none of the precious warmth would be lost) (19–21). In this same scene, Maria looks out of the little window, becoming the centre of visual, cognitive, and sentimental focalization, and the reader discovers the world outside through her gaze and sensitivity. 'Par la petite fenêtre carrée elle contemplait avec mélancolie les quelques champs nus qui s'étendaient derrière la maison, la grange de bois brut aux planches mal jointes, et plus loin l'étendue de terre encore semée de souches, en lisière de la forêt, qui ne faisait que laisser espérer une récompense de foin ou de grain aux longues patiences' (Through the little square windows she looked in a melancholy way over the scanty cleared fields behind the house, the barn built of badly joined planks, and the land beyond still covered with stumps and encompassed by the forest, from which any return of hay or grain could only be expected at the end of a long and patient wait) (20). After François Paradis's first visit to the home of the Chapdelaines, the window remains open onto the outside. It announces not only changes in the weather but also the opening up of Maria's heart to new sentiments. It is for the stove in winter that the men cut firewood (44), and it is near the stove that the family is sitting with guests when François arrives a second time (62). The stove is also the place of pleasurable fantasy or day-dream. When Maria, all alone in the dark, is watching over the bread baking in the stove (76, 77, 78), she dreams of the future, and François appears vividly in her imagination, described and embodied through her feelings and hopes: 'C'est fait. Le voilà devant elle, avec sa haute taille et sa force, sa figure cuite par le soleil et la réverbération de la neige, et ses yeux hardis. Il est revenu, heureux de la revoir ... Il n'y a pas encore de bleuets à cueillir, puisque c'est le printemps; mais ils trouvent quelque bonne raison pour s'en aller ensemble dans le bois; il marche à côté d'elle sans la toucher ni rien lui dire, à travers le bois de charme qui commence à se couvrir de fleurs roses, et rien que le voisinage est assez pour leur mettre à tous deux un peu de fièvre aux temps et leur pincer le cœur' (That's it. He is there in front of her, tall, and strong, his face baked by the sun and the reflection of the snow, and his bold eyes. He has returned to see her ... There are no blueberries to pick, since it is springtime; but they find some good reason to go into the forest. He is walking next to her without touching her or saying anything, through the massed laurel that is beginning to bloom with rose flowers, and their closeness is enough to make their temples throb and their hearts beat) (79). Again, much as in Jogues's narrative, where critical moments are presentified by a shift in verb tenses, here, too, focalization shifts radically from the narrator to Maria. This interplay of temporal deixis positions the reader and gives access to Maria's innermost feelings. The stove is a haven from the violent elements and, especially in winter, the centre of all family activity (90, 92).

For Maria, waiting for François's return at Christmas time, the window is the place of dream, of blossoming love, and of hope of future happiness: 'Maria regardait par la fenêtre les champs blancs que cerclait le bois solennel; la ferveur religieuse, la montée de son amour adolescent, le son remuant des voix familières se fondaient dans son cœur en une seule émotion' (Maria looked through the window at the white fields circled by the solemn forests, the passion of religious feeling, the awakening of young love arising within her, the moving sound of familiar voices, fused in her heart into a single emotion) (102). Yet when Maria learns of François's death and looks at the window, her gaze turns inward with all hope vanishing: 'Mais elle ne dit rien ni ne bougea, les yeux fixés sur la vitre de la petite fenêtre que le gel rendait pourtant opaque comme un mur' (But she did not say a thing, she did not move, her gaze fell upon the frosted panes of the little window, as opaque as a wall) (114). After praying for François's soul with the family, Maria again moves towards the window: 'Le gel avait fait des vitres autant de plaques de verre dépoli, opaques, qui abolissaient le monde du dehors; mais Maria ne les vit même pas, parce que les larmes avaient commencé à monter en elle et l'aveuglaient' (The frost upon the panes had turned them into plaques of unpolished, opaque glass, which abolished the external world. But Maria did not even see them, because tears had welled up inside her and she began to cry) (116). She opens the door, crosses the threshold, feels the cold of death that had taken François's life penetrate her, and then, with a shudder, seeks refuge and 's'assit près du poêle, frissonnante' (sits next to the stove, shivering) (116). She continues to imagine François's last moments as he freezes to death; she shivers and trembles as he did: 'Elle se serre contre le poêle avec une grimace d'horreur et de compassion comme s'il était en son pouvoir de le réchauffer aussi et de défendre sa chère vie contre les meurtriers ... Seulement elle se serre contre le grand poêle de fonte, et bien que la chaleur du feu la pénètre elle continue à frissonner en pensant au pays glacé qui l'entoure, au bois profond, à François Paradis qu'elle ne peut encore imaginer insensible, et qui doit avoir si froid dans son lit de neige' (Maria draws nearer the stove with a look of horror and compassion as though she could bring him warmth and shield his dear life against the assassin ... But still she cowers by the great cast-iron stove, and though the fire's heat penetrates her, she continues to shudder as she thinks of the frozen world about her, of the deep woods, of François Paradis, whom she cannot imagine without feeling, who must be bitter cold in his bed of snow) (118–19).

These two figures, the 'stove' and the 'window,' are present throughout the entire novel. They are linked to the illness and agony of Mme Chapdelaine (157, 164, 165). When there is no longer any hope for her, and the family prepares to get the priest to administer the last rights, 'Les regards se tournèrent vers la fenêtre, qui n'était encore qu'une plaque noire, et de là revinrent vers la malade' (Their eyes searched the window, as yet only a square of darkness, and then returned to her who lay upon the bed) (175). When the heroine is tempted to marry Lorenzo Surprenant to escape from the harsh conditions of her life and move to the city in a foreign country, the 'stove' (189) and the 'window' (184, 186) once again accompany her decision. Immediately after trying to look out the window, Maria hears the voices from within: 'and at once it seemed that the question she had just asked was answered,' and she realizes that she can live the life her mother led. 'Oui, elle serait capable de cela' (Yes, she would be capable of that) (192). Finally, after agreeing to marry Eutrope, 'La pluie crépitait sur les bardeaux du toit, et le monde heureux de voir l'hiver fini envoyait par la fenêtre ouverte de petites bouffées de brise tiède qui semblaient des soupirs d'aise' (The rain was pattering on the shingles of the roof, and nature rejoicing in seeing the end of winter sent soft little puffs of warm air that seemed to be sighs of content through the open window) (199). As the preceding examples show, these two figures are of fundamental importance since they basically fix the boundaries of the /closed/ and the /non-open/ for the heroine, to the exclusion of the /open/ and the /non-closed/. To remain true to historical, social, cultural, and religious values, Maria must not cross the frontiers of house and village, which guarantee the identity of self. To cross over into the magical universe of the /open/ and the technological universe of the /non-closed/ inevitably leads to loss of identity. In short, what is being replayed here is the ongoing struggle between the births of nationalism (represented by Abbé Groulx) and of cosmopolitanism (represented by Wilfrid Laurier)[16] – a struggle that continues today within the Province of Quebec, between those who think that identity can best be guaranteed by a policy of closure and those who think it can be maintained when opening up to the world.[17]

CHAPTER TEN

On the Margins of Nation – The Realist Novel: *La Scouine*

C'est toujours énigme pour moi que cette apparente contradiction entre l'homme et son œuvre.

J'ai peine à comprendre comment il peut se faire qu'un artiste au cœur resté si jeune, si riche d'enthousiasme, aimant le beau à s'en mordre les lèvres se complaise dans la description des scènes les moins belles de la vie.

(For me this apparent contradiction between the man and his work will always be an enigma.

I can hardly understand how it can be that an artist who is so young of heart, so full of enthusiasm, who loves beauty with such an appetite revels in the description of some of the least beautiful scenes of life.)[1]

Lionel Léveillé

From the time of its publication in 1918, the novel *La Scouine*[2] has given rise to very different reactions from critics of all persuasions. These go from outright condemnation by, for example, Camille Roy, who considers the author as 'le père de la pornographie au Canada' (the father of pornography in Canada)[3] to the mitigated enthusiasm of Gérard Bessette (1972): 'Son roman est ou trop long ou trop court. Il lui manque une idéologie générale et explicite, des tableaux collectifs, des retours en arrière qui en assureraient l'unité, la plausibilité' (His novel is too long or too short. It lacks an explicit general ideology, descriptions of the group, flashbacks that would ensure unity and plausibility) (xvii).[4] However, as Gilles Dorion (1980) rightly points out: 'une analyse approfondie de *La Scouine* reste à faire' (an in-depth analysis of *La Scouine* still remains to be undertaken) (998). It is obvious, though, that each critic who has analysed this 'livre curieux' (curious book),⁵ is preoccupied and even fascinated by two types of problems linked both to the formal definition of this agricultural novel, 'seul roman purement naturaliste de notre littérature' (the only purely naturalist novel of our literature),⁶ and to 'le réalisme agressif' (the aggressive realism)⁷ or 'la force brutale de son réalisme si souvent décriée' (the brutal force of his realism that has been denounced so often)⁸ that seems to characterize his work. A notable exception to these approaches is that of Mariel O'Neill-Karch (1986), who studies the function of objects in *La Scouine*. Yet of all these critics, Thuong Vuong-Riddick (1977) is the only one for whom 'Laberge a su mettre en œuvre une structure rigoureusement construite susceptible de mettre au service de ses idées et de sa vision du monde la forme la plus apte à les mettre en valeur' (Laberge was able to elaborate a rigorously constructed structure that could serve his ideas and his vision of the world well and that was the form best suited to highlight them) (117). This is an opinion that I generally concur with, while not attaching exactly the same meaning as she does to the word 'structure.' All other critics identify in Laberge's novel, in the main, both a structural ambiguity linked to problems of identification and classification of the genre according to well-established norms⁹ and a real, daring, and innovative treatment of the topic: 'Malgré ses défauts, le roman est remarquable d'originalité' (In spite of its defects, this novel is remarkably original).¹⁰

Vuong-Riddick's analysis has the undeniable merit of being the first to decide to 'laisser de côté les critères externes' (leave aside external criteria) and to consider the text 'comme ensemble clos' (as a *closed* ensemble), 'comme ensemble *structuralement fini*' (as a *structurally finite* ensemble). She does this in an attempt to discover 'une série de structures repérables, fortement accentuées et agencées suivant une logique propre au fonctionnement et à l'optique fondamentale du roman' (a series of identifiable structures, that are strongly accentuated and arranged according to a logic that is inherent in the functioning and fundamental thrust of the novel) (117). Although this undertaking is certainly praiseworthy, her analysis is unfortunately not founded on an acceptable theory of structure *per se* that would, for example, define the narrative as a system of signs that can be articulated at hierarchical levels, each with its own units and its own correlations. In light of such a definition, Vuong-Riddick's notion of structure is both too loose and encompasses too many different and varied phenomena to be operative. She borrows the concept of structure from Georges Poulet's *Les*

Métamorphoses du cercle and reduces it to simple geometric forms, such as a series of consecutive or concentric circles that, hypothetically at least, are supposed to constitute the organizing principle of human reality. Ontological and topological, the structures in question appear more as intuitively apprehended recurring motifs or figures than as constructed and schematized relational structures (in the Kantian sense). Indeed, they describe and metaphorically organize a large number of very different textual realities that can be apprehended differently through their connotative and denotative aspects. Thus the circle is considered to be the explanatory principle of the opening and closure of the text, of the rhythm of the seasons, of the cyclical reproduction of the stages of life (119), of the circular bread and plates at mealtime (120), and so on.

None the less, the other critics mentioned above all have in common the need to define and classify this text in relation to their apprehension of the novel in general. In short, they all implicitly subscribe to the neoclassical and neo-Aristotelian definition of the novel proposed by Claude Bremond (1966): 'Tout récit consiste en un discours intégrant une succession d'événements d'intérêt humain dans l'unité d'une même action' (Every narrative consists in a discourse that integrates a succession of events having a human interest into the unity of a single action) (68). They all also consider the individual chapters in *La Scouine* to be very little or not at all integrated into the unity of a single action, and therefore logically conclude that Laberge's text is not a novel but is made up of a series of 'tableaux' (scenes) organized more or less chronologically. For them, what we are dealing with is the simple succession of uncoordinated events. Jacques Brunet's (1969) judgment exemplifies this attitude: 'si l'on considère que le roman doit être un récit bien structuré, une action dont tous les épisodes s'enchaînent et découlent l'un de l'autre par voie de conséquence, *La Scouine* n'est pas un roman' (if we consider that the novel must be a well-structured narrative, an action in which all the episodes are linked and flow logically from one another, then *La Scouine* is not a novel) (34).

The plot line of *La Scouine*, this 'roman de mœurs de la campagne canadienne' (social novel of the Canadian countryside),[11] is straightforward, and its thirty-four brief chapters are held together by a chronological framework – the life of the main character, Paulima, who is nicknamed La Scouine. The novel opens on the evening of 29 September 1853, with the birth of twin daughters, who, with the three older boys, Raclor, Tifa, and Charlot, complete the Deschamps family; it closes with a scene that takes place towards the end of the nineteenth century. Gilles Dorion (1980) suggests that taking the life of La Scouine as the point of anchor, the novel can be divided into four parts (995). The first begins with the birth of the twins, Carolina and Paulima, nicknamed La Scouine, and covers Paulima's childhood and adolescence in chapters 1 to 10, at which point she is described as resembling a big sixteen-year-old boy. The second part (chapters 11 to 16) opens with Carolina's marriage at the age of twenty. In this section, Paulima's adult life is narrated with all of its ugliness, cruelty, and suffering. In the third section (chapters 17 to 30), the centre of interest starts to shift and focus on Charlot, her older brother, who has a single sexual encounter with an Irishwoman[12] and then subsequently falls from the roof of the house and remains a cripple. Both the second and third parts of the novel relate a number of incidents that affect the life of the Deschamps family. The fourth part (chapters 31 to 34) deals with the old age and death of the father, Urgèle, after which the rest of the family (Mme Deschamps, Charlot, and La Scouine) move to the village, where they are bored to death. Finally, Charlot returns to visit the paternal farm and, on seeing it occupied by another family who enjoy prosperity and happiness, experiences regret at having sold it.

What strikes me in comparing this novel to, for example, Lacombe's *La Terre paternelle* or Hémon's *Maria Chapdelaine*, with their positive, uplifting, and moralizing depiction of rural life, is the negative, brutal, and violent representation of life on the farm. Paulima is portrayed as a character who lies, is lazy, spreads gossip, and dissimulates; she is sly, sadistic, cruel, a bigot, and informs on people, while Urgèle, her father, is insensitive, brusque, rude, blunt, aggressive, savage, a brawler, and a bully. The others who remain on the farm or live in the countryside are either nonentities or near-replicas of La Scouine and Urgèle. From a thematic point of view, most human relations depicted in the novel can be reduced to basic egotism. No love or tenderness motivate the main characters, and only money seems to elicit feelings in them. In short, the novel appears to be merely a disjointed series of vignettes that represent a gloomy vision of the countryside during the latter half of the nineteenth century.

To account for the nature of this novel, a work that has created difficulties for all critics who have examined it, I propose a more semio-narrative analysis of the work, which is unique in early-twentieth-century Quebec literature. Each chapter of *La Scouine*, it has been suggested by most critics of Laberge, is composed of a limited number of tableaux and/or scenes that are not linked by logic or unity of action. This raises serious difficulties if one defines the genre in terms of unity of action based on the relations that link the sequences making up the ensemble of the novel. Claude Bremond's work (1966) makes it possible for us initially to classify the events of the narrative into two fundamental sequences of *improvement* and *degradation* (62–9). This class of functions, distributional in nature and involving metonymical relata, can be completed, as we saw according to Barthes (1966), by another class, indices, that are integrative and involve metaphorical relata (8–11). For methodological reasons, I will not describe in detail and consecutively all the individual sequences of improvement and degradation in each chapter, although this is one of several possible approaches to the work. Instead I will construct a hypothetico-deductive functional model that can account for all the micro-sequences that constitute the logical framework of the novel.

With this descriptive strategy in mind, I now turn briefly to examine a few of the novel's early chapters. It is possible to divide the initial chapter of the narrative, consisting for the most part of the scene of the daily family dinner, into five micro-sequences linked to Urgèle Deschamps, to the hired man, Bagon the Gelder, and to the mistress of the household, Maço. In the first sequence, Urgèle carries out his project: (hunger to be satisfied → process of satisfaction → hunger satisfied). In the second, Bagon attempts to accomplish the same thing but fails and burns himself (hunger to be satisfied → process of satisfaction → hunger not satisfied). In the third, he asks for water, and no one comes to his help (help to be obtained → help asked for → help not obtained); he then decides to get the water himself but finds the pail empty (appeasement desired → process of appeasement → appeasement not obtained). The fifth sequence, which brings the chapter to a close, ends positively and is related to the birth of the twins (birth desired → process of birth → birth realized).

It should be noted, however, that each micro-sequence describing a logic of actions is interrupted on various occasions by semantic units, indices, that refer to a signified and not to operations. So that, even if Urgèle Deschamps, does happen to satisfy his hunger after having 'marqué du signe de la rédemption le pain du souper ... son pouce laissait sur chaque tranche une large tache noire ... il les avala d'un coup de langue ... il se mit à boire à longs traits, en faisant entendre, de la gorge, un sonore glouglou ... il s'essuya les lèvres du revers de sa main sale et calleuse' (marked the bread for supper with the sign of the Redemption ... his thumb left a wide black mark on each slice of bread ... he swallowed them [bread crumbs] with a sweep of his tongue ... he began to drink in long drafts, with a loud glouglou sound emerging from the depths of his throat ... he wiped his lips with his dirty, calloused hands) (1), the logical functions are overdetermined by the indices that take on the status of signs evoking a vulgar, crude, and brutal character as well as an atmosphere of oppressive and sordid poverty. In the same way, the sequences that have Bagon as an agent are, on the one hand, preceded by a physical portrait[13] – 'L'homme de peine, très petit, était d'une laideur grandiose ... une tête énorme de mégacéphale ...' (The man of all work, who was very small, was imposingly ugly ... an enormous megacephalic head ...) (2) – of an indexical nature that corresponds to the functionality of being (ugliness and sterility), and on the other is overdetermined by indices of the grotesque and of animality that define almost all the characters of the novel. 'Comme lui, les autres lappaient rapidement ... il fit une vilaine grimace et ses joues eurent des ballonnements grotesques' (Like him, [Deschamps], the others all lapped up quickly ... He [Bagon] grimaced hideously and his cheeks puffed out grotesquely) (3). From a strictly logical perspective, the last sequence, the birth of the twins, has an undeniably positive result. Nevertheless, the syntagmatic sanction of the sequence, just as for the sequences just discussed, is overdetermined by the same paradigmatic sanction that indexes the character as well as the sordid and base 'natural' sentiments of the agents. When the other children return home after the birth of the twins, the only comment made is that they 'virent une mare de sang à l'endroit où d'ordinaire, on jetait les eaux sales' (saw a pool of blood at the place where ordinarily the dirty water from the household was thrown) (5).

Without dwelling too long on this, I nevertheless note that the overwhelming majority of the other scenes and/or tableaux set up antagonistic agents in a confrontational situation so that the improvement obtained by one agent corresponds necessarily and inversely to the degradation of the other. For example, whether it is a question of vengeance (chapters 5, 26, 30), of deceit (chapters 11 and 14), of humiliation (chapter 10), of fraud (chapters 9 and 28), of theft (chapter 13),[14] of malicious gossip, and so on, all the sequences have a positive result for the instigating agent. By contrast, when it is a question of justice to be administered (chapter 2),[15] religious knowledge to be transmitted (chapter 6), teaching to be done (chapter 8), justice to be obtained (chapter 10),[16] charity asked for (chapters 13 and 26), and so on, the agent inevitably meets with failure. As a matter of fact, the same indexical process overdetermines each sequence in the negative and dysphoric manner underscored above.

As I mentioned earlier, that the actional micro-sequences are motivated by an elementary decisional and indexical logic that constitutes for them a common fundamental syntax. As I also noted, critics of Laberge's work have come up against the problem of the interrelationship of the sequences, insofar as all the episodes of *La Scouine* are of a 'stemmatic' nature, to borrow once again an expression from Barthes (1966). In other words, these sequences are not linked together and do not take on their meaning within the context of the unity of a single action, but instead form separate, discrete units, so that the text is composed of functionally independent episodes. From this point of view, the narrative form of *La Scouine*, that is to say the form of the discourse of the knowledge transmitted, posits new conditions for its existence and articulates its own procedures authorizing its plural narratives. At this most elementary level (functions), the narrative form is realized within the confines of the institutionalized narrative discourse of the novel. Yet it should also be said that, at the very same time, the narrative form is realized against this very discourse insofar as it deconstructs the positive discursive formations of the novel of the land. At the level of functions, the novel sets in place a syntax that subrogates the sequences conveying a unique presupposition – that is, the pre-eminence of an integrated narrative form in the formulation of traditional knowledge and the knowledge of tradition. In short, to paraphrase Lyotard in *La Condition post-moderne*, the practice of the traditional novel legitimizes institutionalized knowledge in terms of the grand unifying narrative, whereas *La Scouine*, an original text of the rupture, inaugurates a discursive practice of protest that shakes the foundations of institutionalized knowledge. It does so insofar as it plays out in its very form and through its pragmatics the troubling and feverish anamnesis of the legitimacy of the grand narrative that has lost its credibility. By refusing, even by deconstructing, the functional law of the genre, this narrative privileges the paradigmatic class of the indices that integrate the functions at the superior level of the actants, playing out at one and the same time the very scenario of dehiscence, of the scene of the other, of the other scene.

À l'école, à cause de l'odeur qu'elle répandait, ses camarades avaient donné à Paulima le surnom de Scouine, mot sans signification aucune, interjection vague qui nous ramène aux origines premières du langage.

(At school because of the odour she gave off, the children had given Paulima the nickname of La Scouine, a word without any signification whatsoever, a vague interjection that brings us back to the very origins of language.) (12)

In *La Scouine*, characters manipulate, they humiliate, they assail one another, they torture, they mutilate. Regardless of sex and age, the actants in Laberge are all cut from the same cloth and are all inscribed within the social constellation of the family. In other words, each logico-decisional functional sequence is articulated at the superior level by actants[17] who actualize through their actions, thoughts, and feelings within the confines of elementary kinship relations. It is possible to suggest that the quasi-totality of the scenes and/or tableaux have either a direct relationship to one or several members of the Deschamps family, or are set off by them. For example chapters 26 and 27, which relate Tofile (*Theo* + *phile* = friend of God) Lambert's brutality *vis-à-vis* his retarded young twin brothers, bringing about the death of the one called 'Le Schno,' are linked to the Deschamps by La Scouine's visit. As she goes by him, Le Schno pinches her. Then he gets a pitchfork and begins to kill a number of chickens in the yard, laughing as he goes about this. Tofile notices this, kicks his brother in the back, and forces both twins to dig up a ditch, all the while depriving them of food. The sun is extremely hot, and Le Schno takes off his hat, gets sunstroke, and falls fatally ill: 'Le Schno continua de gémir et mourut dans l'avant-midi, comme une vieille rosse fourbue' (Le Schno continued to moan and died that afternoon, like an exhausted old nag) (97). He dies in the barn, his corpse dirty and muddy, where Tofile discovers him: 'I a ben crevé, le bougre, dit-il' (The Devil really croaked, he said). When he announces this to his wife, she in turn remarks: 'En v'la un bon débarras' (Well that's good riddance) (98).

I stated above that all the sequences with actants (subject operators) who wish to transform a subject of state (a subject in a disjunctive relationship with a transcendental object of value) into a subject of conjunction with the said value meet with failure. On the other hand, all the actants who want to impose themselves on weaker ones, or to deprive them of any valued object, succeed most of the time. In the first case, the subject (played out by the actors: primary school teacher, priest, judge, etc.) does not succeed in the name of the original sender (God, truth, history, love, etc.) for a receiver (salvation, family, nation, happiness, etc.) in manipulating the will and duty of the anti-subject. The latter's modal competence (theoretical knowledge, and power) is therefore not activated so as to make him/her perform in an acceptable or wished-for manner (sanction). Hence, La Scouine, in spite of all her teacher's goodwill and best efforts, will not learn the rules of grammar: 'La Scouine apprit avec terreur qu'elle devrait étudier la grammaire et l'histoire du Canada. De plus, elle aurait à lire dans le *Devoir du Chrétien* et dans le *psautier*. Non bien sûr, qu'elle n'apprendrait pas tout ça. Jamais de la vie' (La Scouine learned with terror that she would have to study grammar and Canadian history. In addition, she would have to read in the *Christian's Duty* and the *Psalter*. No, of course not. She would not learn all that. Never!) (21). She refuses to learn the lessons assigned to her, and rips out the successive pages of her textbooks. When the teacher tries to punish her, she runs out of the classroom screaming at the top of her lungs. The parishioners hear her and report this to the school trustees, who accuse the teacher of cruelty and decide to dismiss her. After the teacher gives her version to the priest, he recognizes that justice is on her side, but refuses to intervene on the pretext that doing so would constitute an abuse of authority, and 'Mlle Léveillé, la petite demoiselle blonde et mince, si gentille dans sa robe bleue, dut s'en aller après une semaine d'enseignement' (Miss Léveillé,[18] the little blond young lady, so slim, so nice in her blue dress, had to leave after one week of teaching) (25–6). Neither will La Scouine learn her catechism, or again anything about charity or love of her neighbour. In this universe, religion has no hold over the behaviour of the personae. In one scene, after receiving their first Communion and coming out of the church, the twins and Urgèle gather around an old woman selling sweets from a large basket. A young boy, also a churchgoer, asks for five sticks of toffee, and runs off without paying. The old woman comments in anger to the crowd gathered around her: 'Si c'est pas honteux ... un enfant qui vient de faire sa première communion, me voler comme ça!' (It's shameful ... a child who has just received his first Communion, to steal from me like that) (16). La Scouine also swindles the old blind man the night before Christmas (39), and justice is no better served; the Linches' employee will be persecuted for having told the truth about their fraud (29). This is certainly the case for everything that can be considered positive and/or desirable in this agrarian novel. If we consider *La Terre paternelle* (chapter 8) or *Maria Chapdelaine* (chapter 9) as emblematic of the genre, in *La Scouine* not only do the 'voices' remain mute and hence inoperative, but also ancestrality, origins (language, race, religion), and lineage as well as collective memory are totally absent, and hence are non-existent as senders.[19] When they are considered from the perspective of their actorial spheres, the characters are simply figures of an actantial subject searching to transform the anti-subject, making her/him share the same narrative program of *spirituality*. But these programs never come to fruition, and fail when confronted by the anti-program of *instinct*.[20]

The narrative programs that I have just sketched alternate in the first half of the novel with a second series of narrative programs of manipulation starting with chapter 17 when, in anticipation of his son's future marriage, Urgèle decides to build a new house for him. Climbing down from the roof, Charlot falls, is gravely wounded, and becomes a cripple: 'Dans sa famille, ses frères le surnommèrent le Cassé' (In his family his brothers nicknamed him the Wreck) (57). But during the actualization of the program of manipulation, the actant subject is always deprived of the sought-for object of value that the other, the anti-subject, possesses. In Laberge's world, objects of value circulate in an autarchical economy, so that conjunction is always privative. Moreover, these objects of value do not enter into a circuit of communication or of virtual reciprocity, but simply serve to satisfy the instinctive desire of the subject. In this configuration, the subject is at one and the same time the sender and the receiver of the object of value in question, a relation that is simply inscribed in an immanent circuit of ipseity (By Me → Object → For Me). From the beginning to the end of the novel the same narrative programs and anti-programs of *appropriation* and *conservation* will be reiterated and assumed by different actors, who are always in a polemical and non-contractual relation with the other.

Nevertheless, it should be noted that in the desired narrative sequences of manipulation → competence → performance → sanction, the anti-subject never acquires competence in Laberge's imaginary universe. Indeed, one could qualify all the other actors who will never internalize any modalities enabling them to change and progress with the same characteristics used in describing La Scouine when she was haunting the priests in the village: 'Patiente, rusée, elle surgit ... au moment où ils s'attendent le moins à la voir. Vulgaire, familière, elle est devenue un véritable cauchemar ... ils la fuient comme le choléra, mais ils ne peuvent réussir à l'éviter ...' (Patient, sly, she cropped up ... at the moment they least expected to see her. Vulgar, familiar, she has become a real nightmare ... they flee her like the plague, but they never succeed in avoiding her, in getting rid of her ...) (129). For all the members of the Deschamps family, their innate competence at the origin of action is of the order of instinct, and the reflex of appropriation appears at the very instant the other looms up on their horizon.

It would be appropriate here to ask the question regarding the modal articulation and make up of the performing subject in *La Scouine*. None of the actors in this world of 'nightmare' possesses any theoretical or mythical knowledge transmitted through time, but each one, of a 'sly' nature, possesses an agrarian or domestic practical knowledge that is necessary for her/his own survival or for the general survival of the group. Like La Scouine, they are all ignorant, or superstitious. She concludes that the malediction that has fallen on the family is Taon's fault because he has blasphemed. Even his dog becomes suspect in her eyes, and she decides to get rid of it by throwing it into the well. This she does, and the dog meets an untimely and very cruel death as it swims around for an hour before drowning from exhaustion. All these characters are endowed with knowledge of the other that corresponds to the projection of their intuitive system of understanding. For example, Urgèle Deschamps, on learning of his neighbour Ernest Lecomte's imminent death, attempts to persuade the dying man's sister to sell his cows at an undervalued price and pocket the money so that the other members of the family do not get their inheritance (chapter 16). For both sexes, their power is mainly physical, and each and every one of them is a tireless worker. Women as well as men are involved in heavy outdoor farm labour, and they work side by side at harvest time. However, with respect to masculine subjects, corporeal strength permits one to overcome the other and acquire the desired object of value: 'Deschamps qui était un rude batailleur' (Deschamps who was a powerful fighter) (62), wishing to vote in an election, is prevented from doing so by three solid Irishmen. He begins to fight with them and, after an extremely arduous combat, is vanquished and dragged along, with a rope around his neck, behind a wagon drawn by a horse. 'Moulu, essoufflé, nu-tête, la figure tuméfiée et sanglante, les côtes, les jambes et les reins meurtris, Deschamps courait derrière la charrette, butant contre les pierres et écumant de rage impuissante' (Black and blue, out of breath, hatless, his face bruised and bloody, his ribs, legs and back covered with bruises, Deschamps ran behind the wagon, stumbling against the stones and boiling with helpless rage) (64). La Scouine, as a joke, is shaved by two boys of the village (31). Taon beats his horse to death (36). Bagon castrates La Scouine's favourite calf, and she feels that 'd'avoir vu s'accomplir un meurtre' (she has just witnessed a murder) (92). Tofile's beating of his brother, the idiot, is indirectly responsible for the brother's death. Raclor and Tifa, the two older brothers, attack the rest of the family and beat Charlot, Maço, and La Scouine (112). The feminine subjects are less violent because physically weaker. Sometimes, though, they attack defenceless animals (La Scouine drowns a dog that she believes is a bearer of malediction), and also children (she threatens recent orphans with the return of their dead mother). But most of the time their power is at the tip of their tongues as they lie, deceive, manipulate, and denounce others. In all of these 'naturellement gourmands' (naturally greedy) (10) and 'cupides' (grasping) (74, 75) beings, wanting or desire arises immediately at the instant the other appears. In brief, the presence of the other automatically sets off a reflex of manipulation, founded on violence if one is physically strong, or deceit (making believe) when one is in a position of physical inferiority. From this perspective, the subject actant undergoes no modal transformations insofar as she/he simply reproduces the same antagonistic situation motivated by an innate competence that instinctively triggers performance.

This instinctive privative model of appropriation traces and reproduces the elementary reflex of the biological survival of the individual and the group actualized through the predator–prey, dominating–dominated relations within a single space/territory. In a fundamental way, Laberge's tale realizes and dramatizes, configures and reconfigures, the biological situation of encounter and attack, immobilization and conquest, that, in the novelist's imagination, governs the ambient animal domain. In this novel of origins, the family, grouped around a dominant male, is organized hierarchically according to the dual principle of instinctive force and ruse in such a way that the place of each member of the group is biologically and physically determined. Hence, the family will remain stable in this chosen territory, defended and governed by its head as long as he has the physical strength and power to impose himself at home and within the larger community. It is Urgèle, the father, who, when they reach their majority, gives each of the older sons a farm so that they, in turn, can found a family. For the same reason, he has a house built for his youngest son, Charlot. It is only when the father is old, weak, and impotent that the oldest sons will literally attack his territory along with that of the weaker and dependent members of the family. Again, it is after the father's death that the aged mother, who is now sterile, the barren spinster La Scouine, and Charlot the 'Wreck,' an infertile bachelor, abandon the farm and retire to the village: 'Maintenant que *le père* était mort, ils allaient se reposer, vivre de leurs rentes' (Now that *the father*[21] was dead, they were going to rest and live on their income) (123).

The destiny of the Deschamps family is to consume daily this bread 'au goût sur et amer ... marqué du signe de la rédemption' (having a sour and bitter taste ... marked by the sign of the Redemption) (1) – a sign that, ironically, will remain inoperative throughout this domestic drama. Its patronymic, on the contrary, etymologically arrives at the place where the original scene is dramatized and assumes the status of an eponym as the tale unfolds.[22] Furthermore, this hereditary scenario of kinship does not concern the other families described in the text to the same degree. Ironically, the Lecomtes, those 'good people' whom Urgèle tried to take advantage of (chapter 16), after he becomes 'crippled and impotent' and can no longer digest his own bread, exchange 'l'une de ses galettes sures et amères, lourdes comme du sable, contre l'une de leurs miches blondes et légères' (one of his sour and bitter biscuits, as heavy as sand, for one of their light and blond loaves) (119). In the same vein, the mistress of the Bougie family, the new owners who bought their farm and who live together in harmony on the Deschamps land, 'vive, plaisante, aimable ... apporte sur la table un gros pain blond, chaud et odorant, qu'elle vient de sortir du four. La croûte est de la belle couleur du blé et la mie est blanche et appétissante' (lively, pleasant, friendly ... places on the table a large loaf of blond, hot and sweet-smelling bread that she had just taken out of the oven. The crust is a beautiful wheat colour, and the inside is white and appetizing) (132). In addition, Laberge's narrative is placed under the enigma of the nickname 'la Scouine, mot sans signification aucune, interjection vague qui nous ramène aux origines premières du langage' (la Scouine, a word without any signification whatsoever, a vague interjection that brings us back to the very origins of language) (12). Yet this nickname/title, empty signifier, apparently non-motivated, if we are to believe the author, designating the single, unmarried woman, runs through and works on the narrative, so much so that LA SCOUINE, anagram of LA COUSINE (cousin), inscribes the hallucinatory scene of the primary interdiction, the separation, break, rupture in the elementary structure of kinship linked to the 'very origins of language.'[23]

The trauma of origins, of the break, of the passage from nature to culture, from life to death, from the imaginary to the symbolic, plays out, in this tale of origins, both through the reiteration and concatenation of the haunting image of the disruptive oedipal scene, and the refusal of the oppressive letter of the law that can be linked to all the narrative programs of *spirituality*. It is through violence and repression that the law of the father imposes itself in *La Scouine*. Having abandoned 'the paternal house,' after 'marrying and raising' in their turn, 'a family,' the two older sons, now 'settled on the land that Deschamps had bought for them next to his' decide to avenge themselves and impose their own law on the family through violence. Tifa, 'l'homme de sa nourriture, l'homme dont le chair, le sang, les os, les muscles, le cerveau, le cœur, étaient faits de pain sur et amer. Et le pain était comme le levain qui aurait fait germer dans cette pâte humaine, la haine, le crime, le meurtre' (man of his food, a man whose flesh, blood, muscles, brains, heart, were made up of sour and bitter bread. And the bread was like the yeast that would have made germinate hate, crime, murder in this human dough), beats his brother Charlot, shoves and jostles his mother, seizes his sister by the throat, and 'vomissant une litanie d'horribles blasphèmes ... le bras levé s'avança sur son père' (vomiting a litany of horrible blasphemies ... with raised arm moves towards his father) (113). In front of the broken and used body of 'le vieux Deschamps, si vigoureux autrefois, qui cognait sur tout le monde et à tout propos, invalide maintenant' (old Deschamps, so vigorous in the past, who beat up on everyone for no reason at all, now an invalid), the son stops, turns to the garden, and begins to destroy it with an axe. Meanwhile Raclor, the eldest, with the help of a team of horses, uproots the trees planted by his mother: 'les chevaux tiraient, et les racines de l'arbuste cédaient, craquaient, cassaient, s'arrachaient, *comme les membres d'un homme que l'on aurait écartelé*' (the horses were pulling, and the roots of the tree gave way, cracking, breaking, being pulled out, *like the limbs of a man being drawn and quartered*).[24] Their Mother Nature is subjected to the imposition of the law, this access to the symbolic, and lives it as a physical gash, a radical separation: 'Maço avait la sensation qu'on lui arrachait le cœur, les entrailles' (Maço felt as though they were tearing out her heart, her entrails). The law of violence, the violence of the law, the passage from the universe of the dual, of the imaginary and the symbolic – from the natural mother–child dyad to culture – is somatically experienced in her innermost being as a rent, a radical loss, and is expressed by the extended metaphor woman–garden, child–tree: 'ce jardin dont elle avait bêché la terre, ces arbres qu'elle avait plantés elle-même, qu'elle avait soignés, comme s'ils avaient été *des êtres humains, d'autres enfants*; ces arbres qu'elle avait vu *grandir*, tout cela était rasé, dévasté en un jour de malheur et par la main de ses fils' (This garden whose soil she had dug up, these trees that she had planted herself, that she had nurtured, as though they had been *human beings, other children*, these trees that she had seen *grow up*,[25] everything was razed, devastated in a single day of calamity and by the hands of her sons) (113).

The incision and the lesion of the law are dramatized and enacted one last time, but in reverse, in chapter 32 – an actual retracing of and return to origins – describing Urgèle Deschamps's end and reversing the passage from nature to culture noted above. The father regresses to a natural maternal state of a pre-cultural order: 'Dans sa tête, les choses s'embrouillaient, se confondaient, *comme le soir dans la nature, lorsque vient la nuit*' (In his head, things got mixed up, confused, *like evening in nature when night falls*) (118). Furthermore, the pre-cultural state is marked by separation, by a return to the pre-phallic stage of the imaginary: 'il montait au champ, allant devant lui, indécis, *comme un animal qu'on vient de châtrer*' (he would go up to the field, walking along, indecisive, *like an animal that had just been castrated*) (118). This regression continues inevitably until the mirror stage and is accompanied by a loss of verbal communication: 'Deschamps regardait les choses d'un regard vague, restant pendant des heures appuyé sur une clôture, ou assis sur une pierre près d'un puits, se parlant à lui-même' (Deschamps looked at things in a very vague way, staying for hours on end leaning against a fence, or sitting on a stone near a well, talking to himself) (118–19). Finally, he literally reverts to infancy and identifies the woman-mother before returning to the primary stage of fragmentation: 'il souillait maintenant son pantalon *comme enfant il avait sali ses langes* ... la machine humaine détraquée, ne fonctionnait plus, ne valait guère mieux *qu'un amas de débris*' (he now soiled his pants *as he had soiled his diapers as an infant* ... the human machine unhinged, no longer functioned, was worth no more than *an old pile of debris*) (119).[26] In death, he rejoins nature and is integrated with it, while his body takes on a troubling characteristic that had been elided and unarticulated until now in the text: 'le soleil se couchait. Au dehors, ses rayons rouges mettaient des reflets d'incendie à la fenêtre et ensanglantaient le vieux lit sur lequel le grand corps reposait inerte' (the sun was setting. Outside, its red rays cast reflections of fire on the window and bloodied the old bed on which the big body rested inertly) (120). What is played out to the letter is the final regression to the separation and the fusion, reproducing backwards the paradoxical quest of the difference of the symbolic and the unity of the imaginary.

It is possible that in 'this apparent contradiction between the man and his work,' noted in the quotation by Lionel Léveillé with which this chapter opens, the enigma remains in its entirety. However, in a way, the contradiction vanishes. The fragmentary narrative of *La Scouine* both challenges the law of the genre and unfurls according to the letter of the law. This text, which does not succeed in structuring itself syntagmatically, projects on the paradigmatic axis the hallucinatory scenario of subjects obligated to the dictates of the symbolic productions that position them. It is these very productions that they pointlessly desire to cast off and against which they must, when all is said and done, in desperation define themselves. The structure of *La Scouine* maintains through its stemmatic singularity the tensions between individual and collective historicities and succeeds in deconstructing, through its very specificity, the meanings and forms of the contradictions of a given culture that seems still to believe in the unifying legitimacy and efficiency of the grand family narrative.[27]

CHAPTER ELEVEN

History and the Urban Novel: *Bonheur d'occasion (The Tin Flute)*[1]

In chapter 9, I attempted to show the various hypothetical solutions to the question of the identity of the subject raised in *Maria Chapdelaine* and suggested that this narrative explored a number of options and, in the end, proposed and endorsed an 'ideal' one that would guarantee collective or national distinctiveness. In this novel of colonization, much as in *La Terre paternelle* before it, and *Trente arpents*[2] twenty years later, the wilderness and the city are considered as forbidden and dangerous spaces that lead to tribalism and sexuality, as well as to cosmopolitanism and the isolated couple. They are mapped out as the *beyond*, the *elsewhere*, the *contingent*, and the *impossible* – spaces that dissolve the subject into an ego defining itself in and by its own desire. What these novels do is establish the boundaries, the limits within which each subject can determine itself in terms of the collective aspirations of the group. The frontier and the village are positive spaces that are permitted and necessary, for they lead directly to the family and nationalism. They are the *here* and the *there*, the *necessary* and the *possible* that ensure the survival, continuity, and prosperity of the French-Canadian nation. This is the case with all novels of the land written in Quebec from the mid-nineteenth century to the mid-twentieth, except for *La Scouine*, which, as we have just seen, deconstructs the euphoric, moralized space of the family, village, and group where the subject can blossom and prosper within a commonly shared project of identity. Yet, in spite of this widely iterated nationalistic program, by the end of the Second World War the subject of the novel became firmly ensconced in the city. Whereas historical and territorial novels clearly delimited the positive spaces in which the individual could define and affirm his or her cultural identity – the manor, the village, or the frontier – they also determined the negative spaces – the city[3] and the wilderness[4] – in which individual identity was dissipated and lost. With *Bonheur d'occasion* (translated as *The Tin Flute*), the most widely read postwar Quebec novel of the 1940s and 1950s,[5] not only do individuals migrate to the city, not only do they live and die there, but their offspring are born, raised, and grow up in an urban environment.

The novel is divided into thirty-three chapters, each of which deals with a specific event concerning one or more characters, within a three-month time frame, from the end of February to the end of May 1940. Four plot strands are intertwined.[6] The first deals with Florentine Lacasse's sentimental experiences, first with Jean Lévesque, then with Emmanuel Létourneau. Florentine, a young waitress in a five-and-dime store, ardently desires to escape the poverty of her working-class neighbourhood, Saint-Henri, in Montreal, and becomes emotionally attached to a young and ambitious worker, Jean Lévesque, whom she starts to date steadily. Their relationship becomes rather complex as each of them attempts to control the other. At the same time, Florentine is courted by a soldier on leave, Emmanuel, from a middle-class Montreal background, who is infatuated with her. She, in turn, pursues Jean, with whom she falls madly in love. As she would like to confirm her conquest of him, she abandons herself on a single occasion, becomes pregnant, and, after much anguish, decides not to tell him that he is the father to be. Not wanting to get attached to anyone, Jean subsequently rejects her, along with, unknown to him, the child she is expecting. In an attempt to legitimize her future offspring and to ensure her own financial security, after a very brief courtship, she marries Emmanuel, whom she does not love but who is very much in love with her. Ignorant of her condition, he embarks for England almost immediately afterwards. At the end of the novel, Florentine makes plans to leave Saint-Henri and settle in a much better Montreal neighbourhood, Boulevard Lasalle.

The second plot strand deals with the trials and tribulations of the Lacasse family, and especially of the mother, Rose-Anna, who is desperately trying to prevent the break-up of the family despite ever-increasing financial constraints and endemic poverty. Her son Eugène, despondent and chronically unemployed, ends up enlisting in the army to fight in the war, as does her husband, Azarius, who, unable to find and keep a steady job, sees this as the only solution to guarantee his family a regular income. Her youngest son, Daniel, is felled by leukaemia and dies alone in the hospital, while Florentine seemingly becomes more and more remote and indifferent to everyone in her family. Life follows death, and Rose-Anna gives birth to another son. The third strand deals with the young men of the neighbourhood, in particular Alphonse, Pitou, and Boisvert, victims of structural unemployment linked to the Great Depression. Most of these – except for Boisvert, who becomes an accountant – after having spent a good deal of their adolescent and young adult life in endless discussions in Ma Philibert's restaurant, end up joining the army as their first paying job. The fourth strand is the war that looms over all of the individuals or groups and is considered by them to be the short-term or long-term solution to their economic and social problems.

A careful examination of the different characters in this novel reveals that there exist classes of subjects whom we can differentiate according to the various modalities that enable them to act. However, before undertaking this level of analysis it is necessary, first, to examine briefly the nature of the object of value or desire that motivates each personage. Florentine, for example, wishes to escape the miseries of her condition or class and attain happiness by marrying Jean Lévesque. To do so, she sets out a complex strategy of seduction. In effect, the modalities of the series regulating her actions are governed by her volition by which she can identify the object of her desire and say *I*. To attain her goal, she must draw on a knowledge of the world that is neither technical nor theoretical, but rather instinctive and transmitted by the cultural media of the ambient consumer society. In this vein, one notes the great number of references throughout the novel to movies, fashion, clothing, and bric-à-brac that are shared and valued by most of her acquaintances. What sets Florentine apart from the other characters are the motifs of the mirror, the compact, lipstick, and nylons, which attract her gaze or the gaze of the other, and can be considered simple indices of a world in which the values defining the subject are mediated by and through the other.[7] Every time she is with one of her suitors, the young woman inevitably checks her make-up in a mirror on the wall, or in her compact, appraising herself with respect to lower-class models handed down by the social and economic systems of the times. When Florentine meets Jean in the opening chapter, the reader is caught up in a whirlwind of shifting gazes, as focalization alternates from one character to the other while they converse.[8] And when, later on, he takes her out for dinner in a chic restaurant, she keeps staring at her reflected image, speculating on the effect she is creating: 'Ce qui la grisait surtout, c'était dans une glace profonde derrière le jeune homme, sa propre image vers laquelle elle se penchait fréquemment. Elle s'y voyait, les yeux brillants, le teint mat et clair, les traits dilués; et parce qu'elle se plaisait ainsi, elle avait l'air en s'approchant de Jean de vouloir sans cesse lui communiquer son instant de triomphe. Elle ne pouvait pas ne pas aimer bientôt quelqu'un auprès duquel elle se trouvait si jolie' (73) (What intoxicated her most was her own reflection in the mirror behind Jean. She leaned forward frequently to admire her shining eyes, her transparent complexion, her blurred features, and finding herself so desirable, she wanted to convey her sense of triumph to Jean. It needed little more for her to fall in love with a man in whose company she made such a pretty picture) (53).

Yet this instinctive knowledge of self serves only as a measure of the reification of the subject into a desiring, desired body. In all her personal relations, Florentine attempts to exhibit her body as a sign system to be read and emotionally invested by her male interlocutor. But the gaze of the other, the other's gaze, carries with it a fundamental ambiguity, insofar as, when she attempts to project an image of self, the other reads the constructed body through a system of signs that escapes her, which is the case with Jean, whom she is trying to entice and who is different from others of her class. During their first conversation in the restaurant, after initially observing her, Jean examines her once again and re-inscribes her body into her class of origin: 'et il la vit mieux; il la vit reflétée à mi-corps dans la glace du mur, et il fut frappé de sa maigreur. Autour de sa taille, elle avait pourtant tiré jusqu'au bout le ceinturon de son uniforme vert, mais on devinait que ses vêtements adhéraient à peine à son corps fluet, presque débile. Et le jeune homme eut soudain une vision de ce que pouvait être sa vie, dans l'inquiet tourbillon de Saint-Henri, cette vie des jeunes filles fardées, pimpantes qui lisent des romans-feuilletons de quinze cents et se brûlent à de pauvres petits feux d'amour factice' (12) (and he saw her more clearly. Catching her reflection in the mirror against the wall, he was startled to see how thin she was. She had pulled the belt of her green uniform about her waist as far as it would go, but her clothes still hung loosely on her slender body. The young man had a sudden insight into the narrow life of such a girl afloat in the turbulent eddy of Saint-Henri. Like all girls of her type, she had probably been scorched by the meagre little fires of fictitious love in the pages of cheap novels) (3). Thinking about a possible date that evening, Jean projects her into a future very different from what she herself imagines: 'mais il ne la voyait plus telle qu'elle était là, de l'autre côté du comptoir. Il la voyait parée, prête à sortir le soir, avec beaucoup de fard pour couvrir la pâleur de ses joues, des bijoux cliquetant sur toute sa maigre personne, un petit chapeau ridicule, peut-être même une voilette derrière laquelle ses yeux avivés de khôl brilleraient: une petite fille drôlement attifée, volage et toute tourmentée déjà par le désir de lui plaire' (12) (but he no longer saw her as she was. He saw her in his mind's eye all primped up, ready to go out in the evening, her cheeks plastered with rouge to conceal her pallor, cheap jewellery rattling all over her skinny person, wearing a silly little hat, perhaps a veil, her eyes glittering with make-up, a flighty girl, bent on making herself attractive to him, Jean Lévesque) (3). When she is with Emmanuel, she also deceives him into thinking she is responding to his love, whereas all she wants is a paternal name for the child she is expecting. But perhaps the most telling case occurs when her mother, Rose-Anna, observing her daughter's behaviour, deduces from her bodily symptoms that she is pregnant and questions her, while Florentine steadfastly denies it. 'Lorsqu'elle se redressa, pâle, le visage humilié, sa mère la regardait. Elle la regardait comme si elle ne l'avait jamais encore vue, et la découvrait soudain. Elle la regardait avec des yeux agrandis, fixes, et une expression de muette horreur. Sans pitié, sans amitié, sans bonté: rien que de l'horreur plein les yeux. Presque violente, d'une voix qui montait, elle s'écria: "Mais qu'est-ce que t'as donc, toi! Hier, à matin, pis encore à soir ... On dirait que t'es ..." Elle s'était tue et les deux femmes se regardaient comme deux ennemies' (232) (When she sat up again, pale and shamefaced, her mother was staring at her. She was staring as if she had never seen her before, speechless with horror. There was no pity in her regard, no sympathy, only horror. Her voice rising with hysteria she cried: 'What's wrong with you! Yesterday morning, and now tonight ... You act as if you were –' She was silent, and the two women glared at each other like two enemies) (184). In brief, we are dealing with a complex sign system of manipulation and deception that grounds personal relations in perception, where being and seeming and non-being and non-seeming establish intricate relations between truth, falsehood, secret, and lie. Here subjects endlessly interrogate each other through the gaze and constantly observe and interpret the fluid and ever-changing expressive, gestural, vocal, and dress systems that constitute the form and content of the acting, thinking, feeling body. Within this context, signs are not abstract signifiers and signifieds but are always incorporated, incarnated, and mediated by the flesh. They are unstable by nature, since the polysystems and multiple processes defining them vary and evolve according to the uncertain and unpredictable situations in which the protagonists are projected.

Florentine's ability to act is again dependent on her physical strength, genetic make-up, character, and beauty. She is a capable worker, slender, desirable, and somewhat moody. She is able to interest suitors and hold sway over them by means of both her corporeal attributes and her shifting character. She is also, initially at least, bound by a sense of duty to preserve the family, handing over much of her salary to her mother, living at home, and sometimes even depriving herself of small luxuries to ensure that they have enough money to survive. Yet, in the end, her desires and individual ego manifest and express themselves independently of the traditional family. Upon learning that her brother Eugène, who was earning regular wages in the army, had not returned the money she had given her mother for groceries, and that he had borrowed for his own pleasures, Florentine reacts violently to her memory of him on his last leave as she passed him on St Catherine Street with a flashy-looking girl on his arm. That same evening, Rose-Anna had served the others in the family bread and scraps of cold meat for supper, saying she had not had time to go shopping. 'Oh! le misérable goût de ce repas! Florentine l'avait encore à la bouche, comme une nourriture de peine, de chagrin qui jamais ne se digérerait. Alors, elle avait perdu tout bon mouvement envers sa mère, tout désir de l'aider, par rancune contre Eugène' (224) (The wretched taste of that meal came back to her now; it was food that never could be digested. By yielding to Eugène's demand, Rose-Anna had forfeited Florentine's good will) (177). As a result, Florentine loses all interest in the family and feels increasing resentment towards her brother, whose actions have destroyed her illusions about him and people in general. None the less, at the end of her actantial trajectory, after she marries Emmanuel and the men have gone off to war, Florentine decides to share her new-found financial security with her mother, her sisters, and her remaining brothers. She assumes the status of subject, albeit a desiring subject, but desiring for herself and others as she contemplates an uncertain future: 'Parfois elle éprouvait encore cependant comme un saisissement à la pensée de cet argent qui leur serait donné à elles, les femmes, pendant que les hommes risqueraient leur vie' (345) (And yet at times she thought of all the money that would be given them, the women, while their men risked their lives) (274).[9]

Jean Lévesque, her counterpart of modest origins, is also determined at all costs to escape the conditions of his class. From beginning to end, he is systematically depicted as an ambitious, hard-working, obsessively driven individual who wishes to succeed within the current economic system, no matter what. Everything he does is governed by his drive and aspiration to acquire status by attaining material and social success on the home front. 'C'est qu'il venait de se voir à travers les yeux de Florentine: blagueur, méchant garçon, dangereux même ... Et c'est qu'il venait aussi de saisir toutes les contradictions qu'il y avait entre lui-même, le vrai Jean Lévesque, et le personnage qu'il s'était créé aux yeux de tous ... Le vrai Jean Lévesque était tout autre' (23) (He had just seen himself as Florentine had seen him: a dangerous fellow ... In that same moment of illumination he recognized also all the contradictions within himself, the wide difference between the real Jean Lévesque and the personality he had created for the eyes of the world ... The real Jean Lévesque was another person entirely) (12–13). He sees himself as obstinate, reserved, a hard worker not a silly dreamer. He loves work not for itself but for the ambitions it nourishes, for the success to which it will lead him, and he dedicates himself to work almost in a spirit of revenge on the world. He has all of the characteristics of the self-made man, and nothing must stand in his way. Moreover, he has no illusions about what motivates individuals in the current social, historical, and economic climate. In what began as a political discussion about pacifism at The Two Records with a number of men from the older generation, he cynically states, 'Moi, je vois que des profiteurs. Regardez, depuis six mois seulement que la guerre dure, combien de gens déjà en profitent? À commencer par ceux qui se font une job dans l'armée ... Puis les gars des usines de munitions ... D'un bout à l'autre de l'échelle, c'est le profit qui mène. On est tous des profiteurs, ou si vous aimez mieux, pour ne pas nuire à notre effort de guerre, disons que nous sommes tous de bons patriotes' (42) (To me most men seem like profiteers. Have you any idea how many men have made a good thing out of this war, even though we have only been in it six months? Starting with those who found a job in the army ... Then take the fellows in the munitions plant ... All up and down the ladder, everybody's after the jack. We're all profiteers, but if you'd rather not hurt the war effort, let's say we're all good patriots) (27–8). Yet, in contrast to most of the others born in Saint-Henri, Jean, who has a background of theoretical knowledge related to his field of work, is relatively well educated and spends most of his free time studying on his own to become an engineer. Night after night he closets himself in his tiny room and pores over his correspondence courses. 'Aucun obstacle ne pouvait le rebuter. Son instruction étant insuffisante, il y suppléait. D'ailleurs, qui donc a appris quoi que ce soit des professeurs? Il était lui-même son propre maître, rude et inflexible. Il se tenait bien en main' (24) (No obstacle could dishearten him. If his knowledge proved inadequate to the tasks he had set for himself, he would add to it. Anyway, who ever learned anything from teachers? He was his own teacher, a harsh and inflexible taskmaster. He had complete control over himself) (13). Such knowledge will enable him to master the complex technology related to his immediate job of foreman in a foundry, and to succeed to positions of greater responsibility. In this world, where to know is to have, Jean possesses the intellectual capacity, tenacity, and physical and moral strength to realize his personal ambition. In addition, he feels no duty or obligation to any person or group that could stand in his way. Here, his ego wants and aspires for itself and in itself, and no transcendental values related to ethics or to the survival of the family or group play a role in his behaviour. In short, the capitalist system of self-interest and survival of the fittest motivates the subject to attain success for itself, aided by the war and with little regard for hypothetical, ineffectual sentiments or ethics. From the perspective of desire that permits the individual to say *I*, Florentine is a pale reflection of Jean, the differences being that she does not possess theoretical or technical knowledge and that, in spite of her resolve to break with the family, she oscillates between it and the imminent manifestation of self.[10]

Rose-Anna and Emmanuel form another complementary pair. Rose-Anna's desire, knowledge, and ability to act are regulated by duty, the obligation to ensure the survival of the traditional family within a religious framework where the father, the main wage earner, goes out into the world, while the mother stays home and oversees all the family activities around the warmth of the hearth or stove. When her husband finds work between his many bouts of unemployment, she daydreams about how Azarius felt more cheerful when he heard her slippers shuffling across the kitchen floor while he shaved, and how he liked to come into a room with the fire crackling in the stove[11] to take the chill out of the air, and the steam from the kettle misting the windows. She believes that his toast had a better taste when she served it to him all buttered, and his coffee had more flavour when she poured it for him, while holding back the full sleeve of her kimono (110–11). Her household knowledge is of a practical nature, transmitted through time by tradition and handed down to her daughters, who, in turn, are expected to function within the same frame of reference. Hence, Rose-

Anna spends much of her time doing domestic chores, ensuring that the rent is paid and the children are clothed and fed. Although she has dreams of her own, they are mainly related to improving the traditional family situation; she therefore functions as a subject that desires for the other and not for itself. When praying to God for help in finding a home for the family, a yearly occurrence for them, 'Elle aborda le côté matériel sans trop se presser, car il lui apparut qu'une certaine adresse était peut-être aussi nécessaire dans la prière que dans toute autre requête. Tout cela était instinctif et se jouait, inarticulé, dans les profondeurs de son être. Pour elle-même, elle eût éprouvé de la gêne à demander la moindre chose, mais pour les siens, elle ne craignait pas de préciser ce qu'elle espérait' (89) (She took her time when she came to material problems, for it seemed to her that a certain address was perhaps as necessary in prayer as in any other petition. All this was instinctive, and more or less buried in her subconscious. It would have embarrassed her to ask for anything for herself, but for her family she was not afraid to set forth just what she wanted) (66–7). As we can see, traditional Catholic family values condition the subject, who desires survival and betterment of the family. Yet, when all is said and done, these values remain inoperative and cannot change the lot of the alienated and impoverished individual, being countered by the forces of capitalism and neutralized by the war. All they can do is ensure the emergence of a truncated family amputated of its men.

As noted above, Emmanuel is also motivated by transcendental human values. He too wants, in part, for others, but instead of simply focusing on the family, he strives for the betterment of mankind in general. Emmanuel, who left school and enlisted in the army in order to fight totalitarianism and injustice, is a close friend of Lévesque's but his opposite, because, instead of wanting for and by himself, he acts with the common good in mind. Jean reminds him during a conversation at a tavern that they differ on one very important issue. Emmanuel thinks that it's the soldiers who change the world and lead the people, whereas Jean believes that it's the fellows who stay home and make money out of the war (41). In addition, Emmanuel loves Florentine for herself; unlike her, however, his interpersonal relations are founded on reciprocity rather than manipulation. He stands for openness, truth, and honesty, rather than deception, falsehood, and lies. None the less, deceived and seduced, he marries Florentine, not knowing she is carrying Jean's child, and goes off to war leaving her in a sound financial situation. Humanism conditions the subject to desire openness, truth, and happiness and to strive for a just society. Ironically, to attain even partially this end for the benefit of all, which is, in itself, presented as highly utopian, the humanitarian ideal is furthered by war and countered by the powerful force of modern-day capitalism and self-interest as represented by Jean and Boisvert.

Azarius, the father, much like the youths who hang around in Ma Philibert's restaurant, is able to envisage and identify clearly the material goods necessary to survive and prosper, but, like them, he cannot adopt the necessary strategies, or establish concrete plans to attain them. He is one of the first to be affected by the Great Depression, for he is a carpenter by trade, and construction has virtually ground to a halt in the 1930s and early 1940s. At the same time, though, he is too proud to take just any job and looks for work only in trades allied to his own. At length, and much to his shame, he is forced to apply for public relief. Reacting against being on welfare, he starts up several small businesses that inevitably go under. When the novel opens, he has just lost his job as a taxi driver. An eternal optimist and dreamer, he meets with failure in everything he undertakes. In a heated debate with Emmanuel and Azarius regarding society's concern for the destitute and unemployed, one of the youths categorically states that society doesn't give a damn about any of them and has given them nothing. However, another, Alphonse, interjects and retorts that of course society has given them something – temptations. 'Avez-vous déjà marché, vous autres, su la rue Sainte-Catherine, pas une cenne dans vot' poche, et regardé tout ce qu'y a dans les vitrines? Oui, hein! Ben moi aussi, ça m'est arrivé. Et j'ai vu du beau, mes amis ... Qu'est-ce que vous voyez-t-y pas su la rue Sainte-Catherine? ... Oui, des tentations, c'est ça que la société nous a donné ... Des tentations d'une boutte à l'autre' (52) (Have any of you guys ever walked on St. Catherine Street without a cent in your pocket and looked at all the stuff in the shop-windows? I guess so. Well, I have too. And I've seen some fine things, boys ... What can't you find on St. Catherine Street? ... That's what society gives us, temptations. From beginning to end that's all we get) (35–6). This group has neither the modern technical skills nor the theoretical skills necessary to participate in the trained work force, since its knowledge base is inadequate or inapplicable to current urban economics. The youths have little or no education, and the older workers have skills that have become redundant or irrelevant in the immediate wartime context. Men are being replaced by machines, while the chronically unemployed are losing their skills. A conversation between Azarius and Sam Latour is interrupted by a stranger, a mason by trade, who states that he has not worked at his own trade for eight years and that he has had to take on numerous jobs. He has worked as a gardener at the convent, as a paperhanger, and once, during an epidemic, earned a living as an exterminator, killing bedbugs and cleaning the lice out of mattresses. There's nothing he hasn't tried: 'Ils disent qu'il faut être spécialisé de nos jours pour se trouver de l'ouvrage. Ben, voulez-vous que je vous le dise: un métier, de nos jours, c'est pus rien. On passe la moitié de sa vie à l'apprendre son métier, pis le reste de sa vie à l'oublier' (134) (They say you have to specialize these days to find work. Well, let me tell you, a trade doesn't mean a thing any more. A man spends half his life learning a trade and the rest of his life forgetting it) (103). The scene ends with the mason's words: 'C'est entendu ... C'est la même chose partout. L'habileté se perd ... le métier se perd ... Y a plus que la mécanique' (135) (Right you are ... It's the same all over. We're losing our skills. We're forgetting our trades. Everything's done by machine) (104).

All of the endemically unemployed are emaciated and hungry, while some are even in a state of physical dilapidation that would prevent them from working if there were jobs available, or even, for that matter, from getting into the army. Alphonse describes to Emmanuel the medical visit he failed. After having told him to strip, they took him to the doctor, who told him to open his mouth and blurted out, 'Bonguienne! qu'il me dit, j'ai jamais vu tant de dents pourries de ma vie. Vous êtes donc jamais allé voir un dentiste!' (279) (By jingo, I never saw so many rotten teeth in my life. I can tell you've never been to a dentist!) (222). After that, another one bawled him out because instead of buying eyeglasses when he was ten years old he bought himself candies. 'Mais le plus drôle de la bande, c'est ct'ui-là qui m'a jeté une bordée de bêtises à la face parce qu'au lieu de bon lait pasteurisé j'avais été élevé aux binns pis aux fricassées d'oignons' (279) (The funniest guy of the lot was the one who gave me hell because I'd been brought up on canned beans instead of pasteurized milk) (222). In this universe of economic necessity, individuals are unable to affirm themselves, and all appear in the form of the undifferentiated mass, or 'it,' lost and destitute in a world no longer their own. War brings a solution to their problems since, by enlisting, they are able to look after their needs or to send money to the remaining members of their families. This is the case with Azarius, who, immediately after the birth of his last son, in the dark bedroom, dressed in a private's uniform that she cannot see, confesses to Rose-Anna his numerous failures and his inability to care for his family. He tells her that she will be rid of him and receive a cheque from the government for ninety-seven dollars every month. She at first thinks he has found work elsewhere in the country, until, in a dramatic and ironic turn of events, he switches on a light hanging from the ceiling, and she is shocked to discover that he is dressed in a soldier's uniform and ready to go to war. Once again, capitalism is seen as maintaining the working-class subject in a state of dependency. It can be curbed or even overcome by the war, but all that survives is a depleted family, deprived of its physically fit, adult male subjects.[12]

Whereas the historical novel attributes a specific stratified space to the subject, and the novel of the land or of colonization delimits a stable, unchanging, closed space within which the individual can realize his or her aspirations in light of a common national goal, the urban novel presents an ever-changing, unstable, polymorphous, dangerous, frustrating, and heterogeneous space that can engulf those who inhabit it. In the novel of the frontier, cleared land first becomes stabilized, develops into farmland, then is handed down to one's son and transmitted from one generation to another, before becoming grist for the novel of the paternal farm. In this genre, when subjects leave the farm to err in the city they either become morally and physically lost, or, having learned from their experience, return enlightened and content to the circumscribed space of their birth. Here, subjects live in harmony with nature, and in the world of the eternal return where events reoccur cyclically on a predictable basis. This regulated bi-dimensional temporality of iterated occurrences in a delimited space introduces a tempo of duration, symmetry, and order that can be interrupted by singular eruptions deregulating the stability of this peaceful universe. Subjects remain mainly in control of events and end up, year in and year out, tracing the same paths, with the same ritualized gestures and movements in an enclosed and constant space, alternately focalized through either the all-knowing and moralizing narrator or the thinking, feeling actor. In contrast to these two genres, the most striking characteristics of the urban novel, and in this case *Bonheur d'occasion*, is related to the fact that subjects are constantly on the move, walking, running, strolling, but also stopping, looking, discovering, and being discovered. In the narrative of the city, it is in the horizontal mazes that the body is described and discovers the fragmented urban text without being able to read and to totalize it as a whole. These different urban spatial practices uncover the city as a fragmented form, inscribing and defining the actors in spatiality constructed through the experience of mobility, which, at the moment it is apprehended by them, prevents them from understanding the signification of the object or the event perceived.

As I have suggested, the novel opens *in medias res*, immediately putting in place actors through whom events are focalized. This approach is not maintained throughout the narrative, since focalization is either concentrated within the actor who is speaking or about to speak, or shifts and is relayed by a sentient and cognizant narrator. Such a technique situates what occurs in a particular timeframe that, in the present of enunciation, mimes events as they unfold. At the same time, this technique solicits an expectation and an explanation about the whys and wherefores of what is occurring, while also postulating an indeterminate and unpredictable future. Internal scenes within a small number of confined spaces (the five-and-dime store where Florentine works, the foundry where Jean works, Ma Philibert's restaurant, The Two Records, the Létourneaus' apartment, the Lacasses' house, the church, the tavern, other restaurants or meeting places) alternate with outdoor scenes in which protagonists (internal focalizers), on the move, appropriate the topographical urban system, combined with a spatial description of the place and the articulation of differentiated positions. Furthermore, these spatial practices are founded on a system of nomination based on proper names. Walking corresponds to an external movement, to the mobility of the signifier itself as well as an attempt to mobilize the signified. The names of the actual streets and the city of Montreal evoke within the reader a trace, a past, a story, and the virtual anguish of an unknown future – a possibility – orienting the narrative in an unexpected direction. All the proper names of streets, neighbourhoods, parks, and areas that actually exist, and of shops, boutiques, restaurants, and cinemas that could exist, act as kernels and catalysts for the reader between spatial and signifying practices, introducing the *probable*, *memoria*, and the *possible* – 'ces trois dispositifs symboliques [qui] organisent les *topoi* du discours sur/de la ville (la légende, le souvenir et le rêve)' (those three symbolic systems that organize the *topoi* of the discourse on the city [legend, memory, and dream]) – in the words of Michel de Certeau (1988: 158).

In addition to sanctioning and making credible what is perceived, felt, and described, the observer imposes a rhythm, a tension, and a release by lengthening, shortening, and investing the scene observed or experienced. In effect, it is through the observer-focalizer that the regularity and rhythm, the tension and relief of the predictable and unpredictable aspects of the lived event are discovered and apprehended. It is thanks to the experience of these wanderers that the actions, thoughts, and feelings of other characters are transformed into processes inscribed in urban time and space. Space and time unfold as resistances to be overcome, as coefficients of adversity or assistance, through the mediation of the focalizers, and it is also through their mediation that the event and/or the scene are experienced as slow or fast, as duration. The time of the observer and wandering actors thus becomes anthropomorphic time, or temporality. Although not everyone walks and meanders through the city in *Bonheur d'occasion*, certainly the main protagonists do. Rose-Anna, who remains within the confines of Saint-Henri while trying to find another home for the family, wanders in the streets, stopping, reading signs, thinking, and planning for the future. The reader experiences the urban landscape of poverty through her eyes, through her body, through her fatigue, and through her expectations. As with all other characters, the events and things perceived trigger both thoughts about the past and hopes for the future, inscribing in a temporal arc the here and the now in the then, and the there in the could be and the elsewhere.

Jean, Florentine, Eugène, Azarius, Alphonse, and Emmanuel crisscross the maze of the city by day and by night, but often alone, searching, seeking to understand what they have experienced and what has happened to them. Even when they walk the streets in the company of another, they rarely succeed in communicating their thoughts and feelings. Florentine and Jean both live in their own worlds, as do Emmanuel and Florentine. The second chapter of the novel illustrates the complex and intricate interplay of the meandering observer-focalizer. At lunchtime, Jean, in jest, asks Florentine for a date to go to a movie, to which she gives a noncommittal answer. Her image haunts him all afternoon in the foundry, and he regrets having been so foolish as to ask her out. Thinking about the singular moment with Florentine sets off a stream of consciousness about his own behaviour in the past with other women, and how he had always pursued his ambitions to the detriment of sentiment. Walking home to his furnished room on St Ambrose Street he becomes irritated and cannot drive Florentine out of his mind. During this stroll, he imagines how she judges him on appearances, contrary to what he considers to be his true self. His self-evaluation effectively gives the reader what Jean believes to be his own moral portrait. Arriving home, he sits down to begin work and still cannot get her off his mind. His thoughts wander over his weekly entertainment and work habits and, while speculating about Florentine's home life and character, he wonders if she has taken him seriously and whether she will keep their date. He tries to settle down to work once more, but cannot. As he looks out onto the street, feeling the wind and the snow, his mind constantly wanders back to the young woman. Seeking distraction from his thoughts, he turns around and examines his room, describing the contents and the reasons for its sparseness. In this description, the experience of duration, of time stretched, is felt through the errant gaze, thoughts, and feelings of the focalizer. The description and history of the space – the room, its objects, and its inhabitant – are given in detail and incorporated by the observer-focalizer, who temporalizes and sensitizes them in what seems to be an interminable length of time.

Curiosity finally gets the better of Jean; he dresses, goes out, and walks briskly down the street. At this moment, the central point of focalization shifts to the narrator-observer. It is through those eyes that this part of town and the many changes that have occurred over a long period of time are described, the narrator thereby historicizing them by endowing them with a social and environmental past: 'Autrefois, c'étaient ici les confins du faubourg; les dernières maisons de Saint-Henri apparaissaient là, face à des champs vagues ... De ces bons temps, il n'est resté à la rue Saint-Ambroise que deux ou trois grands arbres ... Les maisons sont toujours là ... Jean avait choisi de s'y établir parce que, dans cette rue éloignée, presque inconnue, le prix des loyers restait fort modique ... Il est vrai qu'au printemps les nuits n'avaient plus de silence' (28) (At one time the suburb had ended here; the last houses of Saint-Henri looked out on open fields ... Of the good old days nothing is left now on St Ambrose Street but two or three great trees ... The houses are still there ... Jean had chosen this remote, little-known street because the rent was low ... In the spring, to be sure, the nights ceased to be quiet) (16–17). A detailed description follows, both of the house where Jean lives opposite the drawbridge at the corner of St Augustine Street and of the activity in the streets and canal. The narrator then shifts focalization back to Jean by investing the description with Jean's own feelings and habits: 'Jean avait cru être en voyage, tantôt sur un cargo, tantôt dans un wagon-lit ... Jean s'appuya un instant au seuil de la porte ... il descendit ... il aperçut ... le visage épanoui et rose de la mère Philibert' (29) (Jean often had the sensation of being on board a steamer or a Pullman car in motion ... Jean leaned against the doorframe for a moment ... he went off down the street ... he saw the bright, ruddy face of Ma Philibert) (17). He peers into the window, identifies some of the regular customers, and comments on them. This sets off a long flashback reaching back to before the first narrative, evoking the times when he worked as a spinner in a cotton mill, as well as the tradition the group had of going to the movies together every Saturday evening. He thinks of how he has distanced himself from his former friends over the last few years and of how Ma Philibert always acted as a den-mother for them. Finally, he decides not to go in and continues down the street to the centre of the suburb. He stops in the middle of Saint-Henri Place, and the railway tracks and trolley-car lines unfold before his gaze. Hearing the sound of a locomotive, he stops, and focalization reverts back to the narrator-observer who mentions that 'À la rue Atwater, à la rue Rose-de-Lima, à la rue du Couvent et maintenant place Saint-Henri, les barrières des passages à niveau tombent' (32) (At Atwater Street, at Rose-de-Lima Street, at Convent Street and now at Saint-Henri Place the railroad barriers fell) (20), and continues by describing the daily activities in and around the crossroads before focusing on the surrounding area. Comments flow from the narrator about the church built in Jesuit style, the Sacred Heart, the parish buildings, the school, the convent rooted not only in the heart of the city but 'comme au creux des vallons laurentiens' (32) (in the whole Saint Lawrence Valley as well) (20). Other parts of Saint-Henri are evoked before the focalization returns to Jean as he continues his walk in the night. He stops at the station and is replaced once more by the narrator, who provides information, generalizes, and makes value judgments on Westmount 'dans son rigide confort anglais. Il se trouve ainsi que c'est aux voyages infinis de l'âme qu'elle invite. Ici, le luxe et la pauvreté se regardent inlassablement, depuis qu'il y a Westmount, depuis qu'en bas, à ses pieds, il y a Saint-Henri. Entre eux s'élèvent des clochers' (33) (in all its stuffy English comfort, spread out over the mountain. Thus the little station invites the mind to journeys of another kind, journeys without end. Here wealth and poverty stare each other in the face, Westmount from above, Saint-Henri at its feet. Between them rise the belfries) (20). Focalization is taken up again by Jean, who continues on his way, thinking about the war in general, but then in a flash seeing it as his own personal opportunity, his chance for rapid advancement: 'Il se voyait lâché dans une vie qui changeait ses valeurs, elle-même changeante de jour en jour, et qui, dans cette mer démontée des hommes, le porterait sur une vague haute' (33) (He saw himself in a world of constantly changing values, afloat in a raging sea of men, in which he would be carried to the top of the highest wave) (21).

Thoughts of Florentine continue to haunt him and, arriving in front of the cinema, he crosses the street, slips into a store entrance, and waits, trying 'de se rappeler ses mots vulgaires, ses gestes maladroits' (34) (to recall her vulgar intonation, her awkward gestures) (21). The observer begins the description, then pursues and finishes it by and through his nervous gaze. The tempo of the scene, the rhythm (slow, then fast) of its incorporated experience, and the spatial unfolding of the description are presented through the watchful eyes of an anguished, impatient, and tense subject. 'Cinq minutes s'écoulèrent ... Il se donna encore cinq minutes de répit et, par la suite, il devait souvent se demander quelle force l'avait retenu ainsi sous le couvert de la pierre ... Pourquoi ne venait-elle pas? Ne se souciait-elle pas du tout de lui? ... Florentine se moquerait-elle de lui?' (34) (Five minutes passed ... He gave himself five minutes more respite, and later he was often to wonder what kept him there in the shelter of the building ... Why didn't she come? Didn't she care for him at all? ... Was Florentine making fun of him?) (21). Suddenly she appears before his gaze, and he is overcome with contradictory feelings: 'Il avait pitié d'elle. Une parcelle de pitié venait de percer à travers sa curiosité brutale. Il fut même troublé, quelque peu ému, qu'elle s'en vînt ainsi rapidement vers lui dans le vent froid, malgré la tempête. Il aurait voulu courir vers elle ... Et cependant il se retirait dans l'angle le plus obscur ...' (34) (He was sorry for her. A particle of pity had pierced his hard shell. He was troubled, he was deeply moved to see her flying to meet him through the wind and storm. He had a momentary impulse to run to her ... And yet he shrank farther back into the darkest corner of the recess ...) (21). This singular event in the present, expected but none the less unpredictable, one that will or will not have a future, takes on its meaning in and by a past that must be evoked and rendered intelligible. The observer needs to know why she has come, why she has been so reckless, and begins to invoke hypothetical reasons for her presence in front of the cinema. She meets, by chance, a group of her friends, one of whom asks her if she is waiting for someone. She does not respond, scans the horizon, and follows them into the lobby, disappearing from sight. It is only then that Jean draws a breath of relief, his arms relaxing, and his fists gradually becoming unclenched. He wonders if he is actually through with her – 'Un doute cependant l'accompagnait et, au bout d'un moment, il s'aperçut qu'il n'était point satisfait' (36) (A certain doubt remained in his mind, however, and a moment later he realized that he was not completely satisfied) (22) – as he is uncertain whether she came to meet him or her friends. He understands neither her character nor her motives and continues to ask himself all sorts of questions about her, finally losing patience with himself. The scene ends abruptly with the observer walking off once more; but this journey into the night, at the narrative level, creates suspense, an uncertain future, regarding possible sequels to the events the observer has just experienced.

The narrative technique in this chapter, where focalization switches from the actor-observer to the narrator, who interprets and glosses the actions of the protagonists, establishes a relationship between alternating tableaux of domestic and enclosed space describing repetitive or iterated actions of Jean's daily life on the one hand, and of urban wandering, of discovery, of the exterior, of the singular on the other. The changes in focalization not only construct a Montreal space of the street and the interior but also temporalize it by incorporating it in the actions, thoughts, and passions of the observer-subject. In this way, the temporal duration of the singularity of urban practices and the iterativity of gestures, thoughts, and desires of the internal domestic space of the individual are integrated into one and the same action. The shuttling to and fro between the focalization and temporalization of the narrator and the character establishes a temporal measure and cadence of the perceived, the understood, and the felt, experienced by the latter. A scansion of strong and weak moments (inchoate, durative, terminative), a tempo (slow, fast), and a tensitivity (crescendo, decrescendo) is thereby created in the urban novel. The walk into the night along the streets of Montreal founds, institutes, and sanctions the credibility and memorability of the very first scene of the novel, the meeting between Jean and Florentine at the five-and-dime store. Its function is also to open urban space to the other and to otherness. The movement of the exploratory memory of the observer-actor or enunciator invites the reader to return to an anteriority, to construct, even to invent, a new spatial practice by reassembling the dispersed fragments of the past, giving them signification and direction while projecting them into a realizable future. But the textualization of the fragments of the past by the observers during their travels in the night must incorporate the surplus and the heterogeneous in the urban network imposed by the city by producing in the trajectory of the existence of the characters possible openings and instituting a 'more' and 'another' that at one and the same time diversify their experience while also signalling the memorable by instituting a temporal arc through the very act of narration.

In *Bonheur d'occasion*, most characters live and evolve within the narrow confines of Saint-Henri, depicted as a poverty-stricken, /open/ space, dependent on social, economic, and historical world events. Sometimes characters will break out and explore either other parts of Montreal[13] or the countryside, but all dream of escaping this destitute neighbourhood. The Lacasses' rented house, dilapidated but clean, is a /non-closed/, transient space that can be opposed to either the Létourneaus' apartment (/non-open/ to Florentine and her family), or to the house of Rose-Anna's mother in the country[14] (/closed/ to all strangers). Moreover, the Lacasses are forced to move often, whenever they cannot pay the rent, and Rose-Anna spends a great deal of time exploring the more sordid quarters of Saint-Henri in search of lodgings. When the family is evicted, they decide to move in the middle of the night, after the new tenants have shown up and invaded the house with their own possessions, even occupying several of the rooms. In this space, /non-closed/ to outside influences of every sort, the family can aspire to no collective goals. Subjects simply inhabit their own private universe, cut off, even isolated from one another in relations of seriality, following their own directions, adrift in the imaginary fulfilment of their own obsessions: 'Ils sont tous ici, dans cette maison, éloignés par les songes qu'ils élaborent chacun de son côté' (148) (Every one in the house lived in a world of his own. No two of them desired the same thing, penned together though they were, close enough to touch one another. No two of them were bound in the same direction: each went on his way privately ...) (114).

The members of the Lacasse family function in a world where their knowledge and frames of reference are informed by the rural values of the isolated pre-industrial village and parish, while they inhabit an open modern world of technology.[15] Within this universe, subjects cannot come to grips with the rapidly changing social and economic structures of an advanced, modern, urban economy. Their incessant wanderings and displacements, generally alone, by night and day in the maze of city, looking for solutions to material problems beyond their control, is a reiterated leitmotif throughout the novel. The only common projects that actually succeed in mustering the energy of the participants are the two recruiting parades, when marching soldiers constituting a group in fusion attract a large number of recruits. The

The Urban Novel: *Bonheur d'occasion* 227

army and war are the only movements that can orient individuals trying to survive in the pursuit of a collective goal – liberation of the motherland. Yet, one remarks that the slowly degrading family, made up of father, mother, and children, is further reduced and dislocated, since most capable and physically fit adult males must go off to war to ensure the continuity of a further diminished household. Incapable of functioning in the new, urban, economic, dynamic order, and weighed down by old, rural, static belief systems, the subject can ensure the continuity and survival of the dismembered group only through risking impending violence and possible death. What occurs throughout the narrative is that manipulating subjects are generally, in turn, manipulated by others or by events they cannot control. Nothing can ensure the cohesion or success of their projects. They are decentred and fractured beings, unable, by and in themselves, to give either sense or direction to experiences that escape them.

Unlike the agents depicted in *La Terre paternelle*, *Les Anciens Canadiens*, or *Maria Chapdelaine*, their very being grounded in a presupposed sender – a common language, race, and religion – that confirmed their unity while their every act signified in terms of duty destined to guarantee their distinctiveness as a group or nation, the agents in *Bonheur d'occasion* are manipulated by social, economic, and historical forces beyond their control. These forces institute individual, alienating, non-reciprocal desire as a libidinal energy driving them along a labyrinthine, endless quest for survival and personal fulfilment. This is not to say that some of the characters are not moved from time to time by ideas or sentiments above and beyond themselves, but these remain contradictory and for the most part inoperative. A number enlist to defend France, their country of origin, but for Emmanuel this is not the real reason for fighting in the war. Returning home on leave, and having left The Two Records Café after listening to Azarius's defence of France and the need to go to war, Emmanuel thinks through his relationship with his mother country and his reasons for enlisting. He perceives the glory and the beauty of France, but he knows that this is not the only reason for his decision. 'Il aimait la France, il aimait l'humanité, il s'apitoyait sur la détresse des pays conquis, mais il savait que la détresse régnait dans le monde avant la guerre et qu'on la soulage autrement qu'avec les armes. Et, malgré sa nature sensible, étant plus accessible au fond à toute idée de justice qu'à la simple pitié ...' (266) (He loved France, he loved humanity, he felt compassion for the people of the conquered countries, but he knew that there had been plenty of suffering in the world before the war and that it could not be relieved by force of arms. And in spite of his sensitivity, the idea of justice had a stronger hold on him than pity) (212). He is very much aware that, like all young French Canadians educated in traditionalist schools, he had formerly entertained many conservative ideas, such as belief in racial survival and the importance of faithful observance of ancestral traditions and the cult of the national holiday. These he considers to be 'expressions figées qui n'avaient rien, songeait-il, pour échauffer ni nourrir les jeunes imaginations, ni même exalter vraiment le courage' (266) (stuffy notions that had no power to nourish the imagination of the young, nor even to fire their courage) (212). His own father, a fervent nationalist who subscribes to the cult of origins, does not consider it contradictory to do everything in his power to dissuade his son from taking up arms to defend France, even though he fervently considers it to be the ancestral fatherland of his countrymen.

Many of the older French-Canadian protagonists who enrol in the army to fight on the side of the hereditary enemy, Britain, and defend the homeland against German aggression are aware in varying degrees of the distinctive origins that constitute their national identity. But it is only Emmanuel, among the current generation, and Azarius and his colleagues among the economically disenfranchised class, who consciously link nationality to language, race, and religion. For the younger generation, the past is not part of their discourse, nor is it a fundamental defining characteristic of their identity. By a strange turn of events, the chronically unemployed, caught up in the throes of international economic forces that maintain them in a state of alienation, can fuse together only when war defines them as a group with a common purpose. Colonial identity is no longer guaranteed by the mixed institutions of the French homeland and the political and military power of the country of the colonizers, Britain, but a new identity can emerge only within the nascent New World socio-economic global order.

Women subjects in *Bonheur d'occasion* do not participate in the debate on nation and national identity, which remains a male preserve. Florentine and Rose-Anna, in a very sentimental way, reflect the war and its impact on them, but do not think beyond the family and their own maternal roles and/or instincts. On the few occasions when Rose-Anna is able to concentrate on anything beyond the survival of her family, she inevitably thinks about the war in terms of mother–son relations. Walking through Saint-Henri looking for a house to rent she happens upon a recruiting poster representing a soldier with a fixed bayonet. 'Ses yeux brillaient et sa bouche juvénile lançait un cri de ralliement. Dans du bleu, au-dessus de sa tête, s'enroulaient de grosses lettres noires: "Allons-y les gars! Le pays a besoin de nous."' (87) (His eyes were shining and his mouth was open in a rallying cry. In the sky over his head, great black letters were printed: 'Let's go, fellows! Our country needs us!') (64). She is overcome with emotion since the young man looks very much like her son Eugène, as their mouths and their eyes are the same. As she spells out the words, she thinks they read: 'Let's go. Fellows! Our mothers need us!' A *mater dolorosa*, she clasps her hand over her coat and imagines that Eugène is standing there in front of the whole district, 'jetait un cri d'angoisse qui se prolongeait et clamait leur pauvreté aux quatre coins du ciel' (87) (uttering a cry of anguish that trumpeted their poverty to the four corners of the world) (65). As for Florentine, who is pregnant, the war is experienced as providing the necessary income to move up the social ladder and away from the squalor of the working-class district of Saint-Henri. No effective transcendental values motivate the new errant urban subject, nor do any emerging values loom up in the future. Ironically, though, the very last lines of the narrative link war and capital, for even as Florentine thinks her troubles are over thanks to her soldier husband's pay, we are told that: 'Très bas dans le ciel, des nuées sombres annonçaient l'orage' (345) (Low on the horizon, a bank of heavy clouds foretold a storm) (274).

CHAPTER TWELVE

Utopia, Family, and Nation – The Wilderness Novel: *Agaguk*[1]

In the previous chapter, I stressed the fact that the imaginary subject of the urban novel is represented as a fractured, decentred being, driven by global socio-economic and historical forces beyond his or her control. Indeed, until the beginning of the 1960s, urban subjects generally continue to be buffeted to and fro, disenfranchised because they can function only in terms of traditional rural value systems. They have not yet learned to objectify, contest, and come to grips with their past, and the city still remains a diabolical space where forces of good and evil physically and morally assail individuals who are incapable of constituting their identity. However, with the publication in 1958 of *Agaguk*[2] by Yves Thériault, the first Québécois author to live solely from the proceeds of his writing, in what could be considered an anachronistic move, the subject is displaced from an alienating urban environment to the wilderness. Although such a displacement was not totally unknown in Quebec fiction, Thériault's originality lay in situating his tale not in the forest of the Amerindian, the space beyond the village or the frontier, but on the barren tundra of the Inuit of the 1930s and early 1940s, a space that had not, up to then, been considered as a possible imaginary landscape within which subjects could define and construct new identities.[3]

The forty-nine brief chapters of the novel, covering a period of some six or seven years, alternate between simple daily, iterated, ordinary events and more critical, singular, extraordinary ones. The tale opens when the central character, Agaguk, son of Ramook, the chief, comes of age and decides to leave the tribe and live on the tundra with Iriook, whom he has just chosen as his partner. Although he attempts to break all links with the village, he does not succeed, and, learning of the presence of a trader amid the tribe, he decides to barter his furs for arms, tools, and foodstuffs. The trader, Brown, who uses illicit alcohol to cheat the Inuit, threatens Agaguk and robs him of some of his furs. Mortified, the latter decides to seek revenge: he recovers his furs in the dark of night, pours kerosene on the trader, and sets fire to his tent, burning him to death. When he returns to the tundra, Agaguk says nothing about what has occurred to Iriook, who informs him shortly afterward that she is pregnant. In need of supplies to get through the winter, he travels to the village of the Hudson's Bay Company, which holds a monopoly on trading in the North. Once more he feels cheated when the clerk refuses to give him true value for his furs, offering him only half of what he expected. Helpless again before an oppressive system that exploits the Native population, he is tempted to take violent revenge but controls himself. He decides to barter his last prime mink skin to an Ojibway trader for four bottles of alcohol. He holes up alone in a shelter, where he drinks all four bottles and remains drunk for two days, before returning home to face Iriook; but again he does not tell her what has happened. Three or four months later, their son, Tayaout, is born. During the birth of the child, Agaguk is unable to understand and bear Iriook's cries of suffering. He beats her to kill the pain and make it flee her body. After Tayaout's birth, the child becomes the centre of their universe.

In the meantime, unknown to the family on the tundra, Henderson, a police officer, comes to the village to investigate Brown's disappearance. The tribe says nothing about what has happened to the trader, closing ranks. Henderson remains in the village and counts on his knowledge of tribal ways and his patience to learn what has happened. The family leaves for the Top of the World to hunt for seals along the Arctic coast. The hunt meets with extraordinary success, and the couple returns to the tundra loaded down with game. Meanwhile, Officer Henderson's stay in the village causes more and more resentment among the villagers, who begin to threaten him. Two separate sequences of events occur simultaneously in the village and the tundra: Ayallik is ready to break ranks and reveal to Henderson that Agaguk has killed the trader; and a mysterious white wolf appears, threatening to kill Tayaout. These events, described in a number of alternating chapters, are followed by two different violent denouements. Ramook orders Ayallik, the potential traitor, to be put to death. He then shoots Henderson, who had decided to leave, and, with the help of the sorcerer and other villagers, mutilates his body. Meanwhile, Agaguk confronts and eventually overcomes the white wolf, but is seriously wounded and disfigured in the long, bloody battle.

With Agaguk close to death, contrary to tradition Iriook must assume the role of the hunter in order to save the family, a form of behaviour that radically modifies relations between them. She begins by treating his wounds and mangled face with great tenderness and skill, and in so doing saves his life. More importantly, she gives him confidence in himself, as he regains his strength through her care. Their trials and tribulations continue, however, for the following summer, a plane carrying four policemen and two scientists lands near the huts of the villagers. Menaced by the officer leading the investigation, Ramook decides to denounce Agaguk. Three officers then come to interrogate Agaguk, who is terribly scarred and not recognizable because of the wounds to his face inflicted by the white wolf. He cannot be identified for certain, and even Ramook remains doubtful as to his exact identity. Iriook, who learns during this conversation about Brown's death at the hands of Agaguk, contrary to Inuit tradition, speaks up. She saves him a second time by stating that he is gone and she does not know what has happened to him. When the officers return to the village, they find the rifle that killed Henderson in Ramook's tent, and Scott tricks the chief into admitting that Henderson actually lived in the village. Ramook is subsequently denounced by a young woman of the tribe, and other members also accuse him of having killed Ayallik, with Ghorok as his accomplice. Both are taken away, put on trial in the city, found guilty, and hanged.

The tribe is now without a chief, and each member who is competent to take on the role refuses because of the constraints and the dangers involved. The dominant persons of the village approach Agaguk, who also declines, both for love of Iriook and because of his real need for solitude. Iriook is again with child. Because of the harsh environment on the tundra, Inuit tradition does not permit the nuclear family to feed those who do not contribute directly to survival, but Iriook wants Agaguk to agree to let the infant live even if it is a girl, hoping that his remorse at killing Brown means that he has evolved morally. A girl is born, and Agaguk is torn between his male pride and his love for Iriook, between Inuit tradition and a new moral order. When finally, first under the threat of a rifle and then with the prospect of a life without love, he allows the child to live, he is rewarded by the birth of another child, a second boy.

In *Agaguk*, two distinct types of objects of value can be identified:

those having a *practical* function and those having a *mythical* one. Practical objects are most often the end result of hunting, and are mainly defined by the quest for and appropriation of variable, quantifiable, and bivalent mammals and fish that are part of the natural world. They are both necessary for survival and can be converted and circulated through the socio-economic channels of trade. Mythical objects of value are always defined by a process of reciprocity in which a unique and progressively revealed spiritual object is shared by two equal subjects. This is expressed in the narrative in the form of love-passion.

Objects belonging to the material universe of daily existence are first distinguished in terms of their diversity. And so one encounters in the narrative long lists of the fur-bearing mammals that preoccupy the waking moments of the inhabitants of the plain. Yet in spite of the proliferation of detail, it is possible to classify the numerous species according to one or several of the following functions: food, clothing, utensils, and exchange. The first three classes – food, clothing, and utensils – fall within the province of individual biological subsistence, whereas the fourth – exchange – introduces a socio-economic dimension because it is not only founded on interpersonal relationships but also institutes and mediates them at one and the same time. As a general rule, game, which is widely dispersed on the vast tundra, is sought after by solitary male subjects, a strategy that greatly increases their chances of locating it. The successful hunter transmits his prize to the group (family or tribe), which transforms it into material goods. The subject's quest must be understood solely in terms of the survival of the group, and so individual will is, of necessity, subordinated to the common project and functions as an adjunct of the collective subject. The individual subject, as such, plays a secondary role, and traditional skills, progressively acquired, make possible the transfer and preparation of objects of value communicated to the community at large. In this constellation, the subject is indeed a *we*, and the modality of duty governs knowledge, power, and will.

Another consequence of the extremely tenuous living conditions in this harsh environment is the imposition and distribution of prescribed tasks for every adult in the group, so that each member assumes a specific role dictated either by tradition or by his/her particular status. This role can be considered as both a duty or obligation, and a necessity that ensures the continuity of any social configuration, be it the family or the tribe. Men's activities are directed towards erecting the conjugal home and supplying it with food, while women prepare the game or the fish procured. Consequently, all interpersonal relations in this universe are mediated through the physical possibilities inherent in the material field. The economical division of labour, the allocation of clearly defined tasks, not only assures the survival of the couple, but also forms the basic structuring principle that governs and organizes the social interactions of all the other Inuit.

The possession of goods, as previously stated, is the sign of a specific activity that defines the attributive agent. Since the appropriation of any object or thing is the end result of a process initiated by a distinct subject, it follows that we should turn to the means used to acquire it. First and foremost, goods can be worked and reshaped into utensils and implements for use either in the household or in the hunt: these include such things as rawhide thongs made of sealskin and needles made of bones (5), ivory knives (19), traps, precious oil from animals that give plenty of fat (33), or harpoons made from long pieces of ivory tipped with a crook like a fishhook (151). Handmade and produced on the spot by artisans who apply simple and proven techniques transmitted by tradition over time, these objects can be fabricated from accumulated stocks without recourse to any intermediaries.

However, more important to the Inuit are the many foreign-made utensils and tools, available at the white man's trading post, that facilitate the capture and conservation of game. The usefulness and necessity of these objects in daily life is constantly stressed: guns, iron pots and tools, a metal stove to burn oil or fat (5), steel traps, white man's traps (19), salt (38), kerosene (45), metal knives (79), the metal box, their most precious possession (80), or the metal axe (150). The introduction of mass-produced objects and their unconditional acceptance by the Inuit signal the weighty presence of modern culture and technology within a society in the throes of dramatic change. The availability and daily use of these objects engender networks of complex relations linking agents to their material space and environment. Fabricated elsewhere, by methods totally unknown to the Inuit, such objects demand a degree of upkeep to ensure their proper maintenance. Moreover, since the Inuit have not assimilated the necessary knowledge and technical know-how to produce these objects industrially, they are completely dependent upon their suppliers, who in turn take advantage of every opportunity to exploit the Inuit.

It is nevertheless true that imported objects do help the Inuit in their daily struggle for life. Because of these tools and weapons, Agaguk is able not only to kill a greater variety of game than was previously possible, but also to defeat his most feared enemy, the white wolf. The same rifle and knives permit Iriook, on an incredibly cold day, to kill and quickly butcher two caribou and by her own strength and skill to ensure the family's winter supply of meat. And when five-year-old Tayaout is attacked by a bear, Iriook runs out of the hut, rifle in hand. She follows the animal in her sights, and fires at it as it flees. The bullet shatters its skull (208). Furthermore, although indigenous weapons, such as the harpoons used to hunt seals (90–1), necessitate a long apprenticeship over time and a great deal of physical strength to use effectively, and hence confine each agent to a marked cultural or sexual role, modern arms have the property of liberating individuals from traditionally determined situations. However, although foreign-made objects do provide a certain degree of material comfort and increase the chances of survival, they are also a source of servility and/or alienation. An imported tool imposes real constraints on its owner and can become a simple end in itself. All of the Inuit are caught up more or less in the same economic processes, laid down and controlled by aliens (Sender): using modern weapons and tools in order to kill the greatest number of commercially valuable fur-bearing animals; preparing the skins and trading them for more rifles, bullets, and metal traps to achieve further gains in efficiency and yield.

In light of the preceding analysis of material goods, we can define the subject as he/she who internalizes the many contradictions of the group in the quest for survival. The category of mythical objects, or various stages of love, however, principally concerns the couple Agaguk and Iriook. What *is* the status of the mythical, however? It was implied that practical objects cannot be understood simply in terms of the appropriation, conversion, and exchange of a passive object of value, since this object actually regulates, through the interplay of complex non-posited relations, the subjects' very being as they interact with their natural and social environments. Conversely, the mythical is primarily defined by factors of choice and reciprocity, where the modality of will governs knowledge, power, and duty. Agaguk frees himself from paternal ascendancy and authority before choosing Iriook, an orphan, as his spouse. She unconditionally consents to leave the village and live alone with him on the tundra. We cannot help but note that the liberty of the two protagonists is intimately associated with parental death. When Agaguk returns from his exploratory trip, he refuses to visit the chief's hut. The fact that Ramook is his father no longer matters to him: 'Depuis que le vieux avait pris une Montagnaise pour remplacer la femme morte, Agaguk considérait que la lignée était rompue. Il pouvait se sentir libre' (4) (Since the old man had taken a Montagnais woman – [the hated breed] – to replace his dead wife, Agaguk considered that all ties were broken. He could feel he was free ...) (3). Iriook is completely unattached: 'Elle aussi était libre, car son père et sa mère étaient maintenant morts. Elle habitait seule dans la hutte autour de laquelle Agaguk et d'autres venaient rôder' (4) (She too was free, for her father and mother were both dead now. She lived alone in a hut around which Ayallik and the others came to prowl) (4). Only after the death of Agaguk's mother and both of Iriook's parents can the formation of the couple take place. Freed from all parental bonds, they hope to start a home and family alone on the vast plain without any interference from others, and so, one morning, the man and the girl take to the trail (5). Having severed all ties with the tribe, they consecrate their new-found communal life by sexual union, but it is only after they reach their final objective three days later that they make love: 'Quand il n'eut plus rien à donner, quand tout en lui fut vidé, il roula aux côtés de la fille et, tous deux demi-nus sous le ciel aux reflets de plomb, ils s'endormirent' (8) (When he was spent, when all of him was emptied, he rolled over beside the girl and they both slept, half naked under the leaden sky) (6). Here the discovery of self is linked to the discovery of the other, and emotions are linked to cognitive processes through the sensate body motivated by sexual desire.[4]

But if the death of parents and the physical separation from the group are the primary and necessary conditions that make the initial formation of the couple possible, its final consolidation depends on the questioning, rejection, and ultimate dissolution of cultural attitudes hitherto accepted unequivocally by Agaguk. The first stage in the couple's constitution, defined by the sudden appropriation of the woman, is basically exclusive. A month before setting off on their journey, Agaguk had expeditiously snatched the screaming girl from the arms of Ghorok the sorcerer, declaring that she belonged to him and that he was her protector. This basic opposition – monogamy (couple) versus polygamy (tribe) – is followed, at the level of sexuality, by a second opposition: exclusivity versus promiscuity. Agaguk refuses the honour of becoming the youngest of all chiefs mainly because of Iriook. He realizes that she is attractive and that if he were to leave the village, even for a short time, men would surround the hut and harass her. Moreover, he is aware that there exist tribal laws of sharing one's spouse with others (200–3). Here the modality of empirical knowledge governs will, power, and duty.

For the tribe, sexual behaviour fulfils specific biological and social functions that guarantee the tribe's continuity and the harmonious well-being of its members, whereas for the couple, sexuality is essentially a sign of the transformation, or of the different stages reached by the protagonists during their last progressive discovery of the significance of love. From the outset, like all the other women, Iriook is assimilated to goods inscribed in a circuit of scarcity, and to all intents and purposes is considered as a completely subservient being. Docile, she passively awaits the male's surging desire and accepts her traditional role of utter dependency. Sexual relationships simply confirm the social hierarchy, since they are established on the model dominant–dominated, master–slave. Men take and possess women: 'Sans attendre, il renversa Iriook, arracha le pantalon de peau de caribou qu'elle portait, détacha lui-même ses chausses et la prit, silencieusement' (8) (Without waiting, he pulled Iriook down, slipped off the caribou pants she wore, then his own, and possessed her silently) (6).

After having killed Brown, the trader who tried to cheat him, Agaguk returns to the river, enters his hut, and 'd'une main ferme il tira le pantalon de la femme, le lui arrache des jambes et le rejeta au loin. Iriook s'éveilla à demi, gémit bellement et ouvrit grandes les cuisses fortes et grasses) (44) (with a firm hand he pulled off her pantaloons and threw them far off. Iriook half-woke, moaned happily and opened her heavy thighs) (30). Next morning, when she informs him that she is expecting a child, her words bring 'une immense lumière, une joie qu'il ne savait pas exprimer. Comme une merveilleuse attente et une sorte de tendresse, un besoin de bercer et d'aimer qu'il ressentait mais dont il ne devinait pas le sens' (45) (a great light into his soul, a happiness he did not know how to express. Like a marvellous hope and a kind of tenderness, he felt a need to solace and love, of which he did not know the meaning) (30). The motif of light marks the threshold to a new life that is intuited, intimately felt, and non-verbalized. Agaguk is aware of a break with the past and, through the experience of paternity, discovers unprecedented joy, which again is expressed by a radical change in his sexual behaviour and an evolution in his relations with his spouse: 'Il accédait à une vie neuve, à des façons qui ne ressemblaient en rien à autrefois. Il avait conçu la vie en cette femme. Il acquérait soudain une force, la plus grande de toutes, une puissance qui lui semblait quasi magnifique' (46–7) (He attained a new passion, gestures which did not resemble anything they had done before. He had generated life in this woman, he acquired suddenly a force, the greatest of all, a power which seemed to him almost magical) (31–2).

However, if we re-examine love, not in relation to the Sender and the Receiver, but on the polemico-conflictual axis of intersubjective relations, we note the fundamental transformation brought about in Agaguk's behaviour by the discovery of paternity. He becomes much more aware of Iriook as subject and giver of life, and the child to be begins to affect them so that the relations between two emerging cognizant and feeling beings are transformed. 'La nouvelle, venue d'Iriook, lui mettait en l'âme une immense lumière, une joie qu'il ne savait exprimer. Comme une merveilleuse attente et une sorte de tendresse, un besoin de bercer et d'aimer qu'il ressentait mais dont il ne devinait pas le sens' (45) (Iriook's news brought a great light into his soul, a happiness he did not know how to express. Like a marvellous hope and a kind of tenderness, he felt a need to solace and love, of which he did not know the meaning) (30). His break with the past and understanding of change is expressed in and by means of his sensate body engaged in passionate lovemaking: 'Alors, sauvagement, en un grand élan de tout son corps, il fut sur elle ... Ce qu'ils découvraient dépassait le monde fermé de leur entendement, la tribu, le sol fertile, les accoutumances. Ils n'étaient plus unis seulement dans la chair, mais aussi par l'âme, et le cœur, et les pensées ... C'était la délivrance des années d'autrefois et l'entrée dans des pays merveilleux et doux' (46–7) (Then savagely, in a great surge of his whole body, he was upon her ... What they discovered surpassed the closed world of their understanding, that of the tribe, the barren soil, the daily drudgery. They were united not only by the flesh, but through the soul, the heart, the mind ... It was a deliverance from the past years and an entry into wonderful and gentle realms) (31–2).

The next stage in their development takes place under the sign of procreation that inevitably modifies the couple's relationship. But first, it is silence, or the 'unsaid,' that regulates interpersonal communication. Agaguk is tempted to describe his frustrating encounter with the Hudson's Bay Company factor. He remains silent for a moment, then decides to tell at least part of the truth, what happened, although he hides the hurt to his pride which is for him the worst thing of all: 'Le secret était lourd. Si lourd qu'Agaguk vint près de raconter la rage qui l'avait empoignée, sa saoulade d'ensuite' (78) (The secret was heavy. So heavy that Agaguk came near to telling of the rage that had struck so deep and the drunkenness that had followed) (53). Nevertheless, in spite of his resolution, he is unable to speak out and thinks it best to say nothing. In the same way, Iriook does not reveal the fears she felt when he was alone for three days in the storm: 'elle se garda de dire un seul mot ... Il n'était pas aisé de rester impassible, sans rien révéler des dures journées qu'elle venait de vivre' (76) (she was careful not to say a word ... It was not easy to remain impassive, without revealing anything of the hard days she had just lived through) (51). However, the forbidden word can supersede the unspoken word.

Iriook is also absorbed in her own personal dream world, for she desires a daughter: 'Elle aussi rêvait, mais autrement. Elle rêvait de douceur et de tendresse' (102) (She too was dreaming, but differently. She dreamed of gentleness and tenderness) (69). Her unspoken wish, originally frustrated and censured by the unwritten law of men, is firstly experienced as a fantasy. Eventually, her desire is oriented, finds its release, and expresses itself through prohibited erotic acts. Even though Iriook, contrary to all tradition, did not conceal that she received pleasure from Agaguk, 'Il ne lui était pas vraiment arrivé de céder à des impulsions, normales physiologiquement, mais qui eussent été réprouvées immédiatement par son homme' (123) (She had not really come to yield to the normal physiological impulses which would have been immediately reproved by her husband) (84). Until the trip to the Top of the World, she had obediently adhered to the dictates of tribal mores: 'Il y a des initiatives refusées aux femmes esquimaudes. La suprématie de l'homme et sa domination restreignent la femme à un rôle de complète passivité' (123) (There are initiatives denied to Eskimo women. The male supremacy and his domination limit the woman to a completely passive role) (84). Nevertheless, against all reason, she is tempted to obey her primary instincts and to give in to her first and immediate reaction. And when she makes a sudden impulsive gesture, an intimate caress to which he is not accustomed, startled he murmurs in her ear that women shouldn't act that way. But soon he stops resisting, willingly assumes a passive role, and is aroused by her extraordinary behaviour, 'tandis qu'Iriook, les yeux fermés, s'initiait à ce dont elle avait souvent rêvé: d'être ainsi maîtresse d'une joie à donner, selon sa passion et son habileté à elle' (124) (while Iriook, her eyes closed, began the experience she had often dreamed of, to be a mistress of a pleasure she could give, according to her own passion and her own ability) (85). The full acknowledgment of the other's intimate desire and the complete acceptance of its legitimacy leads to total complicity in its final satisfaction and fulfilment: 'Après ce fut une folie magnifique, un paroxysme de désir qui les jetait l'un sur l'autre, également possédés. Ils furent repus bien plus tard ...' (124) (Afterwards came a magnificent madness, a paroxysm of desire which threw one on the other, equally possessed. They came to themselves much later ...) (85).

During his mortal struggle with the mysterious white wolf, the hunter is critically wounded, disfigured, and mutilated. But, in spite of all, he manages to vanquish this seemingly all-powerful creature. When he returns to the hut, Iriook murmurs '"Le chef est mort" ... Soudain elle se sentit fière. "Le chef de tous les loups, continua-t-elle, de tous les loups de la terre et du dos de la terre, et c'est mon homme, le père de Tayaout, qui l'a tué"' (199) ('The chief is dead,' ... Suddenly she felt proud. 'The chief of all wolves,' she went on, 'of all the wolves on earth and the back of the world, and it is my husband, Tayaout's father, who killed him') (138). In spite of his spouse's care and encouragement, however, Agaguk has lost his will to live. He no longer sees himself as absolute master of the hut, the igloo, and the tundra, and instinct makes Iriook aware of the correct gestures to make, the proper words to say, that will convince him of his continuing power. The couple's reversal of conventional roles, noted when analysing the practical, takes place once again. But this time it involves their basic attitudes towards sexuality. Not only does Iriook take the initiative, she literally inverts traditional bodily positions in lovemaking: 'Il faisait un geste d'impuissance. Il souffrait même, elle le sentait. Comment fallait-il agir à partir de là? Iriook connaissait mieux les gestes de soumission que les autres' (222) (He made a gesture of impotence. She felt he was miserable. How ought she to behave after that? Iriook was more familiar with gestures of submission than with others) (152). She takes off the caribou skin in which he is wrapped and notices how thin he has become since the accident. She too undresses, then straddles him, 'et lentement, pieusement presque, avec des soupirs et des geignements qui étaient presque des pleurs, elle tira de son homme d'abord l'avant-joie et ensuite l'accomplissement' (223) (and slowly, almost piously, with sighs and moans that were sobs, she drew from him first the beginning of pleasure, and then the full accomplishment) (153). Their pleasure, consummated in simultaneous gratification (she is astonished to reach her climax at the same time that he does) and total fulfilment, activates a need in him to function as before: '"J'irai chasser. Il faut des pelleteries pour le troc ..."' (223) ('Soon I'll go hunting. We must have some furs to trade ...') (153). Sexuality, freely assumed and accepted by the couple, becomes a motivating life force (this is the first time since the accident that he expresses any hope), consolidating a harmonious alliance based on the recognition of the other as an individual subject.

The last stage is again set in motion by a conflict resulting in the death of a chief. Ramook betrays his son and tries to deliver him over to the police by accusing him of killing both Brown and Henderson. Iriook thwarts his plan, outsmarts him, and stands up to the officer in charge of the investigation by answering instead of her husband (170). Yet, contrary to all tradition (in Inuit culture 'the woman has no right to palaver'), Iriook expresses herself openly and speaks her mind without Agaguk's sanction. To Scott's surprise, when she does so, neither her husband nor Ramook protests. When she originally spoke out, she was immediately censured and prohibited from doing so, but now she openly claims the privilege of voicing personal wishes, sentiments, and thoughts normally outlawed by tribal mores. After the constables' departure, she explains herself to Agaguk: 'il est dit, par les Inuit ... qu'une femme n'a ni le droit de penser, ni le droit de parler. Il est possible que je ne sois pas comme les autres. J'ai des choses à dire, et si je pense, c'est que je ne puis m'en empêcher' (249) (our people say ... that a woman has no right to think, or to speak. Possibly I am not like the others. I have some things to say, and if I think, it's because I can't prevent myself) (172). To speak freely, as far as she is concerned, is not only to appropriate all the resources of language founding ego, in and by language, but is also to externalize her innermost desires spontaneously and thereby attain the status of an equal individual. It is also to be accepted as a unique subject and to assert the right to be treated on equal terms. Iriook is aware of her husband's evolution and grateful for his apparent understanding. Commenting on his attitude, she remarks to him that 'Depuis ce temps, il a changé. Il a fait Tayaout. Mais ce n'est pas seulement ça. Il a changé. Je ne peux dire comment, ni de quelle façon. Vois-tu, autrefois Agaguk n'aurait pas permis que je lui parle comme je te parle aujourd'hui. Il m'aurait battue ...' (250) (Since that time, he has changed. He has made Tayaout. But it is not only that. He has changed. I cannot say how, nor in just what fashion. You see, in former days Agaguk would have beaten me ...) (172).

For Iriook, love must also be understood in terms of the exclusive and unequivocal choice of her spouse over all other beings and things. When she discovers the extent of his wounds, sees his maimed body and ravaged face, Iriook is despondent, completely demoralized, and in despair because she cannot see in the half-conscious, revolting, and bloody individual before her the proud, handsome hunter of former days. However, after he groans out in pain, this minute spark of life permits her to recognize and accept him as he is. Nothing matters any more, neither the exposed teeth, nor the mutilated ear, nor the gap where the nose should have been: 'Il restait sa possession la plus précieuse. Plus précieuse même que ce Tayaout qu'il lui avait fait' (223) (He remained her most precious possession, more precious even than Tayaout whom she had made) (153). For his part, Agaguk, even though he previously considered her 'la femelle précieuse, dépendant de lui, mais à laquelle il tenait autant qu'il pouvait tenir à son fusil, à ses pièges, aux balles, au poêle de métal, à la lampe pendue dans l'igloo' (307) (a precious female, dependent upon him, to whom he was attached as he was to his rifle, his traps, his bullets, to the metal stove or the lamp hanging in the igloo) (214), learns to appreciate her intrinsic qualities – her endless devotion and true merit. She ultimately becomes more than a female in his eyes (214). Even so, she must constantly remain aware that for him the child is more precious than any woman (153). In spite of tradition, through his own lived experience, Agaguk does, in the end, admit that she is no longer a simple female, but a woman who can have power over him, a hold over him. Finally, however, love manifests itself as a structure of reciprocity that requires both compassion and understanding from two equal subjects. And this conclusive structure can be instituted only following the eradication and destruction of Agaguk's most profoundly anchored cultural values. For reasons dictated by tradition, he decides to take his newborn daughter's life, but after a long and agonizing struggle he accepts the legitimacy of his wife's desires and hands the child back to her. He helps her onto the caribou skin and places the infant in her outstretched arms: 'En lui montait une tiédeur, une plaisance toute chaude qu'il n'avait jamais encore éprouvée. Il était heureux. La fille vivrait, parce qu'Iriook le voulait ainsi' (326-7) (Within him rose a warmth, a pleasure he had never before experienced. He was happy. The baby would live because Iriook wished it so) (228). In short, reciprocal love is founded on the choice, the understanding, and the respect of the uniqueness of the other. The masculine principle of unconditional domination subsides in Agaguk, who attains a state of harmonious equilibrium when the feminine principle of generosity is revealed to him. He will in the end 'regretter un crime ... Un sentiment qu'aucun Esquimau ne s'avouerait jamais. Un sentiment de femme' (304) (regret a crime, a sentiment which no Eskimo would ever avow, a woman's sentiment) (212).

The mythical object of value has a more complex structure than the practical. As such, the former not only has a greater potentiality than the latter, but also makes it possible for the subject to discover and to reveal his/her internalized world as value through intersubjective relations. Moreover, love does not simply signify for the subject at the cognitive level but, indeed, reveals the subject as body related to the other in a reciprocal tensive relation that defines him/her. In short, love sensitizes the subject's perceiving and feeling body and reveals his/her world as meaning. As love is continuously invested by both subjects at ever-increasing levels of sensitization and is transmitted from one subject to the other, signification is constructed figuratively in this novel by love scenes that are more and more intense.

After Ramook's arrest, the tribe must choose a chief because the absence of an uncontested leader disrupts daily life in the village. The narrator explores the various ways in which the tribe selects a new leader, who must demonstrate particular qualities to be considered for this honour: 'Comment y arrivait-on? Excellence de l'homme, mais en des arts propres à la tribu. Barèmes parfois étonnants. Oonak était bon chasseur. Il savait bien apprêter les peaux. Il n'avait pas de femme ... Il construisait l'igloo le plus solide et le plus rond, il pêchait le phoque comme un homme des pays d'eau. Il savait parler et ne craignait plus personne maintenant' (278) (How did they reach that conclusion? By the excellence of the man, but in the arts that belonged to the tribe. The standards were sometimes surprising. Oonak was a good hunter. He was skilful in preparing skins. He had no wife ... He built the most solid and the roundest igloo, he hunted seal like a man of the sea country. He knew how to speak, and was not afraid of anyone now) (193). The chief is not chosen in accordance with 'Inuk peu respectueux des lois et de la morale' (laws and morality ... [for which] ... Eskimos have little respect) but entirely in terms of 'le bien de la collectivité procédait selon des lois bien différentes' (284) (the well-being of the community which proceeds according to very different laws) (198).

But the exercise of power is not without danger, for it automatically entails unexpected results. Horrendous punishment is inflicted on the chief who errs in his judgment or fails out of ignorance or lack of foresight. Stories passed from village to village and from tribe to tribe tell of the fate that befalls the leader who neglects his duties, betraying the trust and interests of the group. Public disgrace, exile, and even mutilation are common penalties incurred by imprudent tribal heads: 'Celúi-dont on trancha l'oreille, l'autre qui fut émasculé, un autre encore, exilé, devenu apatride parmi les siens et dans la plus immense patrie du monde? Cet autre encore à qui l'on a craché au visage, celui à qui les femmes furent enlevées?' (278–9) (This one's ear had been cut off, that one had been emasculated, another had been exiled, became homeless among his own people and in the biggest country in the world. They spat in the face of another one, and took away his wife) (194). The chief is organically linked to his tribe and, as spokesman for the group, exemplifies ancestral wisdom. Power invested in him must be used to promote the common good. To become chief is to subjugate the other to one's authority and enforce the laws of the tribe, and it is also to accept the consequences for all deviations from the norm. Since errors or omissions are unpardonable and are cruelly punished, the chief uses any means available to gather information in order to neutralize the tribe and consolidate his power base. Hence the necessity to lie, cheat, and deceive and bully the tribesmen, who have 'little respect for the laws and morality.' When Ramook accepts the position of leader, he passes from the state of anonymity and asserts himself as a collective subject mediated by the customs and usages of the group. Here, individual will is governed by duty that regulates knowledge and power.

The passage from the state of anonymity to that of representative subject takes place in several stages: the male's merit is first recognized by all the men of the tribe; a unanimous consensus is then reached as to his qualities of leadership; and finally a formal request is made by delegates, followed by a public oral acceptance. Once more, the appropriation of all the resources of language by the subject establishes and founds a dialogical relation with the male members of the tribe that confirms and maintains the hierarchical status of all the interlocutors. The entire process takes place without apparent ceremony, but the given word solemnly binds each and every member of the group faithfully to respect the contractual oath. It is precisely this internal bond that determines the status and role of all members of the community. The collective desire expressed through the mediation of the chief confirms and ratifies the traditional values of the group. When interrogated by Henderson, Ramook peremptorily states that 'La volonté de tous, c'est la volonté de Ghorok. Il n'a pas à être mécontent. Il obéit' (151) (The will of all, that is Ghorok's will. He was not displeased. He obeyed) (103).

As noted above, space, whether that of the tundra, the family, the village, or the tribe, is generally expressed through the sensitized bodies of the main protagonists, Agaguk and Iriook. As such, perception, feelings, and judgments of cultural, physical, and personal space are always experienced, tensitivitized, and moralized (euphoric, dysphoric) and, ultimately, incorporated and focalized by and through the body.

Yet, much as in *Bonheur d'occasion*, the protagonists' focalized vision of the experienced is relayed by the enunciator, who, in so doing, takes on an explanatory, judgmental, and moralizing role, thereby both positioning and manipulating his enunciatee. Again, this shift from showing to telling is always accompanied by a change in deixes, whether of spatial, temporal, or personal pronouns. Hence, the great number of gnomic value judgments and pronouncements of a sapiential nature that attempt to explain to his virtual readers the morals and the mores of the Inuit in this distant space and distant time. For the narrator, the Inuit of this period are considered as being generally bound by the ancestral principles transmitted to them, members of the group regulating their behaviour according to the dictates of tradition. Barely capable of admitting or feeling guilt, seldom able to reason in terms of elementary moral considerations, the Inuit is motivated by tribal solidarity and an instinct of self-preservation: 'il tue comme il aime, comme il mange, comme il se débarasse d'une puce au poil' (185) (he kills as he lives, as he eats, as he gets rid of a louse in his hair) (128). For the narrator, in this society governed by laws imposed from the outside, the Inuit tries to dominate his neighbour and outwit his oppressors, even though he accepts the possibility of defeat and admits the superior force of the white men. 'Mais le jeu, c'est de vivre sa vie ancestrale, en défi constant aux Blancs. Céder aux instincts: voler, rapiner, violer, tuer, et pourtant rester libre dans la tribu. Sport de tous les jours, habitudes, mode de vie' (185) (His game is to live his ancestral life in constant defiance of the white man, to yield to his instincts, to steal, rob, rape, kill and still remain free within the tribe. This is his everyday pastime, his habit, his way of life) (128). Globally described in negative terms, the group's activities are reduced to the level of instinctive animal behaviour. The tribe is generally presented as an oppressive and cruel institution, not far removed from the 'natural' world, and organized along the same lines as the wolf pack, where cunning and instinct ensure survival. Within this tribal structure, the individual relies on natural instincts both to protect himself and to control others successfully. This representation of the group is not far removed from the one described by Laberge in *La Scouine*.

Ramook is completely at ease in such a world of being and seeming, of duplicity and ruthlessness. He manipulates the villagers and openly breaks tribal laws by marrying a foreigner. Yet he meets an untimely end because of a force he cannot comprehend. Iriook, an outsider who 'descendait par ceux venus avant elle, des peuples du dos de la terre'

(202) (descended from the people on the other side of the world) (139), confounds his plans to incriminate his own son. 'By some instinct,' she connects the presence of the constables and tribesmen with Brown's death. She intuitively begins to form a plan to save Agaguk: 'Brusquement, tout devenait plus facile. Esquimaude elle-même, les ruses ne lui étaient pas étrangères, lors même qu'elle répugnait le plus souvent à leur usage' (243) (In a swift turn everything became more easy. Eskimo tricks were not foreign to her mind, even though she often disliked using them) (167). On returning to the village, Ramook is once more defeated by a woman. He demands that the tribe hold together as a solid block, a block including him, but Tugugak's wife breaks ranks. 'Elle était plus jeunes que les autres, elle était, comme Iriook, plus évoluée, plus tendre aussi, et la vie des siens parfois la dégoûtait. "C'est lui," s'exclama-t-elle. "C'est lui qui a tué Henderson. Il a tué Ayallik aussi. Nous avons peur de lui!"' (270) (She was younger than the others, and like Iriook, more advanced, more tender also, and the life of her people sometimes disgusted her ... 'It's he,' she exclaimed. 'He killed Henderson. He killed Ayallik too. We're afraid of him') (188). Some of the younger women of the tribe instinctively judge their own people according to unlearned ethical values. They weaken tribal solidarity and undermine accepted norms by speaking out, openly questioning the legitimate representative of the group. In short, when they appropriate language and use it in a dialogical situation, they become more powerful than the men, that is to say, dominant moral subjects of and in language as a social institution. What is of note in this universe is the existence of the commonplace presupposition of biological determinism linked to age and physical maturation. Predetermined natural feminine knowledge activates verbal power, which brings about the rejection of the leader by his own people: 'Dans l'histoire de la tribu, pour peu qu'on la consignât dans les chants de veillée, Ramook avait cessé d'être' (271) (In the history of the tribe, as it would be entrusted to the songs at night, Ramook had ceased to exist) (189).

In the course of the slow evolution of his identity, Agaguk, unlike the other actants, undergoes several marked changes. At the age of eighteen, he possesses an elementary grasp of the physical laws governing his immediate environment – the understanding indispensable for survival on the plain. His uncontrolled rages are a sign of powerlessness when confronted with his wife's mysterious nature. And his ignorance of the fundamental laws regulating tribal behaviour is a problem with which he is unable to come to grips: 'Il n'avait jamais été habile à cette vie de la tribu. Il n'avait jamais su se préoccuper des subtilités de la vie collective, des courants d'opinions, des zones de force ... Il avouait sa complète ignorance' (294) (he had never known how to become interested in the subtleties of the collective life, the currents of opinions, the levels of power ... He avowed his complete ignorance) (163). Inuit tradition requires that a man respect his father, that he passively obey his every command: 'Il n'avait jamais eu confiance en son père. Il le savait cupide et rusé. S'il avait quitté le village, c'est qu'il n'en pouvait plus d'accepter cet homme comme chef ... s'il était parti, c'est qu'il craignait justement d'avoir à obéir à des ordres dangereux, de servir les intérêts personnels de Ramook' (237–8) (He had never had any confidence in his father, he knew he was avaricious and tricky. He left the village mainly because he could no longer accept that man as chief ... He left because he feared he might have to obey dangerous orders – to serve Ramook's personal interests) (163). Suspicious of his father's deviousness, in order not to fall under Ramook's domination, Agaguk leaves the tribe and asserts himself as an independent subject: 'Quand il était parti du village, il avait cédé à un instinct de protection plus qu'à un sentiment réfléchi' (238) (When he departed from the village, he was yielding to an instinct for self-preservation rather than acting on considered reflection) (163). In his dealings with the tribe or with the dishonest factor, his behaviour is not inspired by egoism or rational considerations, but rather stems from a unique natural force that sets him apart from all other Inuit. He simply obeys an elemental instinct invested in him by chance at birth. In other words, programmed by biological determinism, his acts spontaneously result from a predetermined intuitive awareness of right and wrong. Instinctive knowledge governs power, will, and duty.

While Ramook is carrying out his plot to murder the constable in cold blood in order to consolidate his power within the tribe, Agaguk attempts to protect his son, Tayaout, against his most dangerous enemy: 'Vers quel destin sanglant le loup blanc aurait-il mené Tayaout? Tayaout, joie, richesse, la seule joie, la plus grande richesse. Tayaout, pour qui Agaguk eût donné la peau de son corps, le sang de ses veines, sa force et sa survie' (178) (To what bloody fate would the white wolf have taken Tayaout? Tayaout, joy and riches, his only joy, his greatest riches, Tayaout for whom Agaguk would give the skin off his body, the blood from his veins, his strength and his life) (125). When the knowledge gained from his long experience of hunting on the plain fails him, 'quelque chose, une alerte intérieure, un rythme nouveau dans le sang, un rien l'avertissait de la présence' (194) (something, some inner alertness, a new rhythm in his blood, a nothingness warned him of its presence) (135). As soon as the beast senses him at a distance, Agaguk likewise perceives it. An uncanny power that he is unable to explain, 'une faculté physique venue de générations multiples' (194) (a physical faculty inherited from many generations) (135), and not his vision, the organ of all practical knowledge, warns him of the imminent danger. Agaguk pits his instinct and skills against the wolf and overcomes it. His victory, however, is not without serious physical and spiritual consequences. The white wolf represents a danger unheard of on the plain and never before encountered by any other male Eskimo. Agaguk successfully passes this unprecedented test and triumphs where all others would have failed. In spite of his accomplishment, however, he cannot find within himself the strength to rekindle his taste for life. A sense of diminished power and dependence on his wife, accompanied by feelings of lethargy and self-doubt, create a situation similar to the one that caused him to leave the tribe. Physically and mentally helpless, unable to function as an independent subject, powerless to generate self-motivated acts, Agaguk, completely demoralized, cannot 's'accommod[er] de sa déchéance' (222) (adjust himself to his fall) (152). If an instinct for self-preservation induced him to leave the tribe and permitted him to accede to the status of personal subject, this time, in contrast, the desire to act must be attributed to woman's power. Activity becomes possible and finds its release only because of her direct intervention. Masculine desire, stymied by its very reflexive nature, is activated and motivated by woman's transitive instinct. Iriook, through sexuality, motivates Agaguk's will and instils in him fresh hope, so that he manages to recreate a personal identity by conceiving new projects.

Having saved him from passively accepting his loss by restoring his instinctive will and duty, Iriook must once again assume the role of a catalysing agent. When she instinctively speaks up and confronts Ramook, not only does she guarantee the continuity of the couple, she also puts into question the tribe's collective values. This fundamental denegation of an intuitive nature constitutes a model of behaviour internalized by Agaguk. Articulated at a rationally posited level, it is at the origin of his rejection of the honour bestowed upon him when he is asked to become chief. His categorical refusal is at one and the same time founded upon his personal evaluation and radical questioning of collective values, as well as upon his deep-felt appreciation of Iriook's individual qualities. Initially, he tries to understand the tribe's motives for offering him the post. He then methodically examines what collective life would mean for him and his family: 'L'Inuk réfléchissait, prenant sa décision. L'on n'est pas chef si jeune, dans les tribus. L'honneur était alléchant. Mais il signifiait le retour à la vie de village. Agaguk ne voulait point perdre ce qu'il possédait. La paix surtout, l'isolement, la liberté qu'il avait de décider de ses moindres mouvements' (291) (The Eskimo reflected, considering his decision. A man does not become chief so young in the tribes. The honour was attractive. But it meant a return to the village. Agaguk did not want to lose what he had, most of all the peace, the isolation, the liberty to decide his own least movements) (203). The need to act according to his own desires, the necessity to achieve his potential according to his own will and sense of duty, take precedence over any social obligations he might feel. Moreover, the tribe, because of its restrictive social structures, offers him limited opportunities to live as his conscience dictates. In spite of the many reasons evoked, however, he wavers temporarily, but in the end refuses, fearing that he may have to give over his wife to other men, who, through no fault of their own, may need a woman. Agaguk, 'sans qu'il lui fût possible d'exprimer par quel transmutation il en arrivait à cette jalousie d'instinct ... il ressentait le mal, il ne voulait pas l'entretenir en lui' (291) (without being able to express by what process he had come to feel this instinctive jealousy[,] ... felt the evil, and wished to have nothing to do with it) (203). Once he has reasoned through the different aspects of the problem, he declines the offer and opts for family life on the tundra. His conclusion sanctions rationally chosen individual values over collective customs. 'Il ne partageait avec personne cette contrée qu'il habitait, avec personne, sauf sa femme qu'il avait choisie et à qui il était attachée' (293) (He shared with no one this country he inhabited, with no one save his wife, whom he had chosen and to whom he was bound) (204). Freely assumed, independent of the group's traditions, family life is presented as being intrinsically superior to gregarious, social cohabitation. 'Iriook avait raison. Quoi de meilleur que cette vie choisie?' (295) (Iriook was right. What better than this chosen life?) (206).

His suspicions of the perils inherent in tribal living, initially awakened by an instinct for self-preservation as well as an awareness of good and evil, are at the origin of his refusal of the offer. His conclusion, arrived at by means of deductive reasoning, presupposes the free choice, according to the dictates of his conscience, of the other as absolute ideal and marks the male subject's accession to the mythical. By slow degrees, his will is conquered by reason and is instituted by means of the progressive discovery of Iriook. The final obstacles preventing Agaguk from attaining peace and happiness will be overcome thanks to the logical development of this ultimate transformation: the validation of feminine power by masculine knowledge founded on empirical criteria actually confirms his dual nature. Originally provided with a rudimentary understanding and a primary instinct partially grounded in tradition, Agaguk, over time, gains knowledge of self as he discovers woman's complementary nature. This learning experience is accompanied by a further discovery: his awareness of the other is inversely proportional to the power and influence of collective values. 'Il lui faudrait convaincre la femme que ce n'est pas seulement une habitude à perpétuer, mais la nécessité de survie. L'enfant mourrait ...' (317) (He would have to convince his wife that it was not only a custom to carry on, but the necessity of survival. The baby would die ...) (221) versus 'Agaguk la regardait, inquiet. Il savait que si elle se mettait à pleurer, il ne pourrait refuser la vie à la petite' (323) (Agaguk looked at her, disturbed. He knew that if she began to cry, he could not refuse life to the baby girl) (226), and 'La petite vivrait, parce qu'Iriook le voulait ainsi' (327) (The baby would live because Iriook wished it so) (228). Iriook intuitively attenuates Agaguk's impulsive nature and awakens his latent moral faculties so that he finally becomes aware of good and evil, the ethical dimension of existence. He behaves compassionately and even tenderly towards her and, although 'Il n'était pas de sa race et de sa tradition de laisser une femme dépasser le rôle de femelle que les millénaires lui imposaient' (307) (it was not in his race and tradition to let woman transcend the female role that thousands of years had imposed on her) (215), he sacrifices all of his ancestral beliefs for her. In short, the 'new-found happiness,' the 'joie soudaine et grandiose' (326) (sudden and tremendous joy) (228) he experiences at the end of his personal journey, corresponds to a freely arrived-at and accepted harmony between two equal and complementary subjects. Here deductive knowledge governs power, will, and duty.

On the figurative level, the text privileges the rational subject's progressive discovery of the equilibrium that ideally exists between the masculine and feminine traits of his character. Under Iriook's influence, far from the tribe, the existence and meaning of Agaguk's moral conscience are revealed to him. He undergoes a long apprenticeship and, by means of logical, natural thought, he succeeds in overcoming 'l'atavisme millénaire' (324) (the old atavism) (226) that imposes an obligatory death sentence on the newborn girl. Following this rational gesture, which erases all trace of traditional values and marks the institution of a new moral order, he is recompensed by the birth of a long-awaited second son – 'Comme tantôt, il tendit les mains. Cette fois, c'était un garçon' (327) (As before, he held out his hands. This time, it was a boy) (229) – and this final scene is played out as an illustration of the Socratic maieutic: Agaguk delivers his wife's twins (first the girl, then the boy) after feminine instinct has delivered their shared love.

Written at the advent of the Quiet Revolution, which, beginning in the early 1960s, heralded great social, cultural, and economic transformations in Quebec society following the long and stifling rule of Maurice Duplessis's ultraconservative, Ultramontain, moralistic, and nationalistic party, *Agaguk* was one of the most widely read and widely taught novels in the province. During the 1960s and 1970s, it was perceived by its readers as representing the mentality of the Inuit, simultaneously maintaining the mystery and difference of these people while making them familiar. For the very first time, sexuality was expressed openly and without guilt in a Québécois novel, and the sensual body became a part of the intrigue.

In attempting to work out a socio-semiotics, I have considered this novel as a cultural artefact that strives to resolve, at the level of the imaginary, contradictions that could not be reconciled within the socio-historical situation of a particular group. Thus, for me, *Agaguk* transcodes Thériault's significant personal reactions to his historical situation in the late 1950s. From this perspective, what we are dealing with are not foreign characters situated in an exotic setting but the transcription, at the level of the imaginary, of social and individual situations that are linked to the Quebec society of the time, prior to the Quiet Revolution of the 1960s. At this level of analysis, Thériault's novel describes the separation of two individuals from the group and the formation of a unique couple whose subjective interactions progressively grow in the direction of complete reciprocity and through which the male instincts of domination and violence are systematically eradicated thanks to a woman's instincts of gentleness and comprehension. Sexuality is considered as the bodily expression of woman's mythical qualities, which are seen as essential for the liberation of man. Moreover, the consolidation of the couple, and subsequently of the family founded on new emerging values, can take place only with the disappearance of the name of the father, which attempts to inscribe the son in the symbolic order, then to destroy him when he refuses to be so manipulated. In the end, a nuclear family that breaks with tradition is created, whereby, isolated in their hut away from the group, two equal, liberated subjects give life to twins. Yet, it is essential to note that, unlike all the other subjects represented in the text, the couple as a unit is confronted with a large number of tests of increasing complexity that it succeeds in overcoming. It progressively passes from the hierarchical and material plane of survival of the group to the moral plane of reciprocity in intersubjective relations. In short, the partners evolve from feeling, instinctive, sensual, unequal subjects into reasoning, sentient, loving, equal subjects.

Such an evolution – which could be considered a revolution, or the construction of a new identity – is possible only through the creation of an original, imaginary, unexplored, and unoccupied space that defines itself with respect to all others. For in setting up specific mythical, social, natural, and supernatural spaces, Thériault also proposes a radical critique of the group/nation, and of group political, moral, and religious structures that condition each and every subject and constitute the interactional frames necessary for the group's cohesion and survival. He deconstructs the conventional representations of the family and the nation that constrained the individual, as represented in the historical, agrarian, or urban novel, a genre that could not foster the emergence of subjects with sentient, eroticized bodies, striving to forge their identities independently of existing value systems or ideologies. Such a turn expresses both the refusal of an ideology and the depoliticization of an identity based on the unity of language, race, and religion of a vanquished and exploited people. Though *Agaguk* could be taxed as an imaginary, idealistic, or even utopian resolution of the fundamental contradictions that thwart the advent of new forms of interpersonal relations, it none the less remains significant, since it sketches a strategy for an alternative politics of identity, freed from traditional, hierarchically ordered moral and social relations. In fact, it actually negates all that is prescriptive in interpersonal relations and establishes a dialogue affirming the primacy of the plurality of sexual identity, a plurality that not only liberates individuals from socially constructed roles but also redefines the passage of self to other, imposing an identity founded on the indistinct frontiers of ambiguity.

In this universe, relations between subjects are mediated through hierarchical patterns determined by tradition, and, as such, the individual subjects of the group are motivated and governed by external, collective values that are independent of them, since they can express their desires only in terms of the norms of the community. Yet, the values that ensure the cohesion of the group/nation and motivate the collective social subject must be overcome, negated, and even eradicated for a new moral and sexual identity to develop, independent of the traditional body politic. The historical novel and the novel of the land and of colonization constructed /closed/ and /non-open/ stable, traditional, homogeneous, predetermined and prescribed spaces within which the subject could safely define its collective identity, or delimited /non-closed/ and /open/ changing, unstable, heterogeneous, polymorphous spaces that shattered the identity of the individual subject. When /closed/ and /non-open/ spaces are presented as alternatives, they most often correspond to the ideality of a fleeting, illusory return to the paternal and/or maternal household or village, which in turn represent ineffectual and futile attempts by the subject to ground and anchor his or her subjectivity in the past. Such a return to the bygone topoi of ancestrality and tradition is doomed to failure, as is the only other option, an urban existence, which offers no centre or core values through which individuals can institute and define their egos independently of the forces constraining them.

Thériault's originality is to have established an ambivalent imaginary space in which the existing cultural topoi are either indexed in filigree (e.g., through modern technological tools, arms, and instruments or through the presence of white men, factors, traders, and policemen, and their means of locomotion, such as planes) or fundamentally redistributed and transformed. The couple can construct its identity in both the /closed/ space of the igloo and the /open/ space of the tundra, mythical and natural domains of evolution and maturation. These are clearly opposed to the /non-closed/ social space of the village or trading post and the /non-open/ space of the supernatural, both of which represent zones of domination within which an independent ego is stifled and vanquished. The latter are social spheres where, within the confines of a politics of unity of language, race, and belief (Ghorok, the sorcerer, is the second most powerful person in the tribe, after the cunning and deceitful chief, Ramook), the subject can forge its collective identity. In contrast to this process, the couple begins by distancing itself from the collective topoi, and negating them at every possible level by successfully passing a prolonged series of complex tests. Through the principle of shared verbal exchange that recognizes and asserts the multiplicity of sexual identity freed from traditional roles, the couple institutes a family that confirms the primacy of liberated dialogical subjects who discover, found, and assume their own interpersonal values.

CHAPTER THIRTEEN

Conclusion

I would like to address a number of issues that follow from this study, and comment briefly on what can be learned from the examination not only of exploratory and ethnohistorical writings of first and early encounters and conversion, but also of founding or best-selling novels over the first hundred years of the production of indigenous French-Canadian literature in Quebec. I have argued that these representative texts all articulate a problematic of identity, of self and otherness, whether written before the fall of Quebec in 1759, or after it. In exploration and conversion texts of New France, the writing self and the speaking self emerge as difference, as positively valorized and moralized subjects on the backdrop of alterity, hostility, and omnipresent menace. In contrast, the other is constructed as the third, the one absent in intersubjective relationships of communication, to be expropriated, dispossessed, and colonized. The other is also imagined as ready to be converted to the 'true' faith and 'civilized' by repudiating the past, along with his/her religious, social, and cultural values, all the while being projected as a decentred 'barbarian,' easy to manipulate but unable to internalize readily the symbolic structures and presuppositions that regulate the activity and behaviour of the incomers.

A version of this same scenario is played out in historiography and the novel of the nineteenth and early twentieth centuries, in works that elaborate a politics of identity after the fall, rooted in a glorious pre-Conquest past peopled by heroic explorers, colonizers, military men, and missionaries. Three of the six novels examined – *La Terre paternelle*, *Les Anciens Canadiens*, and *Maria Chapdelaine* – define the individual, the group, and, I dare say, the imaginary nation, as founded on unity of language, race, and religion, while mapping out heterogeneous spaces where the subject's integrity is threatened, diluted, and even dissolved. To guarantee survival of the group, all eroticized individual desires must always be subservient to the family constellation. The first novel in Quebec to present a radically different form of identity,[1] *La Scouine*, actually reduced its main protagonists to instinctive, aggressive beings, imploding the family back onto itself as a group of individuals linked together by primitive relations of seriality that prevent their fusion through the identification of, and quest for, common goals and projects.

With the Second World War, the Quebec novel, as exemplified by *Bonheur d'occasion*, massively migrates to the city, where the forces of history and the new international order decentre the desiring, impoverished subject, whose identity is no longer guaranteed solely by long-established tradition and values. The self is now opened up to the external world, as the new, transformed, and truncated family reconstitutes itself through and by means of a perceived common language, race, and origin. In this disquieting and anguished universe, part of the past is recuperated and continues to inform the subjects as they desperately attempt to come to grips with omnipresent and menacing forces of internationalism, anxiously awaiting the end of the war that, it is hoped, will bring a different kind of stability to the members of the group, defined by shared speech, beliefs, and ancestors.

It is against the new emerging order that continues to integrate the imaginary French-Canadian subject in the constricting space of family, religion, and race that Thériault, in *Agaguk*, defines a new sexual, moral, rational, and emotional identity based on the rejection of the past. In this universe, the main protagonists put into question the collective social and institutional structures that assign individuals to predetermined hierarchical roles and that dictate norms of behaviour and govern their status in the group. Once again, the elaboration of a liberated, cognizant, and sentient subject who is reborn through relation to a complementary and equal partner can be envisaged only in an elsewhere, a mythical space, where the socio-economic, historical, and sexual contradictions of the Quebec society of the late 1950s can find a form of resolution, albeit one that is totally tentative and utopian.

What all the texts examined in this study do is to work out a solution, at the level of the imaginary, to the problem of identity of the individual and the group. They propose partial answers to the question of how, despite the Conquest and the progressive pressures of international socio-economic forces beyond their control, subjects of French-Catholic origin who have been planted on the North American continent for some four centuries can best maintain their identity. Various divergent and oscillating responses are elicited in these narratives, ranging from subjects who open up to the world to those who fold back onto themselves.

I chose to end this study with the discussion of *Agaguk*, a novel that appeared one year before the death of Maurice Duplessis, the leader of the Union nationale and the premier of the province from 1936 to 1939 and 1944 to 1959. It also predated the advent of new forms of the novel that ceased to define imaginary French Canadians in terms of traditional ideology, replacing them instead with new subjects, the Québécois. As Maurice Arguin (1989) demonstrates in his detailed study of the Quebec novel from 1944 to 1965, the question of identity is the essential question that defines the new Québécois literary hero in most of the novels written between 1960 and 1965 (177–232). For him, the death of the French Canadian is a necessary condition for the birth of the Québécois, an individual who strives to repossess his universe fully through revolution, love, and writing (256).

The corpus in my study both represents the canon and articulates value systems of identity, nation, and survival. Even the later part of Arguin's work, focusing on the production of the first half of the 1960s, deals with what I call the transitional novel with respect to its form and techniques and to the ideology represented in it. Since then, the preoccupations of Quebec novelists and critics of francophone literatures have evolved considerably, as can be attested by the emergence of new concepts of writing[2] as well as the strong multicultural and feminist voices in the creative and critical[3] domains, voices that pose a real challenge to the literary establishment, with its more traditional readings of the canon. Yet this is not to say that the past is no more, that the issues raised today in Quebec literature are completely divorced from those that arise in the pre–Quiet Revolution corpus that I have chosen to examine. Questions of identity, group formation, and the status of the subject continue to be raised, but are played out differently. Since 1968, with the founding of the Parti Québécois under René Lévesque, two referenda have been held on Quebec independence – the first, in 1980, garnering 40 per cent of the popular vote, and the second, on 'Sovereignty Association' in 1995, missing a majority by less than 1 per cent of the votes cast.

It does seem, though, that this imaginary movement of openness and closure to the outside, to the different, to the heterogeneous, in the formation of subject, group, and nation noted in our corpus, has been and is currently being articulated most vehemently in the political domain today, if one judges by the position stated by the current premier of the province, Bernard Landry, in a speech given in February 2001 at Saint-Jean-de-Matha. In his address, he laid out a program of independence, arguing that the province is the fifteenth economic power in the world and, given that there are many less wealthy states that have sovereign control over their own affairs, Quebec should also enjoy the right to represent its own interests on the international scene. Moreover, he stressed that, for him, Quebec nationalism is not based on ethnicity: 'Whether you're born in Santiago in Chile or in Saint-François-Xavier-les-Hauteurs, we are Québécois – let's not forget that.'[4] Yet such a vision of an independent Quebec is certainly not shared by all Québécois, including provincial or federal politicians. Indeed, it may be that this never-ending tension between federalist and sovereignist views is what actually defines what Canada is, and will be, with respect to Quebec. Following former Quebec premier Lucien Bouchard's sudden and unexpected resignation (over comments made by a member that split the party along the lines of traditionalists, who define the nation in terms of those whose ancestors go back to the pre-1759 *'pure laine'* settlers, and non-traditionalists, who define it in terms of the fundamental rights of all individuals, regardless of race, creed or origins), the federal minister of intergovernmental affairs, Stéphane Dion, stated that 'The separatist movement is going down, even with the most charismatic leader they ever had.'[5] This is, however, far from the last word on the subject. Bernard Landry's and Stéphane Dion's very divergent attitudes and beliefs represent two opposite and extreme positions on the fundamental question that has been raised in Quebec in the political arena from the middle of the eighteenth century, even before it was imagined and instituted in literature and historiography: 'How can subjects best maintain and strengthen their identity in a clearly defined geographic region, where they have a history, a culture, a language, institutions, and values that set them apart from other inhabitants of Canada?'

Notes

Preface

1 Sartre, *Situations I* (1939: 71).
2 A glossary is provided following the notes to clarify technical terminology that appears in this work. For more detailed definitions, readers should consult Greimas and Courtés (1982), *Semiotics and Language: An Analytical Dictionary*.
3 As I shall demonstrate in chapters 7, 8, and 9, the society depicted in the novel examined is an oral society made up mainly of characters who can neither read nor write, a fact born out by sociologists such as Dumont et al. (1971).
4 For a literary account of the function of censorship in the province of Quebec, even after the middle of the twentieth century, see the very humorous and ironic novel *Le Libraire* by Gérard Bessette, first published in Paris by Julliard in 1960.
5 For a detailed analysis, see my *Semiotics and the Modern Quebec Novel: A Greimassian Analysis of Thériault's Agaguk* (1996).

1 Introduction to Narratology

1 The same critique of their work could be made as was made by Ferdinand de Saussure in his *Course in General Linguistics* (*CGL* 1966) of the Comparative School of Indo-European linguistics at the beginning of the twentieth century: 'although it had the indisputable merit of opening up a new and fruitful field, [the Comparative School] did not succeed in setting up a true science of linguistics. It failed to seek out the nature of its object of study.

Obviously without this elementary step, no science can develop a method' (4).
2 See É. Benveniste, *Problems in General Linguistics* (1971) chapter 10, 'Levels of Linguistic Analysis' (101–11).

2 A.J. Greimas and Narratology

1 Quoted in J.-C. Coquet. 'Éléments de bio-bibliographie,' liv. This frequently cited and difficult-to-locate article was reproduced in Broden's (2000) edition of *Algirdas Julien Greimas. La Mode en 1830* (371–82).
2 In his Preface to *Algirdas Julien Greimas. La Mode en 1830* (2000), Michel Arrivé notes that Greimas's statement that Saussure was virtually unknown by French linguists of the 1940s and 1950s was somewhat of an overstatement, since Georges Goughenheim, from 1938 on, gave Saussure a fundamental role in his linguistics course at L'École Pratique des Hautes Études in Paris, especially regarding the Saussurian distinction between synchrony and diachrony. Robert-Léon Wagner also gave the *CGL* a central role in a 1953 course on Grammar and Philology published by Centre de Documentation Universitaire (CDU) (Arrivé, 2000: xv).
3 For all page references to articles by Greimas see Greimas (1987a), *On Meaning: Selected Writings in Semiotic Theory*.
4 For definition and interdefinition of terms used by Greimas, consult A.J. Greimas and J. Courtés (1982), *Semiotics and Language: An Analytical Dictionary*; and (1986) *Sémiotique. Dictionnaire raisonné de la théorie du langage, II*.
5 Semes can be defined as the minimal unit of signification. Located at the level of content, a seme corresponds to the pheme, the unit at the level of expression. Hypothetically, a semantic system can account for the level of content of a semiotic system that is comparable to the level of expression of a phonological system.
6 One of the major tasks that had to be completed in the general semiotic theory of the 1960s and 1970s was to free it from the theoretical constraints of structural linguistics. For example, André Martinet (1960) proposed the hypothesis that all languages were organized according the principle of double articulation. On the first level, or first articulation, the utterance is articulated linearly by means of units having meaning (sentences, syntagma, words, etc.), the smallest of which he called morphemes: the sentence 'The baby will sleep' is articulated by means of four morphemes (The [1] baby [2] will [3] sleep [4]), each of which can be replaced in a different environment by other morphemes on the paradigmatic axis, or can end up in a different environment combined with other morphemes on the syntagmatic axis.

At the second level, or second articulation, each morpheme is articulated in turn at the level of the signifier in units having no meaning (distinctive units), the smallest of which are phonemes that are limited in number in every language. Hence, the morpheme sleep (sli:p) is made up of four phonemes each of which can be replaced by another in the same environment or combined with others to form a different morpheme. The signified can also be broken down, but not linearly, into units of meanings or semes: baby = [human] + [very young].
7 *Les Structures anthropologiques de l'imaginaire.*
8 The appearance of the first volume of the dictionary titled *Sémiotique. Dictionnaire raisonné de la théorie du langage* in 1979, co-authored with J. Courtés and published in English in 1982, as *Semiotics and Language: An Analytical Dictionary*, constituted a milestone, since it definitively fixed the first two stages of what has been defined as the 'standard theory' of the Paris School, or Greimassian semiotics.
9 The concept of isotopy designates both the repetition of classemes and the recurrence of semic categories, be they thematic or figurative.

3 First Encounters and Myth Making: Jacques Cartier's *Voyages* to New France

1 See Ramsay Cook's exemplary edition of *The Voyages of Jacques Cartier* (1993), ix and following. All quotations in English are from Cook's edition of *The Voyages of Jacques Cartier*, whereas the French are from R. Lahaise and M. Couturier, *Voyages en Nouvelle-France*.
2 The English translation was originally published in Hakluyt (1600), *The Third and Last Volume of the Voyages, Navigations, Traffiques and Discoveries of the English Nation* (etc.), 232–7.
3 Cartier's grand-nephew, Jaques Noel, in an undated letter to Jean Growte, notes that he has searched everywhere in Saint Malo to recover the writings of Captain Jacques Cartier (1491–1557), his deceased uncle, but was only able to find a 'certaine booke made in manner of a sea Chart, which was drawne by the hand of my said uncle, which is in the possession of master Cremeur ...'; quoted in Cook (1993), *Voyages*, 105.
4 It should also be said that a number of translations of the narratives of exploration undertaken in the sixteenth century also contributed to the importance of Cartier's founding narrative on New France: for example, Ramusio's *Navigationi et viaggi* (1556), which was utilized by two French cosmographers: André Thevet in his *La Singularité de la France antarctique* (1558) and François de Belleforest in his *Cosmographie universelle* (1575).

5 *Des Sauvages ou voyage de Samuel Champlain de Brouage, faict en la France Nouvelle, l'an mil six cens trois* (1603) and *Les Voyages de la Nouvelle France Occidentale, dicte Canada* (1632).
6 1634. Republished in R. Twaites, *Jesuit Relations and Allied Documents*, 73 vols. (Cleveland: 1896–1901).
7 For the definition of technical or unfamiliar terms, see the glossary, following the notes.
8 For a discussion of this see Perron and Thérien (1990), 'Ethno-historical Discourse: Jean de Brébeuf's *Jesuit Relation* of 1636.'
9 This development owes much to Réal Ouellet's seminal article: 'Épistolarité et relations de voyage' (1996).
10 Parataxe is the rhetorical strategy adopted by most exploration or discovery literature when attempting to describe what has never been seen to an audience in the homeland that can only imagine it in relationship to what is common knowledge. Gabriel Sagard (1632), almost one hundred years later, in a chapter devoted to birds in Huronia, tries to depict for his reading public a humming-bird, which, at that time, was unknown in France: 'Premièrement, je commencerai par l'oiseau le plus beau, le plus rare et le plus petit qu'il soit, peut-être, au monde ... Cet oiseau, en corps *n'est pas plus gros qu'un grillon*, il a le bec long et très délié, *de la grosseur de la pointe d'une aiguille*, et ses cuisses et ses pieds *aussi menus que la ligne d'une écriture* ... Sa plume est *aussi déliée que duvet* ...' (First, I shall begin with the most beautiful, the rarest and the smallest bird there is, perhaps in the world. The body of this bird is *no bigger than a cricket*, it has a long and very fine beak, that is *as thick as the point of a needle* and its thighs and feet are *as slight as a line of writing* ... Its feathers are *as fluffy as down* ...) (301). The same paratactic rhetorical device is used in other descriptions, for example, of the moose: 'Pour l'élan, c'est l'animal le plus haut qu'il soit *après le chameau*, car il est *plus haut que le cheval* ... Il a le poil ordinairement grison et quelquefois fauve, *long quasi comme les doigts de la main*. Sa tête est fort longue et il porte son bois double *comme le cerf*, mais large et fait *comme celui d'un daim* et long de trois pieds. Le pied est fourchu *comme celui du cerf*, mais beaucoup plus plantureux ...' (As for the moose, it is the tallest animal alive *after the camel*, for it is *taller than a horse* ... Its coat of hair is ordinarily grey and sometimes fawn-coloured, *almost as long as the fingers of a hand*. Its head is very long and it has *two antlers like a stag*, but wide and *resembling those of a buck*. Its hooves are *cleft like a stag's*, but much more imposing ...) (310; translation mine; emphasis mine).
11 Emphasis mine.
12 The gnomic tense can be considered as the eternal present that can be

defined from the point of view of deixis as indicating neither time nor place.
13 For example, Cartier in his second *Voyage* decides to seize Donnacona the leader of the nation at Stadacona and take him off to France, 'pour conter et dire au Roi ce qu'il avait vu en ces pays occidentaux des merveilles du monde; car il nous a certifié avoir été à la terre du Saguenay, où il y a infinité d'or, rubis et autres richesses, et où sont les hommes blancs, comme en France, et accoutrés de draps de laine' (124) (so that he might relate and tell to the king all that he had seen in the west of the wonders of the world; for he assured us that he had been to the land of the Saguenay where there are immense quantities of gold, rubies, and other rich things, and that the men there are white as in France and go clothed in woollens) (82). Moreover, for Cartier, Donnacona's language is transparent, and they share the same presuppositions regarding the monstrous. Here the belief system of what is considered possible in the New World rejoins that of the Old Continent: 'En plus dit avoir vu d'autres pays, où les gens ne mangent point et n'ont point de fondement et ne digèrent point; mais font seulement eau par la verge. En plus, dit avoir été outre au pays des *Picquenyans*, et autres pays où les gens n'ont qu'une jambe, et autres merveilles, longues à raconter' (124) (He told us also that he had visited another region where the people, possessing no anus, never eat nor digest, but simply make water through the penis. He told us furthermore that he had been in the land of the Picquenyans, and to another country whose inhabitants have only one leg and other marvels too long to narrate) (82). Not even considering he could be misled by the other's tale, Cartier, on his return to France, decides to produce before the king the witness, who 'est homme ancien, et ne cessa jamais d'aller par pays depuis sa connaissance, tant par fleuves, rivières, que par terre' (124) (is an old man who has never ceased travelling about the country by river, stream, and trail since his earliest recollection) (82), along with his narrative, his witnessing, founded on his own lengthy experience and observation.
14 In themselves, these narratives would merit an onomastic study of their toponyms from both a semasiological perspective (an approach that aims at describing significations, taking minimal signs or lexemes as a starting point) and an onomasiological perspective (starting from the signified in order to study the manifestations at the level of signs).
15 Genesis 4: 12: 'When thou tillest the ground, it shall not henceforth yield unto thee her strength.'
16 For a discussion of the role of the portrait in the novel, see Perron (1996), 68–75.

17 This corporeal description would, in itself, necessitate an in-depth analysis concentrating on the passage of the unknown-known: nature/culture; civilized/barbarian (etc.), 'hair/twisted hay; nail/bird's feathers.'
18 Which Cartier interprets as 'We want to be friends.'
19 This development owes much to Marie-Christine Gomez-Géraud (1995).
20 For example, Sagard (1632) in chapter 10 of his *Le Grand Voyage*, entitled 'Des danses, chansons et autres cérémonies ridicules' (On Dances, Songs and Other Ridiculous Ceremonies), borrowing freely from Lescarbot (1609), writes: 'les danceurs ne se tiennent point par la main comme par deçà, mais ils ont tous les poings fermés ... et les hommes les tiennent aussi fermés, élevés en l'air et de toute façon, en la manière d'un homme qui menace, avec movements du corps et des pieds, levant l'un et puis l'autre, desquels ils frappent contre terre à la cadence des chansons et s'élevant comme en demi-sauts ... Et ceux ou celles qui se démènent le mieux et font plus à propos toutes les petites simagrées sont estimés entre eux les meilleurs danseurs ... En cela fait, ils s'écriaient d'une façon et hurlement épouvantable l'éspace d'un quart d'heure, et ils sautaient en l'air avec violence jusqu'à en écumer par la bouche ...' (The dancers do not hold hands but they all have clenched fists ... and the men also hold them clenched and in the air and any other way, like a person menacing, moving their bodies and their feet, raising one foot after the other with which they beat the earth in cadence with the songs and jump up ... And those men or women who thrash about the most and make the greatest fuss are considered by them to be the best dancers ... Having done this they cry out in the most horrifying screams for a quarter of an hour, and they jump up in the air so violently until they froth at the mouth ...) (190–4; translation mine).
21 See Perron and Thérien 9190), 'Ethno-historical Discourse.'

4 Settlement and Conversion: Jean de Brébeuf's Jesuit *Relations* of 1635 and 1636

1 All quotations from the Jesuit Relations have been translated by me from the facsimile edition of the original seventeenth-century edition of the *Relations des Jésuites* published in 1972 (Montreal: Éditions du Jour).
2 For a discussion of the specificity of epistolary discourse and its strategies of representation in realist fiction, see Le Huenen and Perron (1984b).
3 'Introduction à l'analyse structurale du récit.' *Communications* 8: 7–33.
4 For Ricœur (*Time and Narrative II*, 1985), 'What the historical narrative and the fictional narrative have in common is the use of the same operations of configuration that I have placed under the sign of mimesis II. But what

opposes them does not concern the structuring activity invested in the narrative structures as such, but the claim to truth by which is defined the third mimetic relation' (12). However, I would like to suggest here that the specificity of the ethnohistorical discourse of the Relations, a mixed genre, is at one and the same time to claim the same finality as historical discourse – to tell the truth – and, in contrast to the fictional and historical narratives, to have as its structural specificity the investment of the narrative structures so that the stemmatic nature of the functions – non-integrative of the events – is not only subordinated to the indices but systematically converted into the grand paradigm of the intemporal and of eternal truth.

5 Objects of value are terminal effects that permit the logical reconstruction of motivating causes. The sought-after or desired object, a sort of medium or vehicle of values, remains unknowable in itself but can be perceived by means of its discrete determinants, whose differential nature confers upon them a status analogous to that of the linguistic sign. The object of value, be it *mythical* (object of the mind – or noological) or *practical* (object of the world – or cosmological), is thereby considered as the locus of fixation, as a topos of the manifestation of determinant-values. From this point of view, the semiotics of cognition and passions can be considered as a semiotics of the values acquired, lost, suspended, re-acquired, and so on, by the subject.

6 A thin soup made of ground corn meal to which were sometimes added pieces of fish, meat, or squash.

7 In the previous paragraph the enunciator, Paul Le Jeune, and subsequently the narratee possessing European modal competence, are clearly demarcated by the narrator. He calls upon shared knowledge founded on the impression of what has been seen – or, rather, what has already been seen – through the mnemonic evocation of the evanescent trace of a memory or of a shared cultural reminiscence. In short, he does this by the intermediary of a sign that carries out a topological translation in the space of the commonplace of reading: 'Ayant donc arrêté de nous tenir où nous sommes, il fut question de bâtir une cabane. Les cabanes de ce pays ne sont ni des Louvres ni des Palais, ni rien de semblable aux riches bâtiments de notre France, non pas même aux plus petites chaumines; c'est néanmoins quelque chose de meilleur et plus commode, que les taudis des Montagnais. Je ne vous saurais mieux exprimer la façon des demeures Huronnes, que de les comparer à des berceaux ou tonnelles de jardin, dont au lieu de branches et de verdue, quelques-unes sont couvertes d'écorce de cèdre, quelques autres de grosses écorces de frêne, d'orme et de sapin' (Having

therefore decided to remain where we are, we set about building a cabin. The cabins of this country are neither the Louvre nor Palaces, nor in any way do they resemble the rich buildings of our France, not even the tiniest of our huts. They are nevertheless somewhat better and more comfortable than the pigsties of the Montagnais. I cannot better describe how the homes of the Huron are built than to compare them to cradles or arbours in a garden. Instead of branches and greenery, some of them are covered with cedar bark, others with great pieces of ash, elm, pine or spruce bark) (1635: 31). See also Le Huenen and Perron (1984a) for a discussion of representation in realist fiction.

8 This brief description of some of the reactions of the Huron to several inventions of measure, to grids, to symbolic notations, and to inventions that fix relations in the space of theoretical knowledge is considered by the narrator to be proof of their admiration for the superiority of European culture and knowledge. These ethnocentric inventions in fact mediate the 'relations' of the missionaries to the 'savage nature' of the New World. The description, none the less, is preceded by a long explanation of the strategic reasons for choosing *Ihonatiria* as the Jesuit headquarters from among over twenty villages of the Nation: 'parce que la moisson des âmes y est plus mûre qu'en aucun autre endroit, tant à cause de la connaissance que j'ai avec les habitants du lieu, et de l'affection qu'ils m'ont témoignée autrefois, que pour ce qu'ils sont déjà à demi instruits en la Foi ... La seconde raison est, que hormis ce village, il n'y avait que la Rochelle où nous dussions avoir inclination de nous arrêter, et ç'avait été notre pensée dès l'an passé ... Mais ayant considéré, qu'ils devaient à ce Printemps changer de place, comme ils ont déja fait, nous ne voulûmes point bâtir une cabane pour un hiver ... D'ailleurs, quoiqu'il ne soit fort à désirer, pour cueillir plus de fruit, d'avoir beaucoup d'auditeurs en nos assemblées, ce qui nous peut faire choisir les grands villages, plutôt que les petits; néanmoins pour le commencement, nous avons trouvé plus à propos de nous tenir comme à l'ombre, près d'une petite bourgade, où les habitants sont déjà faits à hanter les Français, que de nous mettre tout à coup en une grande, où l'on ne fût point accoutumé à nos façons de faire. Autrement c'eût été exposer des hommes nouveaux et ignorants en la langue, à une jeunesse nombreuse, qui par ses importunités et moqueries eût pu apporter quelque désordre' (because the harvest of souls is better than in any other place, because of the knowledge I have of the inhabitants and the affection they formerly showed me, as well as the fact that they are already partially instructed in the Faith ... The second reason is that except for this village there was only La Rochelle where we were inclined to inhabit, and this

was what we even thought last year ... But having considered last year that they would have to change the place of their village in the Spring, as they had already done, we did not want to build a cabin to spend only one winter ... Moreover, as it is very desirable, to harvest more fruit, to have many auditors in our audience, we are more inclined to choose large villages rather than small ones; however, at the beginning we thought it more prudent to remain in the shade of a small village, where the inhabitants were not used to our ways of doing things. Otherwise we would have exposed new men who did not know their language to the large number of their young people who, through their importunities and mockery, could have created some disorder) (1635: 30–1). In addition, this brief fragment is bracketed by two evaluative moments, the first, situating the actors' space and time, sets up a virtual program of manipulation: 'Cependant, comme j'ai dit, on ne laisse pas de nous venir visiter par admiration, principalement depuis que nous avons eu deux portes de menuiserie, et que notre moulin et notre horloge ont commencé à jouer. On ne saurait dire les étonnements de ces bonnes gens, et combien ils admirent l'esprit des Français' (However, as I said, they continue coming to visit us through admiration, especially since we installed two doors made by our carpenter, and that our mill and our clock have begun to work. We can hardly describe the astonishment of these good people, and how they admire the intelligence of the French) (1635: 32); the second justifies the establishment of a series of programs of 'conversion': 'Tout cela sert pour gagner leurs affections, et les rendre plus dociles, quand il est question des admirables et incomprehensibles mystères de notre Foi: car la croyance qu'ils ont de notre esprit et de notre capacité, fait que sans réplique ils croient ce qu'on leur annonce' (All of this helps us to gain their affection and make them more docile, when we are dealing with the admirable and incomprehensible mysteries of our Faith. For the belief they have in our intelligence and our abilities, makes them believe unconditionally what we tell them) (1635: 32).

9 In *Semiotics and Language* (1982), Greimas and Courtés define *disengagement* as 'the operation by which the domain of the enunciation disjuncts and projects forth from itself, at the moment of the language act and in view of manifestation, certain terms bound to its base structure, so as thereby to constitute the foundational elements of the discourse-utterance ... The language act appears as a split which creates, on the one hand, the subject, the place, and the time of the enunciation, and on the other, the actantial, spatial, and temporal representation of the utterance ... *actantial disengagement*, then, in its first steps, will consist in disjuncting a "not-I" from the

subject of the enunciation and projecting into the utterance, temporal disengagement in postulating a "not-now" distinct from the time of the enunciation, spatial disengagement in opposing a "not-here" to the place of the enunciation' (87–8). Moreover, they accentuate the fact that the subject of enunciation having produced the utterance always remains implicit and presupposed: 'there is only a semblance of enunciation, a case of uttered or reported enunciation' (88). One cannot, in any case, confuse the subject of enunciation who is actualized during an act of communication with the actantial subject of the uttered enunciation.

10 In the brief introductory text of the *Relation* of 1636, Brébeuf himself writes: 'Mais en voilà assez en général, il faut descendre plus en particulier; ce que je ferai volontiers, et amplement, *vous assurant que je n'avancerai rien que je n'aie vu moi-même, ou que je n'aie appris de personnes dignes de foi*' (But enough about the general, one has to get down to particulars, which I shall willingly do in detail. *I assure you that I shall only report what I have seen myself, or what I have learned from trustworthy people*) (77; emphasis mine). For a study of the status of eyewitnesses and reported witnesses in the constitution of the narrator-Sender actant in the *Jesuit Relations*, see Perron and Thérien (1990).

11 In contrast to *disengagement*, which constitutes an expulsion from the domain of enunciation of the category terms that serve as support to the utterance, '*engagement* designates the effect of a return to the enunciation. This effect is produced by the suspension of the opposition between certain terms belonging to the categories of actor and/or of person and/or of space, and of time, as well as by the negation of the domain of enunciation. Every engagement thus presupposes an operation of disengagement which logically precedes it' (Greimas and Courtés, 1982: 100).

12 We can define isotopy as the recurrence of semic categories, be they thematic or figurative. Semes in turn can be defined as designating the minimal unit of signification.

13 Although our perspective is somewhat different from Bakhtin's (1977) insofar as it focuses more on the problematic of enunciation as enunciated-utterance, none the less, we could adopt the definition proposed by him: 'In fact, the speech act, or more precisely its product, enunciation, can in no way be considered as individual in the narrow definition of the term: it cannot be explained with respect to psychophysiological conditions of the speaking subject. *Enunciation is social by nature*' (119).

14 J. Authier-Revuz (1984). See also M. Pecheux (1975): 'Le propre de toute formation discursive est de dissimuler dans la transparence du sens qui s'y forme, l'objectivité matérielle contradictoire de l'interdiscours déterminant

cette formation discursive comme telle, objectivité matérielle qui réside dans le fait que *"ça parle"* toujours, *"avant, ailleurs et indépendamment"'* (What characterizes any discursive formation is to dissimulate in the transparency of the meaning that is created, the contradictory material objectivity of the interdiscourse that determines this discursive formation as such, material objectivity that resides in the fact that '*it speaks*' always, '*before, elsewhere and independently*') (147; translation mine). Quoted in J. Authier-Revuz (1984), 100 (her emphasis).

15 'C'est sur ces dispositions et fondements, que nous espérons avec la grâce de Dieu bâtir l'édifice de la Religion Chrétienne parmi ce peuple, qui déjà d'ailleurs nous est grandement affectionné, et a une grande opinion de nous. C'est à nous maintenant à correspondre à notre vocation et à la voix de N.S. qui nous dit, *videte regiones quoniam albae sunt iam ad messem*' (It is through these dispositions and foundations, that we hope by the grace of God to build the edifice of Christian Religion among these people who, moreover, has already great affection for us and a very high opinion of us. It is now up to us to correspond to our vocation and the voice of our Lord, who says to us, *videte regiones quonian albae sunt iam ad messem*) (1635: 37).

5 Founding Nations: Jesuit–Huron Relations in Seventeenth-Century New France

1 Cf Lagarde (1980), where the phonetic sign transcribed as 8 is a sound approaching and interpreted by a known sound [u] (39).
2 Even taking into account the rhetorical conventions of the 'Preface,' Sagard himself warns the reader that his is not the work of a scholar, and that it may contain errors since it was rapidly put together: 'Et bien que je sois très peu versé en langue Huronne, et fort incapable de faire quelque chose de bien ... il m'y eut fallu employer un grand temps au delà de dix ou douze petits jours que j'y ai employés en fournissant la presse' (Although I am very little versed in the Huron language and quite incapable of doing anything well ... I would have needed much more time than the short ten or twelve days I had to get this copy to press) (1632: 5–10; translation mine). Lagarde (1980: 12) points out that the dictionary must be considered with caution, since it may contain a mixture of dialects. The inaccuracy of bilingual French–Native dictionaries at the beginning of the seventeenth century is attested by Paul Le Jeune in his attempts to learn Montagnais: 'Mais venons au départ des vaisseaux de l'an passé, pour suivre les mois qui se sont écoulés depuis ce temps-là que nous avisâmes le Père de Nouë et moi, qu'il fallait chercher les moyens de s'adonner à

l'étude de la langue, sans la connaissance de laquelle on ne peut secourir les Sauvages. Je quittai donc tout autre soin, et commençai à feuilleter un petit Dictionnaire écrit à la main, qu'on m'avait donné en France; mais tout rempli de fautes. Le 12 octobre voyant que j'avançais fort peu, apprenant avec beaucoup de peine des mots décousus, je m'en allai visiter les cabanes des Sauvages à dessein d'y aller souvent, et me faire l'oreille à leur langue' (But let us return to the departure of last year's ships, to follow the months that have gone by since then during which Father Nouë and I decided we needed to find the means to study the language, the knowledge of which is essential to save the Indians. I therefore gave up all other occupations and began to study a small hand-written Dictionary given to me in France: but it was full of errors. The 12th of October, seeing that I was making very little progress and learning with great difficulty disconnected words, I went to visit the Indians but with the idea in mind of returning often in order to get accustomed to hearing their language) (1633: 2; translation mine).

3 Because of the strategic geographic, economic, and political importance of the Huron Nation, learning their language was considered the key to the evangelization of numerous other neighbouring nations: 'Je fis mention l'an passé de douze Nations toutes sédentaires et nombreuses, qui entendent la langue de nos Hurons; si le reste est à proportion, en voilà plus de trois cent mille de la seule langue Huronne' (Last year I mentioned twelve Nations that were all sedentary and numerous and that understood the Huron language; if the others are as numerous, then there are more than three hundred thousand people for the Huron language alone) (1636: 138). For a discussion of the role the Huron played as intermediaries between the neighbouring tribes and the French in the fur trade, see Heidenreich (1971) and Trigger (1976). As Lagarde (1980) remarks, the Huron regularly came to the trading posts of Trois Rivières and Quebec to barter, and first the Recollet missionaries and then the Jesuits took advantage of their presence to return to Huronia with them.

4 J. Lemercier also writes, 'Depuis environ le 20 février jusqu'à la semaine de la Passion, notre principal emploi fut l'étude de la langue ... pendant le Carême il nous a expliqué quelques Catéchismes que Louis de ste. Foy nous avait tournés l'an passé ... Nous avons bien sujet de remercier cette infinie bonté, qui nous donne une si grande affection pour cette langue barbare: après nos exercices de dévotion, nous n'avons point de plus grande consolation que de vaquer à cette étude; ce sont nos entretiens les plus ordinaires, et nous recueillons tous les mots de la bouche des Sauvages comme autant de pierres précieuses pour nous en servir par après à faire éclater à leurs yeux la beauté de nos s. mystères' (From

roughly 20 February until the week of the Passion, our principal activity was studying the language ... during Lent he [Father Superior] explained several catechisms that Louys de Sainte Foy had translated for us last year ... We are right in giving thanks for this infinite good which gives us such great affection for this barbarous tongue: after our exercises of devotion, we have no greater consolation than to undertake this study. These are our most common undertakings and we glean all the words from the mouths of these Indians as so many precious stones to be used by us afterwards to make shine before their eyes the beauty of our secret mysteries) (1637: 158).

5 The success of the narrative program of conversion can be seen at the onomastic level through the avatars of the name, or by the motivation and re-motivation of the manipulated subject's signified. Whereas the Huron who challenges the missionaries' belief system through argumentation based on observation (his people have been dying since the missionaries have been speaking about their faith) has both a Christian and an indigenous name (François *Kok8eribabougouz*), the convert, who has totally accepted the new value system, is called only by his new Christian name, erasing the past and thereby sanctioning the success of the program of conversion.

6 This still remains true four years later, as Jérôme Lalemant states: 'Si des peuples civilisés ont été des siècles entiers à reconnaître Jésus Christ, peut-on raisonnablement exiger une plus prompte obéissance des peuples qui sont nés dans la barbarie? S'ils les considéraient de près, ils prendraient pour un vrai miracle que même un seul eût été converti: car il semble que ni l'Évangile, ni l'Écriture sainte n'aient été composés pour eux. Non seulement les mots leur manquent pour exprimer la sainteté de nos mystères, mais même les paraboles et les discours plus familiers de Jésus-Christ leur sont inexplicables: ils ne savent ce que c'est que sel, levain, château, perle, prison, grain de moutarde, tonneaux de vin, lampe, chandelier, flambeau; ils n'ont aucune idée des Royaumes, des Rois et de leur majesté, non pas même de pasteurs, de troupeaux et de bergerie: en un mot l'ignorance qu'ils ont des choses de la terre semble leur fermer le chemin du ciel. Les motifs de crédibilité pris de l'accomplissement des prophéties, des miracles, des Martyrs, des Conciles, des saints Docteurs, des histoires tant sacrées que profanes, de la sainteté de l'Église, et de l'éclat extérieur qui la rend vénérable aux plus grands Monarques du monde, tout cela n'a point ici de lieu: par où la Foi peut-elle entrer dans leur esprit?' (If civilized people took entire centuries before recognizing Jesus Christ, can we reasonably demand more prompt obedience from people who wallow in barbarity? If we consider this carefully, then it is a true miracle that even a single one has been converted, for it seems that

neither the Gospels nor the Sacred Scriptures have been composed for them. Not only do they not have the words to express the sanctity of our mysteries, but even Christ's parables and most familiar discourses cannot be explained to them: they do not know of the existence of salt, yeast, castle, pearl, prison, grain of mustard, bushel, lamp, candle holder, candle. They have no idea about Kingdoms, Kings and princes, nor even about shepherds, flocks and sheep. In short, their ignorance of the things of this earth seems to prevent them from reaching the road to heaven. The motifs for belief, taken from the accomplishment of the prophecies, miracles, Martyrs, Councils, the holy Doctors, sacred as well as profane stories, the Sanctity of the Church, and of external pomp which makes it venerable even for the greatest Kings of the world; none of this exists here: how can the faith then enter their spirits?) (1640: 101).

7 In the same vein Sagard gives the example 'to read' in his dictionary.
8 Cf Lagarde (1980: 35), where õ corresponds to the vowel [o] or semi-vowel [w] according to the context.
9 Several years earlier Paul Le Jeune, writing to the Father Provincial about the people encountered at Tadoussac in 1632, states: 'De superstition ou fausse Religion, s'il y en a quelques endroits, c'est bien peu. Les Canadiens ne pensent qu'à vivre et à se venger de leurs ennemis. Il est vrai que celui qui saurait leur langue, les manierait comme il voudrait ... Ces exemples font voir la confiance qu'ils ont en nous. En vérité qui saurait parfaitement leur langue, serait puissant parmi eux' (Regarding Superstition or false Religion they hardly exist here. All the Canadians think about is living and taking revenge against their enemies. It is true that whoever would know their language would be able to manipulate them at will ... These examples show the confidence they have in us. In truth, whoever would know their language perfectly would be all-powerful among them) (1632: 6–12).
10 These can be represented by means of a semiotic square:

The relation between French and Huron microsemantic universes

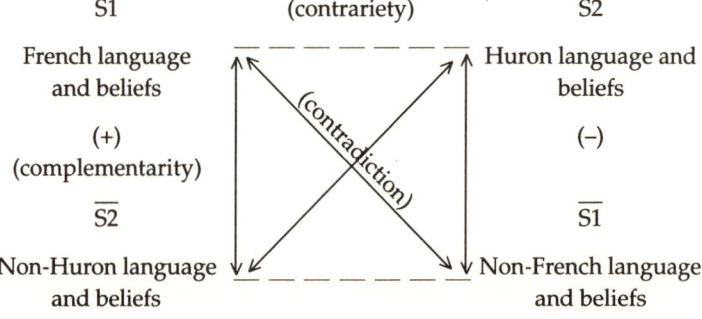

11 Étienne Brulé, who remained in Huronia after the fall of Quebec in 1629, was 'barbarement et traîtreusement assommé' (barbarously and treacherously clubbed to death) (1635: 28) by the Huron of *Ossosanné* before the French returned in 1634. During the Solemn Feast of the Dead, two chiefs from different villages wished to bury Brulé in separate pits 'c'est le plus grand témoignage d'amitié et d'alliance qu'ils aient dans le Pays' (as this is the greatest sign of friendship and alliance they have in the Country) (1636: 137). But in order not to take sides in a delicate political dispute, the Jesuits decided to leave Brulé's body where it was, and Brébeuf concludes: 'Véritablement il y a de quoi admirer ici les secrets jugements de Dieu: car cet infame aussi bien ne meritait pas cet honneur; et pour dire le vrai, nous eussions eu assez de peine à nous résoudre de faire à son occasion un Cimetière particulier, et de transporter en Terre sainte un corps qui a mené une vie si scandaleuse dans le Pays, et donné aux Sauvages une si mauvaise impression des mœurs des Français' (Truly, one can admire God's secret judgments, for this vile creature did not merit such an honour; and to tell the truth it would have been difficult for us to agree to bury him separately and to transport to sacred soil a body that has lived such a scandalous life in the Country, and given the Indians such a bad impression of the morals of the French) (1636: 138).

12 'Il est vrai que j'ai quelque peu d'appréhension pour le temps auquel il faudra leur tenir un langage nouveau sur leurs mœurs, et leur apprendre à clouer leurs chairs, et les retenir dans l'honnêteté du Mariage, en retranchant les dissolutions par la crainte des jugements de Dieu sur les luxurieux' (It is true that I feel some apprehension regarding the time when we will have to employ a new language in reference to their own morals, and teach them to keep down the flesh and hold them in honesty of Marriage, preventing divorce by fear of all judgments of God on the lewd) (1636: 138).

13 'Universellement parlant, ils louent et approuvent la Religion Chrétienne, et blâment leurs méchantes coutumes; et quand sera-ce qu'ils les quitteront tout à fait? Quelques-uns nous disent: Pensez-vous venir à bout de renverser le Pays? c'est ainsi qu'ils appellent le changement de leur vie Payenne et Barbare, en une vie civile et Chrétienne' (Universally speaking they praise and approve the Christian Religion, and blame their evil customs; and when will they abandon them altogether? Some of them say to us, 'Do you think you will succeed in overthrowing the Country?' That is how they speak about changing their Pagan and Barbarian lives into Christian and Civil lives) (1636: 80).

14 One of the important captains replies to Brébeuf in the following terms: '*Echon*, dit-il, il faut que je vous parle franchement; je crois que votre proposition est impossible. Ceux d'*Ihonatiria* disaient l'an passé qu'ils

croyaient afin qu'on leur donnât du pétun, mais tout cela ne plaisait point; pour moi je ne saurais dissimuler, je dis nettement mes sentiments, j'estime que ce que vous proposez ne servira que d'une pierre d'achoppement. Au reste nous avons nos façons de faire, et vous les vôtres, aussi bien que les autres nations; quand vous nous parlez d'obéir et de reconnaître pour maître celui que vous dites avoir fait le Ciel et la terre, je m'imagine que vous parlez de renverser le pays. Vos ancêtres se sont autrefois assemblés et ont tenu conseil, où ils ont résolu de prendre pour leur Dieu celui que vous honorez, et ont ordonné toutes les cérémonies que vous gardez; pour nous, nous en avons appris d'autres de nos Pères' (*Echon*, I must speak frankly with you; I believe that your proposal is impossible. Last year the inhabitants of *Ihonatiria* said that they believed so that you would give them tobacco, and I was displeased by this. As far as I am concerned I cannot dissimulate, and openly say what I feel. I feel that what you propose would be a stumbling block. Moreover, we have our ways of doing things and so do you, just like other nations. When you speak to us about obeying and recognizing as master he whom you say has created Heaven and earth, as far as I am concerned you are speaking about overthrowing the country. Formerly your ancestors assembled and held council and they resolved to take for their God the one you honour, and they organized all the ceremonies that you hold; as far as we are concerned, we have learned different ones from our Fathers) (1637: 137).

15 In Greimas and Courtés (1986: 203), the concept of semi-symbolic or 'molar' language is opposed to monoplanar languages or systems of symbols. 'Contrary to pure systems of symbols (formal languages, for example), semi-symbolic are signifying systems characterized not by conformity between the units of the plane of expression and the plane of content, but by the correlation between *categories* belonging to the two planes.'

16 For an analysis of this sequence see chapter 4. For the function of 'admiration' in conversion see Perron (1985).

17 In 1635, shortly after Brébeuf's arrival in Huronia, the estimated population according to him was thirty thousand souls. Five years later, a census revealed that the population had diminished by roughly two-thirds. 'Ensuite nous avons eu le moyen de faire le dénombrement non seulement des bourgs et bourgades, mais aussi des cabanes, des feux et même à peu pres des personnes de tout le pays, n'y ayant autre moyen de prêcher l'Évangile en ces contrées qu'au foyer de chaque famille, dont on a tâché de n'omettre pas une. Il se trouve dans ces cinq missions trente-deux tant bourgs que bourgades, qui comprennent en tout environ sept cent cabanes, de feux environ deux mille, et environ douze mille personnes. Ces bourgs

et cabanes étaient bien autrement peuplés autrefois, mais les maladies extraordinaires et les guerres depuis quelques années en ça, semblent avoir emporté le meilleur, ne restant que fort peu de vieillards, fort peu de personnes de main et de conduite' (Then we had the means to count not only the villages and hamlets, but also the cabins, the fires, and even most of the people in the entire country, since we had no other way of preaching the Gospels in this country except by visiting the household of each family. And we tried not to forget a single one. In the five missions there are thirty-two villages and hamlets, with in all approximately seven hundred cabins, two thousand fires, and twelve thousand people. These villages and cabins were much more populated in the past, but extraordinary illness and wars over the last few years seem to have carried off the best of them, and only a few old people are left, and very few people to work and to lead them) (1640: 62).

18 For a discussion of the use of images and pictures to convert the Native people of New France, see Gagnon (1975).

19 'L'ordre que Monsieur le Chevalier de Montmagny notre Gouverneur apporta l'an passé, au temps qu'ils étaient descendus en traite, pour punir et réprimer les insolences qu'ici haut ils avaient commises contre nous, a eu déjà de bons effets dans l'esprit de ces Barbares, qui après leur retour n'ont pas moins admiré la sagesse de sa conduite et de sa justice sur le passé, qu'ils ont redouté ces menaces pour l'avenir; jusque là même que quelques nations entières nous ont ici rendu justice du tort que nous avions reçu de quelques-uns d'entre eux, pour éviter la punition et le reproche qu'ils craignaient de recevoir là-bas aux Trois Rivières' (The order given by Monsieur le Chevalier de Montmagny our Governor last year when they came down to trade, to punish and reprimand the insolences that they had committed here against us, has already had positive effects in the minds of these Barbarians. After their return they still admired the wisdom of his behaviour and his justice in the past, to such a degree that several of the nations here rendered justice to the harm we received from some of them, in order to avoid punishment and admonition that they feared they would receive in Trois Rivières) (1641: 62).

6 Narrating and Reading the Body: The Martyrdom of Isaac Jogues

1 On 29 September 1642, René Goupil was killed by an axe blow to the head, at *Ossernenon* in Iroquois territory, while he was a captive with Isaac Jogues, who was liberated in 1643. Jogues returned to the missions but was recaptured and subsequently killed by an axe blow at *Ossernenon* on

18 October 1646. On the very next day, Jean de La Lande, a domestic who accompanied him, was also killed there by an axe blow. On 4 July 1648, Antoine Daniel was killed by arrows and the shot of an arquebus during the siege of *Teanaostaiae* in Huronia. On 16 March 1649, Jean de Brébeuf was tortured and executed at *Taenhatentaron* in Huronia. Gabriel Lalement, who was captured with Brébeuf, was also tortured and put to death the next day in the very same village. They are the only two missionaries who were tortured before being put to death by the Iroquois. On 7 December 1649, Charles Garnier was killed during the siege of the village of *Etharita* in the land of the Petun. He was shot, and later his head was crushed by one of the attackers. The next day, 8 December, Noel Chabanel froze to death on his way to Ste Marie among the Huron, after having left Charles Garnier on 5 December.

2 On occasion the woman recounts in her own words what had occurred in the past tense: 'Pour moi, disait celle qui a raconté cette histoire, si j'eusse été baptisée, j'aurais estimé à faveur de mourir de la sorte; mes yeux n'auraient pas été contraints de voir les horribles spectacles et les cruautés étranges qu'ils ont vus. Entre toutes les femmes prisonnières, nous étions trois qui avions chacun un petit enfant d'environ deux mois; nous n'avions pas fait grand chemin que ces malheureux nous les ravirent' (As for me, said she who told this story, had I been baptized, I would have been happy to die in that way; my eyes would not have been forced to see these horrible scenes and the strange cruelties they witnessed. Among all the captive women there were three of us who each had a small child about two months old. We had not travelled for long when these wretches grabbed them from us) (1642: 46).

3 The narrator's change of verb tense is significant. For the most part, the tale is narrated in the past, hence maintaining a temporal distance between the time of the event and the time of the narration, which, as Émile Benveniste demonstrated (1967), is the time of the historical enunciation and the historical narrative. Collapsing the temporal framework into the present (gnomic, neither time nor place) abolishes temporal distance, which defines the historical narrative, maintaining it in the past, and the time of the event and the time of the narration become co-present – that is, simultaneous for the narrator and the narratee. In short, historical time (past-present-future) is enfolded into the timelessness of the eternal present. The narrator and the narratee are no longer experiencing the event as distance, a present related to a past, but are, in fact, participating in it as a presence that is none other than a co-presence. Moreover, this temporal shifting in and out of the narratee not only positions her/him before the events being de-

scribed, but also, in its semiotic function, indexes and points to an impression of *déjà vu* that revives an imprint woven in memory by knowledge and experience. To re-present, is always to evoke the anteriority of a trace, to induce a reference, that is to say, to establish by the intermediary of sign systems a topological transfer that affects the space of reading. See Le Huenen and Perron (1984b).
4 Perron and Thérien (1990) argue that the description of an event presupposes a visual witness deemed 'trustworthy.' For the initial description of an event to be considered as a founding text, it must articulate according to a specific order, those elements constituting an event (the praxis) that cannot be substituted for each other without abolishing the traces of the event and invalidating the fact of its having been witnessed. When there is no founding text, the traces of the event disappear, and so do its constituent elements. This is the thesis defended by W. Arens in *The Man-Eating Myth* (1979), when he maintains that cannibalism does not exist as a widespread cultural phenomenon in 'primitive societies' as Western colonizers have claimed. Cannibalism is of the order of the 'presupposed' in anthropological discourse about 'primitive people' only because there has never been a verifiable account of direct visual witnessing. This is certainly the case in the *Relations*, where no cases of cannibalism are directly reported by a missionary who has escaped his torturers and who actually records the event; rather, such events are always verbally reported by a witness who supposedly saw what occurred and then related it to the missionary. Such is the case in point. The only way to verify Arens's thesis is to prove the non-existence of a founding text on the topic (56).
5 The Iroquois are constructed as an unstable mixed class of actants comprising three different isotopies or iterated semes – that is, semantic nuclei that permit a coherent reading of them. They are at one and the same time natural beings who, by instinct, belong to the predatory order of the world ('Wolves,' 'lions,' 'tiger,' 'hounds,' etc.). They are also supernatural beings mandated by evil forces that control them ('Werewolves,' 'Demons'). Finally, they are powerful cultural beings who integrate and manipulate both European arms in warfare and the French themselves. Evangelization and conversion are the only elements that can fix a volatile solution that is waiting to break out and engulf the colony at the slightest provocation.
6 From time to time the narrator addresses his virtual readers directly, interrupting the flow of narrative and positioning them through the interplay of deixes in an intersubjective relation of co-presence. On hearing the tale of their cruelty to women and children, he slows the unravelling of

his tale to a standstill and invites his reader to identify and commiserate with the horror he has just described. '*Commota sunt viscera mea,* je fus touché jusqu'au cœur' (*Commota sunt viscera mea;* I was touched to the heart) (1642: 46).

7 This brief sequence in chapter 11 dealing with Isaac Jogues's capture will also be narrated and expanded on two separate occasions by Jérôme Lalemant in subsequent *Relations* evoking his death in 1646.

8 Again, the enunciator's metatextual comments in the present articulate the temporal arc of the past event that will presently be elucidated in the future, reconstituting the temporal tri-dimensionality of the reader reconfiguring the narrative through her/his personal and cultural lived experience.

9 Note the use of the possessive 'our' versus Iroquois, the implied non-person in the act of communication, armed by the Dutch.

10 In Gerard Genette's terminology (1980), these anachronies or flashbacks are *analepses* that can relate to events internal to the first narrative, which he calls *homodiegetic,* or events external to the first narrative, which he labels *heterodiegetic.* What will characterize the tale of Jogues's martyrdom is, on the one hand, the retelling of events that occurred only once and, on the other, the reiteration of the haunting and graphic scenes of torture and mutilation. The various acts of overwriting will not bring a great deal of new factual or graphic information to the narrative, but the same scenes, motifs, and images will be revisited, played out, and relived every year over a five-year period by the same readers of the *Relations,* thereby mobilizing and creating a unique and powerful text of memory and memory of text.

11 'Une femme, ou plutôt une Mégère, lui prend le bras et lui coupe, ou plutôt lui scie avec un couteau, le pouce de la main gauche: elle fait un cerne et s'en va rechercher la jointure, avec moins d'industrie, mais avec plus de cruauté qu'un boucher n'en exercerait sur une bête morte; bref elle lui décharne et enlève tout le gros du pouce. Un autre lui mord un des doigts de la main droite, offense l'os, et rend ce pauvre doigt perclus et inutile; d'autres lui arrachent les ongles, puis mettent du feu sur l'extremité de ces pauvres doigts dépouillés pour rendre le martyre plus sensible. À tous ces maux le pauvre Père n'eut point d'autre Médecin ni d'autre Chirurgien que la patience, point d'autre onguent que la douleur, point d'autre enveloppe que l'air qui environnait ses plaies' (A woman, rather a shrew, takes his arm and cuts off, no rather saws off the thumb on his left hand with a knife. She cuts a gash and locates the joint with less art but much more cruelty than a butcher would on a dead animal; in short,

she removes the flesh and cuts off the main part of his thumb. Another bites one of the fingers of his right hand to the bone, crippling this poor finger and making it useless. Others tear out his nails, then put fire on the ends of these poor stripped fingers making his martyrdom more keenly felt. For all of these pains the poor Father had no other treatment or other surgeon than patience, no other salve than pain, no other cover than the air to wrap them) (1643: 67–8).

12 In fact, the Iroquois and the Huron treated their male prisoners in the same way – that is, executing on the spot those who were not too gravely wounded during battle, after putting them through a ritualized torture ceremony. The description of Jogues's torture is rewritten in terms of the Passion of Jesus Christ and standard martyrology of the early saints and Fathers of the Church who suffered the most extreme mutilation and pain passively and stoically without showing emotion of any sort. This will be the case with the narratives of all the eight Jesuits who were killed from 1642 to 1649. The earliest accounts, as well as the numerous graphic representations of their martyrdom that appeared both in France and in Quebec over the years, relay, reinforce, and represent iconically the written descriptions of their immolation. The very first, most widely distributed engraving by Grégoire Huret in 1650, entitled *La Mort de quelques pères de la Compagnie de Jésus*, depicts a group of martyrs in various states of torture and execution. The scene represented is an account, indeed a narrative, that unifies in one place and at one time the deaths by violence of all the Jesuits in New France from 1642 to 1649. In the foreground are Brébeuf and Gabriel Lalemant, each tied to a stake and naked except for loincloths. Light falls on these two martyrs, who are illuminated behind two great bonfires, each with boiling water roiling in large cauldrons, but Brébeuf, clearly in the foreground, is the central focus of the composition. One of the torturers is slicing the missionary's arm with a red-hot knife; another is pouring boiling water over his shoulder in obvious mockery of baptism; a third also holds a cauldron of boiling water, ready to pour it over him; while a fourth is preparing to place a collar of red-hot axes around his neck. Lalemant is to the left, standing back from Brébeuf, next to the second smoking bonfire, also with a cauldron of boiling water suspended above it. In all, there are eleven Iroquois preoccupied with these two central figures, but each and every gaze, including Lalemant's, is turned towards Brébeuf. To the extreme left, in the foreground but in the shadows, is Isaac Jogues, whom an Iroquois is about to kill with an axe blow to the head, with René Goupil and Jean de La Lande in deeper shadows, about to be executed in the same way by two other warriors. The three victims are kneeling, with

their heads bent downwards, each having an inward contemplative gaze. In the background, to the right, we can identify Antoine Daniel being shot at point-blank range in front of a flaming chapel surmounted by a large cross, with, far behind him, Charles Garnier undergoing the same fate. Both are gazing upwards towards the sky. Further back, along the same axis, a Christian Huron warrior is being burned at the stake. In the centre of the composition, at the very back, near the forest, Noel Chabanel is lying on the ground; finally, in the extreme background, to the left, Anne de Noüe is kneeling in the position in which he was discovered frozen during the winter of 1646. All of the Christians are passive, immobile, and resigned, whereas their torturers and executioners are active, mobile, and aggressive.

The spectator's gaze is attracted to the largest and most dominating group of thirteen personages of the main narrative, and is arrested, suddenly, by the prominent figure who is the focus of all eyes in this group. Brébeuf, indifferent to all that is going on around him, is looking at a spot to his left towards the centre of the engraving. His body is slightly turned in the same direction, his head is slightly bent at the neck, and he is staring out at the place occupied by us, the spectators – by our gazes, our faces, our bodies. This spot is not contained in the engraving, but Brébeuf, who is the only figure in the composition looking outward, transfixes and freezes the spectator, forcing her/him to occupy the very centre of the composition. His eyes trace a direct line to those on the other side of the engraving, turning our gaze to his tortured body, making us feel and identify with the martyr who passively and stoically accepts his suffering. However, like all the protagonists he is frozen in a hieratic pose. There is no brutal representation of a racked, tortured, bloody body, and the viewer glances at each, in turn, with their classic proportions, before quickly turning to the expressionless faces that show no emotion and remain fixed in timeless beauty. Brébeuf's gaze captures us once more and leaves us with an impression of acceptance and dignified resignation to his fate of martyr. After examining in detail the principal scene, the spectator's eye is attracted to and caught up counter-clockwise by the two priests being massacred in front of the burning chapels blazing in the background, before continuing to explore the entire scene and ending up with the shaded group of Jogues, La Lande, and Goupil. In the end, we focus once more on the martyr's gaze before breaking off and taking leave with the representation of his martyrdom firmly inscribed in our minds.

13 'Un vieillard fameux magicien parmi ces nations Iroquoises, qui leur a promis depuis plusieurs années qu'elles se rendraient victorieuses de tous

leurs ennemis, monta tout le premier sur ce théâtre. C'est, dit-il, les Français que j'ai pour ennemis, les Hurons ne méritent pas ma colère, j'ai de la compassion pour eux. Et en disant cela, il bâtonne rudement nos Français les uns après les autres, puis ordonne à une femme de monter et de couper le pouce au Père' (An old man who was a well-known magician among these Iroquois nations, and who for several years had promised them victory over all their enemies, was the first to leap up onto the stage. It is, says he, the French that I consider as enemies, the Huron do not deserve my anger. I feel compassion for them. Saying this he violently beat our Frenchmen with a cudgel, then ordered a woman to come up and cut off the Father's thumb) (1644: 73).

14 He actually writes 'and the entire day was a spectacle of cruelty,' as though he were literally present seeing the events unfold before his eyes, all the while positioning and inviting the reader to imagine and experience Jogues's physical and moral suffering, in all its horror, along with him (*spectaculum, spectare, specere*, to look).

15 This thesis (to which I fully subscribe) is outlined in Laflèche (1989), 'Le Martyre d'Isaac Jogues par Jérôme Lalemant.'

16 The *Relation* of 1647 not only cites previous *Relations*, but also quotes generously from them as well as expanding on, glossing over, or alluding to certain events that are mentioned. This intricate citational integration and use of other texts belonging to the same series can be considered as the intratextual dimension that constitutes the specificity of all the Jesuit Relations, whereas the Scriptures and Lives of the Saints make up their impassable and unskirtable intertextual dimension.

17 In Jean-Paul Sartre's *Nausea*, Roquentin, alone in his room, attempts to come to grips with the question the Self-Taught Man had asked him, about whether or not he had ever had an adventure. Roquentin methodically analyses the fundamental difference between living and telling, between experience and its textualization ('But you have to choose: live or tell'), and concludes that, although 'a man is always a teller of tales [and] he lives surrounded by his stories and the stories of others,' in living 'there are no beginnings.' In telling 'you seem to start at the beginning ... And in reality you have started at the end ... the end is there transforming everything ... the story goes on in reverse' (1964: 39–40). This very lucid reflection certainly expresses the difficulties encountered in narrating how the other lives when there are no beginnings and no end; but here, death, and its aftermath, eternal life, are the finalities that organize and structure Lalemant's narrative in the *Relation* of 1647, serving as interpretants of all the events relating to Jogues before and after his arrival in New France.

18 A flashback, or analepse, to Jogues's first capture in 1642 informs the reader that the Iroquois, who had suffered severe illness and crop failure at that time, accused him of having hidden the devil in a small coffer, and this was the reason given for killing him and Jean de La Lande.

19 Lalemant then immediately enters into the very *raison d'être* of the *Relations*, which have become an apology for martyrdom: 'Il est temps de parler du massacre ou plutôt du martyre du Père Isaac Jogues' (It is time to speak of the murder, or rather the martyrdom of Father Isaac Jogues). But before describing his last sufferings, the narrator states that he would like to 'disons deux petits mots en passant des grâces qui ont précédé le premier moment de son éternité' (say a few brief words about the graces that precede the first moments of his eternity) (1647: 17).

20 The reader is led to believe that Lalemant is the Superior in question, when, in fact it was Buteux himself who coerced Jogues in the winter of 1644–5 to write up his experiences as a captive with the Iroquois. Buteux then composed the 'Narrative of the capture of Isaac Jogues' from Jogues's own report, which was written in Latin. In addition, Jogues sent a letter dealing with this episode to a Jesuit priest in France, a copy of which Lalemant had in his possession. Lalemant also asked Jogues for a written account of 'The capture and death of René Goupil.' The narrator also had in his possession a copy of a letter sent by the Dutchman Jan Labadie to the governor of New France, and he then melded these texts together when finally composing the narrative in the summer of 1647 (see Guy Laflèche, 1989: 11–14).

21 Oral reports of Jogues's travails from Native informants would not be sufficient to guarantee the authenticity of what occurred since, in contrast to Brébeuf and Lalement, whose remains were recovered by the missionaries in Huronia, Jogues and de La Lande were decapitated and their bodies never recovered. This is why it is imperative that Jogues's own narrative becomes the founding text of his martyrdom.

22 Only the written, after the fact, can guarantee the truth of the events that took place in the past and orient their ultimate meaning in the future, when time is to be abolished at the Last Judgment. At any moment in this Christian teleological trajectory constituting the narrative of martyrdom, the act of reading activates the same temporal arc, at one and the same time re-presenting, reconfiguring and reinterpreting the events as they are configured by means of the temporalized actional. Again, the memory of the text negotiates with the *memoria* of the reader in terms of common knowledge and beliefs.

23 The very act of writing (*graphein*) is what founds, creates, and guarantees

the entire process of canonization of the exemplary life of a sacred (*hagios*) person.
24 See Perron and Thérien (1990: 61–4). From beginning to end, the Jesuit *Relations* are strewn with cartographical, geographical, and astronomical measures (longitudes, latitudes, meridians, etc.), and indications of distances – in short, measures of all kinds organize this discourse. It is argued that, in the order of the presupposed, measure, in the *Relations*, does serve to evaluate scientifically the space of the other, to grid it, to fix it, to make it enter the space of the symbolic – in other words, to appropriate it – since measure belongs to the common law and therefore the canon that governs the right to property.
25 For an enunciator to be deemed competent to perform in the *Relations* – that is, for his narrative to organize or to be included in the main body of the text – his modalities must be ordered as follows: /duty-will/→ /knowledge-power/ (S1). The enunciator thus endowed with these modalities will then be competent to transform, through narration, a state of ignorance into a state of knowledge or truth for the enunciatee, or reader, who shares the same modal competence and presuppositions. The act of narration can therefore be considered as a speech act where saying is doing, since it will effect a cognitive and pathemic manipulation of the enunciatee, who, through the act of reading, will be transformed into a knowing, sensitized, and giving subject who adheres to the mandate of conversion.
26 One should note here that at this level of analysis the class of actants literate–Christian (Protestant/Catholic) is positively valued with respect to the class illiterate–Heathen. In this semantic universe one can determine four classes of actants that are opposed in terms of positive and negative. Literate–Catholic (positive, good) is opposed to illiterate–Iroquois (negative, evil), and literate–Protestant (not positive, not good) is opposed to illiterate–Huron (not negative, not evil). In this case, literate and illiterate can be considered as those who do and those who do not read and hear the word of God.
27 In this solipsistic universe, God is both the Sender who mandates and the Receiver who tests and sanctions all the activities of his Subjects in terms of the successful or unsuccessful overcoming of the trials and tribulations visited upon them. The quest comes to an end in death, the glorifying test, when the Subjects receive a penultimate sanction to be confirmed at the moment of the Last Judgment.
28 The Jesuit New France hagiographical narrative must, of necessity, be organized in two parts. The first, the foundational tale, covers events and moments related to the acquisition of modal competence in France, quali-

fying the hero to leave for the missions; the second comprises a series of qualifying tests leading up to the ultimate glorifying test of death for propagating the faith. Both parts can be considered as testing the validity of the hero's modal competence as he reacts to and overcomes greater and greater cruelty and evil.

29 For Paul Ricœur (1984), historical and fictional discourse share the same discursive means for textualizing personae in narrative that can be defined as the temporalization of action. Their only difference is in their finalities. The finality of historical narrative is to tell the truth, whereas that is not the case with fiction.

30 See Pierre Fontanier (1968), *Les Figures du discours*, 425–9, originally published in two parts in 1816 and 1827.

31 We can define the *anaphoric* function of the name, or signifier, of the persona as that which refers back to the sum of his/her acts, be they physical, moral, or spiritual. The *cataphoric* function would be the projection of these same acts into the future.

32 See note 3, above.

33 See Roland Barthes 'L'Écriture du roman' in *Le Degré zéro de l'ecriture* (1958), where he establishes a link between historical discourse and the novel through the use of the past tense to express not time but causality, an inevitability between events as they unfold. For him, the past-definite tense presupposes an elaborated, detached, constructed world, rather than one that is projected, spatially organized, and offered. The past-definite tense is the operative sign by which the narrator brings the eruption of reality to a thin and pure verb, without density, without volume, without spread, whose only function is to unite as quickly as possible a cause and an end.

34 Once more, the configuration and reconfiguration of Jogues's suffering through the shared motifs of the Passion and Crucifixion of Christ activate in the reader tri-dimensional, temporal, individual, and cultural cognitive, beliefs, and pathemic reactions to re-presentations called up and evoked by memory.

35 'Nous trouvâmes sur ces rives de part et d'autre quantité d'hommes et de jeunes gens armés de bâtons qu'ils déchargèrent sur nous avec leur rage accoutumée: il ne me restait plus que deux ongles, ces Barbares me les arrachèrent avec les dents, déchirant la chair de dessous et la découpant jusqu'aux os avec leurs ongles, qu'ils nourrissent fort longs' (We found on both sides of these banks many men and youths armed with sticks that they used to beat on us with their usual rage: I only had two nails remaining, these Barbarians tore them out with their teeth, tearing the flesh

beneath and cutting my fingers to the bone with their nails which they allow to grow very long) (1647: 22).

36 'Un vieillard me prend la main gauche et commande à une femme Algonquine captive de me couper un doigt: elle se détourna trois ou quatre fois ne se pouvant résoudre à cette cruauté; enfin il fallut obéir, elle me coupe le pouce de la main gauche ... Cette pauvre femme ayant jeté mon pouce sur le théâtre, je le ramassai et vous le presentai, ô mon Dieu! me ressouvenant des sacrifices que je vous avais présentés depuis sept ans sur les Autels de votre Église' (An old man takes my left hand and orders a captive Algonquin woman to cut off one of my fingers: she turned away three or four times unable to carry out this cruel act; finally she had to obey, she cuts off the thumb of my left hand ... This poor woman having thrown my thumb on the stage, I picked it up and offered it up to you, oh my God! Remembering the sacrifices that I had offered up to you for seven years on the Altars of your Church) (1647: 23).

37 'Puis on nous fit coucher sur une écorce, nous liant par les bras et par les pieds à quatre pieux fichés en terre en forme de Croix de saint André ... ô mon Dieu! quelles nuits! demeurer toujours dans une posture extrêmement contrainte, ne se pouvoir remuer ni tourner, dans l'attaque d'une infinité de vermines, qui nous assaillaient de tous côtés, être chargés de plaies récentes et d'autres toutes pourries ... de vérité ces tourments sont grands, mais Dieu est immense' (Then we were forced to lie on pieces of bark, tying our arms and legs to four stakes planted in the ground in the form of Saint Andrew's cross ... oh my God! What nights! To remain always in a very constrained position, to be unable to move or turn, under the attack of countless vermin that came at us from all sides, to be burdened with wounds, some recent, others rotting ... in truth these torments are great, but God is infinite) (1647: 23).

38 'Ma peau se détachait de mon corps en plusieurs endroits, et afin que je pusse dire que j'avais passé *per ignem et aquam*, par le froid et le chaud pour l'amour de mon Dieu, étant sur l'échafaud trois jours durant comme en la première bourgade, il tomba une pluie froide qui renouvela grandement les douleurs de mes plaies' (The skin was detaching itself from my body in several places, and so that I could say I had gone through *per ignem et aquam*, the cold and the heat for the love of my God, having spent three whole days on the scaffold, as in the first village, a cold rain fell that renewed the pains of my wounds) (1647: 23–4).

39 'Quelque temps après la mort de son compagnon, Dieu lui communiqua dans son sommeil, comme il faisait jadis à ces anciens Patriarches, ce que je vais raconter, c'est lui-même qui l'a couché par écrit de sa propre main:

voici comme il parle en langue latine, rendu en notre français ... Il eut dans cette retraite quelques communications avec Dieu, que je traduirai fidèlement du latin de son mémoire' (Some time after the death of his companion, God communicated to him in his sleep, as he did in the past to Patriarchs of old, what I am about to relate. He himself wrote it with his own hand: here is how he speaks in the Latin tongue, translated into our French ... He had during this retreat some communications with God, that I will faithfully translate from the Latin of his memoir) (1647: 26–8).

40 '[E]t pour augmentation de mes biens, c'est-à-dire de mes croix, la blessure qu'un chien m'avait faite, la nuit que je me sauvai d'entre les Iroquois, me causait une si grande douleur que si le Chirurgien de cette habitation n'y eût mis la main, j'aurais non seulement perdu la jambe; mais encore la vie, car la gangrène s'y mettait déjà' ([A]nd to increase my blessings, that is to say my crosses, the wound a dog inflicted upon me, the night I escaped from the Iroquois, caused me such pain that if the surgeon of the settlement had not intervened, I would not only have lost my leg; but my life, for gangrene was setting in) (1647: 34).

41 Gérard Genette (1973: 123), notes that it is possible to evaluate the duration of the story, measured in seconds, minutes, hours, days, months, and years, or the speed with which it unravels, by comparing time evoked with the length of text measured in terms of lines and pages. For example, Lalement describes in 9 lines Jogues's birth in 1607 in Rennes, France, his arrival in Canada in 1636, and his trip to Quebec from Huronia in June 1642, before his departure for the land of the Iroquois at the beginning of chapter 4. His capture and torture in August last several hours and are related in 282 lines; the eight-day trip in 31 lines; his second torture, spanning several hours, in 140 lines; the next two-day trip in 1 line; the third torture scene, covering several hours, in 27 lines; his running the gauntlet and fourth torture lasting one day in 146 lines; his visit to the second village and three-day torture in 47 lines; the visit to the third village, his two-day torture, and death sentence in 48 lines; his pardon, taking a few minutes, in 48 lines; life in the village and Goupil's death in 88 lines; his seven-month sojourn in the village in 636 lines. His departure for Europe and arrival in England, taking two months, are told in 35 lines; his arrival in Brittany and his thirteen-day stay there are related in 53 lines; his visit to the Jesuit Collège de Rennes, taking a few hours, is recounted in 41 lines; his one-and-a-half-year stay in France and visit with the Queen are told in 9 lines; his return to New France and two-year sojourn there in 71 lines; his third one-and-a-half-month voyage to the land of the Iroquois in 9 lines; and his sudden death in 3 lines.

42 It is rather difficult to understand how, according to Lalemant, Jogues was able to understand that the young Lutheran traveller cried out 'Martyr, Martyr of Jesus Christ' when the former found out he spoke only in Polish, a language he did not know, unless, of course, he cried out in Latin. It does seem, though, that the finality of martyrdom structures and organizes all events narrated in Jogues's tale of suffering and death.

43 Indeed, Lalemant constructs his narrative as a palimpsest, with each successive layer filling in gaps, changing the focus slightly, concentrating on a different face of an event or an image, and thereby giving a kaleidoscopic and haunting density that creates the maximum effect of adherence, identification, sympathy, and horror in his reader.

44 This segment constitutes a textual *mise en abyme* of what the narrator is attempting to make happen with his community of readers who form and give form to public opinion.

45 It should be noted that the text devoted to Jean de La Lande's hagiography covering his entire life is less than fourteen lines long. By simple contiguity, his adventure will be carried along and given ultimate significance by Jogues's narrative.

46 See Roquentin, note 17 above.

47 The narrator continues the Christic analogy, stating: 'Cela fit croire au Père, que le Royaume des Cieux lui appartenait et qu'il n'en était pas éloigné' (This made the Father believe that the Kingdom of Heaven belonged to him and that he was not distant from it) (1647: 40).

48 *Introduction à la sociologie générale*. Cited in Denis Martin (1988: 2).

7 Before and after the Fall – The Historical Novel: *Les Anciens Canadiens*

1 The second son of Philippe Aubert de Gaspé. He was born in Quebec in 1814. After studying for two years (1827–9) at the Collège Nicolet, he became a journalist and was condemned to one month in prison for a verbal altercation he had with Edmund Bailey O'Callaghan, a deputy from Yamaska. He wrote the first Quebec novel in 1837 and became a journalist at the *Telegraph* in Quebec City. Disappointed by the criticism his novel received, he went to Halifax to find a position and subsequently died there, of cirrhosis of the liver, in 1841.

2 Between 1820 and 1845 more than forty newspapers and journals were founded in Quebec, most of which, according to the flyers distributed to potential customers, had some literary preoccupations. See Hayne (1993).

3 *Le Chercheur de trésor ou l'influence d'un livre*, by Philippe Aubert de Gaspé, *fils*, was followed that same year by *Les Révélations du crime ou Cambray et*

ses complices, by François-Réal Angers. Although the exact status of the genre is still debatable (see Senécal, 1993), between the publication of these two novels in 1837 and the appearance of *Les Anciens Canadiens* in 1863 only nine novels saw the light of day in Quebec: *La Rebelle*, by R. Trobriand, 1841; *Les Fiancés de 1812*, by Joseph Doutre, 1844; *Charles Guérin*, by Pierre-Joseph-Olivier Chauveau, and *La Terre paternelle*, by Patrice Lacombe, both in 1846; *La Huronne*, 1854, *L'Héroïne de Chateauguay*, 1858, and *Le Pirate de Saint-Laurent*, 1859, all by Henri-Émile Chevalier; *Une apparition*, by Jean-Éraste d'Orsonnens, 1860; and *Jean Rivard, le défricheur canadien*, by Antoine Gérin-Lajoie, 1862.

4 For a detailed analysis of the process of production and reception of the literary text, see the four excellent volumes of *La Vie littéraire au Québec*, edited by Maurice Lemire, who is also the general editor of the comprehensive *Dictionnaire des œuvres du Québec*, of which seven volumes have appeared to date.

5 At the time of the appearance of *Les Anciens Canadiens*, of the one million inhabitants in the province of Quebec, seven hundred thousand were of French origin and more than 77 per cent of the population was rural and mostly illiterate. Most of the city dwellers lived in either Montreal or Quebec City. See Dumont, Montminy, and Hamelin (1971: 14–25).

6 All translations are mine unless otherwise indicated

7 See Senécal (1993: 223–9).

8 See Le Huenen and Perron (1984a).

9 On this point, in France, see Iknayan (1961: 51–84).

10 Quoted in Hayne (1977: 39–40).

11 Not only were these revered codes of behaviour to be followed by heroic subjects presented in official histories or historical novels; they also permeated a good deal of the poetry of the period, most notably the works of Octave Crémazie and Louis Fréchette. Moreover, in a comprehensive work on the didactics of discourse in Quebec from 1852 (the founding of the University of Laval) to 1967 (the dissolution of the 'Cours Classique'), in which textbooks and 3,500 student compositions from 'Belles-lettres' and 'Rhétorique' were analysed, Melançon, Moisan, and Roy (1988) study the institutionalization of the said codes in the educational system corresponding to desired forms of social behaviour.

12 Use of the term 'Québécois' to designate the inhabitants of the province of Quebec is a twentieth-century phenomenon. Throughout the nineteenth century, and in Philippe Aubert de Gaspé's novel, the inhabitants of New France before the Conquest are called 'Canadiens.' It is only with the settling of the United Empire Loyalists in what is now Ontario, and the

splitting of the country into Upper and Lower Canada, that the inhabitants of the latter designated themselves by the hyphenated term 'Canadiens-Français,' to distinguish themselves from their neighbours in Upper Canada, 'Canadiens-Anglais.' The evolution and emergence of the deixes denoting geographical 'Québec' and the 'provincial' and even 'national' identity 'Québécois' materialized only in the latter part of the twentieth century.

13 This first translation, published by Desbarats, Quebec, was reissued under the title of *Seigneur d'Haberville* by Musson Books, Toronto, in 1929. A second translation, entitled *The Canadians of Old*, undertaken by C.D. Roberts for Appleton, New York, in 1890, also appeared under the title *Cameron of Locheill*, with L.C. Page, Boston, 1905.

14 The 1864 Desbarats edition (407 pp) was followed by numerous other editions: Quebec: A. Côté & Cie (1877, 2 vols: 298 pp, and 240 pp); Montreal: Beauchemin (1899: 279 pp), (1913, 361 pp), (1955, 298 pp), (1956, 188 pp, School Edition); Montreal: Fides (1961, 351 pp), and the present edition, Montreal: Fides (1970).

15 See C. Bremond, 'La Logique des possibles narratifs,' in Barthes (1966).

16 By his very name Jules's only son ensures the integration on its own terms of the English presence in this society. Arché, a diminutive and gallicization of Archibald, programs the future of the family, since he not only assumes the name of his father's closest friend, who will remain childless, but also becomes his sole heir, as he is the Scotsman's only godson.

17 M. Lemire's (1994) political reading of *Les Anciens Canadiens* complements the reading presented here, as he understands the novel as an attempt to harmonize various contraries: English/French, aristocrats/plebians, masters/servants, and so on. He further concludes that, if the British had recognized the status of the Canadian aristocracy, the face of the colony would have been changed since, because of their hold over the common people, the nobles would easily have won over the Canadians to the British cause. The two races would have been united into a single people. His reading of the relationship between Arché and Blanche is different from the one I propose, since for him, by demeaning the nobility, the English made this marriage impossible. Blanche and Arché live next to each other. 'This was the beginning of the two solitudes' (173).

18 This is in contradistinction to the agrarian novel, which circumscribes four spaces in which subjects can evolve and define themselves in relation to the common good. See chapters 8 and 9 below.

19 The agrarian novel iterates and reiterates the same bi-dimensional, temporal, semantic, and mythic universe of continuity and reproduction. See chapters 8 and 9 below.

20   Perché comme un aiglon sur le haut promontoire,
     Baignant ses pieds de roc dans le fleuve géant,
     Québec voit ondoyer, symbole de sa gloire,
     L'éclatante splendeur de son vieux drapeau blanc.

     Et, près du château fort, la jeune cathédrale
     Fait monter vers le ciel son clocher radieux,
     Et l'Angélus du soir, porté par la rafale,
     Aux échos de Beaupré jette ses sons joyeux.

     Pensif dans son canot, que la vague balance,
     L'Iroquois sur Québec lance un regard de feu;
     Toujours rêveur et sombre, il contemple en silence
     L'étendard de la France et la croix du vrai Dieu.

     (Perched like an eagle on the lofty promontory,
     Dipping its feet of stone in the gigantic river,
     Quebec sees as a symbol of its glory floating,
     The splendid splendour of its ancient white flag.

     And, near the fort, the youthful cathedral
     Pushes towards the heavens her radiant belfry,
     And the evening Angelus, carried by the wind,
     To the echoes of Beaupré casts its joyous voice.

     Thoughtful, in his canoe, bobbing in the waves,
     The Iroquois casts burning glances on Quebec;
     Always dreamy and sombre, he contemplates in silence
     The flag of France, and the cross of the true God.)

21   Although some research has been undertaken on the role of the First Nations people in the literature of Quebec, notably by Gilles Thérien and his research group at the Université du Québec à Montréal (UQAM), a comprehensive study of the representation of the Amerindian in Quebec culture remains to be done. As such, the Amerindian remains the unsaid or unspoken of critical discourse attempting to come to grips with the definition of the subject in relation to otherness.

22   In this it is in contrast to *La Terre paternelle*, where the concept of nation or nationality has to be inferred and where there is no mention of the Conquest and English presence except for the reference to the Anglo-Saxon person who has bought the family property (see chapter 8).

23 In *Les Anciens Canadiens*, warfare is solely the preoccupation of male subjects. Indeed, Blanche is caught in a double bind. Convention makes it impossible for her to be other than a passive observer of war, and yet she feels that since she did not actively participate in warfare – which is not possible – she cannot marry the conqueror.

24 Again, at the onomastic level the play on the French 'Blanche' is quite explicit. In French 'blanc' or 'blanche' is polysemic, since in addition to white it also means innocent or non-consummated: 'une âme blanche,' 'mariage blanc.' Jules, the conquered Frenchman, integrates the new order and maintains his family name and lineage by marrying an unnamed Englishwoman. He hence possesses her, whereas Archibald, the 'English' or possessing conqueror, does not possess Blanche, who maintains her French identity. In short, in this imaginary universe, though the French are dispossessed in Canada, they none the less possess the English by integrating their women into the symbolic family order, thereby preserving it, whereas, even though England does possess the French in Canada, it does not possess its women and remains without family or progeny.

25 He is referring directly to F.-X. Garneau's four-volume *Histoire du Canada*, published from 1845 to 1852.

26 De Gaspé was admitted to the bar in 1811 and was nominated by the governor general as sheriff of the district of Quebec in May 1816, a position he occupied until November 1822, when he was removed from office. He was obviously not a gifted administrator, to say the least, and was condemned in October 1834 to pay a fine of £1,974, 4 s, to creditors. Unable to do so, he served three and a half years in prison from May 1838 to October 1841, when he was pardoned and released.

8 Family, Group, and Nation in the Nineteenth-Century Agrarian Novel: *La Terre paternelle*

1 It is notable that, by the mid-twentieth century, two-thirds of the French-Canadian population of Quebec lived in urban centres. Throughout this period, more and more rural inhabitants immigrated to the city, to the rest of Canada, and to New England. However, the reading public continued to be given and to read texts that defined the identity of the subject in terms of a fast-disappearing culture. French Canadians were living the adventure of urbanization, with all of its changing complexities, while being presented with imaginary worlds in which subjects found solutions by imploding back into the unchanging, cyclical universe of the land.

2 This is true especially for the first half of the twentieth century; as we saw,

in the second half of the nineteenth century, of the fifty-three novels published, twenty-six can be defined as historical novels.
3 At the onomastic level, the choice of names and surnames has a good deal of significance. They are not simply empty signs, since they contain at the outset the virtual and actual kernels of the positive narrative programs of the consolidation and the prosperity of the nation that will be expanded and realized in the novel. The concession was initially given to Jean Chauvin, who will remain chauvinistically devoted to the land and pass it on to his son, who will do the same. Finally, from John (the apostle who adheres to the land) it will be transmitted to John the Baptist, who will lose it, cry out in the wilderness, then reclaim it through his son, Charles, and, ironically, in the very last sentence of the novel, proclaim the truth of the land, but not the saviour. 'Nous aimons à visiter quelquefois cette brave famille, et à entendre répéter souvent au père Chauvin, que la plus grande folie que puisse faire un cultivateur, c'est de se donner à ses enfants, d'abandonner la culture de son champ, et d'emprunter aux usuriers' (We sometimes like to visit this good family, and hear Père Chauvin often repeat that the greatest folly for a cultivator is to give himself over to his children, abandon the cultivation of his fields, and borrow from userers) (119). All translations mine, from *La Terre paternelle* (Montreal: Hurtubise, 1972).
4 For the function of analepses, the iterative and the singular, as distinctive features of the agrarian novel, see chapter 9.
5 Following Genette (1972), the 'singular' or 'singulative' characterizes an event that has occurred once and is narrated once, whereas the iterative is an event that has occurred several times but is narrated once (146–78).
6 It should be noted that the narrator shifts out of the historical past into the present in these last scenes of the novel, as the characters themselves are ejected from the bi-dimensional temporality of the narrative and fade into the gnomic (neither time nor place) presence of intemporality.
7 This, we saw, is what happened with Étienne Brulé, who went 'native', and who was soundly condemned by Jean de Brébeuf for doing so, in his *Relation* of 1635.
8 This is the opposite of what happens in *Maria Chapdelaine*, where the stove is the giver of life. See chapter 9, 223–6.
9 My analysis is somewhat different from that in François Paré's (1986) subtle article on identity and filiation in *La Terre paternelle*. Inspired by Northrop Frye's notion of displacement as the technique used to adjust formulaic structures to a roughly credible context, he argues that this novel defends individual identity, but that the problem rests on maintaining the filiation and hierarchy of family roles (299).
10 See Dumont, Montminy, and Hamelin, eds (1971).

11 'La paix, l'union, l'abondance régnaient donc dans cette famille; aucun souci ne venait en altérer le bonheur. Contents de cultiver en paix le champ que leurs ancêtres avaient arrosé de leurs sueurs, ils coulaient des jours tranquilles et sereins. Heureux, oh! trop heureux les habitants des campagnes, s'ils connaissaient leur bonheur!' (Peace, union, abundance therefore reigned in this family; no worries troubled their happiness. Happy to cultivate in peace the fields that their ancestors had watered with their sweat, their days were happy and serene. Happy, oh! too happy are the inhabitants of the country, if only they appreciated their happiness!) (43).
12 The old friend of the family constantly repeats the same phrase to her during her son's absence: 'Allons, allons, la mère, consolez-vous. Tenez, je ne suis pas prophète; mais je vous l'ai dit souvent, et je vous le répète encore, que Dieu est bon, qu'il se laissera toucher par vos prières et qu'il vous rendra tôt ou tard votre fils' (Come, come, Mother, console yourself. Here now, I am not a prophet; but I have often told you, and I say it once more, that God is good, that he will be touched by your prayers and that he will sooner or later give you back your son) (101).
13 When the son Charles returns to the paternal farm, he finds that it is occupied by a foreigner, an Englishman, who bought it after his father's bankruptcy. Charles does not understand English, and he is greeted brusquely and rudely by this foreigner, who addresses him in English and broken French. 'What do you say? Moi pas connaître ce que vous dire ... No, no, moi non connaître votre père, moi havoir acheté le farm de la sheriff ... No, no, goddam, vous pas d'affaire ici, moi havoir une bonne deed de la sheriff' (108). Soon afterwards, the owner passes on, Charles buys back the farm, and 'cette famille, après quinze ans d'exil et de malheurs, rentra enfin en possession du patrimoine de ses ancêtres' (this family, after fifteen years of exile and sorrows, finally takes possession of their ancestors' heritage) (117). One can certainly read this allegorically as the dispossession of the family, group, nation's rightful heritage by socio-economic forces beyond their control, the occupation of what is rightfully theirs by a foreign power that legally justifies its appropriation, and, finally, as the actual revenge by nature/God and the legal re-appropriation of their rightful legacy, while remaining under the British laws and institutions.

9 Nationalism and the Novel of Colonization: *Maria Chapdelaine*

1 All translations of *Maria Chapdelaine* are mine from the critical edition prepared by Nicole Deschamps (Montreal: Boréal Express, 1980).
2 Lionel Groulx is a twentieth-century historian who also published a novel

in 1922 entitled *L'Appel de la race* (*The Call of the Race*). He was an advocate of the right-wing ideology of *L'Action française* and adhered to the views of the two French authors of the early twentieth century whose ideas he shared, Paul Bourget and Maurice Barrès. He had numerous disciples, especially among the younger elements of the literate population in Quebec.

3 Between 1851 and 1901, the population of the province of Quebec grew from 890,000 to 1,648,900 and that of Montreal from 57,700 to 267,700. In 1851, 80 per cent of the population was rural and 20 per cent urban, whereas in 1901, 60 per cent was rural and 40 per cent urban. Between 1901 and 1931, the population of the province grew from 1,648,900 to 2,874,250; by 1931, 37 per cent of the population was rural and 63 per cent urban, with 950,000 concentrated in Quebec city and Montreal. The economic situation of urban Quebec between 1913 and 1963, for example, corresponds very little to the situation described in *Maria Chapdelaine*. Yet, the ideology portrayed in the novel, written by a foreigner, continued to be projected by those in power over this fifty-year interval. For an in-depth discussion of the relationship between ideology and economies in Quebec during this period see Dumont, Montminy, and Hamelin, eds (1971 and 1974).

4 In his introductory chapter, Dumont (1971) notes that in 1850 the social structure of Quebec already contains the imperatives that will condition the society's ideologies for a long time. Quebec is predominantly rural and agricultural; its inhabitants are poorly educated; communications are badly developed. A large percentage of the population has traits that make it possible to define it in terms of what anthropologists call a folk society. He states that for a long time the bourgeoisie of business has been predominantly British and the control of economic life is not in the hands of French Canadians. The infrastructure of Quebec society depends on another parallel society whose ideals have not penetrated the province. Since the beginning of the nineteenth century the opposition between these two societies appears in their ideologies and in the violent polemics in which each attempts to justify itself to the other. On the one hand, we have a defence of the seigneurial system and French civil rights along with a condemnation of commerce and merchants, and on the other, the exaltation of the virtues of commerce and the condemnation of the 'ignorance' and inertia of the Québécois.

5 This first voice covers all of the activities of the cultivators and clearers of land over an entire yearly cycle. Initially, the voice describes the transitions of nature. 'La neige redoutable se muant en ruisselets espiègles sur toutes les pentes; les racines surgissant, puis la mousse encore gonflée d'eau, et

bientôt le sol délivré sur lequel on marche avec des regards de délice et des soupirs d'allégresse ... Un peu plus tard les bourgeons se montraient sur les bouleaux, les aulnes et les trembles' (The dreaded snow stealing away in prankish rivulets down every slope; the tree roots cropping up, then the mosses drenched with dampness, soon the ground freed from its burden whereon one walks with delighted glances and sighs of happiness ... A little later, the birches, the alders, aspens, the massed laurels beginning to bloom with rose flowers) (193–4). It goes on to evoke the work of the farmers. 'Le bétail enfin délivré de l'étable entrait en courant dans les clos et se gorgeait d'herbe neuve. Toutes les créatures de l'année: les veaux, les jeunes volailles, les agnelets batifolaient au soleil ... Après cela c'était l'été; l'éblouissement des midis ensoleillés, la montée de l'air brûlant qui faisait vaciller l'horizon et la lisière du bois, les mouches tourbillonnant dans la lumière ... Puis la moisson, le grain nourricier s'empilant dans les granges, l'automne, et bientôt l'hiver qui revenait ... la neige amoncelée, la paix, une grande paix ...' (The cattle at last set free from their shed, gallop to pasture and stuff themselves with fresh grass. All the new-born creatures – the calves, the fowls, the lambs, gambol in the sun ... And then summertime; the dazzle of sunny noons, the heated quivering air that blurs the horizon and the outline of the forest, the flies swirling in the sun's rays ... Then the harvest; the grain that gives life heaped in barns; then autumn and soon the return of winter ... deep drifting snow, peace, a great peace ...) (194). The voice then immediately contrasts this with the city. 'Dans les villes il y aurait les merveilles dont Lorenzo Surprenant avait parlé, et ces autres merveilles qu'elle imaginait elle-même confusément: les larges rues illuminées, les magasins magnifiques, la vie facile, presque sans labeur, emplie de petits plaisirs' (In the cities there were the strange and wonderful things that Lorenzo Surprenant had told her about, along with the others that she imagined herself confusedly: wide lighted streets, beautiful shops, an easy life almost without toil with a round of small pleasures) (194–5).

6 The second voice chimes in immediately after she dreams of the American cities. 'Là-bas c'était l'étranger: des gens d'une autre race parlant d'autre chose dans une autre langue, chantant d'autres chansons ... Ici ... Tous les noms de son pays, ceux qu'elle entendait tous les jours comme ceux qu'elle n'avait entendus qu'une fois, se réveillèrent dans sa mémoire: les mille noms que des paysans pieux venus de France ont donné aux lacs, aux rivières, aux villages de la contrée nouvelle qu'ils découvraient et peuplaient à mesure ... lac à l'Eau-Claire ... La Famine ... Saint-Cœur-de-Marie ... Trois-Pistoles ... Sainte-Rose-du-Dégelé ... Pointe-aux-Outardes ... Saint-André-de-l'Épouvante ...' (Over there were the foreigners, with

people of another race speaking of other things in another tongue, singing other songs ... Here ... All the names of her country, those she listened to every day, those she heard only once, came crowding back in her memory: a thousand names piously bestowed by peasants from France on lakes, rivers, on the settlements of the new country they were discovering and settling as they went – lac à l'Eau-claire ... La Famine ... Saint-Cœur-de-Marie ... Trois-Pistoles ... Sainte-Rose-du-Dégelé ... Pointe-aux-Outardes ... Saint-André-de-l'Épouvante ...) (195).

7 'Alors une troisième voix plus grande que les autres s'éleva dans le silence: la voix du pays de Québec, qui était à moitié un chant de femme et à moitié un sermon de prêtre. Elle vint comme un son de cloche, comme la clameur auguste des orgues dans les églises, comme une complainte naïve et comme le cri perçant et prolongé par lequel les bûcherons s'appellent dans les bois. Car en vérité tout ce qui fait l'âme de la province tenait dans cette voix: la solennité chère du vieux culte, la douceur de la vieille langue jalousement gardée, la splendeur et la force barbare du pays neuf où une race ancienne a retrouvé son adolescence ... Elle disait: "Nous sommes venus il y a trois cents ans, et nous sommes restés ... Nous avons apporté d'outre-mer nos prières et nos chansons: elles sont toujours les mêmes ... Ici toutes les choses que nous avons apportées avec nous, notre culte, notre langue, nos vertus ... Autour de nous des étrangers sont venus ... ils ont acquis presque tout l'argent; mais au pays de Québec rien n'a changé ... Nous sommes un témoignage ... C'est pourquoi il faut rester dans la province où nos pères sont restés, et vivre comme ils ont vécu, pour obéir au commandement inexprimé qui s'est formé dans leurs cœurs, qui a passé dans les nôtres et que nous devrons transmettre à notre tour à de nombreux enfants"' (Then a third voice, mightier than the others, broke the silence: the voice of Quebec, that was both the song of a woman, and the exhortation of a priest. It came to her like the sound of the church bell, like the majesty of an organ's tones, like a simple lamentation, like the long high call of woodsmen in the forest. For in truth, all that makes up the soul of the province was in this voice: the dear solemnities of ancestral faith; the softness of the ancient language guarded with jealous care; the grandeur and the barbaric strength of this new land where an ancient race again found its youth ... It said: 'We came three hundred years ago, and we have remained ... We carried our prayers and our songs overseas; they are ever the same ... We brought with us our faith, our language, our virtues ... Strangers have surrounded us ... they have acquired most of the wealth; but in this land of Quebec nothing has changed ... We are a testimony ... For this is why we must live in this province where our fathers dwelt,

living as they have lived, so to obey the unwritten command that once shaped itself in their hearts, that passed to ours, which we in turn must hand down to innumerable children') (197–8).
8 Just as with François Paradis, Maria's first love, who is from a place having a Amerindian ('foreign') toponym, *Mistassini*, Lorenzo Surprenant, the other suitor whom she will not marry, is also from a region having a toponym of Native origin, *Kiskising*.
9 A scene with the town crier after Sunday mass occurs in Patrice Lacombe's *La Terre paternelle* (1846), the first novel of the land published in Quebec. Here, though, the narrator gives a long explanation about the importance of such an event in the parishes of the province, before describing the interaction between characters. This is a common occurrence in *Maria Chapdelaine*, where the narrator constantly interrupts the flow of the narrative in the past by a change in verb tense to the present, suspending the unravelling of the diegesis by his explanatory and evaluative interventions. These gnomic interruptions of the time of the fable are unnecessary for the Quebec reader and are evidently intended for the metropolitan French reader with very different presuppositions and encyclopedic knowledge. 'Ces criées qui se font régulièrement, le dimanche, à la porte des églises, sont regardées comme de la plus haute importance par la population des campagnes; en effet, toutes les parties des lois qui l'intéressent, police rurale, ventes par autorité de justice, les ordres du grand-voyer, des sous-voyers, des inspecteurs et sous-inspecteurs s'y publient de temps à autre et dans les saisons convenables; c'est pour eux la gazette officielle. Ensuite viennent les annonces volontaires et particulières; encan de meubles et d'animaux, choses perdues, choses trouvées, etc., etc., tout tombe dans le domaine de ces annonces; c'est la chronique de la semaine qui vient de s'écouler' (These events that occur regularly on Sunday, at the entrance to the churches, are considered of the greatest importance by the people of the countryside. Indeed, every law that interests them, rural police, auctions by authorization of the courts, inspectors and deputy inspectors are announced in public from time to time and in good season. For them this is the official newspaper. Then come the specific announcements: the auction of furniture and animals, things lost and found, etc., etc. Everything is in the domain of these announcements; it is the weekly chronicle of all that has occurred) (59). However, the scene in *Maria Chapdelaine* of the sale of a piglet brought to the auction in a sack and offered for one dollar, with its humorous ending, resembles very much the scene in *La Terre paternelle* where two men carry a calf and stop at the crier's feet, who auctions it off: 'Messieurs, continua celui-ci, un veau pour l'Enfant-

Jésus. Qu'est-ce qui veut du veau? ... Une piastre, pour commencer; ... rien qu'une piastre pour ce beau veau bien gras ... deux piastres ... il s'en va, il va s'en aller ... Une fois ... deux fois ... trois fois ... Adjugé ... à moi – c'est moi qui l'achète' (Gentlemen, he continued, a calf for the Child Jesus. Who wants a calf? ... One dollar, to begin with; ... only one dollar for this beautiful fat calf ... two dollars ... It is going, going ... Once ... twice ... three times ... Sold ... to me – I am buying it) (60). Perhaps it is sheer coincidence, but it is not impossible that Hémon borrowed his inspiration for this scene from Lacombe's novel of 1846.

10 Following Greimas and Courtés (1982: 245), we are attempting to establish the various narrative programs (NPs) by taking successively into consideration the following criteria: (a) the nature of the junction corresponding to the acquisition or deprivation of values; (b) the nature of the invested values: modal values of the subject (knowing, wanting, having-to and being-able) as well as the descriptive values; and (c) the nature of the subjects present together.

11 If one projects these four terms on the semiotic square one gets:

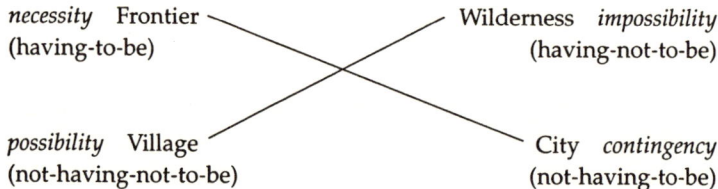

necessity Frontier   Wilderness *impossibility*
(having-to-be)   (having-not-to-be)

possibility Village   City *contingency*
(not-having-not-to-be)   (not-having-to-be)

12 If one projects these four terms on the semiotic square one gets:

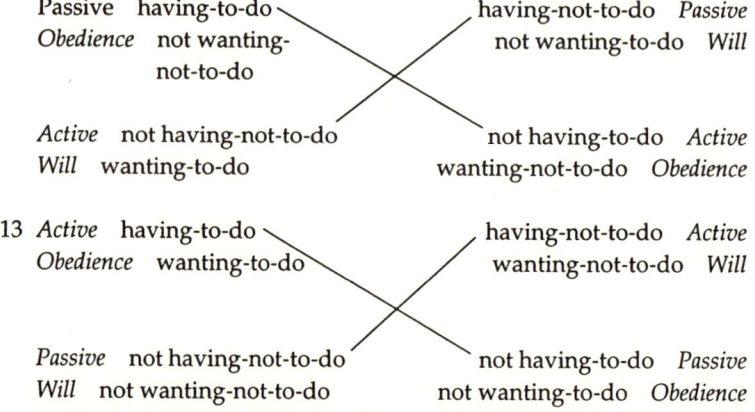

Passive   having-to-do   having-not-to-do   *Passive*
Obedience not wanting-   not wanting-to-do *Will*
          not-to-do

Active not having-not-to-do   not having-not-to-do *Active*
Will   wanting-to-do   wanting-not-to-do   *Obedience*

13 *Active*   having-to-do   having-not-to-do   *Active*
   Obedience wanting-to-do   wanting-not-to-do   *Will*

   Passive not having-not-to-do   not having-to-do   *Passive*
   Will   not wanting-not-to-do not wanting-to-do *Obedience*

14 The differential character of the semantic values grouped under the opposition /closed/ versus /open/ can be projected on the semiotic square:

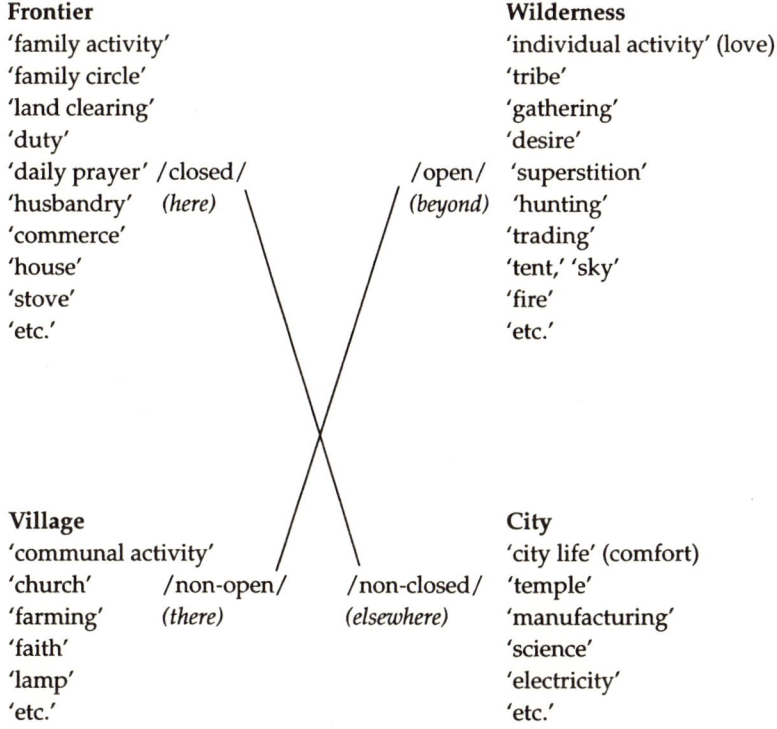

15 A third figure, the 'door sill,' plays a fundamental role in the novel, since it functions as the threshold through which characters can enter the /closed/ space of the family from the outside and also represents a potential escape into the /open/ space of the exterior, the wilderness, and the /non-closed/ space of the city.
16 Born in Quebec in 1841, Wilfrid Laurier was head of the Liberal party and the first French Canadian to be Prime Minister of Canada (1896–1911). Laurier preserved the autonomy of Canada and established closer ties with the nations of Europe than had his predecessors. He was also of the opinion that Quebec could best survive and prosper by opening up to the world and increasing immigration.
17 The following two schemas recapitulate and trace Maria's personal and social trajectory and various options in this novel:

300 Notes to page 191

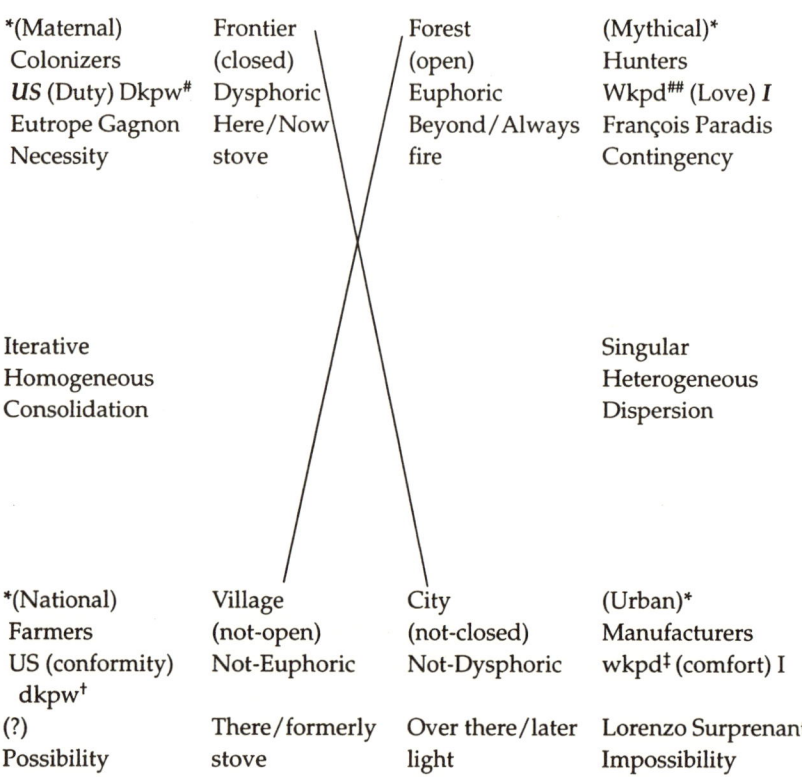

---

* Various tongues (voices) valorized positively as contributing to in the narrative to ensure the consolidation of the group, and negatively as contributing to its dissolution.
# Modal series of competence. Read: Duty (active obedience) regulates knowledge, power, and will. This is the strongest manifestation of the collective subject = **US**.
Read: Will (desire/love/reciprocity) regulates knowledge, power, and duty. This is the strongest manifestation of the desiring ego = *I*.
† Read: duty (passive obedience) regulates knowledge, power, and will. The most common manifestation of the collective subject that always conforms to the norms of the group = US.
‡ Read: will (desire of material goods) regulates knowledge, power, and duty. The weakest manifestation of the individual subject = I.

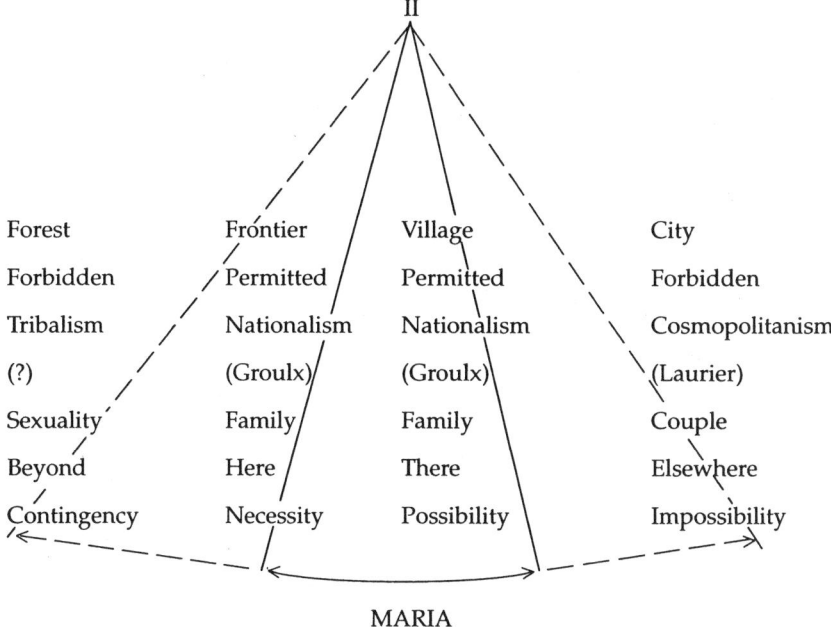

10 On the Margins of Nation – The Realist Novel: *La Scouine*

1 Unedited letter from Lionel Léveillé to Albert Laberge, 23 June 1951. Translation mine.
2 All translations mine from Albert Laberge, *La Scouine* (Montreal: L'Actuelle, 1972).
3 Camille Roy, quoted in Bessette (1972: ix). Translation mine.
4 All translations of critics mine.
5 Jacques Brunet (1969: 36).
6 Ibid., 33.
7 Gabriel Pascal (1976: 35).
8 Thuong Vuong-Riddick (1977: 117).
9 Brunet (1969: 43).
10 This is the criticism, among others, addressed by Olivar Asselin: 'le livre de Laberge est ... plutôt qu'un roman, une série de scènes sans autre lien entre elles que l'intérêt que comporte par elle-même la vie rurale' (Laberge's book ... instead of being a novel, is made up of a series of scenes without any link between them other than interest generated by rural life

itself) (quoted in Bessette, 1972: xvii). Jacques Brunet writes in the same vein: 'La Scouine n'est pas un roman. C'est un groupe de tableaux et de récits plus ou moins indépendants, reliés par le lieu, le temps et les personnages' (La Scouine is not a novel. It is made up of a group of more or less independent scenes and narratives that are linked by place, time, and characters) (Brunet, 1969: 34). As for Gérard Bessette he states more or less the same thing: 'Au lieu de présenter une intrigue suivie, Laberge brosse une série de brefs tableaux sans progression dramatique et sans liens organiques entre eux ... C'est ce qui fait dire à Gérard Tougas que La Scouine souffrait du "même défaut que le roman canadien du XIXe siècle," celui d'obéir "à une mécanique"' (Instead of presenting a consistent intrigue, Laberge paints a series of brief tableaux without any dramatic progression and without any organic links between them ... This is what makes Gérard Tougas conclude that La Scouine has 'the same shortcomings as the nineteenth-century French-Canadian novel,' that of obeying 'simple mechanical techniques') (1972: ix). Mireille Servais-Maquoi (1974) considers that: 'ce petit livre ... se situe à mi-chemin entre le recueil de nouvelles et le véritable roman. Il serait vain d'y chercher l'évolution d'une intrigue ... Un épisode quelconque pourrait disparaître sans nuire à l'intelligence du suivant' (this little book ... is situated half-way between a collection of short stories and a real novel. It would be hopeless to look for the evolution of a plot ... Any single episode could disappear without affecting the understanding of the one that comes after it) (101). And this is certainly the case with Gabrielle Pascal: 'Aucun thème central ne relie les trente-quatre chapitres de l'œuvre qui n'est ainsi composée que d'intrigues secondaires, d'ailleurs fort peu élaborées, et n'ayant entre elles aucun lien causal. En ce sens La Scouine est davantage la chronique d'un moraliste qu'un roman' (No central theme links the thirty-four chapters of the work that is composed only of secondary subplots; moreover, they are hardly elaborated, and have no causal link between them. From this perspective, La Scouine is more the chronicle of a moralist than a novel) (1976: 15). Finally Gilles Dorion writes: 'la deuxième et la troisième parties contiennent un groupe assez disparate d'anecdotes hétérogènes – ou même hétéroclites – rapportant des incidents de la vie quotidienne de la famille Deschamps ... on remaque la structure très lâche de ce roman à tiroirs, où la place de divers éléments ou anecdotes se combine de façon aléatoire selon les caprices du rédacteur. Le romancier procède sciemment par tableaux séparés, par tranches de vie ou par scènes précises, en les raccordant par quelques artifices de vocabulaire ou par des notations sommaires de temps' (the second and third parts contain an ill-assorted group of heterogeneous anecdotes – or even heteroclitical – that relate incidents from the daily life of the Deschamps family ... This novel has a very loose structure. It is made up of episodes, where the diverse elements or anecdotes are combined in a random fashion according to the whims of the writer. The novelist proceeds cleverly by presenting separated tableaux, slices of life, linking them together through some simple artifices of vocabulary or by brief temporal notations) (1980: 995–6).

11 This is the actual subtitle of the novel.
12 Both of these characters are depicted in a drunken state with extremely negative language that de-realizes and debases their actions: 'Ses trente-cinq ans de vie continente, ses nuits toujours solitaires dans le vieux sofa jaune, allumaient à cette heure en ses entrailles de luxurieux et lancinants désirs ... Toute la meute des rêves mauvais, des visions lubriques, l'assiégeait, l'envahissait ... La pluie battait la couverture de la grange, chantant sa complainte monotone, et la sempiternelle et lugubre plainte des grenouilles s'entendait comme un appel désespéré.

Alors Charlot se rua.

Et le geste des races s'accomplit.

Ce fut sa seule aventure d'amour.'

(His thirty-five years of continence, his constant solitary nights sleeping in the old yellow sofa, lighted up in his innards lustful and burning desires ... All of the packs of bad dreams, lustful visions, attacked him, invaded him ... The rain was beating on the roof of the barn, chanting its monotonous lament, and the lugubrious moaning of the frogs was heard like a cry of despair.

Then Charlot pounced

And the gesture of the races was accomplished

This was his only experience of love.) (68)

13 It is tempting to underscore in passing a possible effect of intertextual deconstruction and/or a parody linked to the portraits of the two hired men: Edwige Légaré in *Maria Chapdelaine* (see chapter 9) and Bagon the Gelder. Moreover, we know that Louis Hémon's novel was published in serial form at the beginning of 1914 in Paris, then in Montreal in 1916, whereas chapter 1 of *La Scouine*, entitled: 'Le Pain sûr et amère' (Sour and bitter bread), appeared in the newspaper *L'Autorité* on 8 April 1916. The complete version of the novel appeared in 1918 in an edition that was not for commercial distribution. It is therefore not impossible that Laberge was aware of a version of *Maria Chapdelaine*, the most widely read Quebec novel of the twentieth century, when he was composing his work.

Edwige Légaré	**Bagon le coupeur**
Court et trapu	très petit, laideur grandiose, *tronc* très court
Il avait les yeux d'un bleu étonnement Clair ... à la fois aigus et simples	il était borgne
Un visage *couleur d'argile* surmonté de cheveux d'une *teinte presque pareille* (couleur d'argile)	une tête énorme de mégalocéphale
	teint d'un homme souffrant de la jaunisse
	le chef presque complètement dépourvu de cheveux ressemblait *une aride butte sur laquelle ne poussent que quelques brins d'herbes*
son visage n'exprimait qu'une *rusticité* terrible	la picotte avait outrageusement *labouré* ses traits
visage éternellement *haché* de coupures	sa bouche édentée ... quelques *chicots gâtés comme des souches*
vêtu d'une chemise et de pantalons en étoffe du pays, d'un *brun terreux*, chaussé de grandes *bottes poussièreuses*, il était en vérité *tout entier couleur de terre*	vieux chapeau de paille
	chemise de coton

Edwige Légaré	**Bagon the Gelder**
Short and stocky	very short, grandiose ugliness, very short *trunk*
He had eyes that were astonishingly clear blue ... at one and the same time piercing and simple	he was blind in one eye
His face was the *colour of clay* and his head was covered with hair almost of *the same colour*	an enormous megacephalic head
	complexion of a man suffering from jaundice
	his head almost devoid of hair resembled an *arid mound* on which *only a few blades of grass grew*
His face expressed an incredible *rustic simplicity*	chickenpox had outrageously *ploughed* his face

An extraordinary face *chopped with cuts*	His toothless mouth ... a few remnants *rotted like stumps*
He was dressed in a shirt and pants made of local cloth and wore great *dusty boots*. In truth, he was the *colour of the soil from top to bottom*	old straw hat cotton shirt

(Italics reflect my emphasis.) This mirroring effect is dependent on the metaphoric inscription that organizes the somatic trace so that the two men are compared and integrated into the ambient environment, all the while maintaining a close relation of 'correspondences' and/or conjunction with it. Yet in contrast to Edwige Légaré, whose depiction maintains the positive and euphoric relationship of man and land – the two are cut from the same fertile matter – Bagon's portrait retraces, as by an echo of counterpoint, the corporeal inscription of the negative and dysphoric relationship of man and land, suggesting that both emerge from the same sterile substratum. From this time on, the indexical translation that is set off at the moment the body is described as linking the agent to land – in one case positively, but in the other extremely negatively – will continue throughout both narratives, and will progressively unravel and be embodied at the superior level of the actants.

14 In this episode, a blind man comes to beg for money the day before Christmas and La Scouine swindles him out of money by asking him to give her change for a coin, which just happens to be counterfeit. This sequence of successful theft (from the point of view of La Scouine) or of charity not obtained (from the point of view of the old blind man) is marked, as in the book's last chapter, by a change in verb tenses (in both chapters, from the past-definite tense to the present). One could also say that the verb tenses play the role of indices, insofar as the theft sequence of chapter 13 takes place on the day before Christmas, the feast of the birthday of Jesus, and, as implicit signifier, indexes the ineffectualness of all religion and/or of all transcendental values (good, justice, charity, truth, etc.) in motivating and, consequently, influencing in any meaningful way the behaviour of an agent who is dependent only on a decisional logic of survival. Chapter 34, which ends the tale, is also narrated in the present tense since, after the father's death, the three old and sterile remaining protagonists, Maço, La Scouine, and Charlot, sell the farm and move to the village to lead an idle life. Incapable of maintaining themselves in the logico-temporal and causal unravelling of the action imposed by the past-definite tense (see Barthes,

1958, 'L'Écriture du roman'), they literally leave the order of (hi)story and vanish and fade into the inactive atemporality of the eternal present of the idle retired.

15 The twins, in class, witness the following event. One of the schoolchildren, Corinne Galarneau, was quite naughty, and the schoolteacher, to punish her, made her kiss the ground, kneel down, then stand up and receive five blows of the strap on each hand. The child cried for an hour, then went home for lunch and complained to her mother, who, as it turned out, happened to have a violent character. The mother came back to school and began insulting and menacing the teacher in front of the pupils. To end the affair, she turned around, and 'd'un large geste de mépris, avait montré à la jeune fille un panorama qui avait scandalisé les enfants' (with a grand gesture showed the children a panorama that scandalized them) (8–9). Pale with rage, the schoolteacher could not say a word after that damning insult.

16 The Linches, who owned the main general store in the village and sent their yearly billings to the farmers, mailed Urgèle Deschamps a bill for goods he did not receive. He refused to pay. They sent the bailiff and, after hiring a lawyer, Urgèle went to court. Deschamps was condemned to pay the bill and the costs. Years later, an employee who had asked the Linches for a raise and did not get it, revealed that most of the items appearing on the bills were non-existent. He was then arrested and faced with a lawsuit for defamation, and so 'le commis indiscret fit trois mois de prison pour avoir, dit le juge, diffamé ses patrons' (the indiscreet employee ended up with three months in prison for having, said the Judge, slandered his employers) (29).

17 In this section I have chosen to concentrate on the first two levels of analysis, the functions and the actants, but not the third (enunciation), which I have analysed in detail in other chapters of this work. I should point out, though, that a narrative pragmatics modalizes the utterances relating to the functions and actants, and that the dominant tropes are paralepsis, irony, understatement, and metalepsis.

18 At the onomastic level, the name of the teacher, Ms Léveillé (from l'éveillé – bright, sharp, awakened), is in the ironic mode, since she does not in any way succeed in awakening the desire to learn in any of these schoolchildren.

19 The discontinuity of the temporal structure – hence the ahistorical nature of *La Scouine* – can be especially noted by the fact that, to paraphrase Genette (1972), once the 'first' narrative is set in motion at the beginning of the first chapter, the story unfolds with a quasi absence of flashbacks or analepses.

In addition, most of the events that are narrated are singular in nature (are narrated once and occur only once), in contrast, for example, to *Maria Chapdelaine*, where there exist a great number of flashbacks of an iterative nature that reach far back in time and have a great amplitude much beyond the first narrative. This constitutes an actual historicizing anteriority that anchors the iterative event in a distant past. This is also the case with Lacombe's genealogy at the beginning of *La Terre paternelle*, which situates the present owners in relationship to the acquisition of the land by their first ancestors. Hence, with Laberge, the impression of atemporality, since each narrated event is enfolded into its own singular present and is inexorably cut off from a past that could found it as continuity. From this perspective there exists no duration, no temporality, in this text where each scene or tableau vanishes – with no past foundation or future horizon – at the very moment, the very instant, it occurs and unfolds.

20 At the end of the novel, though, Charlot does help Bougie (= candle/light), the new owner of the paternal farm, to cover the roof of the barn. At this point, however, Charlot has already sold the farm and retired to the village and has left the time of historical activity to melt into the timelessness of the eternal present.

21 Emphasis mine.

22 The three characters are installed in the village, where 'on n'attend que la mort' (they are only awaiting death) (129). None of them, though, will be granted the privilege of being called by their given name and surname, or even by their surname alone – the group will be designated as such on only one occasion – for the name will have disappeared with the death of the father and the decision of all the other protagonists to abandon the land to live in the village, this place of inactivity where 'il ne vit plus; il attend la mort' (he no longer lives; he only awaits death) (134).

23 The name 'Urgèle' lends itself to a number of meanings with reference to its etymology – *Ur* (primitive, original, earliest) and *gèle* (frozen) – which establishes a relationship of origins. In addition, the synthesis of the given name with the surname ('Deschamps' = of, from the fields) retraces and strengthens the identity and the actantial trajectory of the overbearing father.

24 Emphasis mine.

25 Emphasis mine.

26 Emphasis mine.

27 My conclusions join those of Annie Alexandre (1985) who, in an insightful article on *La Scouine*, notes that in this novel the French Canadian is no longer the son of his glorious ancestors. He has no contact with a distant

national future and is caught up in a final immobility. Laberge's characters 'have no national future, no glorious past; only the present of the flesh tormented by its indigestions, its appetites. A new *experienced time* now appears in the French-Canadian literary text' (103).

11 History and the Urban Novel: *Bonheur d'occasion*

1 Published in 1945 (Montreal: Beauchemin) and translated into English as *The Tin Flute* by Hannah Josephson (Toronto: McClelland and Stewart, 1947). All page numbers for English quotations refer to the latter edition.
2 Novel by Ringuet (Philippe Paneton's pseudonym) first published in Paris by Flammarion in 1938 before being published in English as *Thirty Acres* in 1940 by McClelland and Stewart. When it appeared, it was widely acclaimed both in Quebec and in Europe and was considered a masterpiece of French-Canadian literature.
3 The representation of the city in novels before Roger Lemelin's *Au pied de la pente douce* (1944) and *Les Plouffe* (1948) and Roy's *Bonheur d'occasion* is to a large extent agriculturalist. The city is depicted as a non-closed heterogeneous space where forces of evil, darkness, and temptation besiege the subject's physical and moral integrity. It is the space of theoretical knowledge, science, and material goods, where the subject's deepest beliefs are constantly assailed. It is also represented as a space of transition where the desiring subject either fails to acquire the knowledge necessary for integration and success, and hence is defeated and disappears, or recognizes the error of his or her ways and gains wisdom before being reintegrated into the homogeneous cultural, social, religious, and linguistic space of the village, farm, or frontier.
4 In addition, the wilderness and the city represent the obvious danger of hybridization which, in effect, brings about the dissolution into the world of the other, the elsewhere, and the beyond of the specific characteristics and even the symbolic order that define the subject in terms of nation. Regarding the wilderness, the motif of the loss of French-European identity through contact with the Amerindian religion and culture can be traced back to Jean de Brébeuf's *Relation* of 1635, in which he describes the necessity of adopting the other's value system in an attempt to convert the Huron to Catholicism (see chapter 5). Moreover, in the *Relation* of 1636 he alludes to the dissolute life of Étienne Brulé, who was sent to Huronia by Champlain as a young man to learn the Huron language and serve as interpreter. As I noted before, he remained there from 1629, after the conquest and evacuation of Quebec by the Kirkes, to 1634 when the French

Notes to pages 209–15   309

returned. He was assassinated by the Huron, and Brébeuf was quick to condemn him for adopting the life and mores of his hosts, especially with respect to sexual customs.

5   First published in Montreal in 1945, this work was republished in Montreal and Paris in 1947 and won the very prestigious *Prix Femina* in France the same year. It sold 130,000 copies in Quebec as well as more than one million copies in translation, including 130,000 in English Canada.

6   My plot summaries follow those suggested by Sirois (1982).

7   For an analysis of the gaze in *Bonheur d'occasion* see the study by N. Bourbonnais (1988) on the representation of the female body, as well as D. Drummond's (1986) article on identity in this novel.

8   This 'existential' motif of the times is reinforced when Jean, observing her for the first time, brazenly stares at her: 'Elle avait un visage mince, délicat, presque enfantin. L'effort qu'elle faisait pour se maîtriser gonflait et nouait les petites veines bleues de ses tempes ... Sa bouche était mal assurée, et parfois esquissait un tremblement, mais Jean, en regardant les yeux, fut soudain frappé de leur expression. Sous le trait surélevé des sourcils épilés que prolongeait un coup de crayon, les paupières en s'abaissant ne livraient qu'un mince rayon de regard mordoré, prudent, attentif et extraordinairement avide. Puis les cils battaient et la prunelle jaillissait entière, pleine d'un chatoiement brusque' (11) (She had a thin, delicate, almost childish face. As she struggled to get a grip on herself the small blue veins in her temples swelled and throbbed ... Her mouth quivered from time to time. But Jean was particularly struck by the expression in her eyes. Under the high arch of her plucked and pencilled eyebrows, her lowered lids concealed all but a glint of bronze, but he could see that the eyes were watchful, and yet extraordinarily eager. Then the eyelids fluttered open and the whole pupil became visible, full of sudden iridescence) (2–3).

9   In a particularly insightful and lucid study, Patricia Smart (1991) provides us with an original feminist reading of what she calls 'realism in the feminine' in *The Tin Flute* that enhances and enriches considerably the socio-semiotic interpretation of the feminine characters I have given.

10 After her husband's departure overseas, at the very end of the novel, Florentine, 'âpre au gain' (344) (greedy for the money) (273), decides to continue to work until the very end of her pregnancy. She also 'devenait ambitieuse et secrètement solidaire aux siens' (344) (was growing ambitious and secretly felt closer to her kin) (274) and thinks about renting a house in a much better district of Montreal than Saint-Henri, using her newfound wealth to provide better shelter and food for what is left of her family: 'elle recommençait ses calculs; elle se trouvait riche, elle se

proposait d'acheter ceci et cela, elle se réjouissait au fond de la tournure des événements, car sans la guerre où seraient-ils tous?' (345) (she returned to her calculations. Good gracious, she was rich! There were so many things she could buy for her mother and the children as well as for herself. At heart she rejoiced at the course of events, for without the war where would they all be?) (274).

11 One notes again the motif of the fire in the stove, a motif which, as we saw, has such a fundamental role in the novel of the land, notably in *Maria Chapdelaine*, where it corresponds to all the positive values that define the family and ensure its continuity. Here, though, the stove is relegated to the universe of dream, of desire for what is no longer and can never be.

12 For a detailed analysis of the role of money and capitalism in the novel see the very perceptive chapter 'On the Outside Looking In: The Political Economy of Everyday Life in Gabrielle Roy's *Bonheur d'occasion*' in Purdy (1990: 41–61).

13 This is the case in chapter 29, when Emmanuel and Florentine decide to visit Verdun on the outskirts of Montreal where, as a young child, she used to go fishing with her father. They spend the entire day together, taking the bus, walking, and stopping, and at twilight they find a place to sit down in sight of a little cove where they can hear the rumble of the city in a faint murmur. Choosing a spot on a large boulder near the water, they hold each other in their arms, and Florentine manoeuvres Emmanuel into asking her to marry him, a proposal she immediately accepts with relief: 'Toute tempête était apaisée. Il n'y aurait plus d'extase, plus d'abîmes dans sa vie, rien qu'une route plane, tranquille, où, s'y voyant sauvée, elle ne s'étonnait plus de se trouver engagée' (305) (The storm was over. There would be no more heights of ecstasy in the depths of horror in her life, only a smooth quiet road ahead of her. She was saved) (243).

14 Only once do the Lacasses actually leave the city, to visit Rose-Anna's mother and brother in the country, the first time in seven years. This trip, which begins as a return to origins, quickly takes on tragic and nightmarish proportions. First of all, Florentine refuses to accompany the family, invites Jean to her parents' place, and succumbs to his advances, with potentially disastrous consequences for her. Second, the physical and material degradation of the city dwellers who have abandoned the farm is further accentuated by the comparison with their healthy, robust cousins. Rose-Anna's children have thin little faces and skinny limbs: 'L'avant-dernier de Réséda s'était traîné vers elle sur de grosses pattes courtes, à demi arquées, potelées aux genoux; et, tout à coup, au-dessus du bébé, elle avait aperçu une rangée de petites jambes grêles. De ses enfants, assis contre le mur docilement, elle ne voyait plus que les jambes, des jambes

pendantes, longues et presque décharnés' (171) (Réséda's next youngest was crawling toward her on short fat legs, with plump knees, and suddenly, beyond the baby, she saw a row of spindly shanks. Her children were seated in a row against the wall, and all she could see was their legs, their long scrawny legs) (134). Finally, returning to the city, Azarius has an accident with the truck he had borrowed from his boss, without telling him, and loses his job. Struggling in the city, no longer able to cope in the country, the Lacasses are amputated from their roots and do not have the means to function as a cohesive group in their harsh urban environment.

15 Both Azarius and Rose-Anna dream of a home in the city that would have all the trappings of the country: 'Il parlait d'avoir une maison avec un jardinet où il planterait des choux et des carottes. Et elle, qui venait de la campagne, était tout émue, toute joyeuse, à l'idée de voir pousser des légumes sous ses fenêtres' (83) (He would speak of having a house with a little garden where he would plant cabbages and carrots. And she, being a country girl at heart, would brim with joy at the prospect of seeing vegetables grow under her window) (61–2). But this desire that never materializes – they always move near factories and ramshackle houses – encapsulates their dilemma of living in a different world with values from the past that have no impact on the present.

12 Utopia, Family, Nation – The Wilderness Novel: *Agaguk*

1 For a detailed semio-narrative analysis of this novel see my *Semiotics and the Modern Quebec Novel* (1996).
2 All quotations in English are from Miriam Chapin's translation (Toronto: McGraw-Hill Ryerson, 1963).
3 Paulette Collet (1986), points out, however, that two French authors, Henri-Émile Chevalier and Victor Forbin, both of whom spent some time in Canada, published novels in France with an Eskimo setting, the former in 1866, entitled *La Fille des Indiens rouges*, the latter in 1926, *La Fée des neiges*.
4 In an ironic twist, as both protagonists fall asleep on the tundra, high in the sky and unknown to them, a small plane flies overhead, marking the presence of the other and of modern technology in this seemingly remote and isolated world

13 Conclusion

1 Other novelists wrote satirical and ironic works that were censured or negatively viewed by ecclesiastical authorities – for example, Rodolph Girard's *Marie Calumet*, published in 1904, and condemned by the Archbishop of

Montreal – but none deconstructed, or even questioned, the dominant ideology of identity and survival based on unity of language, race, and religion.
2 See for example Purdy's (1990) illuminating essay on the sociocultural codes at play in a representative number of Quebec novels, as well as the translation and expanded version of J. Paterson's (1994) pioneering work on postmodernism and the Quebec novel.
3 It is not possible to reread the Quebec canon of the twentieth century in the same way since the appearance of Patricia Smart's groundbreaking *Writing in the Father's House* (1991). This work, which appeared originally in French and which studies the emergence of the feminine in the Quebec literary tradition, has inspired a good deal of feminist criticism. See also S. Simon's (1991) edited volume on minority writing in Quebec.
4 *Toronto Star*, 5 February 2001: A7.
5 *New York Times*, International edition, 12 January 2001: A10.

Glossary

This glossary is designed to facilitate the reading of this work. For more in-depth definitions, readers should refer to A.J. Greimas and J. Courtés, *Semiotics and Language: An Analytical Dictionary* (1982).

actant   That which accomplishes or undergoes an act independently of all other determinations. The actant – be it subject, object, predicate, or other – exists only in a junctive relation with other actants. As such, it accounts for the organization of narrative discourse at the level of narrative syntax.

actor   Character or entity containing at least the seme of individuation that gives it the appearance of an autonomous figure.

actual   *See* virtual.

anaphora   A relation of partial identity between two terms that serves to link two figures or actors, whereby the expanded term precedes the condensed term.

aspectualization   The overdetermination of the elementary predicates by a set of semic categories (inchoate versus terminative, punctual versus durative, etc.) that diversify the way in which the processes unravel.

axiology   The paradigmatic organization of the actantial transformations of values. Contrasted to ideology.

cataphora   A relation of partial identity between two terms serving to link two figures or actors, whereby the condensed term precedes the expanded term.

classemes   Recurrent semic categories that guarantee the homogeneity of a discourse.

conjunction   The appropriation of the object of value by the actant subject.

contract   One of the two bases for the organization of narrative discourses, whereby a subject interacts with an anti-subject or opponent in the mode of agreement. Contrasted to polemic.

contract, fiduciary   The exchange of objects of value between two subjects in which they recognize, at the cognitive level, the equivalence of the value of the objects.

cosmological dimension   The perception of events and actions by actant subjects.

culture versus nature   The first elementary investment of the social semantic universe. Contrasted to life versus death, which characterizes the individual semantic universe.

deixis   A linguistic element that refers to the domain of enunciation and to its spatio-temporal coordinates: I, here, now.

description   A surface sequence at the level of discursive organization which is opposed to dialogue, narrative, tableau, and so on.

diegesis   The narrative aspect of discourse. Contrasted to description.

discourse   The result of choices made by a given speaker from the stock of language in order to produce a message in a particular and determined situation.

disjunction   The separation of the actant subject from the object of value.

enunciation   The instance of mediation by which discourse is produced.

ideology   The syntagmatic organization of the actantial transformations of values.

language   The set of elements and rules that a speaker must use in order to produce well-articulated utterances.

life versus death   The first elementary investment of the individual semantic universe. Contrasted to nature versus culture, which characterizes the social semantic universe.

manipulation   An action a subject undertakes on another subject with the aim of having him/her carry out a given program. Manipulation can be praxic, cognitive, passional, or a combination thereof.

mise en abyme   A micro-narrative that recapitulates and announces in an extremely condensed form the story that is about to unravel.

modality   That which modifies a state or an activity. Four modalities – wanting, having-to, being-able, and knowing – can come into play in the semiotic organization of the novel. From our point of view, modalities of competence enable the actant subject to perform at the actional, cognitive, or passional levels.

modality, deontic   A modality in which having-to-do overdetermines and governs the utterance of doing.

mythical   The noological or abstract dimension of discourse.

noological dimension   The abstract interpretation of events and actions by actant subjects.

polemic   One of the two bases for the organization of narrative discourses, whereby a subject interacts with an anti-subject or opponent in the mode of conflict. Contrasted to contract.

practical The cosmological or figurative dimension of discourse.

predicate One of the syntactic functions that are part of the utterance.

realized *See* virtual.

role, actantial The modal investment of the actant and the actant's position within the narrative trajectory.

seme The minimal unit of signification.

sememe The set of semes realized by a term inscribed in a given context.

semiosis The act of the production of signification by the setting up of a relationship of presupposition between a signifier and a signified.

square, semiotic 'The visual representation of the logical articulation of any semantic category' (Greimas and Courtés, 1982: 308).

structure, deep The point of departure of a series of transformations presented as a generative process.

subject, cognitive A subject endowed by the enunciator with a partial or total knowledge.

subject, collective A subject endowed with a common modal competence that characterizes all of the actors it subsumes.

subject, competent A subject endowed with a modal competence composed of a hierarchical organization of the four modalities of wanting, having-to, being-able, and knowing.

subject, semiotic In a narrative, a subject that can exist only in a junctive relation with an object of value and a polemico/contractual relation with an anti-subject.

syntax, fundamental The deep level of the semiotic and narrative grammar.

syntax, narrative The set of procedures or rules that can be used to define the elementary utterance. It is derived from the fundamental syntax.

trajectory, generative The manner in which the components that enter into the mode of production of a semiotic object are linked together, from the simplest to the most complex, from the most abstract to the most concrete.

utterance The state resulting from enunciation, which is the speech act.

utterance of doing The transformations between subjects and objects.

utterance of state The junctions between subjects and objects.

virtual, actual, realized Categories of subject–object relations. Semiotic subjects and objects are 'virtual' when they are situated next to one another without being in a junctive relation. This relation defines the first degree of semiotic existence of subjects and objects before their actualization. They are 'actualized' when they are in a relation of disjunction. They are 'realized' when they are conjoined.

Bibliography

Alexandre, A. 1985. 'Albert Laberge: Aux bords de l'ombre vague.' *Voix et images* 10 (3): 93–112.
Arens, W. 1979. *The Man-Eating Myth*. New York: Oxford University Press.
Arguin, M. 1989. *Le Roman québécois de 1944 à 1965*. Montreal: L'Hexagone.
Arrivé, M. 2000. 'Préface.' *Algirdas Julien Greimas. La Mode en 1830*, xi–xxv. Paris: Presses Universitaires de France.
Aubert de Gaspé, P. 1970. *Les Anciens canadiens*. Montreal: Fides.
Authier-Revuz, J. 1984. 'Héterogéneité(s) énonciative(s).' *Les Plans d'énonciation. Langages* 73: 98–111.
Bakhtin, M. 1977. *Le Marxisme et la philosophie du langage*. Paris: Minuit.
Bal, M. 1985. *Narratology*. Toronto: University of Toronto Press.
– 1986. *Femmes imaginaires. L'Ancien testament au risque d'une narratologie critique*. Paris: Nizet.
Barry, J. 1999. *Art, Culture, and the Semiotics of Meaning*. New York: St Martin's Press.
Barthes, R. 1958. 'L'Écriture du roman.' In R. Barthes *Le Degré zéro de l'écriture*, 29–38. Paris: Gonthier.
– 1966. 'Introduction à l'analyse structurale du récit.' In Barthes, ed., *L'Analyse structurale du récit*. Paris: Seuil.
– 1968. 'L'Effet de réel.' *Communications* 11: 84–9.
– 1970. *S/Z*. Paris: Seuil.
– 1971. *Sade, Fourier, Loyola*. Paris: Seuil.
– 1981. 'Sur *S/Z* et *L'Empire des signes*.' In *Le Grain de la voix*, 69–86. Paris: Seuil.
Belleforest, François de. 1575. *De la cosmographie universelle de tout le monde*. Paris: M. Sonnius.
Benveniste, É. 1966. 'Les Relations du temps dans le verbe français.' In É. Benveniste, *Problèmes de linguistique générale I*, 237–50. Paris: Gallimard.

- 1966. 'De la subjectivité dans le langage.' In É. Benveniste, *Problèmes de linguistique générale I*, 258–66. Paris: Gallimard.
- 1971. *Problems in General Linguistics*. Translated by M.E. Meek. Coral Gables, FL: University of Miami Press.
- 1974. 'L'Appareil formel de l'énonciation.' In É. Benveniste, *Problèmes de linguistique générale II*, 79–88. Paris: Gallimard.

Bérubé, G., and M.-F. Silver. 1996. (Eds.). *La Lettre au XVIIIe siècle et ses avatars*. Toronto: Éditions du GREF.

Bessette, G. 1972. *Anthologie d'Albert Laberge*. Montreal: Le Cercle du livre de France.

Besterman, T. 1957. *Saint Jean de Brébeuf, les Relations de ce qui s'est passé au Pays des Hurons (1635–48)*. Geneva: Droz.

Booth, W.C. 1961a. 'Distance and Point of View: An Essay in Classification.' *Essays in Criticism* 11: 60–79.
- 1961b. *The Rhetoric of Fiction*. Chicago: University of Chicago Press.

Bourbonnais, N. 1988. 'Gabrielle Roy. La Représentation du corps féminin.' *Voix et images* 40: 72–89.

Bremond. C. 1966. 'La Logique des possibles narratifs.' In Barthes, ed., *L'Analyse structurale du récit*, 66–82.
- 1973. *Logique du récit*. Paris: Seuil.

Broden, T.A. 1995. 'A.J. Greimas (1917–1992): Commemorative Essay.' *Semiotica* 105 (3–4): 207–42.
- 1999a. 'Linguistics, Semantics for Literature and the Human Sciences Today.' *Semiotica* 124 (1–2): 81–127.
- 1999b. 'Narrativité et dynamique du corps.' *Recherches sémiotiques/Semiotic Inquiry* 19 (2–3): 219–50.
- 2000. 'Avant-Dire.' *Algirdas Julien Greimas. La Mode en 1830*, xxvii–xliv. Paris: Presses Universitaires de France.

Brunet, J. 1969. *Albert Laberge, sa vie et son œuvre*. Ottawa: Éditions de l'Université d'Ottawa.

Cartier, J. 1977. *Voyages en Nouvelle-France*, R. Lahaise and M. Couturier, eds, Ville LaSalle, Québéc.

Champlain, Samuel de. 1603. *Des Sauvages ou voyage de Samuel de Champlain de Brouage, faict en la France Nouvelle, l'an mil six cens trois*. Paris: Claude de Monstr'oeil.
- 1632. *Les Voyages de la Nouvelle France Occidentale, dicte Canada*. Paris: L. Sevestre, C. Collet, et P. Le Mur.

Charlevoix, François-Xavier de. 1744. *Histoire et description générale de la Nouvelle-France*. 6 vols. Paris: Nyon.

Chatman, S. 1978. *Story and Discourse*. Ithaca, NY: Cornell University Press.

- 1980. 'What Novels Can Do That Films Can't (and Vice Versa).' *Critical Inquiry* 7: 121–40.
Cloutier-Wojciechowska, C., and R. Robidoux. 1986. (Eds). *Solitude rompue*. Ottawa: Éditions de l'Université d'Ottawa.
Collet, P. 1986. 'Avant *Agaguk*, deux romans esquimaux écrits par des Français.' In Cloutier-Wojciechowska and Robidoux, eds, *Solitude rompue*, 47–55.
Cook, R. 1993. *The Voyages of Jacques Cartier*. Toronto: University of Toronto Press.
Coquet. J.C. 1982. *Sémiotique – L'École de Paris*. Paris: Hachette.
- 1985. 'Éléments de bio-bibliographie.' In Parret and Ruprecht, eds, *Recueil d'hommages pour / Essays in Honor of Algirdas Julien Greimas*, liii–lxxxv.
Coste, D. 1989. *Narrative as Communication*. Minneapolis: University of Minnesota Press.
Courtés, J. 1976. *Introduction à la sémiotique narrative et discursive*. Paris: Hachette.
- 1985. *Pour une sémantique des traditions populaires. Actes sémiotiques – Documents VII*. Paris: Centre National de la Recherche Scientifique.
- 1986. *Le Conte populaire: poétique et mythologie*. Paris: Presses Universitaires de France.
Cressolles, P., L. de. 1620. *Vacationes Automnales. III*. Paris: Cramoisy. Trans. B. Lefebvre. *Revue des sciences humaines* (1975) 2 (58): 275–8.
Culler, J. 1981. *The Pursuit of Signs*. Ithaca, NY: Cornell University Press.
de Certeau, M. 1990. *L'Invention du quotidien. 1. Arts de faire*. Paris: Gallimard.
De Lauretis, T. 1984. *Alice Doesn't*. Bloomington: Indiana University Press.
- 1988. *Technologies of Gender*. Bloomington: Indiana University Press.
Deschamps, N. 1980. *Le Mythe de Maria Chapdelaine*. Montreal: Les Presses de l'Université de Montréal.
Doležel, L. 1973. *Narrative Modes in Czech Literature*. Toronto: University of Toronto Press.
- 1979. *Essays in Structural Poetics and Narrative Semantics*. Toronto: Toronto Semiotic Circle.
- 1990. *Occidental Poetics: Tradition and Progress*. Lincoln: University of Nebraska Press.
- 1998. *Heterocosmica: Fiction and Possible Worlds*. Baltimore: Johns Hopkins University Press.
Dorion, G. 1980. '*La Scouine*.' In Lemire, ed., *Dictionnaire des œuvres littéraires du Québec*, II, 993–8.
Doutre, J. 1970. 'Préface.' *Les Fiancés de 1812*. In G. Rousseau, *Préfaces de romans québécois du XIXe siècle*, 23–9. Ottawa: Éditions Cosmos.

Drummond, D. 1986. 'Identité d'occasion dans *Bonheur d'occasion.*' In Cloutier-Wojciechowska and Robidoux, eds, *Solitude rompue*, 85–102.
Ducrot, O., and T. Todorov. 1972. *Dictionnaire encyclopédique des sciences du langage.* Paris: Seuil.
Dumont, F., J.-P. Montminy, and J. Hamelin. 1971. (Eds). *Idéologies au Canada Français 1850–1900.* Quebec: Les Presses de l'Université Laval.
– 1974. (Eds). *Idéologies au Canada Français 1900–1929.* Quebec: Les Presses de l'Université Laval.
Duquette, J.-P. 1982. '*Marie-Didace.*' In Lemire, ed., *Dictionnaire des œuvres littéraires du Québec*, III, 609–14.
Durand, G. 1963. *Les Structures anthropologiques de l'imaginaire.* Paris: Presses Universitaires de France.
Eagleton, T. 1983. *Literary Theory.* Minneapolis: University of Minnesota Press.
Eco, U. 1966. 'James Bond. Une Combinatoire narrative.' In Barthes, ed., *L'Analyse structurale du récit*, 83–99.
– 1979. *The Role of the Reader.* Bloomington: Indiana University Press.
– 1986. *Semiotics and the Philosophy of Language.* Bloomington: Indiana University Press.
– 1987. 'Notes sur la sémiotique de la réception.' *Actes sémiotiques – Documents* 9 (81): 5–27. *Documents de recherche.* Paris: Centre National de la Recherche Scientifique.
Ejxenbaum, B.M. 1965. 'La Théorie de la "méthode formelle."' In Todorov, ed., *Théorie de la littérature*, 31–75.
Entrevernes Group. 1978. *Signs and Parables.* Pittsburgh: Pickwick Press.
Falardeau, J.-C. 1972. *Notre société et son roman.* Montreal: Hurtubise.
Fisette, J. 1991. 'Compte rendu.' *Recherches sémiotiques / Semiotic Inquiry* 11 (1): 180–90.
Fontanier, P. 1968. *Les Figures du discours.* Paris: Flammarion.
Forster, E.M. 1927. *Aspects of the Novel.* New York: Harcourt Brace.
Fortin, N. 1994. *Une Littérature inventée. Littérature québécoise et critique universitaire (1965–1975).* Sainte-Foy: Les Presses de l'Université Laval.
Friedman, N. 1955a. 'Forms of Plot.' *Journal of General Education* 8: 241–53.
– 1955b. 'Point of View in Fiction.' *Publications of the Modern Language Association* 70: 1160–84.
Frye, N. 1957. *Anatomy of Criticism.* Princeton: Princeton University Press.
Gagnon, F.-M. 1975. *La Conversion par l'image. Un Aspect de la mission des Jésuites auprés des Indiens du Canada au XVIIe siècle.* Montreal: Bellarmin.
– 1988. 'L'Iconographie classique des Saints Martyrs Canadiens.' In Laflèche, *Les Saints Martyrs canadiens.* I, 37–79.
Garneau, F.X. 1845–52. *Histoire du Canada.* Quebec: N. Aubin.

Garvin, P. 1955. *A Prague School Reader on Esthetics, Literary Structure and Style.* Washington, DC: Washington Linguistic Club.

Gaudreault, A. 1988. *Du Littéraire au filmique, système du récit.* Quebec and Paris: Les Presses de l'Université Laval, Méridiens Klincksieck.

Gaudreault, A., and F. Jost. 1990. *Cinéma et récit II – Le Récit cinématographique.* Paris: Nathan.

Genette, G. 1972. *Figures III.* Paris: Seuil.

Gervais, B. 1990. *Récits et actions. Pour une théorie de la lecture.* Montreal: Le Préambule.

– 1993. *À l'écoute de la lecture.* Montreal: VLB Éditeur.

– 1998. *Lecture littéraire et explorations en littérature américaine.* Montreal: XYZ Éditeur.

Gomez-Géraud, M.-C. 1995. 'La Perception du geste sauvage et ses enjeux: Regards sur l'Indien de la Nouvelle-France.' In Thérien, ed., *Figures de l'Indien*, 32–45.

Goodman, N. 1980. 'Twisted Tales; Or Story, Study, and Symphony.' *Critical Inquiry* 7 (1): 103–19.

Greimas, A.J. 1956. 'L'Actualité du saussurisme.' *Le Français moderne* 24: 3–11.

– 1966a. 'Éléments pour une théorie de l'interprétation mythique.' In Barthes, ed., *L'Analyse structurale du récit*, 34–65.

– 1966b. *Sémantique structurale.* Paris: Larousse.

– 1970. *Du sens.* Paris: Seuil.

– 1976. *Sémiotique et sciences sociales.* Paris: Seuil.

– 1981. 'Contre-note. Le Carré sémiotique.' *Le Bulletin du groupe de recherches sémio-linguistiques* 17: 42–6.

– 1983a. *Du sens II.* Paris: Seuil.

– 1983b. *Structural Semantics.* Introduction by R. Schleifer. Translated by D. McDowell, R. Schleifer, and A. Velie. Lincoln: University of Nebraska Press.

– 1986. 'En guise de préface.' *Actes sémiotiques – Documents* 9 (81): 3–4. *Documents de recherche*, Paris: Centre National de la Recherche Scientifique.

– 1987a. *A.J. Greimas. On Meaning: Selected Writings in Semiotic Theory.* Translated by P. Perron and F. Collins. Minneapolis: University of Minnesota Press.

– 1987b. *De l'imperfection.* Périgueux: Pierre Fanlac.

– 1988. *Maupassant: The Semiotics of Text.* Translated by P. Perron. Amsterdam and Philadelphia: John Benjamins.

– 1990. *The Social Sciences: A Semiotic View.* Translated by P. Perron and F. Collins. Minneapolis: University of Minnesota Press.

– 2000. *La Mode en 1830.* T. Broden, ed. Paris: Presses Universitaires de France.

Greimas, A.J., and J. Courtés. 1982. *Semiotics and Language: An Analytical*

Dictionary. Translated by D. Patte, L. Crist, et al. Bloomington: Indiana University Press.
– 1986. *Sémiotique: Dictionnaire raisonné de la théorie du language, II.* Paris: Hachette.

Greimas, A.J., and J. Fontanille. 1993. *The Semiotics of Passions.* Translated by P. Perron and F. Collins. Minneapolis: University of Minnesota Press.

Hakluyt, Richard. 1600. *The Third and Last Volume of the Voyages, Navigations, Traffiques and Discoveries of the English Nation.* London: G. Bishop.

Hammad, M. 1973. *Sémiotique de l'espace.* Paris: Groupe 107.
– 1977. 'L'Espace du séminaire.' *Communications* 27: 28–54.
– 1983. 'Énonciation: Procès et système.' In H. Parret, ed., *La Mise en discours. Langages* 70: 73–81.

Hayne, D. 1977. 'Les Origines du roman canadien-français.' In *Le Roman canadien-français,* 37–67. Montreal: Fides.
– 1993. 'L'Influence des auteurs français sur les récits.' In Lemire, ed., *Le Romantisme au Canada,* 43–56.

Heidenreich, C. 1971. *Huronia.* Toronto: McClelland and Stewart.

Hémon, L. 1980. *Maria Chapdelaine. Récit du Canada français.* Montreal: Boréal Express.

Iknayan, M. 1961. *The Idea of the Novel in France: The Critical Reaction, 1815–1848.* Geneva and Paris: Droz-Minard.

James, H. 1934. *The Art of the Novel.* New York: Scribner's.

Jameson, F. 1972. *The Prison House of Language.* Princeton: Princeton University Press.
– 1987. 'Foreword.' *A.J. Greimas: On Meaning – Selected Writings in Semiotic Theory,* vi–xxii.

Jauss, H.R. 1970. *Literaturgechichte als Provokation.* Frankfurt-am-Main: Suhrkamp.

Kristeva, J. 1969. *Recherches pour une sémanalyse.* Paris: Seuil.
– 1970. *Le Texte du roman.* The Hague and Paris: Mouton.
– 2001. *Hannah Arendt: Life Is a Narrative.* Toronto: University of Toronto Press.

Krysinski, W. 1981. *Carrefours de signes. Essais sur le roman moderne.* The Hague: Mouton de Gruyter.

Laberge, A. 1972. *La Scouine.* Montreal: L'Actuelle.

Lacombe, P. 1972. *La Terre paternelle.* Montreal: Hurtubise.

Laflèche, G. 1988, 1989. *Les Saints Martyrs canadiens.* 2 vols. Laval: Les Éditions Préambules.

Lagarde, P. 1980. *Le Verbe huron.* Paris: Éditions l'Harmattan.

Landowski, E. 1979. 'Introduction. Sémiotique des passions.' *Le Bulletin du groupe de recherches sémio-linguistiques* 9: 3–8.

Laurendeau, A. 1950. 'Une œuvre vitale.' *Le Devoir*, 7 October 1950: 4. Quoted in Deschamps, 1980: 215.
Le Huenen, R., and P. Perron. 1980. *Balzac. Sémiotique du personnage romanesque: L'Exemple d'Eugénie Grandet.'* Montreal and Paris: Les Presses de l'Université de Montréal, Didier Érudition.
– 1984a. 'Reflections on Balzacian Models of Representation.' *Poetics Today* 5 (4): 711–28.
– 1984b. 'Les *Lettres à Madame Hanska*: Metalangage du roman et représentation romanesque.' *Revue des sciences humaines* (1984) 3 (195): 25–40.
Le Jeune, Paul. 1634. *Relations de ce qui s'est passé en la Nouvelle France en l'année 1633*. Paris: S. Cramoisy.
Lemire, M. 1978. 1980. 1982. (Ed.). *Dictionnaire des œuvres littéraires du Québec*. 3 vols. Montreal: Fides.
– 1991. 1992. 1996. 1999. (Ed.). *La Vie littéraire au Québec*. 4 vols. Sainte-Foy: Les Presses de l'Université Laval.
– 1994. '*Les Anciens canadiens*, une tradition de lecture.' In Melançon, ed., *La Lecture et ses traditions*, 165–74.
– 1993. (Ed.). *Le Romantisme au Canada*. Quebec: Nuit Blanche Éditeur.
Lescarbot, Marc. 1609. *Histoire de la Nouvelle France*. Paris: A. Périer.
Lévi-Strauss, C. 1955. *Tristes tropiques*. Paris: Plon.
– 1963. 'Structure et dialectique.' In C. Lévi-Strauss, *Anthropologie structurale*, 257–66. Paris: Plon.
Lévy, A. 1979. *Sémiotique de l'espace. Architecture classique sacrée*. Paris: Plon.
Lidov, D. 1980. *Musical Structure and Musical Significance*. Working Paper, Victoria University. Toronto: Toronto Semiotic Circle.
– 2000. 'Music and Consciousness.' In Perron, Sbrocchi, Colilli, and Danesi, eds, *Semiotics as a Bridge between the Humanities and the Sciences*, 229–41.
Lotman, J.M. 1977. *The Structure of the Artistic Text*. Ann Arbor: Michigan Slavic Publications.
Lubbock, P. 1921. *The Craft of Fiction*. London: Cape.
Lyotard, J.-F. 1979. *La Condition post-moderne*. Paris: Seuil.
McHale, B., and R. Ronan. 1990. *Narratology Revisited I & II. Poetics Today* 11 (2, 4).
McKnight, E. 1978. *Meaning in Texts. The Historical Shaping of Narrative Hermeneutics*. Philadelphia: Fortress Press.
Martin, D. 1988. *Portraits des héros de la Nouvelle-France*. La Salle: Hurtubise.
Martinet, A. 1960. *Éléments de linguistique générale*. Paris: A. Collin
Melançon, J. 1994. (Ed.). *La Lecture et ses traditions*. Quebec: Nuit Blanche Éditeur.

Melançon, J., C. Moisan, and M. Roy. 1988. *Le Discours d'une didactique. La Formation littéraire dans l'enseignement classique au Québec*. Quebec: CRELIQ.

Mendilow, A.A. 1952. *Time and the Novel*. London: Routledge and Kegan Paul.

Metz, Ch. 1966. 'La Grande syntagmatique du film narratif.' In Barthes, ed., *L'Analyse structurale du récit*, 120–4.

– 1971. *Langage et cinéma*. Paris: Larousse.

– 1977. *Le Signifiant imaginaire*. Paris: Union Générale d'Éditions.

Morris, C. 1938. 'Foundations of the Theory of Signs.' In *Foundations of the Unity of Science* 1 (2): 1–14.

Mukarovsky, J. 1934. 'L'Art comme fait sémiologique.' In *Actes du Huitième Congrès International de Philosophie à Prague 1934*, 1065–72. Prague: Orbis.

– 1977. *The Word and Verbal Art*. New Haven: Yale University Press.

Nattiez, J.-J. 1976. *Fondements d'une sémiologie de la musique*. Paris: Union Générale d'Éditions.

– 1987. *Musicologie générale et sémiologie*. Paris: C. Bourgois.

– 1993. *Le Combat de Chronos et d'Orphée*. Paris: C. Bourgeois.

– 1999. *La Musique, la recherche et la vie: Un Dialogue et quelques dérives*. Montreal: Leméac.

Nef, F. 1976. 'Entretien avec A.J. Greimas.' In F. Nef, *Structures élémentaires de la signification*, 18–26. Brussels: Editions Complexe.

O'Neil-Karch, M. 1986. 'La Fonction des objets dans *La Scouine*.' In Cloutier-Wojciechowska and Robidoux, eds, *Solitude rompue*, 279–86.

Ouellet, R. 1996. 'Épistolarité et relations de voyage.' In Bérubé and Silver, eds, *La Lettre au XVIIIe siècle et ses avatars*, 179–99.

Panier, L. 1983. 'La Bombe dans le discours.' In L. Millot, ed., *Sur l'énonciation. Études littéraires* 16 (1): 55–77.

Paré, F. 1986. 'Identité et filiation dans *La Terre paternelle* de Patrice Lacombe.' In Cloutier-Wojciechowska and Robidoux, eds, *Solitude rompue*, 294–300.

Parret, H. 1989. 'Introduction.' In P. Perron and F. Collins, eds, *Paris School Semiotics I*, vii–xxvi.

Parret, H., and H.G. Ruprecht. 1985 (Eds). *Recueil d'hommages pour / Essays in Honor of Algirdas Julien Greimas*. Amsterdam and Philadelphia: John Benjamins.

Pascal, G. 1976. *Le Défi d'Albert Laberge*. Montreal: Éditions Aquila.

Paterson, J. 1994. *Postmodernism and the Quebec Novel*. Toronto: University of Toronto Press.

Patte, D. 1976. *Semiology and Parables*. Pittsburgh: Pickwick Press.

– 1978. *Pour une exégèse structurale*. Paris: Seuil.

– 1982. 'Greimas' Model for the Generative Trajectory of Meaning in Discourses.' *American Journal of Semiotics* 1: 59–78.

- 1987. *The Gospel according to Matthew*. Philadelphia: Fortress Press.
- 1990. *The Religious Dimensions of Biblical Texts: Greimas' Structural Semiotics and Biblical Exegesis*. Atlanta: Scholars' Press.

Pecheux, M. 1975. *Les vérités de La Palice. Linguistique, sémantique, philosophie*. Paris: F. Maspero.

Perron, P. 1985a. 'Jean de Brébeuf et le regard émouvant.' *Recherches sémiotiques / Semiotic Inquiry* 5 (2): 145–57.
- 1985b. 'Le Capitaine du jour: Les *Relations* (1635–36) de Jean de Brébeuf chez les Hurons.' *Fabula* 5: 75–93.
- 1986. 'Narratology.' In Sebeok, ed., *Encyclopedic Dictionary of Semiotics*, 596–601.
- 1987. 'Introduction.' *A.J. Greimas: On Meaning*, xxiv–xlv.
- 1989a. (Ed.). 'Introduction.' *Greimassian Semiotics: New Literary History* 20 (3): 523–38.
- 1989b. 'Toward a Semiotics of Manipulation: Jesuit–Huron Relations in XVIIth Century New France.' *Semiotica* 76 (3/4): 147–70.
- 1994. 'Narratology.' In Sebeok, ed., *Encyclopedic Dictionary of Semiotics*. Supplement to Tome 2, 26–9.
- 1996. *Semiotics and the Modern Quebec Novel*. Toronto: University of Toronto Press.
- 1997. 'Pour une typologie du roman de la terre: L'exemple de *Maria Chapdelaine*.' In P. Bhatt, ed., *Hommage à Henry Schogt*, 159–67. Toronto: Scholars' Press.
- 1999a. 'Creating Memory: The Martyrdom of Isaac Jogues in the *Jesuit Relations* of 1642–47.' *Texte* 25/26: 211–42.
- 1999b. 'Terra Incognita: Áltro'e álterità'nei *Voyages* verso la Nuova francia di Jacques Cartier.' In *Eloquio del senso. Dialoghi semiotici per Paolo Fabbri*, 337–51. Ancon-Milan: Costa and Nolan.

Perron, P., and F. Collins. 1989a. (Eds). *Paris School Semiotics I: Theory*. Amsterdam and Philadelphia: John Benjamins.
- 1989b. (Eds). *Paris School Semiotics II: Practice*. Amsterdam and Philadelphia: John Benjamins.

Perron, P., and M. Danesi. 1993. *A.J. Greimas and Narrative Cognition*. Toronto: Toronto Semiotic Circle.

Perron, P., and P. Fabbri. 1990. 'Foreword.' *A.J. Greimas: The Social Sciences – A Semiotic View*, vi–xii. Minneapolis: University of Minnesota Press.
- 1993. 'Foreword.' *A.J. Greimas and J. Fontanille: The Semiotics of Passions*, vii–xvi. Minneapolis: University of Minnesota Press.

Perron, P., L. Sbrocchi, P. Colilli, and M. Danesi. 2000. (Eds). *Semiotics as a Bridge between the Humanities and the Sciences*. New York: Legas.

Perron, P., and G. Thérien. 1990. 'Ethno-historical Discourse: Jean de Brébeuf's *Jesuit Relation* of 1636.' *The American Journal of Semiotics* 7 (1–2): 53–67.
Petitot-Cocorda, J. 1982. 'Introduction. Aspects de la conversion.' *Actes sémiotiques: Le Bulletin du groupe de recherches sémio-linguistiques* 24: 5–7.
– 1985. *Morphogenèse du sens I*. Paris: Presses Universitaires de France.
Pinto, J.C.M. 1989. *The Reading of Time. A Semantico-Semiotic Approach*. New York: Mouton de Gruyter.
Plamondon, A. 1844. *Prospectus, Le Ménestrel* 1 (1), 20 June.
Poetics Today. 1980, 1981. *Narratology I, II, III*. 1 (3); 1 (4); 2 (2).
– 1990, 1991. *Narratology Revisited I, II, III*. 11 (2); 11 (4); 12 (3).
Pouliot, P. 1966. 'Le Jeune, Paul.' *Dictionnaire biographique du Canada*, 464–8. Quebec: Les Presses de l'Université Laval.
Prince, G. 1973. 'Introduction à l'étude du narrataire.' *Poétique* 14: 178–96.
– 1982. *Narratology*. The Hague: Mouton.
– 1987. *Dictionary of Narratology*. Lincoln: University of Nebraska Press.
Propp, V. 1928. *Morfologija Skazki*. Leningrad: Academia. English translation: L. Scott. 1958. Bloomington: Publications of the Indiana University Research Centre in Anthropology, Folklore and Linguistics, 10.
Proulx, B. 1987. *Le Roman du territoire*. Montréal: Université du Québec à Montréal.
Purdy, A. 1990. *A Certain Difficulty of Being*. Montreal and Kingston: McGill-Queen's University Press.
Ramusio, Giovanni Battista. 1556. *Terzo volume delle navigationi et viaggi nel quale si contengono le navigationi al Mondo Nuouo*. Venice.
Rastier, F. 1972. *Idéologie et théorie des signes*. The Hague: Mouton.
Relations des Jésuites 1632–73. 1858. Quebec: Augustin Côte.
Ricœur, P. 1980. *La Narrativité*. Paris: Centre National de la Recherche Scientifique.
– 1984. 1985. 1988. *Time and Narrative I, II, III*. Chicago: University of Chicago Press.
– 1989. 'Greimas's Narrative Grammar.' In Perron and Collins, eds, *Paris School Semiotics I*, 3–31.
Rigault, C., and R. Ouellet. 1978. '*Relations* des Jésuites.' In Lemire, ed., *Dictionnaire des œuvres littéraires du Québec I*, 637–49.
Rimmon-Kenan, S. 1983. *Narrative Fiction*. London: Methuen.
Robidoux, R., and A. Renaud. 1966. *Le Roman canadien-français du vingtième siècle*. Ottawa: Éditions de l'Université d'Ottawa.
Rocher, G. 1969. *Introduction à la sociologie générale*. Montreal: Hurtubise.
Rousseau, Guildo. 1970. *Préfaces des romans québécois du XIXe siècle*. Sherbrooke: Éditions Cosmos.

Roy, G. 1945. *Bonheur d'occasion*. Montreal: Beauchemin. Translated by Hannah Josephson as *The Tin Flute*. Toronto: McClelland and Stewart, 1947.
Ruprecht, H.G. 1984. 'Ouvertures meta-sémiotiques. Entretien avec A.J. Greimas.' *Recherches sémiotiques / Semiotic Inquiry* 4: 1–23.
Ruwet, N. 1972. *Langage, musique, poésie*. Paris: Seuil.
Sagard, Gabriel. 1632. *Le Grand Voyage du pays des Hurons*. Paris: D. Moreau.
– 1636. *Histoire du Canada et voyages que les frères mineurs Récollets ont fait pour la conversion des infidèles*. Paris: M. Sonnius.
Sartre, J.-P. 1964. *Nausea*. London: New Directions.
– 1939. 'La Temporalité chez Faulkner.' *Situations I*, 71–81. Paris: Gallimard.
Saussure, F. de. 1966. *Course in General Linguistics*. New York: McGraw-Hill.
Schleifer, R. 1983. 'Introduction.' *Structural Semantics* by A.J. Greimas, xi–lvi. Lincoln: University of Nebraska Press.
Scholes, R. 1982. *Semiotics and Interpretation*. New Haven: Yale University Press.
Sebeok, T. 1986. (Ed.). *Encyclopedic Dictionary of Semiotics*. Amsterdam: Mouton de Gruyter.
– 1994. (Ed.). *Encyclopedic Dictionary of Semiotics*. Supplement to Tome 2. Amsterdam: Mouton de Gruyter.
Segre, C. 1979. *Structure and Time: Narration, Poetry, Models*. Chicago: University of Chicago Press.
Senécal, A. 1993. 'Ce genre fantastique et sombre.' In Lemire, ed., *Le Romantisme au Canada*, 219–30.
Servais-Maquoi, M. 1974. *Le Roman de la terre au Québec*. Quebec: Presses de l'Université Laval.
Sheriff, J. 1989. *The Fate of Meaning. Charles Saunders Peirce, Structuralism and Literature*. Princeton: Princeton University Press.
Shklovsky, V. 1929. *O Teorii Prozy*. Moscow: Nauka.
Silverman, K. 1983. *The Subject of Semiotics*. New York: Oxford University Press.
– 1984. '*Histoire d'O*: The Construction of a Female Subject.' In C.S. Vance, ed., *Pleasure and Danger: Exploring Female Sexuality*. London: Routledge and Kegan Paul.
– 1988. *The Acoustic Mirror*. Bloomington: Indiana University Press.
Simon, S. 1991. *Fictions de l'identitaire au Québec*. Montreal: XYZ.
Sirois, A. 1982. '*Bonheur d'occasion*'. In Lemire, ed., *Dictionnaire des œuvres littéraires du Québec III*, 127–36.
Smart, P. 1991. *Writing in the Father's House*. Toronto: University of Toronto Press.
Tarasti, E. 1996. *Sémiotique musicale*. Limoges: Presses Universitaires de Limoges.

Thériault, Y. 1961. *Agaguk*. Montreal: Éditions de l'Homme. Translation: Miriam Chapin. Toronto: McGraw-Hill Ryerson, 1963.

Thérien, G. 1987. *L'Indien imaginaire*. Special issue of *Recherches amérindiens au Québec* 17 (3).

– 1995. *Figures de l'Indien*. (Ed.). Montreal: L'Hexagone.

Thevet, André. 1575. *La Singularité de la France antarctique*. Paris: M. de la Porte.

Thivierge, M. 1950. 'Le Roman d'un roman.' *Le Devoir*, 28 December 1950: 4. Quoted in Deschamps, 1980: 215.

Thürlemann, F. 1979. *Trois peintures de Paul Klee. Essai d'analyse sémiotique*. Paris: Klinckseick.

– 1981. 'La Double Spatialité en peinture. Espace simulé et topologie planaire.' *Le Bulletin du Groupe de recherches sémiolinguistiques* 20: 34–46.

Todorov, T. 1965. (Ed.). *Théorie de la littérature*. Paris: Seuil.

– 1969. *Grammaire du Décaméron*. The Hague and Paris: Mouton.

Trigger, B. 1976. *The Children of Aataentsic*. Vols. 1 and 2. Montreal: McGill-Queen's University Press.

Tynianov, J., and R. Jackobson. 1965. 'Les Problèmes des études littéraires et linguistiques.' In Todorov, ed., *Théorie de la littérature*, 138–40.

van Dijk, T.A. 1972. *Some Aspects of Text Grammars*. The Hague: Mouton.

Vuong-Riddick, T. 1977. 'Une Relecture de *La Scouine*.' *Voix et images* 3 (1): 116–26.

Warwick, J. 1978. 'Le Grand Voyage au pays des Hurons.' In Lemire, ed., *Dictionnaire des œuvres littéraires du Québec*, I, 296–9.

White, H. 1980a. 'The Value of Narrativity in the Representation of Reality.' *Critical Inquiry* 7 (1): 5–27.

– 1980b. 'Direct and Third Person Discourse in the Narrative of the *Fall*.' *Semeia* 18: 91–106.

Index

actant (agent), x, 7–8, 21–3, 25–6, 28, 30–3, 37, 43, 50, 66, 70, 72–3, 76, 95, 105–6, 113, 115, 142, 144, 152–3, 176, 182–4, 187, 197–9, 201, 203, 227, 234–5, 246, 248, 277n5, 283n26, 305n13, 306n17
actantial model, 7, 21–31, 35–7, 184
actantial role, 7, 30–1, 36, 47–8, 71, 183–4, 213
actor, xv, 30–3, 36, 43, 45–6, 66–7, 70–1, 73–4, 94, 114–16, 154–6, 159, 173, 182–3, 200–2, 219–25, 267n8, 268n11
actorialization, 25, 32, 36, 71–2, 74, 90
addressee. *See* enunciatee, narratee
addresser. *See* enunciator, narrator
Agaguk (Thériault), xv–xvi, 13, 230–53, 256–7
Alexandre, Annie, 307–8n27
alienation, 166, 216, 228, 230, 235
Anciens Canadiens, Les (Aubert de Gaspé), xiii, 131, 137–50, 152, 164, 255, 288nn5, 12, 289nn13, 14, 16, 17, 290n20, 291nn23, 24
Angers, François-Réal, 287–8n3
Anglo-American criticism, 5–6, 10

anti-subject (opponent), 7, 21, 28, 37, 79, 97–8, 115–16, 131, 200–3, 255
Arens, W., 277n4
Arguin, Maurice, 257
Aristotle, vii, x–xi, 24
Arrivé, Michel, 260n2
aspectualities, 12, 37–8, 175
Asselin, Olivar, 301–2n10
Aubert de Gaspé, Philippe: *Les Anciens Canadiens*, xiii, 137–50, 152, 164, 255, 288nn3, 12, 289nn13, 14, 16, 17, 290n20, 291n26
Aubert de Gaspé, Philippe, *fils*: *L'Influence d'un livre*, 132, 287n3
Augustine, St, x–xi
Authier-Revuz, J., 268–9n14

Bakhtin, Mikhail, 75, 268n13
Bal, Mieke, 8, 14
Barrès, Maurice, 294n2
Barry, Jackson, 13
Barthes, Roland, vii–ix, 3, 6–7, 12–13, 19, 50, 64, 196, 198, 284n33, 289n15, 305–6n14
being-able, 28–9, 31, 33–5, 37, 43, 66, 115, 142, 160, 162, 176, 179–82, 187,

200, 217, 233, 235–7, 244, 246–8, 250, 283n25, 298n10, 300n17
Belleforest, François de, 261n4
Benveniste, Émile, ix–x, 6, 17, 260(ch.1)n2, 276–7n3
Bessette, Gérard, 192, 259n4, 301n3, 301–2n10
Besterman, Theodore, 58–9, 83
body: in action, 116, 121; burial of, 93, 163, 206; eroticized, xv, 175, 178, 211–13, 236–41, 243–4, 248, 251, 256; in motion, 14, 50–1, 219–21, 229; mutilated, xii, 101–2, 104–12, 116–22, 126, 131, 231, 243–4, 275–6n1, 278–81nn11–13, 284–6nn35–40; narrating and reading the, xii, 101–27; perceiving, thinking, and feeling, xi, 17, 243–4
Bonheur d'occasion (Roy), xiv–xv, 136, 208–29, 245, 256, 308nn1, 3, 309–11nn5–15
Booth, Wayne, 5–6
Bourbonnais, N., 309n7
Bourget, Paul, 294n2
Brébeuf, Jean de, 57–76, 79–102, 107, 266–7n8, 268n10, 269n15, 273–4nn11, 14, 17, 275nn17–19, 276n1, 279–80n12, 282n21, 292n7, 308–9n4
Bremond, Claude, viii, ix, 8–9, 13, 194, 196
Bressani, François, 101-2, 110
Broden, Thomas, 11, 13–14, 18
Brulé, Étienne, 59, 79, 86, 273n11, 292n7, 308n4
Brunet, Jacques, 194, 302n10
Buteux, Jacques, 104–6, 114, 116, 282n20

Caën, Émery de, 58
Caën, Guillaume de, 58
Canadians of Old, The. See *Anciens Canadiens, Les*
Cartier, Jacques: *Voyages*, xii, 41–56, 57, 131, 261nn1–4, 263n13, 264n18
Cassegrain, Henri-Raymond, 135
Chabanel, Noel, 276n1, 280n12
Champlain, Samuel de, 42, 53, 58–61, 79, 100–1, 308n4
Charlet, Étienne, 112
Charlevoix, Pierre-François-Xavier de, 42
Chatman, Seymour, 10, 13
Chauveau, Pierre-Joseph-Olivier, 288n3
Cherrier, G.H., 132
Chevalier, Henri-Émile, 288n3, 311n3
city, invested space of, xiv–xv, 136, 143, 145, 153, 156, 158–65, 168–9, 174, 178–81, 183–8, 191, 208–9, 219–26, 230–2, 256, 295–6n6, 298–9nn11–15, 300–1n17, 308n3, 310–11n14
Collet, Paulette, 311n3
colonization, xii, 42–3, 57–76, 77–102, 103–26, 131, 143, 148–9, 153, 166–91, 208, 255, 277n4
comparative parataxe, 46–7, 262n10
competence, 9, 28, 30–7, 43–4, 70, 72, 78–9, 85, 86, 88–91, 114–15, 142, 176, 200–3, 265n7, 283n25, 284n28, 300n17
Conquest, the, xii, 127, 136, 138, 139, 140, 143, 146, 148–9, 154, 164, 255–6, 290n22
conversion and narrative, 20, 25–30, 35–6

conversion, religious, xii, 42, 44–5, 49, 54–5, 57–76, 78–9, 81–90, 94–102, 107, 109, 111–12, 117, 121, 131, 255, 266–7n8, 269n15, 270–2nn3–6, 273n13, 274–5nn17–18, 277n5, 283n26, 308n4; narrative of, 65–70, 131, 255
Cook, Ramsay, 42, 44, 261n1
Coquet, Jean-Claude, 18, 34, 260(ch.2)n1
Coste, Didier, 13
Courtés, Joseph, 3, 10, 24–7, 29–33, 36, 70, 260n4, 267–8n9
Crémazie, Octave, 135
Cressolles, Lois de, 68
Culler, Jonathan, 13

Danesi, Marcel, 15
Daniel, Antoine, 59, 276n1, 280n12
Davost, Ambroise, 60
de Certeau, Michel, 220
De Lauretis, Teresa, 14
deixes, ix, 47–8, 55, 71–5, 87, 117, 123, 173–4, 187, 190, 245, 262–3n12, 277n6, 289n12, 300–1n17
Deschamps, Nicole, 166
discourse: abstract, 32; and actantial theory, 21, 30–1, 70–4, 78, 97; direct, 72, 109; ethnohistorical, xii, 57–76, 77–102, 103–26, 255, 265n4; figurative, 3, 22, 31–2, 34, 93, 115–16, 183; historical, ix–x, 9, 117, 119, 167, 284nn29, 33; indirect, 72, 74, 104; literary, 4; and narrative, 3, 7, 10, 15, 23–5, 30–2, 34, 38, 55, 70–1, 78, 85, 194, 198; and otherness, xii, 72, 75, 78–102; pragmatic, 17; and rhetoric, 89–4; structures of, 20, 25, 30–1, 88; syntax of, 25, 32, 37;

third-person, ix; written, as speech act, viii
Doležel, Lubomir, 5
Dorion, Gilles, 192, 195, 302–3n10
d'Orsonnens, Jean-Éraste, 288n3
Doutre, Joseph, 135, 153
Drummond, D., 309n7
Ducrot, Oswald, 3
Dumézil, Georges, 19–20
Dumont, Fernand, 259n3, 294n4
Duplessis, Maurice, xiii, xvi, 251, 257
Duquette, Jean-Pierre, 152–3
durative, 8, 119, 123, 156–7, 171, 173–5, 219, 221–2, 225, 286n41
Durham Report, 136

Eagleton, Terry, 13
Eco, Umberto, viii, 9
Ejxenbaum, Boris, 4
enunciatee, x–xi, 17, 42–50, 53, 55, 71–2, 114–15, 245, 283n25. *See also* narratee
enunciator, x, 42–50, 54–5, 66–7, 70–2, 114–16, 139–40, 225, 245, 265n7, 278n8, 283n25. *See also* narrator
epistemic act, 33–4
equivalencies, 25–8, 34

Fabbri, Paolo, xvi
family, xiii–xvi, 93, 105, 132, 140–3, 145–8, 152–3, 155–65, 166, 168–73, 176–9, 182–4, 186–91, 195–6, 199–200, 203–5, 207–8, 213, 215–16, 218–19, 221, 226, 228–9, 230–53, 256, 293n13
farm, invested space of, 152–65, 168–70, 180–2, 185, 187, 191, 195, 202–4, 219, 308n3

Fisette, Jean, 16–17
focalization, 5, 10, 42, 52–3, 104, 108, 113–16, 169, 189–90, 210–11, 219–25, 244–5, 276n2, 277–8n6
Fontanier, Pierre, 284n30
Fontanille, Jacques, 12
Forbin, Victor, 311n3
Forster, Edward Morgan, vii, 5
Foucault, Michel, vii
Friedman, Norman, 5
frontier, invested space of, xv, 153, 169, 174, 177, 183–4, 186–8, 191, 208, 219, 230, 298–301nn11–17, 308n3
Frye, Northrop, 5

Gagnon, François-Marc, 275n18
Garneau, François-Xavier, 42, 127, 136, 150–1
Garnier, Charles, 276n1, 280n12
Garvin, Paul, 5
Gaudreault, André, 10
Geertz, Clifford, 43
generative trajectory, 24–5
Genette, Gérard, viii–x, 8, 14, 278n10, 286n41, 292n5, 306–7n19
Gérin-Lajoie, Antoine, 288n3
Gervais, Bertrand, 15
gesture: and narrative, 3; and otherness, xii, 51–4, 87, 89, 97, 117, 119, 121, 239–40; and ritual, 53, 87, 97, 117, 157, 219, 225; semiotics of, 21–2, 50–4, 95, 97–8, 212
Girard, Rodolph, 311(Conclusion)n1
gnomic, 47, 139, 245, 262–3n12, 276–7n3, 292n6, 297n9
Gomez-Géraud, Marie-Christine, 53, 264n19
Goodman, Nelson, 10–11

Goupil, René, 103, 107, 120, 275n1, 279n12, 282n20
grammar: aspectual, 32, 38; deep, 25–6, 28; fundamental, 12, 27, 30; of Huron language, 82–8; modal, 32, 34–5, 38; narrative, 9–10, 13, 22–30, 32, 38; surface, 25–7, 29; text, 7–8, 10; transformational, 8; universal, 7
Greimas, Algirdas Julien, vii–ix, xii, xvi, 3, 9–13, 15, 18–38, 70, 260nn3, 4, 267–8n9, 274n15, 298n10
Groulx, Lionel, 167, 191, 293–4n2, 301n17
group, xiii–xvi, xvii, 4, 49, 132, 138, 142–3, 147–50, 152–65, 167, 170, 173, 176–82, 186–8, 192, 203–4, 208, 210, 215, 217–19, 223, 227–8, 233, 235–6, 243–9, 251–2, 255–8, 293n13, 300n17, 307n22
Guèvremont, Germaine: *Marie-Didace*, 152–3, 156

Hamel, Charles, 135
Hammad, Manar, 12
having-to, 28, 31, 33–5, 43–4, 66, 114–15, 142–3, 160, 162, 176, 181–4, 187, 215–16, 233, 235–7, 244, 247–50, 283n25, 298n10, 300n17
Hayne, David, xvi, 132, 135, 288n10
Heidenreich, Conrad, 270n3
Hémon, Louis: *Maria Chapdelaine*, xiii, 152–3, 156, 166–91, 195, 201, 208, 255, 293–301nn1–17, 303–5n13, 307n19
heterogeneity, xii, xv, 4, 62, 65, 154–5, 158, 160–5, 174–6, 178–9, 184, 187–8, 191, 219, 225, 253, 255–7, 300n17, 308n3

Hjelmslev, Louis, 9, 11, 13, 17, 19–21, 24
homogeneity, xii, xiv, 142, 145, 152, 154–9, 161–5, 174–6, 178–9, 184, 187–8, 191, 219, 253, 300n17, 308n3
Huret, Grégoire, 279n12

identity, xv, xvii, 26, 153–4, 186, 191, 218–19, 252, 255; dual, 146–50; group, xiii, 127, 131–2, 136, 146, 155, 164–5, 188, 208, 228, 252–3, 255–8, 291n24; individual, xiii, 162, 188, 208–9, 230, 232, 246, 248, 252–3, 255–6, 292n9. See also subject: collective; subject: individual
Iknayan, Marguerite, 288n9
industrialization, xiv–xv, 136, 165, 167–9, 174, 178–81, 185–8, 191, 208–29, 230, 234, 256, 291n2, 295–6n6, 310–11n14
intersubjectivity, viii–ix, xvi, 21, 30, 37, 47–9, 51, 114–15, 121, 141–3, 154, 174–5, 183, 233–5, 237–43, 249–52, 255–6, 277n6
isotopy, 9, 21, 34, 73, 124–5, 184–5, 261n9, 268n12
iterative, 119, 123–4, 157–8, 173–6, 219, 225, 230, 300n17, 307n19

Jakobson, Roman, 4–6, 10, 19, 24
James, Henry, vii, 5, 13
Jameson, Fredric, 21
Jauss, Hans Robert, 5
Jesuit Relations, xii, 57–76, 77–102, 103–26, 131, 265–7nn7–8, 268n10, 269n15, 269–72nn1–9, 273–4nn14–15, 274–5nn17, 19, 276n2, 277n6, 278–81nn7–16, 282nn18, 19, 283n24, 284–6nn35–40, 287n47, 308–9n4
Jogues, Isaac, 103–26, 189, 275–6n1, 278–81nn7–15, 282nn18–21, 284–6nn34–41, 287nn42, 45
Jost, François, 10

Kirke, Sir David, 59
Kirke, Sir Lewis, 59
knowing, 28–31, 33, 35, 42, 44, 66, 114–15, 142, 159–62, 176–83, 186–7, 200, 202, 211–18, 233–7, 244, 246–8, 250, 283n25, 300n17
Kristeva, Julia, vii–viii, 3, 12
Krysinski, Wladimir, 13

Laberge, Albert: *La Scouine*, xiii–xv, 192–207, 208, 245, 301n1, 301–8nn10–27
Lacan, Jacques, vii, 19
Lacombe, Patrice: *La Terre paternelle*, xiii, 152–65, 195, 201, 208, 255, 290n22, 292nn3, 9, 293nn11–13, 297–8n9, 307n19
Laflèche, Guy, 282n20
Lagarde, Pierrette, 269n1, 270n3, 272n8
La Lande, Jean de, 112
Lalemant, Charles, 58
Lalemant, Gabriel, 276n1, 279–80n12
Lalemant, Jérôme, 77–8, 106–16, 120, 122–6, 271–2n6, 281n17, 282n19, 286n41, 287nn42, 43
Landowski, Eric, 35–6
Laurendeau, André, 167
Laurier, Wilfrid, 191, 299n16
Le Caron, Joseph, 58
Le Huenen, Roland, 13, 68, 264n2, 266n7, 277n3, 288n8

Le Jeune, Paul, 42, 57, 60, 62, 103–4, 265–6n7, 269–70n2, 272n9
Lemelin, Roger, 136
Lemercier, François-Joseph, 270–1n4
Lemire, Maurice, 289n17
Lescarbot, Marc, 42, 53
Léveillé, Lionel, 192, 207, 301n1
Lévi-Strauss, Claude, 6, 10, 19–20, 22–3, 32, 37
Lévy, A., 12
Lidov, David, 10
L'Influence d'un livre (Aubert de Gaspé, *fils*), 132, 287n3
linguistics: applied, 85; Saussurian, vii; structural, ix, xi, 5–6, 19–20, 260n6
Lotman, Juri, 5
Lubbock, Percy, 5
Lyotard, Jean-François, 198

McHale, Brian, 14
McKnight, Edgar, 9–10
mandate sequence, 37, 43–6
Maria Chapdelaine (Hémon), xiii, 152–3, 156, 166–91, 195, 201, 208, 255, 294–301nn1–17, 303–5n13, 307n19
Marie-Didace (Guèvremont), 152–3, 156
Martin, Denis, 127, 287n48
Martinet, André, 260–1n6
martyrdom, 101–2, 103, 108–27, 131, 275–6n1, 278–81nn11–15, 282nn18, 19, 21, 22, 284–6nn34–40, 287n42
Masse, Enemonde, 58, 110-11
Mauss, Marcel, 37
Melançon, Joseph, 288n11
Mendilow, Adam Abraham, 5
Merleau-Ponty, Maurice, xi, 12, 19
Metz, Christian, viii, 10

mise en abyme, 65–76, 144–5, 174, 287n44
modality, 13, 28–9, 31–8, 43–4, 66, 114–15, 142–3, 160, 162, 176, 184, 187, 201, 210, 233, 235–6, 283n25
Morris, Charles, 15–16
Mukarovsky, Jan, 5

naming, act of, 47–8, 65–8, 78, 94, 98, 131, 148, 161, 171–2, 194–5, 199, 201, 204, 212, 220, 231, 263n14, 271n5, 291n24, 292n3, 307nn22, 23
narratee, ix, 7, 9, 12, 47, 53, 70, 72, 74, 103, 106, 108, 121, 265n7, 276–7n3. *See also* enunciatee
narrative: actional dimensions of, xi, 16, 116, 170–1, 183, 198; apparent level of, 11; cognitive dimensions of, xi, 16, 34, 37, 47, 50, 73, 139, 170–1, 183; of conversion, 65–70, 131, 255; definition of, 3, 29; embedded, 65, 104, 107, 112–14; ethnohistorical, xii, 57–76, 77–102, 103–26, 255; exploration (discovery), xii, 41–56, 131, 255, 261n4, 262n10, 263nn13, 14; first-person, ix, 5, 55, 70, 112; grammar of, 9–10, 13, 22–30, 32, 38; historical, ix–x, 9, 15, 264n4, 276–7n3; immanent level of, 11; of martyrdom, 103, 108–27, 131, 278–81nn7–13, 282nn19, 20, 284–6nn35–40, 287n43; passional dimensions of, xi, 12, 16, 35–6, 38, 47, 170–1, 175, 183; social function of, 15–16; and spatiality, ix, 25, 32, 47, 49, 66, 68, 71, 74, 90, 102, 143–6, 219–20, 224–5, 245, 267–8n9; and temporality, vii–xi, 3, 5, 8, 15–16, 25, 32, 34, 47, 60, 62–6, 68, 71–2, 74, 90,

102–3, 106, 116–17, 119, 123, 138, 143–6, 155–8, 171–7, 190, 219, 221–2, 225–6, 245, 267–8n9, 276–7n3, 278n8, 284n29, 292n6, 305–6n14, 306–7n19; third-person, ix, 43; verbal, 104, 107, 112–14
narratology: and Anglo-American critics, 5–6; definition of, 3; and feminist criticism, 14; and French narrative semiotics, 6–9; Greimassian, viii–ix, 11–12, 15, 18–38; history of, vii–viii, 3–17; and non-literary texts, 9–12; poststructuralist, 14; questioning of, 12–14, 16–17; recent contributions in, 13–17; and reception theory, 14–15
narrator, ix, 7–9, 12, 14, 16, 43, 46–7, 53, 67, 70–3, 78, 85, 87, 89, 90, 92, 94–5, 103–6, 108–9, 112–13, 119–21, 123, 126, 137, 139–40, 144–8, 157–8, 160, 162, 171–3, 176, 190, 219–20, 222–3, 225, 243, 245, 265n7, 266n8, 276–7n3, 277–8n6, 282n20, 284n33, 287n44, 292n6, 297n9. *See also* enunciator
nation, French-Canadian, xiv, xvi–xvii, 127, 131–2, 137, 146–50, 152–3, 155–6, 162–5, 166, 176, 182–3, 188, 192, 200, 208, 219, 227–8, 230, 252, 255, 257–8, 288–9n12, 290n22, 292n3, 293n13, 308n4
nation, Huron, 63, 65–6, 77–102, 107, 122, 263n13, 266n8, 274–5n17, 276n1, 286n41
nationalism, 133–6, 142, 154, 164–5, 166–91, 208, 228, 251, 258, 301n17
Native people, 41–2, 44–6, 48–55, 57–76, 136, 145–6, 158, 160–1, 167, 185, 230, 290n21; Algonquin, 60, 104–8; Huron, xii, 58–76, 77–102, 103–4, 106–11, 113, 117, 119, 121–2, 131, 266–7n8, 269–70nn2, 3, 271n5, 272n10, 273–4nn11–14, 274–5n17, 279–81nn12, 13, 283n26, 308–9n4; Inuit, xv, 230–53; Iroquois, xii, 100–2, 103–27, 131, 143, 275–6n1, 277n5, 279–81nn12, 13, 282n18, 283n26, 284–6nn35–40; Micmac, 51, 55; Montagnais, 58–9
Nattiez, Jean-Jacques, 10
Nef, Frédéric, 27
New Criticism, 5, 13
Noüe, Anne de, 110-11, 280n12
novel, French-Canadian: aesthetics (poetics) of, 137–40, 153; agrarian, 152–65, 192–207, 208, 219, 252–3, 289n19; ambiguous status of, 132–4; of colonization, 153, 166–91, 208, 219, 253; historical, 132, 136–50, 152–4, 164, 208, 219, 252–3; legitimization of, 134–5; origins of, 136–7; realist, 192–207; urban, 208–2, 230, 252, 256; wilderness, 230–53

O'Neill-Karch, Mariel, 193
object: mythical, 76, 93, 178, 181, 202, 233, 235, 242–3, 249, 251; practical, 233–4, 242; of value, 28–31, 35, 66–7, 75, 141, 182–3, 199–202, 210, 232–5, 242–3, 265n5
other, xii, xvi, 14, 37, 41, 43, 48–55, 62–76, 78–102, 104–27, 131, 141, 165, 175, 178, 197–8, 201–3, 209–11, 216, 225, 236, 238–40, 242–4, 249–52, 255, 283n24
otherness, xii, 43, 71, 97, 225, 255, 290n21
Ouellet, Réal, 60, 262n9

Panneton, Philippe (Ringuet), 308n2
Paré, François, 292n9
Parent, Étienne, 132–3, 135
Paris School, viii–x, 6, 11–12, 17
Parret, Herman, 9, 11, 18, 35
Pascal, Gabrielle, 302n10
passion, viii, xi, xv, 12–13, 23, 34–8, 47, 94, 114, 127, 137, 142, 154–5, 168–9, 174–5, 178, 183–5, 187, 189–91, 208, 210–12, 225, 233, 235–44, 248–51, 256
Paternal Farm, The. See Terre paternelle, La
Paterson, Janet, 312n2
Patte, Daniel, 10–11
Pecheux, Michel, 268–9n14
Peirce, Charles Saunders, 9, 12, 13, 16–17
Perron, Paul, 9, 11, 13, 15, 68, 262n8, 263n16, 264n2, 266n7, 268n10, 274n16, 277nn3, 4, 283n24, 288n8
Petitot-Cocorda, Jean, 23–5, 27–8
phenomenology, vii, xi, 12, 15, 17, 27
Pinto, Julio, 16
Plamondon, Aurèle, 134–5
poles. *See* deixes
Pouliot, P., 58
Prague School, viii, 3–6, 11
presupposed, xii, 7, 24, 28, 33, 43–4, 47–9, 51, 53–6, 66–7, 73, 80–1, 86, 96, 113–15, 131, 182, 186, 198, 227, 246–7, 255, 263n13, 268n9, 277n4, 283n24
Prince, Gerald, 7, 13
Propp, Vladimir, 4, 7–8, 22–3, 26, 32–3, 37
Proulx, Bernard, 152
Purdy, Anthony, 310n12, 312n2

Quiet Revolution, xiii, xvi, 167, 251, 257

Ramusio, Giovanni Battista, 261n4
Rastier, François, 9, 22
receiver, 21, 28, 30, 37, 44–6, 49, 66–7, 70, 78, 115, 176, 200–1, 238, 283n27
reception, vii, ix–xi, 5, 14–17, 68
Recollet order, 58–9, 79, 270n3
Renaud, André, 135–6
repetition, 97, 122, 157, 174, 225
Ricoeur, Paul, x–xi, 15–17, 27–8, 43, 264–5n4, 284n29
Rigault, Claude, 60
Rimmon-Kenan, Shlomith, 13
Ringuet: *Trente arpents*, 152–3, 156, 208, 308n2. *See* Panneton, Philippe
Robidoux, Réjean, 135–6
Rocher, Guy, 127
Ronan, Ruth, 14
Roy, Camille, 192, 301n3
Roy, Gabrielle: *Bonheur d'occasion*, xiv–xv, 136, 208–29, 245, 256, 308n1, 309–11nn5–15
Ruprecht, Hans George, 18, 26, 35
Russian formalism, viii, 3–6, 11

Sagard, Gabriel, 42, 53, 58–61, 79–81, 262n10, 264n20, 269n2
Sartre, Jean-Paul, vii–viii, xi, 259(Preface)n1, 281n17
Saussure, Ferdinand de, vii, xi, xvii, 9, 11, 13, 16–19, 35, 259–60n1
Schleifer, Ronald, 11, 18, 21
Schogt, Henry, xvi
Scholes, Robert, 13
Scouine, La (Laberge), xiii–xv, 192–207, 208, 245, 301–8nn1–27
Segre, Cesare, 8
semantic axes, 7, 21
semantic universe, xi, 11–12, 17, 21, 23–4, 48, 83–92, 102, 122, 139, 162, 196, 283n26
semantics, 5, 13, 16, 19, 27, 29, 86–7;

discursive, 25; fundamental, 24–5, 86–7, 90; narrative, 25, 37; structural, xii, 18, 20–1, 23
seme, 20–1, 24, 31, 185, 260n5, 261n9, 268n12, 277n5
semiosis, 15, 22, 96–7, 122
semiotic square, 24, 26–7, 33–5, 272n10, 298–9nn11–14
semiotic system, viii, 12, 22–4, 29, 30, 32, 36, 51, 53, 83, 94–5, 97, 100, 121–2, 260n5
semiotics: of action, viii, 13, 33, 37; and art, 13; of character, 13; of cognition, viii, 13, 265n5; connotative, 20; definition of, 21, 26; denotative, 20; of evaluation, 37; and film, 10; gestural, 21–2; Greimassian, xvi, 11–12, 15, 18–38; history of, 18; of manipulation, 33, 37, 95; and music, 10, 13; narrative, 5–8, 13, 15, 18–38, 142, 146, 251; of passions, viii, 13, 265n5; Peircean, 9, 12; Saussurian, xvii, 9; of time, 16
sender, 21, 28, 30, 33–4, 37, 43–6, 49, 53–4, 66–7, 70, 76, 78, 96, 115, 176, 200–1, 227, 235, 238, 283n27
Senécal, André, 288n7
Servais-Maquoi, Mireille, 302n10
Sheriff, John, 16
Shklovsky, Victor, 4
sign, xi, 8, 13–16, 21, 50–4, 73, 76, 79, 85, 95–8, 100, 110–11, 197, 204, 213, 234, 237–8, 263n14, 265n5, 292n3
sign system, ix–xi, 43, 94–5, 101–2, 121, 193, 211–13
Silverman, Kaja, 14
Simon, Sherry, 312n3
singulative, 119, 125, 157–8, 174–6, 219, 221, 224–5, 230, 292n5, 300n17, 307n19

Sirois, André, 309n6
Smart, Patricia, 309n9, 312n3
Sollers, Philippe, vii
space, xiii, xv, 34–5, 47, 127, 143, 146, 152–65, 173–88, 203–4, 208–9, 219–23, 225–7, 230, 233–4, 236–7, 240, 244–5, 252–3, 255–6, 268n11, 283n24, 308n3
spatiality and narrative, ix, 25, 32, 47, 49, 66, 68, 71, 74, 90, 102, 143–6, 219–20, 224–5, 245, 267–8n9
structures: actantial, 23, 35–6, 156; actional, xi, 16, 38, 170; cognitive, xi, 16, 170; deep, 8–9, 22, 26, 32, 35, 38; discursive, 9, 25, 30–1, 36, 38, 92, 97; narrative, xi, 5–13, 16, 22–5, 30, 33, 35–6, 38, 71–3, 114, 143, 156, 168, 193–4, 207, 242, 265n4; passional, xi, 12, 16, 35–6, 38, 170, 175, 183; semantic, xii, 18, 20, 29, 31, 88; spatial, 71, 143; surface, 9; symbolic, xvi, 43, 255; temporal, vii, x, 143, 156, 158, 171, 193
subject: actant, 21, 23, 25, 28–35, 37–8, 152, 201–3, 265n5, 267–8n9; active, 163, 176, 184; cognitive, 33, 67; collective, xiii, 47, 49, 52–3, 63, 70, 72, 103, 112, 122–3, 142–3, 153–4, 159–65, 167, 170, 176–8, 181–2, 184, 187–8, 201, 213, 218–19, 227, 233–4, 243–7, 249–53, 255–8, 300n17; competence of, 31–7, 43–4, 78–9, 84–5, 88, 114–15, 142, 176; decentred, xiv, 75, 94, 227, 230, 256; desiring, xiii, 160, 181–2, 201, 210–18, 224–6, 236–44, 248–9, 251, 256, 308n3; feminine, xiii, 203, 228, 238–9, 251; individual, xiii, xv–xvi, 47, 70, 142, 146, 154, 159–62, 164, 174, 176, 178, 181–4, 187–90, 203–4, 208–27, 230, 233–43, 246–53, 255–8,

300n17; manipulated, 33, 65, 87, 227; manipulating, 89–90, 94, 96–7, 100, 102, 227; masculine, xiii, 14, 141–2, 202, 219, 233, 249, 251, 291n23; passive, 78, 97, 163, 184; present, 47; violent, 155, 202–6, 213, 256. *See also* identity: collective; individual

subject/object relation, 7, 21–2, 28, 32, 37, 67, 141, 183, 199–200

syntax, 7–8, 23, 29, 37; actantial, 23–4; discursive, 12, 25, 32; fundamental, 25–6, 198; logical, 21; modal, 12, 35; narrative, 7, 25–7, 31–2, 35; surface, 29–30, 33–5; topological, 28

Tarasti, Eero, 10

temporality and narrative, vii–xi, 3, 5, 8, 15–16, 25, 32, 34, 47, 60, 62–6, 68, 71–2, 74, 90, 102–3, 106, 116–17, 119, 123, 138, 143–6, 155–8, 171–7, 190, 219, 221–2, 225–6, 245, 267–8n9, 276–7n3, 278n8, 284n29, 292n6, 305–6n14, 306–7n19

Terre paternelle, La (Lacombe), xiii, 152–65, 195, 201, 208, 255, 290n22, 292nn3, 9, 293nn11–13, 297–8n9, 307n19

Thériault, Yves: *Agaguk*, xv–xvi, 13, 230–53, 256–7

Thérien, Gilles, 262n8, 268n10, 277n4, 283n24, 290n21

Thévet, André, 261n4

Thivierge, Marcel, 167

Thom, René, 12

Thürlemann, Felix, 12

Tin Flute, The. See *Bonheur d'occasion*
Todorov, Tzvetan, viii, ix, 3, 5, 7–8
Tougas, Gérard, 302n10
Trente arpents (Ringuet), 152–3, 156, 208, 308n2
Trigger, Bruce, 270n3
Trobriand, baron de, 288n3
Trubetzkoy, Nikolai, 4
Twaites, Ruben, 262n6
Tynianov, Juri, 5

utterance, 5, 8, 19, 21–2, 26, 28–30, 32, 34–5, 67, 71, 75, 86, 183, 260–1n6, 267–8n9, 306n17

van Dijk, Teun A., 8–9
village, invested space of, 158–9, 161–4, 174, 183–8, 191, 195, 201, 208, 226, 230, 244, 253, 298–301nn11–17, 308n3
Vimont, Barthélemy, 77–8, 103–4, 107
Voyages (Cartier), xii, 41–56, 57, 131, 263n13
Vuong-Riddick, Thuong, 193–4, 301n8

wanting, 28–9, 31, 33, 35–6, 42, 66, 115, 142, 160–2, 176, 181–2, 184, 216, 233, 235–7, 244, 247–50, 283n25, 298nn12, 13, 300n17
Warwick, Jack, 58
White, Hayden, 3, 9
wilderness, invested space of, 143, 145–6, 159–62, 164, 168, 183–4, 186–8, 208–9, 230, 298–301nn11–17, 308n4

OHIO UNIVERSITY LIBRARY

Please return this book as soon as you have finished with it. In order to avoid a fine it must be returned by the latest date stamped below. All books are subject to recall after two weeks or immediately if needed for reserve.

SEP 0 7 2007

CF